Understanding displacement aesthetics

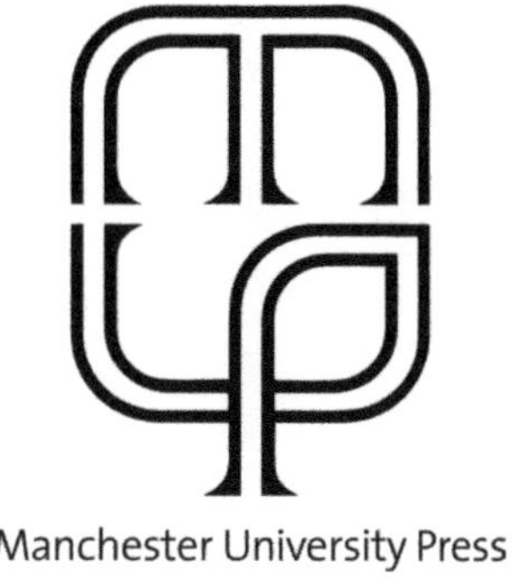

Manchester University Press

Understanding displacement aesthetics

History, art, and museums

Ana Carden-Coyne, Chrisoula Lionis,
Angeliki Roussou, and Charles Green

Manchester University Press

Published by Manchester University Press
Oxford Road, Manchester, M13 9PL

www.manchesteruniversitypress.co.uk

British Library Cataloguing-in-Publication Data
A catalogue record for this book is available from the British Library

ISBN 978 1 5261 8148 0 hardback

First published 2025

EU authorised representative for GPSR:
Easy Access System Europe, Mustamäe tee 50, 10621 Tallinn, Estonia
gpsr.requests@easproject.com

Typeset
by Cheshire Typesetting Ltd, Cuddington, Cheshire

Contents

List of figures

This book is dedicated to all displaced artists. It is for those who live in fear of persecution, who are held in detention, who seek asylum or remain stateless, and for those artists who bring their creativity to enrich other societies.

Acknowledgements

First and foremost, we thank all the artists who have contributed to this book through joint projects, in providing testimonies, and in making or lending artworks for exhibition, including mandla, Azza Abo Rebieh, Safdar Ahmed, Lyndell Brown, Charles Green, and Hiwa K. We are especially grateful to the artists and co-curators Khalda Alkhmri, Yuwai Chung, Ani Daspanyan, Vian K. Hussein, Kani Kamil, Kofo Kego Oyeleye, Cristina Mallai, Gemima Mbuyi Tshimanga, Ambrose Musiyiwa, Mahboobeh Rajabi, Noor Seddiqi, Helena Tomlin, Sonam Tso, and Emmanuela Yogolelo. Working together has been a profound and powerful experience, and a great learning privilege that brings new knowledge to the arts sector which we hope this book can share with the world.

We must thank the galleries we worked closely with, Manchester Art Gallery and the Whitworth Art Gallery, and all the dedicated staff who helped bring this project together. Curatorial practice-led research was essential to this book. It would not have been possible without the consistent and long-term care of co-curators Ruth Edson, Clare Gannaway, and Hannah Williamson at Manchester Art Gallery. Similarly, we appreciate the enormous efforts and sensitivity of co-curators Leanne Green and Hannah Vollam at the Whitworth. These projects were made possible by the leadership of Alistair Hudson Sook-Kyung Lee, Inbal Livne, and Amanda Wallace at the two partner art galleries. There were also curators behind the scenes who supported the exhibitions, including Ann French, Amy George, Natasha Howe, and Liz Mitchell. We are grateful, as well, to Dr Elaine Dewhurst (Manchester University) and Dr Laura Sandy (Liverpool University) for assisting with research and interpretation.

We are especially grateful to our funders, the Arts and Humanities Research Council (AHRC) and the University of Manchester. We owe particular thanks to members of our Advisory board, Dr Suzannah Biernoff, Prof. Anthony Downey, and Ambrose Musiyiwa, who have all offered fundamental advice on the research, exhibitions, and the book. We also received input from Monica Bohm Duchan and Dr Roaa Ali, who brought critical insights to this project in its early stages. We thank our colleagues at the University of Melbourne. We also thank the Centre for the Cultural History of War at Manchester University for inspiration and support:

Prof. Jean-Marc Dreyfus, Emeritus Prof. Peter Gatrell, Dr Laure Humbert, Dr Max Jones Dr Jo Laycock Dr Ewa Ochman, and Prof. Bertrand Taithe.

We are grateful to the organisations In Place of War (IPOW) and Artists for Artists (AfA) for their collaboration, contributing to our understanding of how artists face displacement, occupation, and crisis. Finally, we thank the anonymous readers of the manuscript for sage advice, Manchester University Press Editorial Director Emma Brennan for her support, freelancer Angela Roberts for her careful eye over the final manuscript, and Dan Wand for image assistance.

Introduction

The starting point for this book is that cultural images of refugees are unexpectedly long-standing and historically enduring. The context for this refugee imagery starts with the various displacements that occurred in the first half of the twentieth century, which brought about the formalisation of international refugee law in the 1951 Convention Relating to the Status of Refugees, followed by its 1967 Protocol (which broadened geographic boundaries beyond Europe), and by efforts of the United Nations (UN) and various humanitarian agencies to bridge the gaps left by nation states in relief and resettlement.[1] Thus, more than a century of policies and representations concerned with displaced people flow into the present day. These are always framed by a pervasive, apparently practical and seemingly natural, understanding: refugees, migrants, and asylum seekers are populations marked by crisis.

But this was never the complete picture. Edward Said once observed that nineteenth- and twentieth-century western culture was largely the work of exiles, emigrés, and refugees.[2] His was a dryly romantic observation, but refugee communities in Britain, for instance, have often lacked the resources or places to insert their narratives of exile into the national culture. So, in a sympathetic but nuanced response to Said, this book examines artists who have experienced displacement, and who made a mark in their place of origin and in their new homes, as well as those who faced enormous barriers to re-establishing themselves elsewhere, and who have faced significant barriers to making the contributions that Said envisioned. However, there is a crucial complicating factor that this book will address – the role of artists, curators, and art museums, who play a historically important but ambivalent role in the construction and representation of 'refugeedom'. This book follows in the footsteps of scholars who use this term to articulate how the international refugee regime (a set of rules, norms, and procedures seeking to protect people from persecution and ensure their right to seek asylum outside their country of origin) intersects with the social and cultural world. For instance, how the agency invested in visual creativity and its display responds to the upheavals of displacement and resettlement in the past and present.[3] This book highlights how displaced artists and art museums shape and activate these intersections.

Artists, curators, and art institutions have often generously sought to communicate human rights and the plight of refugees to the broadest publics, and to support displaced artists in their projects. They have also – intentionally, and because museums are a prestigious, cultural focus for both elite and large mass audiences alike – converted the experience of people affected by war and displacement into images with wide currency. Though not as wide-reaching as those of the mass news media, Hollywood films, or social media, the circulation of art is marked by its durability across time and its not is capacity to reflect, emotionally and aesthetically, on the past in the search for meaning that follows wars and conflicts.

Artists sometimes represent refugees and forced migrants through abstractions, as migratory flows on maps for instance, or through material tropes such as boats and suitcases – as traces and absences – or through ecological metaphors, such as migratory birds, and often through engagement with the history of art and paradigmatic stories of exile. Contemporary artists often speak with authority and charisma on behalf of refugee populations, sometimes unconsciously or at other times ironically revealing the artist's and, by extension, society's, presumptions. By virtue of their immense infrastructures and cultural authority, art museums and art biennials (recurring mega-exhibitions of contemporary art that are held regularly around the world) select, collect, conserve, and fully present works of art that inevitably become influential representations of contemporary refugee experiences. But while artists hope to challenge hostile representations of displaced communities, the flip side is that actual opportunities for displaced artists and curators in the contemporary art world remain limited. In addition, art dealer galleries and artist-run spaces are rarely visited by refugee communities, though as we will see, many public art museums have made great efforts to reach diverse communities, both diaspora and recent immigrants. With notable exceptions, there has been little remedy or even recognition of these issues.

Without fully comprehending these challenges, artists, galleries, and museums can inadvertently perpetuate historically constructed misunderstandings when they do work with displaced artists. Compounding this, curators' efforts to decolonise collections, museum displays, and exhibitions, and museum directors' efforts to diversify staff and programming, have not easily included the specificity of forced displacement. Nor can they escape the national laws by which asylum seekers and refugees are bound. The barriers that displaced artists encounter – lack of language proficiency, restrictions on their travel, limited access to education and healthcare, along with economic and psychological precarity – set their lives at the far edge of community experience. In addition, draconian regulations increasingly restrict participation of forcibly displaced people in the cultures of the countries where they have come to live.

Understanding that 'refugeedom' is a historical and cultural construction is a further starting point for this book. We draw here on Peter Gatrell's definition, which connotes a new and distinctive status: a category of humanity defined by displacement.[4] The term draws attention to the multiplicity of relations – between refugees and relief workers; between government and institutional practices that manage refugees – which together constitute refugeedom. However, as Gatrell notes, refugeedom cannot be reduced to power relations alone. Rather, the term encapsulates, as Gatrell along with fellow historians Lauren Banko, and Katarzyna Nowak explain, 'the cultural and social worlds of refugees, including the framing of displacement as something experienced by an individual or by an entire group'.[5] Building on these insights, the present book proposes that both cultural history and art history – two separate disciplines with distinct methods and discourses – are needed to understand the historic and contemporary aesthetics of displacement, and the matrix of refugeedom in culture as it pervades the institutions, rules, metaphors, and practices that inform representation. Gatrell, Ghoshal, Nowak, and Dowdall also explain that the 'modern political category of the refugee' defined in international law is not just specified by the legal and bureaucratic institutions that the postwar era constructed as 'refugeedom'. It is also shaped by 'the diverse social and cultural worlds inhabited by refugees and their encounters with aid workers, government officials, and the broader refugee regime'.[6] Hence this book explores how artists, artworks, and exhibitions activate the cultural arena of refugeedom. In doing so, it emphasises artists' agency and invites recognition by museums and the art gallery system. This approach underpins the conceptual framework of 'displacement aesthetics', which concerns the wider fields of cultural representations, visual art practices, and curation. It also extends beyond the confines of refugees to encompass wider experiences of displacement, forced migration, and statelessness.

Beginning with a discussion of the key concept of 'displacement aesthetics', this Introduction provides an overview of both the aims and the scope of research presented within this book. It elucidates the methods and sources which underpin our interdisciplinary approach and discusses the state of scholarship in the fields of art history, cultural history, and museum studies. Finally, it outlines the impact of displacement aesthetics in contemporary art exhibition history in the Global North and concludes with a summary of the forthcoming chapters and their key arguments.

Displacement aesthetics

This book brings together cultural history and art history to answer pressing questions. Would exploring both how refugees depict themselves, and how refugees are represented, challenge contemporary culture's image of displacement? After all, representations of refugees shape museums' and curators' involvements with artists who have experienced forced displacement. Where is it possible to provide a better understanding of the lived and historic experiences of displaced artists? What might assist in overcoming the limits that displacement imposes on artists, art galleries, and cultural institutions alike? Ideally, the answers will require a sustained effort to share power.

Recognising the existence of a representational and museological system in relation to displacement underpins what this book defines as 'displacement aesthetics'. Displacement aesthetics is *representational, lived,* and *operational.* It produces emotional and sensory responses and encompasses both visible and invisible forces in institutional systems. This means that the legal, social, and economic barriers impacting displaced people's everyday lives *produce aesthetic outcomes,* such as the way art is both created and displayed in galleries. Displacement aesthetics, therefore, highlights the interrelation between representations and the lived conditions of refugeedom. It also recognises that art worlds obfuscate the depth and breadth of this entanglement. This interrelation underscores the framework we have identified in four modes: visual tropes, language and identity, labour, and institutions. Displacement aesthetics is not separate from forcibly displaced people and its impacts on them; they are both agents and subjects of forces.

Displacement aesthetics has historical antecedents stretching back into longer histories of art and representation. But in the first half of the twentieth century, as the international refugee regime was being established, it came to be a powerful force in the visual knowledge system that underpins understandings of displacement. Hence, this book examines the historical formation of displacement aesthetics and describes that system's many visible and invisible aspects, including the entanglements and negotiations between artistic representations, art institutions, and the laws that regulate forcibly displaced people, especially those enacted in the UK. It means stretching the definition of aesthetics well beyond representation. However, we insist that incorporating the factors shaping artistic representation and artists is irrevocably part of the wider contemporary reformation of the idea of aesthetics. The aesthetic outcomes we refer to includes affective emotions such as compassion, pity, and even beauty, for instance in portrayals of female refugees in painting and photojournalism.

Displacement aesthetics can appear to arrange its peoples into neat categories, for instance: mobility and immobility; speech and speechlessness; flight and stasis. But it also encompasses modes of transformation through artistic, collaborative, and institutional practices. As many writers have noted, the aesthetics of displacement is not confined to art or by classical aesthetics' concerns with beauty and sublimity.[7] It is a continual renegotiation between the representational, affective, and operational. It is felt and experienced, constructed and reshaped, by displaced people, as well as allies and advocates, and by a whole range of others including artists who may have deep compassion yet lack practical, first-hand insight into the experiences of displacement. By drawing together cultural history and contemporary art, and bringing practice-based research into curation and exhibition-making, this book will investigate the four different modes of displacement aesthetics.

First, the book explores displacement aesthetics as an image system grounded in historical precedents and repeated in visual themes that are the tropes of refugeedom and of displaced people to persuade us they are figures of concern. Tropes in art and visual culture do not have fixed meanings; they can condense understanding, be meaningful cultural metaphors, and have multiple meanings for different people (mode 1). Second, the book explores the intersection of displacement in contemporary art with the overlooked issue of language. This includes translation and 'mastery' of language, terminologies, ascribed identities, artistic typologies, and moral rights (mode 2). Third, the book explores institutions, including art museums and their curatorial practices (mode 3), turning to artists with backgrounds of forced migration and displacement to better understand their perspectives and art practices. Fourth, the book looks at the experience of displaced artists as they encounter the invisible, covert, and gendered systems of work and labour that artists perform, because the conditions of refugeedom create their own specialised aesthetics of labour (mode 4). These modes resurface across all the chapters.

The first mode of displacement aesthetics consists of the repeated visual themes, motifs, and tropes which form an image system that underpins the historic representation of refugeedom. It encompasses the affective impact that elicits compassion, anxiety, and other emotional responses. A visual trope is a repeated representation, sign, or metaphor in wide use, grounded in the history of displacement and genres of art history, and resonating in the present day. Our description of these is largely consistent with what other writers have described in relation to contemporary art. However, with our longer and wider perspective, we can say that from the first half of the twentieth century to the present, these themes remained relatively familiar even across separate cultural domains: visual art, the mass media, humanitarian photography, and in the UN's visual communications. A prime example is the gendered or racialised configurations of refugees, about which Cynthia Enloe, Heather Johnson, and Marta Zarzycka have separately written.[8] Here, it is important to remark that image manipulation is not unique to images of displaced people. A host of artists have made art about economic migration as well, where migrants move across closed borders in search of better lives for themselves and their children. Thus, the lines between categories of forced and economic migration may be blurred. But we also emphasise that visual motifs and tropes are not intrinsically bad things; they have been highly productive and useful for communities and, indeed, for displaced artists themselves.

The second mode of displacement aesthetics is the language of refugeedom, including terminologies, identities, and typologies of artists. This mode requires more explanation. It includes, firstly, the language of who is speaking about the experience of forced displacement and, second, the rights of those who live that experience to describe themselves and their own experience. These issues involve moral rights. Describing this dimension connects to the recent discourse of decolonisation as it has swept across the arts and museums. Here, debates about who speaks, who translates, and who performs the experience of decolonisation in art spaces are often encapsulated by the demand, familiar from the activism of persons with disabilities, that there can be 'nothing about us without us'. The phrase was popularised by American author James Charlton who in the 1990s gave voice to the electrifying idea that people with disabilities know what is best for themselves.[9]

The second mode involves a typology of artist identities and discursive identities that create representations of displacement. They include war artists, humanitarian photographers, anti-war artists, and activist artists. The problem that is immediately apparent is that it consists of compassionate allies, commentators and observers, not the subjects themselves. They may passionately identify with their subjects but some scholars, such as the Vietnamese feminists Yến Espiritu and Lan Duong, find their identifications unconvincing. On the one hand, they both deplore populist, anti-refugee rhetoric and, on the other, they criticise the 'liberal narratives of tragedy that represent war-displaced refugees as always already suffering feminized bodies'.[10] The second mode has shaped the barriers that displaced artists encounter in the art world (as Chapter 2 explores). When displaced artists and audiences seek collaborations and participation, this second mode explains how they will be identified, classified, and filed away when they approach art institutions other than through the art world's established gatekeeper pathways.

To be sure, works of art are rarely straightforward. They do not actually represent or aim to confirm the views of society, and so it cannot be assumed that a work of art encapsulates wider opinions and prejudices. Art often deliberately misleads viewers, just as stories in books trick readers. Art is an unreliable witness. Its messages may not be the moral clarion calls that activists, or socialist and totalitarian regimes, prefer. Works of art can be ambivalent or even amoral, like their makers, and yet still be powerful, memorable, and inspiring. Artists may gesture at the reprehensible consumption of suffering, but this may ricochet back onto them (as Chapter 4 will discuss).

A further complication is art that deliberately seems to appropriate the moral rights of refugees and displaced persons, or their descendants, including enslaved and colonised Indigenous peoples. To explore the ethical complexity of the second mode, we must understand that themes of human rights and social justice often overlap. From the 1990s onwards, exhibitions were considered to be activist when they sought social justice. Artists and curators across those regions were alert to what was happening beyond their own national borders for they were linked by travel, art journals, and, increasingly, by websites.

Artists can also get their experiments with social justice spectacularly wrong. An example of the problematic misrepresentations of displaced peoples has been typified by Swiss-Icelandic artist Christoph Büchel's *Barca Nostra* (*Our Boat*, 2019). He purchased the wreckage of a fishing boat from the Italian government, which had sunk with hundreds of refugees aboard, then redisplayed it at the 2019 Venice Biennale. Attracting a morass of criticism, Büchel gambled on presenting a work of art that was iconic (that was identical to its referent), knowing that it would then be defended or attacked because it was indexical (because it was still verifiably and causally linked to a real tragedy, which appeared heartless). This apparent careerist exploitation by a privileged artist with little connection to the tragedy appeared to many to be opportunistic or cynical. Trauma theorist Ernst van Alphen had earlier diagnosed the trouble: many artists assumed that they were able, without consequence, to experiment with the confusion between iconic and indexical forms, a confusion that they thought they were legitimately exploring and exploiting.[11]

By contrast, some artists are intensely aware of the pitfalls of speechlessness, othering, and orientalism. For example, a few critics have expressed their disapproval of Irish photographer Richard Mosse's large-scale, immersive, three-channel video installation, *Incoming* (2014–17), on the grounds that he and his team of cinematographers reduced refugees to ghostly, abstract figures of flow, and thus to metonyms. He used a highly specialised surveillance camera and heat map technology, originally designed for military use. The camera produces images by detecting the heat of human bodies. As has often been observed, Mosse walks a tightrope: *Incoming* exposes the refugees' stressful flight, as a rubber boat finally enters the port for processing. Their individuality is reduced to shades of black-and-white, which also provides a veil of privacy, unlike documentary photography. It is important to remember that Mosse is fastidious about gaining permissions from the people on the boats, and the film was made with the active support of refugees on account of his alignment with refugee causes. What does this mean? Many writers and artists have explained that there is a particular strand of art that refuses to disclose its meaning, the artist's identity, or that of their subjects.

Indeed, artists often erase their own biographies and any sense of themselves from their art. Literary theorist Leo Bersani has explored Samuel Beckett's books, Alain Resnais' films, and Mark Rothko's paintings by uncovering their search for secrecy and their denial of identity, as did Mieke Bal of Amerighi da Caravaggio's dark Baroque paintings.[12] The appeal of Mosse's work, seen in various biennials and exhibitions around the world, was to trouble the human story that is not visible to the human eye or even to thermal imaging reserved for militaries. Mosse is more than aware of the historic and ongoing contemporary issue of representing refugees and their suffering. By imbuing the scene with a distanced, aesthetic beauty, the very problem of the representational system is thrown into high relief and becomes the audience's moral conundrum. The interventions made by contemporary artists into displacement tropes and museum collections are discussed further in Chapters 1 and 5.

Artists face many complexities within the matrix of displacement aesthetics, whether they are humanitarian witnesses, anti-war artists, or activist artists. No matter the intention, memorialisation must be consensual; memory cannot be parachuted onto communities. The responsibility for representation could be better shared with displaced communities. Attempts to do good, which Liisa Malkki described as a 'self-humanising' desire to help refugees, are not aesthetically redeeming enough in themselves to constitute ethical memorialisation, no matter how highly we value artistic freedom.[13] Activist artists who seek to do good by representing displaced people or the legacy of forced displacement face a problem that was messy then and remains so now. It is important to note that the ways in which refugees have been culturally represented, even with the best intentions, can nonetheless make us uneasy.

The second mode of displacement aesthetics shows us that, no matter how worthy the cause or the intention, artistic memorialisation, community memory, and wider audience response can be wildly different.[14] While there is no rulebook for the professional art world to adopt, making art about displacement comes with genuine responsibilities and accountability both to displaced artists denied a space in the art world, and displaced communities with whom artists purport to be allied.[15]

The third mode of displacement aesthetics is the dimension that encompasses the experiences of artists as they negotiate the maze of cultural institutions, of curators, of art galleries, biennials, arts councils, and educational institutions, and even of humanitarian organisations and UN agencies. How do artists build reputations that allow them to be invited to exhibit in galleries or art museums? Here, professional training intersects with covert assumptions to shape this dimension of displacement aesthetics. Forms and grant applications have a huge impact on the lives of artists with backgrounds of forced displacement and shape their careers. In this mode, the aestheticisation of displacement in mode 1 is encountered from a different viewpoint. This is what artists and communities encounter as they face the rules and habits of museums which often inadvertently reproduce and reinforce the tropes of mode 1 and the discursive identities of mode 2.

Exhibition formats in art museums, such as single-artist retrospectives or reinstallations of permanent collections, have long been the preeminent vehicle with which to define art, but neither have strayed from established national canons and carefully garnered, highly professionalised reputations. In practice, collecting and purchasing works for permanent collections of art museums have excluded artists from diverse communities. Nor did they explore displacement other than through a narrow representational lens, rather than looking within to their own collections and their colonial histories, which ground our understanding of displacement aesthetics. As for thematic exhibitions, art museums were risk-averse to threats from populist politicians and to donor and tabloid media pressure, which led to threats of defunding.[16] Instead, it has increasingly been biennials, operating in the zone between artistic laboratory and carnival, that have road-tested and licensed the kind of experimentation that included displaced artists, visa problems notwithstanding.

Biennials placed the politics of refugeedom at the centre of attention, even at one point relocating to one of its pivotal geographies (Athens, *documenta14*, 2017), with varying degrees of success. But this trend is not at all new. From the 1970s, the concept of the art museum, its expandability, and its receptivity to diverse communities of artists has been questioned from both the Left and the Right. Dramatic artist strikes during the 1970s on the sidewalk of the Museum of Modern Art demanded change. Further, *documenta5* (1972), assembled by Swiss curator Harald Szeemann, faced widespread petitions and artist protests that he was promoting himself and his own theories, not the artists. Szeemann's methods of contemporary curating during the 1970s and 1980s defined the canon by curatorial fiat rather than through any collaborative model of dispersing curatorship or through a collective process. Nevertheless, artist activists across the world – in New Delhi in 1968, in New York with the Art Workers Coalition during 1969 and 1970, and in Sydney in 1976 and 1979 – urged diverse artist voices upon museum trustees and curators. Increasingly, biennial curators such as Elisabeth Sussman and Thelma Golden at the 1993 Whitney Biennial and biennial directors Okwui Enwezor and Charles Esche assumed responsibility for the concept that art museums should serve communities and artists. Gradually, the rhetoric of activist resistance, of doing good, recognised that it needed to draw on collaborative curatorship. This was the process at *documenta11* (2002) under Enwezor, in gathering the living, actual voices and experiences of artists from multiple backgrounds, and it would involve long-term, practice-led curatorial research, working closely with artists and advisors.

This shift in practice meant the curators and directors of public cultural collections began to seek the ideas of refugees and migrant artists, curators, and communities for solutions that might assist exhibition programming as well as building relationships with displaced artists and communities. For instance, displaced artists emphasised the importance of terminologies and protocols that might serve rather than hinder. These pointed the way toward a new ethics of collaboration. Inside art museums there were already collections of objects resonant with deep emotional and cultural significance for displaced and migrant communities. However, the displays were out of date or intermittent, and, lacking community consultation, the captions were often wrong. The total effects, in short, were muted. There are several different ways of selecting and displaying collections in museums, and of setting up exhibitions closer to what both migrants and refugees know about their own artefacts, signs, and symbols. Community collaboration may include reinstalling historical collections and altering exhibition designs, and community-based consultation may lead to innovative curatorship, which this book explores in the final chapter.

The fourth mode of displacement aesthetics is the labour that artists perform as they create works of art that represent refugeedom, and as they encounter the invisible, covert, and gendered systems of work and labour. Their labour might be that of a lone producer working in a studio as a small business entrepreneur. It might be that of one assistant amongst many in a rich, successful artist's studio, uncredited by their employer when the art they help fabricate is exhibited. It might be as a participant in a friendly workshop welcoming artists with disabilities, or in a remote community art centre for Indigenous artists, which provides the materials and a place to work. The labour might be of a troupe of performers, whose membership shifts, and includes sound engineers and video operators as well as performance artists. This range of labour practices shapes the spectrum of art depicting refugees as well as that made by displaced artists. Understanding labour, however, is sometimes paradoxically constricted by both humanitarian sentiments and the art industry's business practices, as discussed in detail in Chapter 4.

As we shall see, when forms of artistic labour are collaborative and cooperative, creative participants are credited if they wish to be.[17] Social practice art nevertheless involves continual negotiation. Art historians have written critically about performances involving paid assistants. Where many of them did not have the right to legally work, payment was derisory; further, demonstrating indignity was sometimes precisely the artist's intention, as we shall see.[18] The rapidly expanding literature about care and hospitality in art has only just begun to consider the special problems displaced artists face. Their labour can augment the matrix of displacement aesthetics. Indeed, like American artists Joseph Kosuth and, slightly later, Fred Wilson (and his influential method of *Mining the Museum*), they may work as artist-curators and cultural heritage experts, but this can also reveal unequal relationships behind the glossy face of art museums. In the light of the re-evaluation of past practices, contemporary art's claims to foster inclusivity, compassion, and resilience needs to be continually and critically tested.

Sources and methods

The book brings together the methods and source materials used by cultural historians, art historians, and art theorists. Its primary sources include visual art (historical and contemporary) as well as news, humanitarian and UN photography, and are drawn from national and international repositories in the Global North. The approach does not frame the work of artists as exemplary but rather acknowledges that these works have achieved critical recognition in the international art world, in turn impacting scholarship and speaking directly to the challenges and consequences of displacement aesthetics. At the same time, it considers the impact of displacement aesthetics on the lived experiences of early careers artists, and art galleries working today in the UK. The book utilises in-depth interviews with a small group of artists, curators, community advisors, and other arts professionals from backgrounds of forced migration and displacement. These interviews are the result of collaborative projects with artists who have lived experiences of displacement and forced migration. They describe the distinct conditions impacting them: their experiences were more extreme and their recollections more panoramic than other immigrant artists, war artists, or activist artists.

This book concentrates mostly upon refugeedom in Anglo-European history and in the contemporary UK context in the full consciousness that the vast majority of displaced persons remain within their own countries, or in camps and borderlands around the world. We are writing at a time of unprecedented persecution of refugees, including assaults on asylum seeker accommodations in the UK and Germany. Ethnic cleansing and genocidal violence (the intent to destroy, wholly or in part, a national, ethnic, racial, or religious group) are not consigned to the past, for displacing Darfuri people, Rohingya, and Palestinians, especially Gazans, is ongoing.[19] Despite rhetoric, the global imbalance of caring for refugees weighs most heavily on countries outside the Global North and especially neighbouring countries. However, the majority of widely circulated images of refugees at the time of writing have concentrated disproportionally on dramatic arrivals in Europe, which is a gross distortion of the facts.

Given the scale of mass displacement, a focus on post-migrant contexts enables a precise discussion of the UK situation. This refers to societies fundamentally transformed by migration, informing national identity, and underpinning political, social, and cultural institutions. While we understand the limited geographical scope of this research, the hope is that our framework for displacement aesthetics will be adopted and reworked for future scholarship and other geographies.

The research for this book was conducted over three years and was funded by the Arts and Humanities Research Council. The project was titled *Understanding Displacement Aesthetics and Making Change in the Art Gallery with Refugees, Migrants and Host Communities* (2021–24). During this time, the team of researchers – the co-authors of this book – sought to undertake three areas of research. First, to assess the history and contemporary representations of displacement. Second, to enhance the careers of artists and curators with a background of migration and displacement. Third, to assist galleries in using their collection, database, and labelling in new ways through a focus on migration and displacement and to promote engagement with artists and communities. The practice-based research involved working with Manchester Art Gallery and the Whitworth Art Gallery and engaging with the work of many different artists from local and international networks. In formulating the key concept of displacement aesthetics, this book is also seeking to assist galleries to make changes in curating and operating but also to contribute to the scholarship of cultural history, art history and theory, and museum studies. Our methods of practice-based research with collections and curating attempted to break new ground in institutional practices. But we also recognise, as discussed further in Chapters 2 and 5, that academic researchers – like museums – hold positions of privilege and status, and must continually reflect on the invisible power dynamics of collaboration to safeguard collaborators. Finally, this book draws on artworks from international examples of exhibition practice, refugee-led arts initiatives, and artist-run innovations in Europe, the Middle East, and Australia. It is therefore not only concerned with the public-facing outcomes of displacement aesthetics (exhibitions and artworks), but also keenly attuned to the working processes that underline museum-sector activity relating to displacement.

Displacement in contemporary art exhibitions

Experiences of migration and displacement are central to contemporaneity. This term describes the conditions of contemporary art and demarcates the contemporary as a period of art separate but arising from nineteenth- and twentieth-century modernism.[20] Since the 1990s, this has been most evident in exhibition-making, due to the decentralisation of the art world, postcolonial movement, and pushback from artists who felt marginalised and othered by the Global North mainstream. In addition, curators have reflected the dramatic increase in migrant and displaced populations and how that augments post-migrant societies. As recurring survey exhibitions held every two, three, or five years, international biennials are a useful example for this activity.

Since the late 1980s, the worldwide rise of these global mega-exhibitions has been accompanied by Asian and European curators' determination to explode artist selection beyond the established canon of western European and East Coast American modern and contemporary artists. Artists were almost always male, White, and comfortably settled despite earlier lives that might have been marked by the twentieth century's many forced displacements. In Britain, a defining exhibition of resistance was curator and artist Rasheed Araeen's *The Other Story: Afro-Asian Artists in Post-War Britain* (Hayward Gallery, London, 29 November 1989 to 4 February 1990; Wolverhampton Art Gallery, 10 March to 22 April 1990; Manchester City Art Gallery and Cornerhouse, 5 May to 10 June 1990). The exhibition amplified the neglected work of Asian, African, and Caribbean artists at a time of intense racist and political violence in the UK. Some of those artists were from forced migrant and displacement heritages, and the works they produced often critiqued Britain's imperial history and the legacies of racism, nationalism, and inequality.[21] This exhibition, despite its mixed reviews, insisted that Britain was and is a multicultural society, and that art should be understood as a global phenomenon. The exhibition was ahead of its time, but the work of 'decolonising' British art history and the collections of museums is now an urgent concern across the art industry.

To be sure, the canon within the narrow confines of the mainstream had dominated the two great biennials of the contemporary art calendar, the Biennale of Venice and *documenta* (held every five years in Kassel, Germany). The hugely influential global survey exhibition in Paris, *Magiciens de la terre* (1989), which had been initially conceived as a biennial, presented a brief challenge to the ascendancy of the Biennale of Venice and *documenta*. Although it was emblematic of the widening of artist selection and opening to others' voices, the chief curator of *Magiciens*, Jean-Hubert Martin, was accused of 'Third Worldism' – that is, creating a saccharine 'Family of Man' effect similar to Benetton clothing advertisements, and repeating the tropes encapsulated in the first mode of displacement aesthetics (see Chapter 1). Almost simultaneously, and with a similar encyclopaedic inclusiveness, the Studio Museum at Harlem, the New Museum of Contemporary Art, and the Museum of Contemporary Hispanic Art, in 1990 presented *The Decade Show: Frameworks of Identity in the 1980s*. These two exhibitions – *Magiciens* and *The Decade Show* – were amongst the first instances of big art museums across the North Atlantic allowing marginalised artists to impact the dominant art historical narrative taught in art history departments across the Global North.

A year later, across New York's East River, the venerable Brooklyn Museum commissioned veteran conceptual artist Joseph Kosuth to reinstall its own encyclopaedic collection. The resulting exhibition, *The Brooklyn Museum Collection: The Play of the Unmentionable* (1991), included a host of previously ignored homoerotic artworks by gay and lesbian artists from the collection along with Kosuth's new, extended didactic texts. Thereafter, revisionist words and texts would become essential parts of the new curatorial lexicon. In reframing a whole museum collection, *The Play of the Unmentionable* disrupted the historic presumptions of what we might now understand as 'displacement aesthetics'. This was not just a question of bringing marginalised artists into the canon, but of explicitly rendering visible the exclusionary histories and opaque decision-making that often underpin museum collections and curation. We will return to this in Chapter 5, when discussing collaborative projects with the Whitworth Art Gallery and Manchester Art Gallery.

A couple of years later, the 1993 Whitney Biennial of American Art in New York would become the first biennial of activist art. By focusing on the racist legacy of slavery, it also highlighted the forced displacement of enslaved peoples from Africa to the Americas. Curated by Elizabeth Sussman and a team that included influential African-American curator Thelma Golden, it had considerable impact across the English-speaking world, stretching beyond the US to the UK, Canada, and Australia. It therefore warrants extended reflection. A considerable body of literature has developed in recent years about that Whitney Biennial, long after its initially hostile reception as the 'politically correct' or the 'political' biennial.

The 1993 Whitney was accused at the time of constraining the audience's responses, and of rigidly fixing meaning along the lines of a very combative understanding of identity politics focused on race. *New York Times* art critic Roberta Smith's reaction was respectful. She acknowledged that the biennial finally reflected the very different cultural climate of the new decade, and she lauded it for 'breaking the biennial meld'; it was a watershed.[22] However, she also deemed the exhibition didactic, moralising, confrontational, and predictable. Activist art curating was too narrowly focused, in her view: 'this show takes a distinct position. It focuses on a range of art that is political – or at least social – paying scant attention to anything else'. The 1993 Whitney Biennial provoked a special issue of the esteemed journal of art theory, *October*, whose panel of critics and artists observed that the militant art on show was overly affirmative and separatist in its understanding of identity. Quite separately, biennial reviewer Charles A. Wright redefined this criticism and suggested that it was created by the language of curatorship. He wrote that artists were 'articulated in the convenient terms that the museum chose to present them in'.[23]

Pat Ward Williams' *What You Lookn At?* (1992) was one of the Whitney Biennial's clearest instances of art seeking to move covert racism from a place of invisibility to visibility in order to reveal its workings to the viewer – to expose the hidden hatred and fear of the Other imbricating the experience of forcibly displaced people. Ward Williams scrawled over a large and grainy photograph of a group of young Black men the words, 'What you lookn at?'. Curator Sussman installed the work in the Whitney's front window, looking out over Madison Avenue. The statement was rhetorical and the placement symbolic. Situating the work in the museum's front window transported the supposed community of young Black men into the privileged precinct of Upper East Side of Manhattan, with the aim of redressing their invisibility within so-called mainstream culture as stereotypically dangerous and threatening. In theory, Williams' scrawl provided the voice that gave her subjects the ability to subvert the controlling White gaze, denying their silencing by White society. However (White) art historian Hal Foster acerbically commented, 'It assumes [the audience] have no analytical competencies, no reading methods, of their own'.[24] *Art and America* reviewer Eleanor Heartney called this curatorial corralling the tactic of reciprocal intimidation.[25] Ward Williams' window intentionally simulated the process of what was about to become widely known as racial profiling, but Heartney doubted if this tactic would ever elicit enough empathy on the part of the museum visitor to understand the plight of being stereotyped.

The 1993 Whitney Biennial's curatorial statements were grounded in claims about the justice of representing American art's present minorities, often descendants of forcibly displaced people, rather than, as at *Magiciens de la terre*, of recognising former geographic peripheries and their artists. The backdrop to the 1993 Whitney Biennial was the emergent realisation of the art world's globalisation, and the newly urgent need to look beyond Cold War walls to encompass the margins and border regions already witnessing outflows of refugees. At the Venice Biennale and at *documenta*, artists beyond the North Atlantic who had long been invisible on account of the impact of the Cold War were now garnering attention.

The pathfinding of curators like Thelma Golden, who combined social justice with identifying the new wave of important Black artists – Glen Ligon, Gary Simmons, Lorna Simpson, and others – cannot be overestimated. Golden understood there was a need for cultural justice for Black artists, rather than ignoring colour. This would be the case for displaced artists too, as we shall see later in this section and in forthcoming chapters, for with contemporary art even if not in society, a degree of cultural capital can be found in working with artists who have backgrounds of displacement.

Director David Ross wrote in his Introduction to the 1993 Whitney Biennial exhibition catalogue that, 'there is no single set of questions with more relevance at this moment, no set of shared concerns with more relevance of this moment, than those raised by artists concerned with identity and community'.[26] It is important here to explicitly draw out an issue implicit in Ross' assertion: namely that the consequences of forced displacement, enslavement, and settler-colonialism directly underscore issues of identity and community. Sussman and Golden believed that the 1993 Whitney Biennial challenged the art centre from the margins, and if they conceived of those margins as social rather than geographic, the processes through which those maps were to be redrawn was to be confrontational. The co-curators drew upon the African-American philosopher and activist Cornel West's formulation of 'the new politics of difference'. At the start of her catalogue essay, Golden prominently cited West's definition of this new cultural politics whose distinctive features, West wrote, were 'to trash the monolithic and homogenous in the name of diversity, multiplicity and heterogeneity; to reject the abstract, general and universal in light of the concrete, specific and particular; and to historicize, contextualize and pluralize by highlighting the contingent, provisional, variable, tentative, shifting, and changing'.[27]

Influential artist and theorist Coco Fusco's collaborative performance-installation with long-time collaborator Guillermo Gómes-Peña, *Year of the White Bear* and *Two Undiscovered Amerindians Visit the West* (1992–94), was restaged at the biennial, enacting the eighteenth- and nineteenth-century imprisonment and display of displaced Indigenous peoples in cages.[28] Presaging the contemporary wave to decolonise art museums, Fusco's catalogue essay read, 'In the debates and art emerging from the tumult of the present are reflections of the many legacies of the conquest and colonization of the Americas, among them, its limiting views of art and culture'.[29] She continued, 'the mainstream appropriation of subaltern cultures in this country has historically served as a substitute for ceding to those peoples and real political or economic power'.[30] This aligns with the impact of displacement aesthetics' third mode. It is worth noting that many of the artists in the 1993 Whitney Biennial were calling for the redistribution of cultural, social, and political power by increasing their visibility, for which displaced artists are also still calling.

After 1993, the search for new methodologies to challenge displacement aesthetics shifted elsewhere, in 1996 to Paris with the Musée nationale d'art moderne's vast exhibition of art that represented global conflict, *Face à l'histoire*,[31] and to Johannesburg with the second Johannesburg Biennale in 1997, titled *Trade Routes: History and Geography*. The latter was an ambitious exhibition spanning multiple venues across two cities (Johannesburg and Cape Town), and encompassing artists from across the world rather than just a coterie of North American and European art superstars. Directed by the young New York-based Nigerian-born curator Okwui Enwezor, it emphasised dialogue, trade, and migration, but also the power asymmetries between the Global South and the colonising North. Despite the economic focus of its title, *Trade Routes: History and Geography* presented the displacement of peoples as the unifying dark core of globalisation. Displacement, Enwezor observed, was even more fundamental than globalisation's 'economic consolidation and efficient distribution of labour and capital'.[32] The main thrust of Enwezor's argument at Johannesburg was that contemporary globalisation emerged from the earliest developments of European colonialism (between the fifteenth and nineteenth centuries), and that an examination of colonialism (and slavery) breathed new life into thinking about new forms of globalisation.[33] While he emphasised the colonial origin of current developments in global history, Enwezor saw contemporary globalisation as an unprecedented phenomenon.[34]

　　　　　　　　　　　　　　　　　　　　　　　　　　　　　17

Enwezor attracted considerable suspicion and hostility inside South Africa because, in the context of newly liberated South Africa's economic crisis and persisting inequality, his Biennial reflected the international art world at the expense of more humble local projects. To local critics, and in retrospect the same may be said almost three decades later, it seemed that Enwezor and other contemporary art curators imagined that fluidity, trade, and economics, despite being rooted in the violence and forced displacement of centuries before, might soften the contours of conflict through the healing agency of contemporary art. That well-meaning optimism, according to influential Slovenian critical theorist Slavoj Žižek, suggested that 'multiculturalism is a disavowed, inverted, self-referential form of racism … [It] retains this position as the privileged empty point of universality from which one can appreciate (and depreciate) properly other particular cultures', and that a real Other would instead always be 'instantly denounced for its "fundamentalism"'.[35] Those good intentions will be questioned throughout this book.[36]

Despite Žižek's acidic challenge in 1997, artists, curators, and thinkers in subsequent years continued to turn to art practices that spoke with compassion and fury for people suffering. This continues today. An antagonistic approach to this curatorial and artistic approach has been met with audience rage. A notable example was the New York Jewish Museum's exhibition, *Mirroring Evil: Nazi Imagery/Recent Art* (2002).[37] Rather than focusing on images of victims, as earlier artists had done, the artists in that show (who included descendants of both victims and perpetrators of the Holocaust and of Jewish refugees) described the world view of the perpetrators. This was a new and controversial approach. Several works in that 2002 exhibition represented the speaking position – the subjective viewpoint – of Nazis rather than their victims, and so the works were condemned as either carelessly Fascist in their sympathies or irresponsible in their apparent disregard for the wider educative and social function of artistic representation. Writers for the exhibition catalogue had argued that existing theories of memory in contemporary art, particularly well-intentioned writings on Holocaust art, valorised art's memorial function but were oblivious to what they saw as the artificiality and duplicity of cultural memory.[38]

Within the domain of art criticism and art theory, Jill Bennett and Ernst van Alphen made the distinction between the redemptive claims of art and the process of memorialisation clear.[39] In terms of the politics of representation, there had already been considerable thinking about the failure of representation in relation to Holocaust terror. German painter Anselm Kiefer's ambiguous 1977 album of photographs of himself standing on top of German monuments 'performing' Hitler's *seig heil* salute, and his vast paintings incorporating Nazi imagery, had long caused deep critical division. Eventually, in a famous defence of Kiefer, literary theorist Andreas Huyssen claimed that the works moved way beyond either the glorification or caricature of Nazi gestures by, first, betraying the intolerable longing to move beyond that era of German history through mythological sublimation, and second, and more importantly, exposing the viewer to the addictive glamour of sheer, murderous power.[40] This subtlety did not necessarily communicate or travel well.

The years after those exhibitions saw significant displacements from Africa and the Middle East. People visibly fleeing wars and economic dislocations arrived in Europe and the UK to blanket media coverage and a cool welcome. Refugeedom's ubiquity at the 2015 Biennale of Venice, *All the World's Futures*, reflected the phenomenal shift in forced displacement's public visibility and urgency. Works included Kurdish artist Hiwa K's video and sculpture, *The Bell* (2014–15) and the Syrian artist collective Abounaddara's videos, *All the Syria's Futures* (2015), which they withdrew, alleging that they had been censored. It also included Brazilian artist Vik Muniz's *Lampedusa* (2015), a fourteen-metre paper boat coated with a giant reproduction of the Italian newspaper article reporting on a maritime tragedy, and British artist John Akomfrah's video installation, *Vertigo Sea* (2015). Akomfrah, a founding member of British Black Audio Film Collective, launched in 1982, made socially activist documentary films from an explicitly migrant perspective, including documentaries that explored the Windrush generation's emigration from the Caribbean to work in an unwelcoming Britain during the 1950s. From the 2010s on, Akomfrah's immersive video installations focused on displacement reimagined through metaphors of the natural world and using the model of a travel documentary. Curators like Massimiliano Gioni spoke approvingly of Akomfrah updating the decades-old documentary travelogue into new 'sentimental documentaries'. Much of *Vertigo Sea* consisted of long, slow, drifting, aerial sequences of wilderness, wild animals and migrating birds, metaphors for migration, across the wide screens' panoramic, joined breadth. Other sequences included static tableaux by actors in period costumes gazing silently at landscapes blighted by the colonial past.

Enwezor's research culminated in the epochal exhibition at Haus der Kunst in Munich, *Postwar* (2016).[41] This exhibition took up the ambition and revisionist challenge of *Trade Routes*, acknowledging, this time, the continual, massive displacement of peoples across each decade after the Second World War. Intended as merely the first of a gargantuan trilogy, *Postwar* set out a wholesale revision of post-1945 art history, taking into account artists from around the globe and carefully including displaced artists. Enwezor was one of only a very few curators who sought to widen the field of artistic production to include a range of other artists, other thinkers, and other histories beyond those anchored to the North Atlantic. Peak national museums had been remained relatively homogenous, too preoccupied or too timid to acknowledge the sheer scale of slavery, massacre, wars at home, and forced displacement of vast populations. The ability to conceptualise histories that did not relegate art as 'untimely' by freighted, fraught, or often simply incorrect comparisons with canonical North Atlantic art history depended on an ethos of curating that would need to be grounded in collaboration with marginalised and displaced peoples who were given international opportunities rather than merely the dubious privilege of being represented. Fully escaping the civic exclusions and double binds of displacement aesthetics was almost impossible, as the controversies surrounding Abounaddara's videos at Venice in 2015, and then at *The Restless Earth* in 2017 demonstrated.[42] The 2015 Biennale of Venice: *All the World's Futures* was the last major biennial curated by Enwezor before his untimely death in 2019, though several of his planned shows were finished by close colleagues right up to *The 2023 Sharjah Biennale: Thinking Historically in the Present*, which was completed by a team led by Hoor Al Qasimi, Director of the Sharjah Art Foundation.

The Restless Earth (2017), curated by Massimiliano Gioni and supported by the Nicola Trussardi Foundation, was, of all the exhibitions that we survey, the one most explicitly focused on the involuntary displacement of peoples, even more than *documenta 14*, which opened in Athens two weeks before *The Restless Earth* in Milan and a month before the vernissage of the 2017 Venice Biennale. The coincidences were both deliberate and telling, requiring extended pilgrimages by the privileged art world of curators, collectors, critics and the selected artists. At the Athens component of *documenta 14*, director Adam Szymczyk included Artur Żmijewski's video, *Realism* (2017), a grainy, brutal documentary surveying the remains of the makeshift Calais refugee camp known as the Jungle. Greece, where Żmijewski's work was shown, had been a major transit point for refugees as they journeyed towards their extended families already living in northern Europe.

Gioni selected a large percentage of artists with a heritage of displacement and forced migration. German Syrian artist Manaf Halbouni's *Nowhere Is Home* (2015), an installation that toured across art museums in Europe and the UK, was a dilapidated car overflowing with the artist's belongings, evoking his flight to escape Syrian military service. French Algerian artist Kader Attia contributed a monumental installation, *La Mer Morte* (*The Dead Sea*, 2015), consisting of a sea of blue cloth made of scattered jeans, T-shirts, and shoes strewn across the art museum floor. Bouchra Khalili's *The Mapping Journey Project* (2008–11) avoided refugee faces and bodies altogether; instead, their voices describe journeys while maps show their circuitous paths across nations. In a single-channel video, *how to make a refugee* (1999), Phil Collins produced an 11-minute film, in which a group of photojournalists arrange a family of dazed Albanian refugees from the Kosovan War, and direct a baffled, teenage boy. This shocking work exposed media clichés about refugees, and the industry's clinical if not cynical approach to the trauma of genocidal violence.

The artwork broke the so-called third wall, the imaginary barrier through which we maintain the fiction that the people, objects, and landscapes depicted in a film or work of art are 'real'. This third wall prevents the characters in a play or film or work of art from showing us that they know they are fictional constructions. Breaking the third wall disrupts our immersion in a work of art. When the third wall breaks, we are forced to see that we are looking at actors, at flickering images on a screen, or at thin layers of paint. A further, fourth wall is broken when actors not only acknowledge their audience but also address them directly in conversation. Gioni observed that 'the construction of images is never innocent, even when it wants to be supportive of its subjects'.[43] Gioni suggested that the opacity encountered was a moral right: the right of the displaced to own images of themselves, withholding their faces from view as they wished:

> How can we represent certain crises without framing them in the kind of one-dimensional representation so typical of the mainstream media? And who has a right to images of the refugee, immigrant, or migrant? Glissant [twentieth-century poet and postcolonial theorist from Martinique] spoke about the right to opacity, and this becomes particularly relevant today.[44]

The Restless Earth gathered together all the themes and methods that we have thus far discussed: deliberate opacity; documentary methods drawing on older cinema; seductive but open-ended narratives (e.g. Akomfrah's *Vertigo Sea*); memorials owned and created by migrants and refugees, foregrounding the labour of self-presentation.

These decades of international art exhibitions have, however, been considered without the perspective of cultural history and implicitly within the rootedness of displacement aesthetics in the past. To understand this history and its current legacies, this book draws together several disciplines in conversation.

The state of scholarship

This book's key message is the existence of displacement aesthetics. It exists through forms of representation, through a system of art-making, as a language system, and in specific modes of labour. To make this visible requires drawing on research in cultural history, art history, critical theory, and both museum and curatorial studies.

Cultural and social history

The study of refugees and displaced persons (DPs), displaced person camps, humanitarian aid, and the international organisations that underpinned the refugee regime in the aftermath of the Second World War has become a distinct area within the discipline of history. Alongside scholars focused on the creation of international refugee law, in which the 'modern refugee' was made, as Peter Gatrell argues, is a wide scholarship on relief efforts during and after the two world wars. Not content with the top-down approach yielded from the extant sources, scholars have sought to retrieve the missing voices of refugees and DPs.[45] Developing from this field is the realisation that images were powerful conveyors of the political realities of accepting and resettling refugees, and of humanitarian concerns of relief and rehabilitation when millions of people were displaced from their homelands after the Second World War. A landmark volume in this approach is Heidi Fehrenbach and Davide Rodogno's *Humanitarian Photography* (2015), which alerted readers to the colonial origins of humanitarian visuality, even in its attempts to show compassion to those in dire need. Since then, rising interest in the photography of displacement, and its dissemination by UN agencies, and other organisations, such as the United Nations Relief and Rehabilitation Administration and the International Refugee Organisation, has followed.[46] Simone Gigliotti has identified extensive archives of newsreel and documentary films made about Jewish refugees used to represent their humanitarian needs in the postwar period.[47] In depth studies of cultural and visual representation, framed as fundamental to the refugee regime and to visual knowledge, have not yet emerged, and so this book offers a significant contribution to scholarship, concentrated in Chapters 1 and 5.

Furthermore, the book draws, throughout, on the concept of refugeedom. Understanding of refugees in this period tends to focus on Europe and the Jewish experience, which was also reflected in the 1951 Convention Relating to the Status of Refugees, and did not include non-Europeans until the 1967 Protocol. The consequence of this is an absence of representation, and even erasure, of displaced people to, from, or within Africa, Asia, and the Middle East as a result of the Second World War. Moreover, the visual stories of Europeans fundamentally shaped the art industry and the cultural figures that are visible in Chapter 1. Peter Gatrell has explained why historians have systematically begun to describe displaced persons, the camps they were housed in, the humanitarian campaigns, and the international organisations that created the contemporary international order which both cared for and governed the displaced.[48] Within these histories, attention to images of refugees, and to images and objects made by refugees, are often discussed in passing or are cited merely as illustrations. There are of course exceptions, including studies of postwar humanitarian and UN organisations' photography and films of refugees and displaced persons, and, conversely, private, family photographs taken by Jewish refugees.[49]

This brings us to the centrality of war in the remaking of cultural history, and how it intersects with studies of colonial legacies, famine, and ethnic conflict, as well as with postwar reconstruction.[50] A rising interest within cultural history focuses on the relationship between photography and humanitarianism, the representation of refugees, including children, and the photos that refugees themselves have produced.[51] An important volume by key scholars develops the thesis that, since the nineteenth century onwards, images became pivotal in shaping political and social responses to suffering, while also forging international networks of solidarity. Images shaped the interpretation of political violence as humanitarian crises in the international community, 'making and unmaking' the framework of crisis.[52] This research is also influenced by the 'sensory turn' and the history of emotions, although it does not contend with the concept of aesthetics that has been the concern of art history and theory. Hence our concept of displacement aesthetics will offer this field a useful approach, for instance in understanding the emotions that images of displacement arouse and their impact on both artists and influential spheres of cultural representation.

The contribution of cultural history is fundamental to the interdisciplinary purpose of this book. The emphasis on the contemporary in many fields has failed to grasp the full extent of the way in which image cultures cross paths over time, and how visual tropes of displacement are rooted in the past. We argue that such images provided a foundational palette of displacement imagery that has been sustained across the twentieth and twenty-first centuries.

Museum studies and curatorial scholarship

These fields have begun to look closely at refugee and migrant communities, alert to the efforts of art institutions to liaise with refugee communities by commissioning artists. The implicit or explicit expectation is that those artists will work with refugee communities.[53] Domenico Sergi's *Museums, Refugees and Communities* (2021) was based on workshops with refugee communities in Germany, the Netherlands, and the UK; it complemented other studies of museums, migration, and mobility, and the widening scholarly interest in enabling refugee voices through participatory projects and community arts initiatives.[54] Focus on refugees follows on from the study of museums as spaces for social justice edited by Robert Janes and Richard Sandell.[55] With concerns for diversity and the inclusion of marginalised communities and marginalised artists in museum collections, this book engages with scholarship on 'decolonising' or 'Indigenising' museums.[56] While much literature focuses on national museums and international biennials, Nina Möntmann has shown that smaller arts organisations have acted as platforms of both participatory practices and decolonising strategies. In a further work, *Decentering the Museum: Contemporary Art Institutions and Colonial Legacies* (2023), she argues that contemporary art museums can learn from anthropological museums and smaller arts organisations in their approach to collections, interrogating ongoing coloniality and addressing the needs of diverse publics in the present day.[57] This chimes with the practice-based curatorial research undertaken for this book, which, as mentioned, was conducted with two UK art institutions based in the northern region of Manchester (Britain's second largest city): Manchester Art Gallery and the Whitworth Art Gallery.

Art history and theory

Artists from stateless nations have long been part of modern and contemporary art in ways that deeply problematise national histories of art and ideas of contented diasporic adaptation. Art historians have always understood that artists are forced to move from country to country, for example the Surrealist exiles and emigrés fleeing Nazi Europe who had a great impact on the formation of the New York School, which included Jackson Pollock, or German artists who moved from east to west in the decades after the Second World War.[58] However, focusing on individual artists or art movements almost always means celebrating their contributions to their host countries' national art history and ignoring the rich and cosmopolitan cultural scenes that refugees were part of before exile and the art they made within them. Many artists forced to flee, both then and now, had reputations as important artists in their home countries. The dominance of the English language, which has become the lingua franca of the art history discipline, has resulted in a variety of homogenising effects. James Elkins has explored the complex tension between national art histories and this diminution of diversity.[59] National art museums organise their displays into departments that tend to prioritise a national story above all. Refugee experiences are airbrushed into neat, simple, abbreviated contours in order to fit this narrative. The potential but rare exceptions to this national myopia include single artist retrospectives or monographs that are forced to take into account the wider span of a life across borders, but which quickly pass over the artists' displacement in favour of establishing their new lives.[60] The indispensable and distinctive experiences of displaced artists should be embedded within art history along with their art.

Our point is that displacement aesthetics appears in the west in the period that we now call the Enlightenment with its mixed heritage of colonisation, slavery, capitalism, nationalism, and globalism. They intersected again in the period from the end of the Second World War to the present alongside decolonisation and the end of many empires.[61] Contemporary art since the 1970s has been entwined in decolonisation, war, conflict, and refugees' search for safety. However, courageous refugee responses emerged in response to displacement throughout the twentieth century and beyond, and can also be traced back to Black resistance to the forced displacement of Trans-Atlantic slavery. Although most studies of war art ignore histories of exile or refugee perspectives, a few have attempted to take a broader view of the period. One example is Brian Foss' account of the Second World War Official War Artist Scheme; however, it only examines one nation's official war artists during one war in one medium – painting – and is not concerned with displaced artists' perspectives.[62] Monica Bohm Duchen's volume, accompanying an arts festival throughout Britain, *Insiders/Outsiders* (since 2023), highlights European Jewry and their contribution to multiple arts. Far less well known is the role of Polish soldier-artists who were refugees in Iraq during the Second World War, and the Iraqi artists who welcomed them, who collaborated in rendering a version of modern art, and whose British-occupied state supported them by purchasing the Polish artists' work.[63]

No scholarly explanation of any breadth has described either contemporary art's re-picturing of war or displaced artists' places in that reconfiguration. World authorities within art history have instead habitually defaulted to a narrow perspective of perpetual growth that either privileges the perspective of the global art industry, consists of proud but brittle national histories, or defaults to accounts of artists that omit anything of the history and the broader social and political forces that surrounded the world of those artists.[64]

Much art theory (as distinct from art history) focuses on contemporary art and on conditions of contemporaneity.[65] Providing a feminist perspective, Angela Dimitrakaki analyses sexualised depictions of migration between eastern and western Europe, along with the simultaneous rise of female art collectives and performances of masculinity by male art stars. She saw the emergence of new conditions for contemporary art that replace postmodernism, a perspective that we draw on when discussing labour and institutional care in Chapter 4. Furthermore, in contrast to many art historians, Mieke Bal, has defined a capacious 'migratory aesthetic' as 'a condition of sentient engagement'. Bal's use of the term migratory did not denote migrants nor the actual migration of people, but was a 'feature, or a quality of the world in which mobility is not the exception but on its way to becoming the standard, the means rather than the minority'.[66] She identified her migratory aesthetic in the writings of other scholars and curators of the time, including Nicholas Bourriaud's 'relational aesthetics' and art theorist Jill Bennett's 'empathic aesthetics' until, finally, she identified her migratory aesthetic in political art, which is nowadays more generally labelled as activist art. In contrast to the notion of mobile and itinerant artists, this book contends that displaced artists are different: their working lives are more likely defined by waiting, stasis, and restricted mobility, and by the social and political anxieties of their new homelands.

Sociologist Nikos Papastergiadis explains mainstream society's ambient fears of immigrants and refugees, but also explores the role of artists in reclaiming the conditions of hospitality in the aesthetics of culture.[67] By interviewing artists who have backgrounds of displacement, and engaging with art in the past and present, we take a complementary approach to the aesthetics of displacement and its compassionate intentions. Papastergiadis drew, as did many critical theorists, on Jacques Derrida's earlier invention of the ethics of hospitality in which he valorised cooperation and coexistence.[68] For Irina Aristarkhova, contemporary artists' depictions or enactments include gender stereotypes of welcome, and attempts to reclaim civility and amplify the role of guests to push the limits of our hosting traditions.[69] A consideration of displacement aesthetics as a gendered phenomenon will also be highlighted in this book.

Recent scholars have focused on theories of care, empathy, and responsibility in art, on the art world's labour practices, and on art as a social and economic enterprise.[70] Theorists drawing on the new academic field of resilience studies moved away from a focus on individuals and away from the cliché of communities 'bouncing back'. Instead, they looked at the capacity of communities to be adaptive and evolutionary, to be 'bouncing forward'.[71] One of the present book's co-authors, Chrisoula Lionis, has developed the theory of cultural resilience in relation to artists' use of humour as a political strategy in diverse sites of 'crisis', occupation, and denied sovereignty such as Greece, Palestine, and Indigenous Australia. While resilience was reimagined as a capacity to collectively absorb adversity, she offers a critical reading in which resilience is also a key counterpoint to the emphatic role of culture. Instead, humour in contemporary art is a strength-based enactment of cultural resilience that includes authenticity and placemaking, bolstering, belonging, and access in opposition to refugee symbolism often focused on conceptions of 'voiceless' victims.[72] Her research has also shaped this book's approach to investigating modes of collaboration in art museums.

Although we do not explore social practice art at length in this book, we recognise the impact of key debates surrounding community participation, both in terms of contemporary art practice and institutional forms of collaborative co-curation.[73] Furthermore, we recognise its influence on the museums with which we collaborated. For instance, Suzanne Lacy worked with Manchester Art Gallery while we were also collaborating with them on a long-term redisplay of their Grand Tour gallery. Other influential figures include gallery director Charles Esche (associated with the development of Arte Útil (useful art and curating that deepens art's connections with neglected communities) and activist artists such as Tania Bruguera, who also worked with Manchester Art Gallery (School of Integration, Manchester International Festival). Bruguera led the Internationale network; her artistic activism against the Cuban government and representations of incarcerated artists led to her detention and forced exile. Useful art has many historical antecedents that include nineteenth-century aesthetician John Ruskin's democratising philosophy of art; this was the formative influence upon Thomas Horsfall's establishment of the Ancoats

Museum in Manchester, which fostered working-class people to make art themselves. This is important context for the projects we conducted in Manchester.

Scholarship emphasises how art plays an essential yet often overlooked role in community resilience. If writers from the social sciences described the consequences when home is not the place of belonging that is most easily imagined, then a wave of art historians and visual studies scholars located that disquiet in images representing migrants in supposedly post-migration societies.[74] Choosing to pinpoint inequalities and discrimination in the art world, from the 2000s on they located a thread in contemporary art where artists adapted and reinvented documentary forms learned from older documentary and humanitarian photography and cinema. Artists depicted experiences not only of refugees, but also of those affected by the climate crisis, racial division, and inequitable labour. This focus is linked to the political activism that has preoccupied many younger curators, scholars, and artists who allied the figure of the refugee with their aspirations for a just global order, for liberty, equality, and fraternity. T.J. Demos wrote about the connection between exploitation and migration, from the poorest to the wealthiest countries, pointing to artworks like Steve McQueen's videos, including *Western Deep* (2002) and *Gravesend* (2007). Demos saw exile, statelessness, and nomadism as variations of contemporary conditions of mobility. He chose the image of the migrant as a broad concept that might encapsulate, he said, 'multiple forms of movement'.[75] Verónica Tello described similar works of art, noting experimental approaches to reconstructing contemporary history, and linking their effect with the sensation of disorientation when history is fictionalised in video installations, or when recent events are seen only as cryptic aftermaths in mural-sized, colour photographs. She called this 'counter-memorial aesthetics'.[76] This brings us full-circle to Edward Said's comments on the twentieth-century fixation on 'modernity-as-exile'.

The chapters

The book identifies four modes of displacement aesthetics across a succession of chapters that explore the representation of refugees and DPs from the first half of the twentieth century up to the present day, investigating visual representations, art institutions and art collections, and describing contemporary art industry's labour practices since the 2000s. The chapters focus primarily, but not exclusively, on the UK and Europe, and therefore we point out that our references are primarily in English since that language has, for better or worse, become the lingua franca of art history, biennials, and art fairs in recent decades (an issue taken up at length in Chapter 3). Displacement aesthetics is a matrix of western and often Eurocentric interpretations and engagements. It is not immanent, natural, ahistorical, or transcultural, for we are in no way implying that other regions of the globe are exempt from their own cultural forms.

Chapter 1, 'Displacement aesthetics: visualising "refugees" in the twentieth century', describes the visual representation of displacement in the first half of the twentieth century, the defining period when the international refugee regime came to the fore. The two world wars and the Spanish Civil War were particularly influential pivots in visual representation. However, the period after the Second World War was a turning point. The mass displacement of millions of Europeans saw Allied militaries, the UN and humanitarian agencies deploy the term 'displaced person', a bureaucractic category to manage and deliver relief services. However, it often had the effect of ascribing an unwanted 'DP' identity to those seeking resettlement. Throughout this tumultuous period, representations of refugees and displaced persons proliferated in the media, visual art, humanitarian publications, and for UN agencies. The chapter argues that the metaphors and themes that appeared at the very emergence of the contemporary legal category of the refugee in international law have remained constant across different decades and conflicts. This significantly shaped the proliferation of modern art and its collecting in post-migrant countries. The ensuing Cold War saw shifts in consolidating representations of refugees: they became 'figures of concern' and distinct forms of humanity through visual representations. Images were mobilised, then as now, for humanitarian, political, and artistic purposes.

There was a set of visual motifs and themes around which representations of displaced people clustered. The first was mobility and its opposite, immobility, which meant exodus and its opposite, stasis. The second was crowds – that is, vast numbers of displaced, anonymous people. The third was the gendered emotions framing the single category 'womanandchild'. A corollary to this is the trope of the children alone without parents, or the 'waif and stray', a popular way of referring to the new UN discourse of the 'unaccompanied minor'. Such tropes of deserving refugees were particularly useful for humanitarian purposes. There were also racialised refugees that focused initially on Partition and Palestine but continued in the present day as a dominant way of seeing and defining refugees from the Global South. The final motif focuses on the material traces of flight, signified by boats, lifejackets, and the small objects that refugees carried with them. These synecdoches, motifs, and tropes traverse the decades that followed the Second World War, and encompass geographies beyond Europe, such as India, Palestine, Korea, Vietnam, Afghanistan, Rwanda, and Syria, up to and including recent contemporary asylum seekers' boat journeys in the Mediterranean.

Artists, war photographers, humanitarians, and human rights agencies rediscover each of these tropes each decade as if they were new. Sometimes, as we shall see, those orthodoxies were defied but often to the artists' or photographers' cost. In the present day, artists, photographers, and journalists who have not been displaced continue these humanitarian and documentary traditions. Their use of visual conventions can awaken powerful emotions of compassion and pity, but they can also reproduce stereotypes about refugeedom and the cultural figure of the refugee. Some critics have argued that tropes flatten curiosity about the conditions that underpin displacement and refugeedom. This chapter also explores the artists who found particular uses for familiar motifs, often from their own experience and their engagement with art history, as well as the contemporary artists who have understood the tropic history and complicated its representational pathway through time and place.

Chapter 2, 'From representation to lived experience: displaced artists and intersectional barriers', moves from representation to lived experience, turning to contemporary artists who have experienced forced migration and displacement themselves. One key argument is that displaced artists are different to migrants and cannot be placed in the same category. Although it is states that discriminate against different kinds of migrants, this chapter examines the specific conditions in which displacement impacts on artistic practices, shaping, for instance, opportunities and curatorial approaches that differ from other forms of marginalisation. The chapter begins with a discussion between two artists on the trope of the refugee boat. It analyses the political and social issues when artists identify with another and when that 'other' is a refugee. It then explores how displacement aesthetics underwrites the experiences of displaced artists, casting a long shadow over their lives and presenting a set of profound challenges to their careers. This is practical. Refugees have found themselves as the subject matter of art, but they are often stuck: stuck in place without visas to move; stuck with a burden of proof in which displaced artists are often asked to narrate and re-narrate their traumas, both in their art and to access art school entry or arts funding; stuck with financial precarity. The process of seeking asylum and acquiring refugee status raises barriers that other migrants do not experience, and this has had a distinct impact on artists from backgrounds of forced displacement in their encounters with art schools, galleries, and art museums. The chapter describes obstacles such as draconian restrictions that curb international opportunities such as artist residencies. It also looks at artistic collaborations with female asylum seekers, and it explores the burden of proof in re-narration. Significantly, artists have themselves resisted stories imposed on them by governments and humanitarian agencies, and they have resisted the way in which 'Refugee Week' has provided limited opportunities.

Chapter 3, 'The "problem" of language: identifications, definitions, and translations', asks a question that will surface again and again: were photographers and artists presumptuous or ignorant in speaking out on behalf of refugees, even though depicting the interiority of others is part-and-parcel of art and literature generally? We can narrow the question down more usefully: under what conditions does depicting others become either ethically untenable or aesthetically exhausted and unconvincing, or even just plain exploitative? This chapter analyses the political and social issues when artists identify with another when that 'other' is a refugee. It looks at language and terminology, and the complex ways in which refugees are 'spoken for' by others.[77] Critical theory has argued that the words and terms that describe forced displacement are constantly in transition and are also shaped by the dominance of English.

The chapter proceeds with a discussion of the key terms that artists with backgrounds of displacement use to identify themselves, and of the words artists choose to describe their background and heritage. Moreover, displacement aesthetics enables the affective sensation of compassion, but that sensation guarantees neither quality nor the advancement of the subjects that works of art depict. On the one hand, there are works of art that powerfully depict refugees and asylum seekers, but may inadvertently define them as 'speechless emissaries'.[78] Displaced people have so often found themselves as both rhetorical weapons and as the subject matter of art.[79] Whether driven by humanitarian ethics, or a degree of performativity, this attempt to intervene, raise awareness, and do good can also have the opposite effect. The chapter explains the nexus between displacement and testimony, where the question of who has the right to speak on behalf of another may outweigh aesthetic freedom.

Chapter 4, 'Displacement aesthetics and artistic labour: the care of workers', considers displaced artists and their labour as they encounter the world of contemporary art. This chapter examines how employment regulations, legal barriers, and conditions of work shape the artistic labour – paid and unpaid – of displaced artists, whose work must be demarcated from migrant artists, since their opportunities for work and their mobility are so uniquely and absolutely constrained by restrictions. The distinctive relationship between displacement and labour in art addressed in this book has not previously been considered in any depth. We will therefore seek to explain the unique ways in which labour has different implications for displaced artists. The chapter begins by identifying the wide gap between the itinerancy that is valued in art-writing and by artists, and the conditions that displaced artists face. Although one of the dominant tropes describing major contemporary artists is that they are peripatetic, highly mobile, and post-national figures, they often encounter restrictions on movement, economic precarity, and invisibility in a web of controls that disadvantage them.

The chapter considers new forms of participatory art that have considered displacement. It focuses on art from the early 2000s to the present day, particularly on works by Christoph Schlingensief and Santiago Sierra, looking closely at the presence of displaced people as participants, and then examining projects by art collective The Silent University (2012). The point is unambiguous: there is a tension between the artists and their assistants who may have backgrounds of displacement.

This tension is amplified by the anonymity that goes with employee status, even in other projects that seek to care for assistants through anonymisation when the identity of displaced artists and participants must be protected. Finally, the chapter considers how displaced artists collaborate with visual art institutions, pinpointing issues that challenge preconceptions of hospitality and care in artistic and curatorial practices that presume to be engaging with displacement. In other words, the chapter maps the barriers that persist despite institutional policies of equality, diversity, and inclusion, and the discourses of institutional care and hospitality. We may ponder whether open call exhibitions and mentoring between established local and displaced artists will provide more career opportunities.

Chapter 5, 'Displacement aesthetics: collaboration, co-curation, and collections', considers how cultural institutions can both advocate for and share power with displaced communities and those artists who are marginalised from the centres of creativity, while also attempting to act as a force in generating institutional change. In doing so, the chapter explores the 'operational' aspects of displacement aesthetics as it changes from the focus on representing displaced, voiceless 'others', while recognising that all operations are entangled with representation as it stands in for, takes the place and ascribes (unfixed) meanings on behalf of others. The start of this chapter considers the efforts within the art industry that sprung up during the Second World War to assist displaced and interned artists. These efforts revealed the strengths and limits of advocacy and compassion. The chapter also moves towards the present, exploring the challenges that contemporary curators and galleries face in efforts to change the focus from ostensibly pure representation of displaced artists or works that visualise themes of forced migration toward a more considered, inclusive approach of collaboration with artists from displaced heritage. In art museums, the representational world of the collection is shaped by invisible factors. What is encountered is made visible through an invisible and complex set of processes and priorities. When we consider displaced artists, we must be aware of who is selected for rescue, what is selected for collections and exhibitions, and who ends up on the walls of the museum. What is visible can often disguise and even displace a multitude of other stories. The final part of the chapter examines contemporary artists who have worked with museum and archival collections to make decolonial interventions, and offers new ways of thinking about, seeing, and feeling the aesthetics of displacement.

Notes

1   Peter Gatrell, *The Making of the Modern Refugee* (Oxford: Oxford University Press, 2013); for technical definitions of modern refugee processes and protocols, see Peter Adey et al. (eds), *The Handbook of Displacement* (London: Palgrave Macmillan, 2020).

2   Edward Said, 'Reflections on Exile', in Edward Said, *'Reflections on Exile and Other Essays* (Cambridge, MA: Harvard University Press, 2000), p. 173.

3   Alexander Betts, 'The Normative Terrain of the Global Refugee Regime', *Ethics and International Affairs*, 29:4 (2015): 363–375; Peter Gatrell, *The Unsettling of Europe: The Great Migration, 1945 to the Present* (London: Allen Lane/Penguin Books, 2020).

4   Peter Gatrell, 'Refugees: What's Wrong with History?', *Journal of Refugee Studies*, 30:2 (2017): 170–189.

5   Lauren Banko, Katarzyna Nowak, and Peter Gatrell, 'What is Refugee History, Now?', *Journal of Global History*, 17:1 (2022): 1–19.

6   Peter Gatrell, Anindita Ghoshal, Katarzyna Nowak, and Alex Dowdall, 'Reckoning with Refugeedom: Refugee Voices in Modern History', *Social History*, 46:1 (2021): 70–95, 75, 74.

7   Ossi Naukkarinen, 'Aesthetics and Mobility: A Short Introduction to a Moving Field', *Contemporary Aesthetics*, 1 (2005), accessed 3 September 2024. https://search-ebscoh ost-com.manchester.idm.oclc.org/login.aspx?direct=true&db=aft&AN=505099715& site=ehost-live

8   Cynthia Enloe, *Bananas, Beaches and Bases: Making Feminist Sense of International Politics* (Oakland, CA: University of California Press, 2014); Marta Zarzycka, *Gendered Tropes in War Photography: Mothers, Mourners, Soldiers* (London: Routledge, 2016); Heather Johnson, 'Click to Donate: Visual Images, Constructing Victims and Imagining the Female Refugee', *Third World Quarterly*, 32:6 (2011): 1015–1037.

9   James Charlton, *Nothing About Us Without Us: Disability Oppression and Empowerment* (Oakland, CA: University of California Press, 2000).

10 Yến Espiritu and Lan Duong, 'Feminist Refugee Epistemology: Reading Displacement in Vietnamese and Syrian Refugee Art', *Signs: Journal of Women in Culture and Society*, 43:3 (April 2018): 587–615, 588; Kristina Boréus, *Migrants and Natives – 'Them' and 'Us': Mainstream and Radical Right Political Rhetoric in Europe* (London: Sage, 2020).

11 Ernst van Alphen, 'Playing the Holocaust', in Norman J. Kleeblatt (curator and ed.), *Mirroring Evil: Nazi Imagery/Recent Art*, exhibition catalogue (New York and New Brunswick: Jewish Museum and Rutgers University Press, 2002), pp. 65–83.

12 Leo Bersani and Ulysse Dutoit, *Arts of Impoverishment: Beckett, Rothko, Resnais* (Cambridge, MA: Harvard University Press, 1993); Mieke Bal, *Quoting Caravaggio: Contemporary Art, Preposterous History* (Chicago, IL: University of Chicago Press, 1999).

13 Liisa Malkki, *The Need to Help: The Domestic Arts of International Humanitarianism* (Durham, NC: Duke University Press, 2015); Moritz Schramm et al. *Reframing Migration, Diversity and the Arts: The Postmigrant Condition* (London: Routledge, 2021).

14 Eleana Yalouri, '"Difficult" Representations: Visual Art Engaging with the Refugee Crisis', *Visual Studies*, 34:3 (2019): 223–238; Balca Arda, 'Contemporary Art on the Current Refugee Crisis: The Problematic of Aesthetics Versus Ethics', *British Journal of Middle*

Eastern Studies, 46:2 (2019): 310–327; Kaya Barry, '"Artists not Tourists": Ethical Tensions between Creative Mobility and Migration', *Applied Mobilities* (July 2023): 1–15.

15 Bénédicte Miyamoto and Marie Ruiz (eds), *Art and Migration: Revisioning the Borders of Community* (Manchester: Manchester University Press, 2021); Christine Ross, *Art for Coexistence: Unlearning the Way We See Migration* (Cambridge, MA: MIT Press, 2022).

16 For instance, Charles Saatchi's *Sensation* (1999) at the Brooklyn Museum, New York.

17 See Charles Green, *The Third Hand: Artist Collaborations from Conceptualism to Postmodernism* (Minneapolis: University of Minnesota Press, 2001).

18 Dave Beech, 'Inside/Out: On the Fall of Public Art', *Art Monthly*, 329 (September 2009), accessed 22 May 2024. www.artmonthly.co.uk/magazine/site/article/inside-out-by-da ve-beech-september-2009

19 www.un.org/unispal/document/genocide-as-colonial-erasure-report-francesca-albanese-01oct24/; https://www.un.org/en/genocideprevention/documents/USG_and_Special_Adv iser%20Nderitu_Sudan_13_June_2023.pdf

20 Terry Smith, *What Is Contemporary Art?* (Chicago, IL: University of Chicago Press, 2009).

21 See Jean Fisher, 'The Other Story and the Past Imperfect'. www.tate.org.uk/research/tate-papers/12/the-other-story-and-the-past-imperfect

22 Roberta Smith, 'At the Whitney, A Biennial With a Social Conscience', *New York Times* (5 March 1993). www.nytimes.com/1993/03/05/arts/at-the-whitney-a-biennial-with-a-so cial-conscience.html?pagewanted=print&src=pm; also see Christopher Knight, 'Crushed by Its Good Intentions: Under the Banner of Opening up the Institutional Art World to Expansive Diversity, the Whitney Biennial has in fact Perversely Narrowed its Scope to an Almost Excruciating Degree', *Los Angeles Times* (10 March 1993). http://articles.latimes. com/1993-03-10/entertainment/ca-1335_1_art-world. For the chief curator's memoir of the show, see Elisabeth Sussman, 'Then and Now: Whitney Biennial 1993', *Art Journal*, 64:1 (Spring 2005): 75–79.

23 Charles A. Wright Jr., 'The Mythology of Difference: Vulgar Identity Politics at the Whitney Biennial', *Afterimage*, 21:2 (September 1993): 4–8, 6.

24 Hal Foster, 'The Politics of the Signifier: A Conversation on the Whitney Biennial', *October*, 66 (Fall 1993): 3–27, 12.

25 Eleanor Heartney, 'Identity Politics at the Whitney', *Art in America*, 81:5 (May 1993): 42–47, 45; reprinted in Eleanor Heartney, *Critical Condition: American Culture at the Crossroads* (Cambridge: Cambridge University Press, 1997), pp. 166–177.

26 David Ross, 'Preface: Know Thy Self (Know Your Place)', *1993 Whitney Biennial*, exhibition catalogue (New York: Whitney Museum of American Art & Harry Abrams, 1993), pp. 8–11, 9.

27 Cornel West, 'The New Cultural Politics of Difference', in Russell Ferguson, Martha Gever, Trinh T. Minh-ha, and Cornel West (eds), *Out There: Marginalization and Contemporary*

Cultures (Cambridge, MA: MIT Press, 1990), p. 19, cited in Thelma Golden, 'What's White …?', in Elisabeth Sussman (curator and ed.), *1993 Whitney Biennial Exhibition*, exhibition catalogue (New York: Whitney Museum of American Art and Harry N. Abrahams, 1993), p. 27.

28 Coco Fusco and Guillermo Gómez-Peña, 'The Year of the White Bear', *Art & Text*, 43 (September 1992): 52–57.

29 Coco Fusco, 'Passionate Irreverence: The Cultural Politics of Identity', in Elisabeth Sussman (curator and ed.), *1993 Whitney Biennial Exhibition*, exhibition catalogue (New York: Whitney Museum of American Art and Harry N. Abrahams, 1993), p. 85.

30 Fusco, 'Passionate Irreverence', p. 79.

31 Musée nationale d'art moderne, *Face à l'histoire*, exhibition catalogue (Paris: Centre Georges Pompidou, 1996).

32 Okwui Enwezor, 'Introduction: Travel Notes: Living, Working, and Travelling in a Restless World', in *Trade Routes: History and Geography: 2nd Johannesburg Biennale 1997* (Johannesburg: Greater Johannesburg Metropolitan Council and Thorold's Africana Books, 1997), p. 12.

33 Enwezor, 'Introduction: Travel Notes', p. 9.

34 Enwezor, 'Introduction: Travel Notes', p. 12.

35 Slavoj Žižek, 'Multiculturalism, Or, the Cultural Logic of Multinational Capitalism', *New Left Review*, 225 (September–October 1997): 44, 37.

36 *Manifesta 12: The Planetary Garden. Cultivating Coexistence* (2019) took place in Palermo, a city that was host to many refugees. But local artists were pushed aside while famous, international artists were flown in to perform Palermo's sense of community for its people. Ironically, Manifesta's offices, set up in a poor migrant neighbourhood, were burgled; see Arseny Zhilyaev, 'Revisiting Manifesta 12', *e-flux Criticism*, 25 September 2018, accessed 22 May 2024. www.e-flux.com/criticism/241939/revisiting-manifesta-12

37 Norman J. Kleeblatt (curator and ed.), *Mirroring Evil: Nazi Imagery/Recent Art*, exhibition catalogue (New York: Jewish Museum, 2002). See reviews by Linda Nochlin, 'Mirroring Evil: Nazi Imagery/Recent Art', *Artforum*, 40:10 (2002): 167–170; Peter Schjeldahl, 'The Hitler Show; the Jewish Museum Revisits the Nazis', *The New Yorker*, 78:6 (2002): 87; Robert Atkins, 'Bringing Nazi Symbols to the Jewish Museum', *ARTnews*, 101:3 (2002): 46–47.

38 Similar criticisms were made of Kara Walker in exposing stereotypes in the 1990s. See Tommy Lott, 'Kara Walker Speaks: A Public Conversation on Racism, Art, and Politics with Tommy Lott', interview, *Black Renaissance/Renaissance Noire*, 3:1 (2000): 69–91.

39 Jill Bennett, 'Material Encounters: Approaching the Trauma of Others through the Visual Arts', in Charles Green (ed.), *Postcolonial + Art: Where Now?* (Sydney: Artspace, 2001); see Ernst van Alphen, 'Colonialism as Historical Trauma', in B. Atkinson and C. Breitz (eds), *Grey Areas: Repression, Identity and Politics in Contemporary South African Art* (Johannesburg: Chalkham Hill Press, 1999), pp. 269–281; see Jill Bennett and Rosanne

Kennedy (eds), *World Memory: Personal Trajectories in Global Time* (New York: Palgrave Macmillan, 2002).

40 Andreas Huyssen, 'Anselm Kiefer: The Terror of History, the Temptation of Myth', *October*, 48 (Spring 1989): 25–45.

41 Okwui Enwezor, Katy Siegel, and Ulrich Wilmes (curators and eds), *Postwar: Art between the Pacific and the Atlantic, 1945–1965*, exhibition catalogue (Munich: Haus der Kunst, 2016).

42 Massimiliano Gioni (curator and ed.) *The Restless Earth* (La Terra Inquieta; Milan: Trussardi Foundation and Triennale de Milan, 2017); see T.J. Demos, 'Charting a Course: Exile, Diaspora, Nomads, Refugees: A Genealogy of Art and Migration', in Gioni (curator and ed.) *The Restless Earth*, pp. 18–26; on Abounaddara see: https://hyperallergic.com/392565/syrian-collectives-videos-turn-up-in-triennial-after-they-refused-to-participate/

43 Massimiliano Gioni in conversation with Rahel Aima, 'La Terra Inquieta at La Triennale di Milano, Milan', *Mousse Magazine* (August 2017). www.moussemagazine.it/magazine/massimiliano-gioni-rahel-aima-2017

44 Massimiliano Gioni in conversation with Rahel Aima.

45 Gatrell, *The Making of the Modern Refugee*; Jordana Bailkin, *Unsettled: Refugee Camps and the Making of Multicultural Britain* (Oxford: Oxford University Press; 2018); Francesca Piana and Jo Laycock, *Aid to Armenia: Relief, Humanitarianism and Intervention from the 1890s to the Present* (Manchester: Manchester University Press, 2020); Peter Gatrell, *The Unsettling of Europe: the Great Migration 1945 to the Present* (London: Penguin, 2020); Laure Humbert, *Reinventing French Aid: The Politics of Humanitarian Relief in French Occupied Germany* (Cambridge: Cambridge University Press, 2021); Becky Taylor, *Refugees in Twentieth Century Britain: A History* (Cambridge: Cambridge University Press, 2021); Ruth Balint, *Destination Elsewhere: Displaced Persons and the Quest to Leave Postwar Europe* (Ithaca: Cornell University Press, 2021).

46 S. Gemie, S. and L. Rees, 'Representing and Reconstructing Identities in the Postwar World: Refugees, UNRRA and Fred Zinnemann's Film *The Search* (1948)', *International Review of Social History*, 56:3 (2011): 441–473; Christina Twomey, 'Framing Atrocity: Photography and Humanitarianism, *History of Photography*, 36:3 (2012): 255–263; Sylvia Salvatici, 'Sights of Benevolence: UNRRA's Recipients Portrayed', in Heidi Fehrenbach and Davide Rodogno (eds), *Humanitarian Photography* (Cambridge: Cambridge University Press, 2015), pp. 200–222; Antoine Burgard, 'Visualising Holocaust Child-Survivors in Canada: From Post-war Humanitarian Campaigns to National Memory', *Cultural and Social History*, 17:5 (2020): 731–754.

47 Simone Gigliotti, *Restless Archive: The Holocaust and the Cinema of the Displaced* (Bloomington, IN: Indiana University Press: 2024); See also E. Nooter, 'Displaced Persons from Bergen-Belsen. The JDC Photographic Archives', *History of Photography*, 23:4 (1999): 331–340.

48   For an eloquent overview of refugee history, see Peter Gatrell, 'From the History of Refugees to Refugee History', *Refugee History*, 2 November 2016; Lauren Banko et al., 'What is Refugee History, Now?' On post-First World War refugee experiences, see Peter Gatrell and Liubov Zhanko (eds), *Europe on the Move: Refugees in the Era of the Great War* (Manchester: Manchester University Press, 2017); Alice Massari, *Visual Securitisation: Humanitarian Representations and Migration Governance* (London: Palgrave Macmillan, 2021); Lynda Mannik (ed.), *Migration by Boat: Discourses of Trauma, Exclusion, and Survival* (New York: Berghahn Books, 2016).

49   Laure Humbert, 'Picturing Displaced Persons: Exhibiting French Prestige?' Photographs of Humanitarian Aid for Displaced Persons in French-Occupied Germany, 1945–52', *Journal of War and Culture Studies*, 15:22 (2022): 208–232; Lynda Mannik, *Photography, Memory and Refugee Identity: The Voyage of the SS Walnut, 1948* (Vancouver: UBC Press, 2013).

50   Tom Allbeson and Claire Gorrara, 'Visual Histories of Postwar Reconstruction', *Journal of War and Culture Studies*, 15:2 (2022): 125–132.

51   Fehrenbach and Rodogno (eds), *Humanitarian Photography: A History*; Tanya Sheehan (ed.), *Photography and Migration* (London: Routledge, 2018); Simone Gigliotti, 'Displaced Children of Europe, Then and Now: Photographed, Itinerant and Obstructed Witnesses', *Patterns of Prejudice*, 52:2–3 (2018): 149–171.

52   Brenda Lynn Edgar, Valérie Gorin, and Dolores Martin-Moruno (eds), *Making Humanitarian Crises: Emotions and Images in History* (Cham: Springer Nature, 2022).

53   Domenico Sergi, *Museums, Refugees and Communities: Communities, Collections and Representations* (London: Routledge, 2021); Rob Sharp, *Refugee Voices: Performativity and the Struggle for Recognition* (Abingdon, Routledge: 2024).

54   Jan-Jonathan Bock and Sharon MacDonald (eds), *Refugees Welcome: Difference and Diversity in a Changing Germany* (Oxford, New York: Berghahn Books, 2019; Amy K. Levin (ed.), *Global Mobilities: Refugees, Exiles and Immigrants in Museums and Archives* (London: Routledge, 2016).

55   Robert Janes and Richard Sandell (eds), *Museum Activism* (London: Routledge, 2019).

56   Wayne Modest and Robin Lelijveld (eds), *Words Matter: An Unfinished Guide to Word Choices in the Cultural Sector* (Leiden: Research Center for Material Culture, 2018); Wendy Ng, Syrus Marcus Ware, and Alyssa Greenberg, 'Activating Diversity and Inclusion: A Blueprint for Museum Educators as Allies and Change Makers', *Journal of Museum Education*, 42:2 (2017): 142–154.

57   Nina Möntmann, 'Small-Scale Art Organizations as Participatory Platforms for Decolonizing Practices and Sensibilities', *Journal of Aesthetics and Culture*, 13:1 (2021): 1–9; *Decentering the Museum: Contemporary Art Institutions and Colonial Legacies* (London: Lund Humphries, 2023).

58   See Stephanie Barron, Sabine Eckmann, and Matthew Affron (curators and eds), *Exiles + Emigrés: The Flight of European Artists from Hitler*, exhibition catalogue (Los Angeles: LA

County Museum of Art, 1997); Stephanie Barron, Sabine Eckmann (curators and eds) *The Art of Two Germanys / Cold War Cultures 1945–1989*, exhibition catalogue (Los Angeles: LA County Museum of Art, 2009).

59 James Elkins, *The End of Diversity in Art Historical Writing: North Atlantic Art History and Its Alternatives* (Berlin: De Gruyter, 2021); Julietta Singh, *Unthinking Mastery: Dehumanism and Decolonial Entanglements* (Durham, NC: Duke University Press, 2018).

60 Monica Bohm-Duchen (ed.), *Insiders/Outsiders: Refugees from Nazi Europe and their Contribution to British Visual Culture* (London: Lund Humphries, 2019); Siân Roberts, 'Education, Art, and Exile: Cultural Activists and Exhibitions of Refugee Children's Art in the UK during the Second World War', *Paedagogica Historica: International Journal of the History of Education*, 53:3 (2017): 300–317.

61 See Pankaj Mishra, *From the Ruins of Empire: The Revolt Against the West and the Remaking of Asia* (London: Picador, 2012); Pankaj Mishra, *Age of Anger: A History of the Present* (New York: Farrar, Straus, and Giroux, 2017).

62 Brian Foss, *War Paint: Art, War, State, and Identity in Britain, 1939–1945* (New Haven, CT: Yale University Press. 2007).

63 Anneka Lenssen, 'Baghdad Kept on Working: Painting and Propaganda during the British Occupation of Iraq, 1941–45', *Getty Research Journal*, 19 (2024): 92–121.

64 Yves-Alain Bois, Benjamin H.D. Buchloh, Hal Foster, and Rosalind Krauss, *Art Since 1900: Modernism, Antimodernism, Postmodernism* (New York: Thames & Hudson, 2004).

65 Angela Dimitrakaki, *Gender, Art Work, and the Global Imperative* (Manchester: Manchester University Press, 2013).

66 Mieke Bal, 'Lost in Space, Lost in the Library', in Sam Durrant and Catherine Lord (eds), *Essays in Migratory Aesthetics: Cultural Practices between Migration and Art-Making* (Amsterdam: Rodopi, 2007), p. 23.

67 Nikos Papastergiadis, *Cosmopolitanism and Culture* (Boston: Wiley, 2012).

68 Jacques Derrida and Anne Dufourmantelle, *Of Hospitality*, trans. Rachel Bowlby (Stanford, CA: Stanford University Press, 2000).

69 Irina Aristarkhova, *Arrested Welcome: Hospitality in Contemporary Art* (Minneapolis: University of Minnesota Press, 2020).

70 Elke Krasny and Lara Perry (eds), *Curating with Care* (London: Routledge, 2023); Gregory Sholette, *Dark Matter: Art and Politics in the Age of Enterprise Culture* (London: Pluto Press, 2010); Hans Abbing, *The Changing Social Economy of Art: Are the Arts Becoming Less Exclusive?* (London: Palgrave Macmillan, 2019).

71 See Philip Cooke and Luciana Lazzeretti (eds), *The Role of Art and Culture for Regional and Urban Resilience* (London: Routledge, 2018); Catherine Panter-Brick, 'Health, Risk, and Resilience: Interdisciplinary Concepts and Applications', *Annual Review of Anthropology*, 43 (2014): 431–448.

72 Chrisoula Lionis, 'Humour and the Commodification of Suffering: Strategies of Cultural Resilience in Contemporary Art', *Third Text*, 35:5 (2021): 605–623.

73 Grant Kester, *The One and the Many: Contemporary Collaborative Art in a Global Context* (Durham, NC: Duke University Press, 2011); Claire Bishop, *Artificial Hells: Participatory Art and the Politics of Spectatorship* (London: Verso, 2012).

74 Claudette Lauzon, *The Unmaking of Home in Contemporary Art* (Toronto: University of Toronto Press, 2017); Vinh Nguyen and Thy Phu (eds), *Refugee States: Critical Refugee Studies in Canada* (Toronto: University of Toronto Press, 2021); Anne Ring Petersen, *Migration into Art: Transcultural Identities and Art-Making in a Globalised World* (Manchester: Manchester University Press, 2017).

75 T.J. Demos, *The Migrant Image: The Art and Politics of Documentary During Global Crisis* (Durham, NC: Duke University Press, 2013), pp. xv, 2–3.

76 Verónica Tello, *Counter-Memorial Aesthetics: Refugee Histories and the Politics of Contemporary Art* (London: Bloomsbury, 2016); Verónica Tello, 'What is Contemporary About Institutional Critique', *Third Text*, 34:167 (2020): 2–15.

77 Sten Pultz Moslund and Anne Ring Petersen, 'Introduction: Towards a Post Migrant Frame of Reading', in Moritz Schramm (ed.), *Reframing Migration, Diversity and the Arts: The Postmigrant Condition* (New York: Routledge, 2019).

78 Liisa Malkki, 'Speechless Emissaries: Refugees, Humanitarianism, and Dehistoricization', *Cultural Anthropology*, 11:3 (1996): 377–404.

79 Anne Ring Petersen, 'The Square, the Monument and the Re-Configurative Power of Art', in Anna Meera Gaonkar et al. (eds), *Postmigration: Art, Culture, and Politics in Contemporary Europe* (Bielefeld: Transcript Verlag, 2021); Alex Rotas, 'Is "Refugee Art" Possible?', *Third Text*, 18:1 (2004): 51–60.

1 Displacement aesthetics: visualising 'refugees' in the twentieth century

What is conjured in the mind's eye when the word 'refugee' appears? We might imagine family groups traipsing across a horizon with few belongings, or a photograph of people in orange lifejackets crammed into rubber boats, or a close-up of the desperate face of a mother cradling her child, or perhaps a young child whose parents are entirely outside the picture frame. These archetypal images were not only made in recent decades. There is a longer history of aestheticising displacement through a set of familiar and repeated visual themes and metaphors that focus on identifiable cultural narratives and symbols that conjure displaced people and their experiences of being forced out of their homes.

This history is inextricably linked to three visual phenomena: the technical capacity and proliferation of photography, the rising production and consumption of visual media, and the influence of art history and its iconography. Together, they shaped how both affective emotions and cultural memories appeared in response to displacement.[1] Moreover, this forms the basis of our discussion of 'displacement aesthetics', which begins with the seismic events of the Second World War as it instigated the largest displacement of people in modern history. By the mid-twentieth century, such experiences were transformed into a coherent set of images, which are the subject of this chapter.

It is April 1940. German forces have invaded Denmark and are heading to Norway. The battle for France is raging. Refugees pour out of Europe. The front-page of *Picture Post*, the popular pictorial newspaper in Britain, is splashed with a close-up photo of a man and woman huddled on the floor of a train station. The camera is perched just above them, pointing downward, homing in on their dazed expressions and clasped hands. A single suitcase and cloth bundle are their only possessions (Figure 1.1). In this quiet moment of respite from their dramatic exit, the photo demands an emotional response from the viewer.

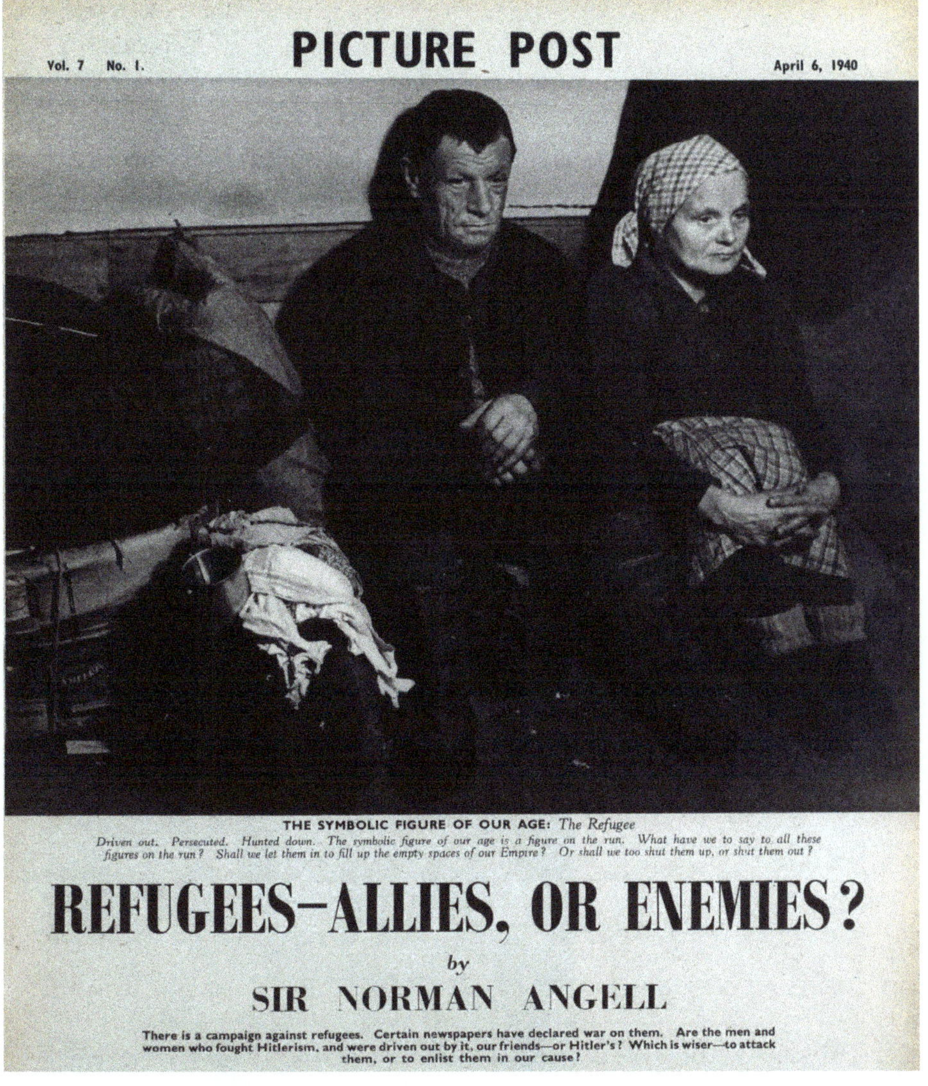

1.1 *Picture Post* (6 April 1940, front page).

Narrating the headline image, renowned English journalist and Nobel Prize laureate Norman Angell declared that the refugees' plight is Europe-wide and prescient. Such pictures reflected a turning point in history:

The Symbolic Figure of Our Age: *The Refugee*. Driven out. Persecuted. Hunted down. The symbolic figure of our age is a *figure on the run*. What have we to say to all these figures on the run? Shall we let them in to fill up the empty spaces of our Empire? Or shall we *shut them up*, or shut them out? Refugees – Allies or Enemies?[2]

Identified neither by nationality nor name, the couple, he notes, are *symbolic figures*. Further inside the paper, additional photographs encapsulate motifs that would become familiar: a convoy of Polish civilians departing on foot, a distraught Spanish woman, a bomb-injured Chinese grandmother and bewildered child, and a despairing, Jewish woman in Vienna (Figure 1.2). Although tacitly acknowledging the worsening refugee situation in China, refugees in this period were mostly represented as White Europeans, the visual personification of the political and humanitarian condition of 'refugeedom' at that time.

Historians use the term refugeedom to encapsulate the emerging political and legal category, 'refugee', in international law during the first half of the twentieth century. Significantly, the term also signifies the creation of a new social category of humanity that humanitarianism shaped. Importantly, refugees' symbolic significance was based on visual representations, and yet these have rarely been the subject of comprehensive examination.[3] This chapter explores mode 1 of displacement aesthetics identified in a set of common visual tropes about refugees, displaced persons, and the conditions of refugeedom. However, the argument offers a distinctive and nuanced interpretation of the role of familiar motifs beyond simply the repetition of normative

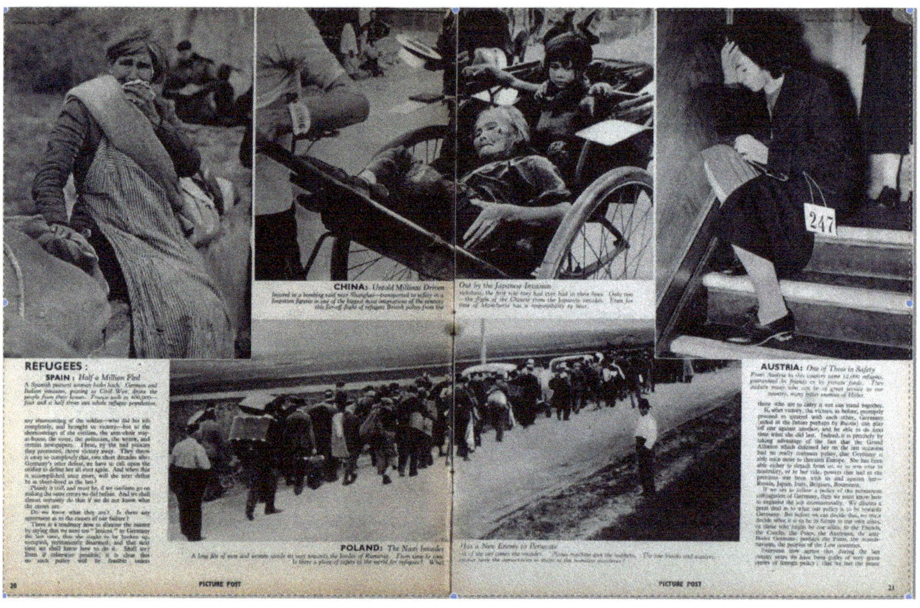

1.2 *Picture Post* (6 April 1940, inside cover).

images or stereotypes of refugees across cultural forms. We will also see how artists play a unique part in experiencing, interpreting, and producing aesthetic experiences of displacement.

These images are as relevant now as they were then. Hence, we begin this study with the historical foundations of displacement aesthetics in the first half of the twentieth century. In art, there is a longer history of European paintings, including fifteenth-century depictions of Muslim and Jewish expellees from Spain and Portugal, and religious images, which point to displacement aesthetics in action. But the twentieth century marks a distinctive period when refugees appeared as cultural figures framed by modern humanitarian and political drivers. Visual narratives supported efforts to assist refugees and displaced persons through charitable aid and international organisations, and they also defined the contours of refugee rights through systems of protection. This chapter examines the role and importance of visual tropes of refugeedom in shaping 'displacement aesthetics' across humanitarian and news media, UN media, and also visual art. Images, we contend, shaped and sometimes universalised visions of the 'modern refugee'. A powerful set of persistent motifs and artistic iconographies migrated across diverse cultural arenas, geographies, and temporalities. Georges Didi-Huberman asks: 'Shouldn't we admit that every image must be thought of as a moment in a movement, a stage in a migration?'[4] The migrated tropes discussed in this chapter are not an exhaustive list and have been selected largely in relation to significant conflicts (the two world wars, Spanish Civil War, Palestine, Partition, Korea, and Vietnam). They have been selected to convey the longevity, portability, and dynamism of displacement aesthetics in the twentieth century and into the present day.

Through an examination of the motifs that aestheticised displacement, the chapter explores how similar images appeared in different cultural arenas, but in many contexts and often with wildly different motivations informing their production. The first set centred on images of mobility and immobility. The second type were crowds, signifying the collective identity of refugees as faceless masses, which contrasted with artists' affinity for refugee portraiture. The third group was gendered, engaging emotions surrounding a singular, apolitical, and idealised category of victimhood, the 'womanandchild'. Connected to this were images of caregiving fathers, emerging from the late 1940s, that could reflect the crisis of the family and of wartime masculinity.

The fourth most common image was of children alone without their mothers, parents, or family. These were particularly important in establishing that ruptured families were deserving refugees, and in eliciting strong emotional responses to their implied vulnerability, stirring the parental drive to care for children. The fifth set was found in the material culture of displacement, associated with mobility and immobility such as transportation, objects carried, and temporary accommodation. Familiar objects of refugeedom aroused affective and embodied emotions in response to the material culture associated with displacement. Particular conflicts conjured specific objects of mobility: the sack, cart, and horse in the First World War; the suitcase and train station in the Second World War. The wooden fishing boat came to define *all* refugees fleeing the Vietnam War because this was the method by which they escaped, and so they all came to be identified as 'boat people'. As a result of the 2011 Civil War in Syria, when over 14 million people fled to Europe, refugees were identified with objects such as orange lifejackets and black rubber boats. They appeared as sensory markers – visual, tangible, haptic – of lived experiences of contemporary displacements. Artists have recently responded to this materiality, aware of how it can elicit emotions beyond a primary signification. Artists activate cultural connections and the affective meanings of displacement.

The chapter also discusses forced displacement as a result of the cruelties of colonial policy, including Palestine and India. However, in the example of the Partition of India (1947) it considers how displacement aesthetics impacts on populations often considered beyond the scope of refugeedom. As scholars have shown, the 'modern refugee' is a geopolitical construction, one made by international legal frameworks, national immigration policies, colonial histories, and humanitarian organisations.[5] As we will see in this book, modern refugees are framed by images with their own histories. Crucially, contemporary artists have engaged with this deeply impactful story, intervening in both historic and contemporary practices of displacement aesthetics with new stories and voices.

The role of images in the emergent refugee regime

Visual images matter. This was amplified in the period when the collective identity of 'refugee' was emerging in international law and as the 'refugee regime' came into force in the first half of the twentieth century. In this period, refugees and displaced persons were gradually transformed into cultural figures. Although displacement is a longstanding human experience, visual culture provided a modern means of making sense of war's upheavals and the emerging legal frameworks to manage population movements. While visual images preceded the period in which the 'modern refugee' was made, common motifs began to be reanimated. As familiar images turned into visual tropes throughout the century, we find a common note: they appear at once highly contemporary, speaking to the moment of a declared 'crisis', whilst also intimating the ahistorical and universal condition of humanity on the move. This is why they are largely unnoticed and unquestioned; they seem natural and realistic rather than constructed.

Moreover, visual tropes entail identifiable motifs within an easily recognisable and accessible iconography of symbols, metaphors, and material objects. They can also become synecdoches – a part or a detail that stands in for the whole story – which is distinct from symbols and metaphors, which also play a role in how images of refugees are routinely interpreted. Over time, conventions are established and images traverse seamlessly, back and forth, across time, space, and conflicts. Geography, too, becomes less and less specific. The tropes of displacement aesthetics provide a pliable, flexible framework that would enable very different audiences to mentally travel from Europe to Asia and the Middle East.

In addition, humanitarian emotions of empathy, pity, and compassion underlie the appeal of such images across geographies and decades. Scholars know that certain iconographies are furnished with more emotional power than others, provoking the sensation of universal truth. Universalising specific political, geographic, and historical moments can dehumanise, generalize, and flatten individuals into symbols outside their reality, which serves the spectator's need to empathise with 'vulnerable others'.[6] The motifs and tropes of displacement aesthetics are not necessarily fixed in a specific time but are networks of iconologies that cross generations and centuries.

Their affect has been debated. One art historian has blamed the public indifference to suffering on the aestheticisation of anguish.[7] This is based on the idea that great western art, from the Elgin Marbles to Goya's *Disasters of War*, has turned the apprehension of war into merely an aesthetic experience of pathos. Scholars have noted the long history of the pornography of pain in enslavement lithography, which thrilled Abolitionists. Conversely, in current media images, it has been observed that a similar 'staging of spectacles of suffering' weakens the intended moral response.[8] We are not arguing, however, that visual tropes of displacement, like iconologies, are to blame for habituation and indifference, or humanitarianism's impotence.

By historicising displacement aesthetics, we argue that visual motifs and tropes are much more complex, meaningful and historically resonant than mere stereotypes or moral entreaties. To grasp this, we turn to early twentieth-century theorist Aby Warburg, and his influential idea of the stored affect that underlies repeated visual tropes of war, displacement, and suffering. Warburg listed and explained the specific but archetypal tropes underlying the temporal and spatial breadth of European art history, photojournalism, and visual culture. He and his iconological successors explained why and how tropes are much more than stereotypes. This distinction must be remembered throughout this and succeeding chapters, for images sustain the capacity to carry radically different meanings and purposes.[9] Warburg traced morphological tropes and specific recurring gestural motifs, categorising them according to a list of allegories – Medea or the Death of Orpheus, for instance – that were governed, he postulated, by sublimations surviving from image to image in frozen, intensely felt gestures. Warburg assumed that a collective mind is connected by the sublimated image's affect. This is different to iconography. Kurt Forster has pointed out that Warburg was inventing the discipline of visual culture studies, giving it a domain far beyond the conventional art history of his time.[10] Warburg was also attempting to develop a psychological history and language of affect, encoded and transmitted in visual images. He called the pathetic affect by a name, the pathos formula, triggered by particular gestures and signs. He gave these signs – the gestures of figures and figure-groups frozen at an instant of maximum intensity or excitement as opposed to moments of ethos, or contemplation – a name: the dynamogram.[11] He was explaining that there is a hidden language of images, like invisible writing. Some tropes produced pathos and others not, and this power was not just produced by context, but was tied to archetypes.

This is why, in many media, in humanitarian and UN photographs, visual tropes shaped refugees into archetypal narratives, at times compressing experiences into stories of abjection and rescue that were already meaningful to viewers. Such imagery was remarkably familiar, despite different aims, such as the emotional spectacle of newsworthiness, attracting charitable donors, or a demonstration of the effectiveness of international policy and its funding. At other times, similar tropes carried very different meanings for displaced communities, such as when displaced artists depicted their experiences, witnessing forced displacement while at the same time conversing with art history through contemporary images. When visual artists repurposed a trope or theme that has been part of art history, they also adapted living history.

The role of categories of tropes outlined above was significant, even more so in the context of the first half of the twentieth century, for this visuality traversed many different arenas – news media, humanitarianism, visual art – at precisely the time when the European refugee regime emerged as an international legal framework. Internally and externally displaced people were seen as problem populations that required international assistance and humanitarian protection. The explosion of images saw refugees become cultural figures framed by aesthetic emotions.

Visual images pervaded the news and humanitarian media in response to mass displacements of populations due to conflicts, changing borders, ethnic cleansing, and 'population exchanges' that accompanied the creation of nation states and territories, nationalism, revolutions, and Fascist occupations.[12] Key points of the widespread visualisation of large displaced populations were seen during the First World War (1914–18), the Armenian genocide (1915), the 'Great Catastrophe' of Asia Minor (1920s), the Spanish Civil War (1936–39), and the Second World War (1939–45), with its prolonged aftermath involving millions of displaced people. In the late 1930s, refugees who crossed the border into France during and after the Spanish Civil War, from the 1939 *Retirada* (the Republican 'retreat'), did not possess any right to asylum.

They were interned in camps, returned to Spain, or were permanently exiled.[13] During the same decade, the 'problem' of Jews escaping National Socialism also dominated international politics and refugee relief.

The Second World War, and then the onset of the Cold War which immediately followed, saw a continued focus on European refugees and displaced persons, featuring first those fleeing Nazism and then Communism. Around 65 million people were displaced into camps after 1945. They were now designated as 'displaced persons' (DPs), stateless, in need of resettlement in another country or at risk of being returned (voluntarily or forcibly repatriated) to their places of origin. Only a few short years later, the Palestinian Nakba (the 1948 'Catastrophe' of expulsions and mass displacement), the Partition of India and Pakistan, and widespread displacement from wars in China and Korea shifted attention eastwards. As Peter Gatrell argued, the making of the 'modern refugee' may have been underpinned by international and national relationships, but there was no singular history of 'the refugee'.[14] Yet the repeated patterns in visual tropes of refugees could at times universalise rather than draw out complexity and diversity.

The evolution of the 1951 Convention was gradual, and subject to national and international self-interest. The creation of the High Commission for Refugees in 1921 and the Intergovernmental Arrangement on Russian Refugees (protecting 800,000 people) in 1922 were two early successes for the League of Nations. In part, this was due to the efforts of the Norwegian scientist and diplomat Fridtjof Nansen. In the 1930s, the Nansen International Office for Refugees in its quasi-diplomatic role continued its work, advocating for refugees. However, while stateless Armenians and undocumented Russians acquired legal status affording protection with the so-called Nansen passports, Jewish Germans and Austrians faced uniquely difficult problems of legal citizenship. The restrictive policies of nation states meant there was a need for Jewish charities in rescue and resettlement.[15] Successive League of Nations' refugee organisations were formed between 1938 and 1947, for example, the League Inter-Governmental Committee for Refugees.

The International Committee of the Red Cross played a significant role in assisting refugees and administering refugee camps throughout the interwar period. However, it was not until the formation of the United Nations Relief and Rehabilitation Administration (UNRRA) in 1943 that a definite international organisation was dedicated to the relief, welfare, and resettlement of postwar displaced persons (DPs). This was soon followed by the establishment of the International Refugee Organisation (IRO) in 1946, which required that refugees apply for refugee status. This was a protracted and bureaucratised system. Applicants had to repeatedly verify their identities and retell their stories of displacement to IRO officers, a dehumanising process that refugees are still familiar with today. While screening out Nazi sympathisers was important, resettlement and repatriation were the IRO's main aims, providing care, protection, and retraining for future employment.[16] Finally, in 1952, the Office of the United Nations High Commissioner for Refugees (UNHCR) emerged as a permanent agency of the UN. The declaration of the UN Refugee Convention in 1951 consolidated this history of international commitment and bureaucracy to manage the flow of refugees and displaced persons.

These colossal efforts required visual communications that would muster support, financial aid, and political will. International organisations deployed photographers and artists, publishing a range of magazines that pictured refugees and displaced persons, such as *The Journal of the British Red Cross Society* or the UN's *The Courier*. After 1945, the political category of the refugee meant focusing on resettlement or repatriation of displaced persons (DPs), and this was a cornerstone of UN activity. As we will see, refugees were not just defined by political and bureaucratic forces but were framed by images that encapsulated the cultural and social worlds of the period. This is crucial and is the observation from which to analyse the foundation of the visual tropes of displacement.

Responding to the negative image of refugees in 1940, Norman Angell raised the issue of their missing voices, a point that resonates to this day. Images of refugees and displaced persons, for instance, impact on public culture and impart political ideas, to the extent that some scholars believe that 'no caption is needed'.[17] Displacement aesthetics has been shaped both by those with lived experienced and those without, both those makers of images who seek to support with compassion and those who seek otherwise. Importantly, this is not to say that when refugees represent themselves or their experiences, normative images are *not* reproduced. Artists were indeed vital players in visualising the harsh realities and intense emotions that displacement aroused, and they often did this through common themes and motifs, such as exodus, boats, and barbed wire.

To that extent, displacement aesthetics does not bifurcate images into normative and non-normative sets, and thus it should not be seen that conventions and stereotypes signify a cultural pathology of displacement imagery. We argue that the same image can elicit radically different meanings and purposes. Didi-Huberman's point that images are not a 'crisis of reason' to be 'reproached for not consisting, for not holding in place, and consequently for only forming lesser realities' rings true for displacement aesthetics.[18] Simply put, these aesthetic conventions are part of cultural and art history. They have staying power. Refugee crises and the emerging refugee regime provided momentum to its visualisation.

Yet it is crucial to recognise that displaced people do not often hold the space of creative agency, whether it be in photojournalism, in the art industry, in humanitarian media, or in the dominant visual culture. David Farrier wrote that to become a refugee is declaratory rather than constitutive, and the discretionary rights of their recognition resides with the nation state so that hospitality is highly conditional.[19] So too is the right of reply – that is, the right to determine one's own representation. In the humanitarian field, one remarkably consistent image is that of refugees as rescued, as recipients of hospitality from donor communities. The point is that compassionate images – the images that arise from the matrix of displacement aesthetics – habitually reflect a humanitarian perspective which is not necessarily proposed by displaced persons themselves. Understanding the contours of displacement aesthetics by identifying the common tropes shaped by compassion and advocacy enables us to see them operating in the present.[20]

Mobility and immobility

The earliest moving images of refugees emerged during the First World War with newsreels of refugees leaving France and Belgium, evacuating towns and cities along roads by foot and by horse-drawn cart, escaping the advancing German army. Silent, black-and-white footage, made by news companies such as Pathè and Topical Budget, were screened in cinemas. Accompanying captions to the silent footage emphasised emotions in poetic terms: 'the deep *unutterable woe* which none save *exiles feel*'.[21] Despite the emerging importance of modern newsreels, visual art continued to be a crucial visual form that conveyed dramatic experiences of forced mobility to audiences. Artwork featured in the illustrated news, in Allied propaganda, and in humanitarian portrayals of European refugees. Richard Jack and Gerald Spenser Pryse in England, Theophile Steinlen in France, and Leo Gestel in the Netherlands, for instance, depicted French, Belgian, and Serbian refugees through images of tightly packed crowds fleeing with just the few possessions they could carry.

Similar sentiments were made about both newsreel and art's capacity to represent the emotional ordeal. One Dutch art critic described Gestel's series *Exodus*, as 'scenes so *throbbing with woe* and *speechless agony* as to *haunt the mind* for days after'.[22] The discursive power of victimhood displaced refugee testimony. Images have thus played an important role in communicating refugees' suffering However, in recent times, speaking for the voiceless has come under scrutiny. Scholars of contemporary humanitarianism argue that refugees are frequently positioned as 'speechless emissaries', that is, depoliticised, dehistoricised, and universalised.[23] We argue that this silencing is intertwined with the rise of the refugee as a pervasive cultural figure, who traverses multiple visual industries and identities, much as Edward Said postulated in the remarks with which this book began – that displacement is a condition of modern life involving a constant renegotiation of identity and belonging.

Forced mobility was an imaginative aesthetic. Departure and arrival were conveyed as columns of people moving in unison in one direction, whether in colourful paintings, black-and-white lithographs and photographs, newspapers, or mass-produced posters. In 1914, Britain's Official War Artist, Frank Brangwyn, turned his art to anti-German propaganda. For Brangwyn, a Belgian-born Welsh artist, the displacement caused by the German occupation was personal. A lithograph, *Refugees Leaving Antwerp* (1914), depicts a dense convoy of civilians leaving their city on a road that stretches behind them. Children cling to fearful parents and men raise their fists at the advancing German Army. Brangwyn was combining anti-German sentiment with sympathy for refugees. But the gestures of defiance enabled British audiences to see that refugees were not completely helpless. Providing them with sanctuary appeared a worthy solution. *Refugees Leaving Antwerp* was circulated in the press. Stamps and posters with the image were made for the Belgian and Allied Aid League, a humanitarian charity. The visual story moved from the drawing to mass-produced material culture.

Throughout the 1920s, depictions of refugee departure were similarly made for the Asia Minor catastrophe (1922) and the Turkish War of Independence (1919–23), during which thousands of Greeks, Assyrians, and Armenians became refugees. Photos and illustrations of the flight to Smyrna on foot or by horse and cart, with burning villages in the background, followed the pattern of the Belgian and French imagery of a few years earlier. Blame for mass departure was clear. Civilians 'terrified by the looting and fires' left in fear of 'bloody reprisals' declared the front page of *La Domenica del Corriere* (the Italian Sunday weekly). Beltram Achille's colour illustration depicted the blazing city and crowds of women and children fleeing.[24] The illustrated news media provided colour and emotion, while black-and-white newsreels conveyed movement and urgency, both supporting Allied actions and humanitarianism. Newsreel intertitles again referred to the 'Exodus', especially resonant with Christian audiences. This was a period of growth in the media industry, one which would dominate public perceptions of refugees for the next century. Artists drew on photographs, and photographers drew on art. In Brangwyn's drawings and woodcuts of *The Exodus* (1918), he drew directly from photographs of Belgian civilians to depict refugees pulling a cartload of people and belongings, while also harkening back to Christian iconography.[25]

Exodus: an enduring visual story

To communicate the emotional upheaval of twentieth-century displacement, artists turned to the story of the Exodus. The aesthetic emotions that surround the imagining and visualising of refugees became anchored in the longer history of Christian and

Jewish religious art, in images created centuries before the advent of photography or film. Exodus was a foundational narrative of Abrahamic religions of the Old Testament story about the Israelites' departure from Egypt and formed a central iconography in western art. It centred around a 'master narrative of border crossing', where sea and desert are spaces of both 'liminality and transit'.[26] Across the history of European painting, Exodus was a popular theme up to the late nineteenth century and the British Pre-Raphaelites. Even though later artists drifted away from religious themes across the twentieth century, a plethora of European and British artists interpreting the flight of refugees in France, Belgium, and Mesopotamia (during the Armenian genocide) often returned to this historically emotional motif.

Again, during the Spanish Civil War (1936–39), the religious and artistic heritage of Exodus was repurposed. Half a million Spanish civilians fled the Fascist military. Photographs and posters played a critical role in conveying the immediacy of the impact by the Luftwaffe barrage on innocent civilians, terrorised into fleeing with their belongings. Photos circulated by Republican agencies and independent freelance photographers, including Robert Capa, Gerda Taro, and David 'Chim' Seymour, called on the world to assist the victims of this new Exodus.[27] Although internally displaced Spaniards were not included in the emerging international legal refugee regime, the visualisations of these people chimed with the Belgian and French refugees of the First World War in making clear their need for protection.

In 1941, the French experience of 'L'Exode' (The Exodus) represented the mass displacement of civilians from Paris, as 6 million people fled to the south of France to escape the advancing German army. Independent freelance photographers documented the mass departure, and photos were disseminated through agencies such as the Roger Viollet company, founded by the couple, Hélène Roger and Jean Fischer. Valerie Holman notes that the French authorities instructed media outlets not to 'overly dramatize' the mass migration. That did not work. The drama and powerlessness of civilians strafed by the Luftwaffe was impossible to downplay. As with the Spanish Civil War, the victimising of civilians was the foremost aesthetic motif, rather than heroic resistance.[28] There were alternatives to photographs of endless 'columns of miserable refugees filing down the roads of provincial France', including Thérèse Bonney's portraits of women and the elderly, makeshift encampments, and worried parents trying to locate their children.[29] But these images did not disrupt common depictions of the exodus that portrayed French refugees as the victims of epic events beyond their control.

French artists were also witnesses to the upheaval. In two works made around the same time, Andre Dupin's *The Exodus from Paris* (painted in June 1940), and in Robert Houdusse's *Exodus* (painted in 1941, when most of France was under German occupation), people become throngs of anonymous bodies, trudging over

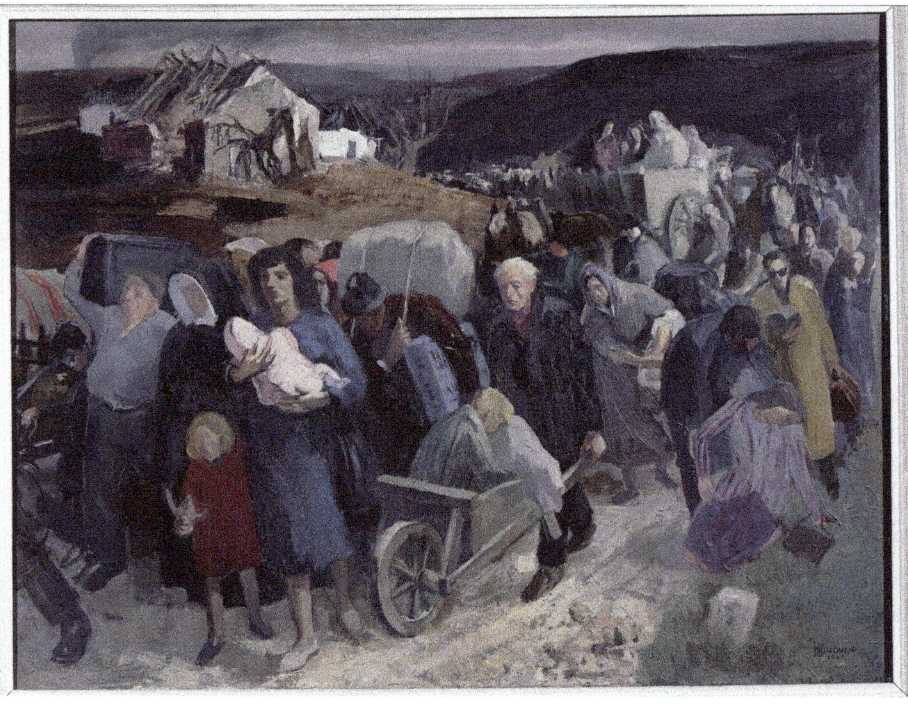

1.3 Robert Houdusse, *Exodus* (1941). Oil on canvas. Courtesy of Bridgeman Images.

roads, burdened by sacks and suitcases. Houdusse depicts a woman collapsing by the roadside, a mother carrying her infant, and bombed buildings reminiscent of 1914 (Figure 1.3 and back cover of this book). Only a few faces stand out, grimacing and dazed. This would become a common way of representing Europeans fleeing violence and occupation.[30] However, the emphasis on flight obscured both the collapse of democracy and the disaster that 90,000 children had been separated from their parents in the panic.

As the legal regime governing refugees emerged, the theme of exodus was continually repurposed for political, humanitarian, and artistic purposes. This travelled with the modernist artists fleeing across the Atlantic. Working for the Emergency Rescue Committee, the American journalist Varian Fry helped European artists and intellectuals to escape, including André Breton, Marcel Duchamp, Max Ernst, Jacques Lipschitz, and Hannah Arendt. The modernist painter Marc Chagall remained committed to the theme of exodus for the rest of his life. In 1941, Chagall fled France to the US on the *SS Sinaia*, the same ship on which Magnum photographer David Seymour, two years earlier in 1939, recorded Spanish refugees bound for Mexico. In New York, Chagall, fluent in Yiddish but not at all in English, was isolated. He blamed the sudden death of his wife, Bella, on their departure, saying that 'exile from Europe had sapped her will to live'.[31] In 1945, his grief deepened with news of the Nazi death camps. As he reflected on the fate of European Jewry, Chagall returned to biblical themes. Ultimately, he struggled to cope with life in America and returned to France in 1947.

The same year, the ship *Exodus*, transporting 4,000 Holocaust survivors to Palestine, was turned back by the British. This tragedy inspired Chagall's *The Boat Exodus* (1947), a painting of a boat crowded with people and of swimmers struggling for shore. Exodus had a profound significance for the artist. After his first visit to the newly declared state of Israel in 1951, Chagall began a colossal painting, *Exodus* (1952–66), depicting Jesus rather than Moses in a Flight from Egypt. In a series of twenty-three lithographic prints, *The Story of the Exodus* (1966), Chagall brought together Jewish and Christian themes, painting the Passover and Easter, set in the Sinai so that Moses and the Ten Commandments comingled with the Madonna and Child. One of his prints also depicted a throng on the move. He returned to similar themes in his *Flight* prints from 1971, which emerged from Varian Fry's idea to raise funds for the International Rescue Committee.[32] Chagall believed in a Jewish homeland, creating colossal works for the Knesset in the 1960s, and massive tapestries depicting the Exodus in 1969. Yet the 1967 Arab–Israeli War profoundly tested his allegiance to the state of Israel.[33] It is more than plausible that the persistence of Christian and Jewish themes of exodus in his work owed a lot to his own personal trauma of displacement.

By 1945, the idea of exodus was used so routinely to communicate mass dis-placement that officials from UNRRA used it to signify the organised repatriation of displaced persons (DPs), as well as the resettlement of unaccompanied or uni-dentified children from occupied zones.[34] Likewise, the United Nations Works and Rehabilitation Administration (UNWRA) described its photographs of refugees flee-ing the 1967 war as 'the second exodus'. Palestinian families were depicted boarding boats to the East Bank of the Jordan River or crossing the temporarily rebuilt Allenby Bridge with suitcases. Close-up portraits of women's and children's strained faces, or children crying, had also become common modes of visually witnessing the distress of forced departure.[35] Artists also made use of these themes, not only as they were rooted in art history, but as their own, life-threatening experiences brought new meaning to art. Exodus lent cultural significance to forced departure.

For some, it was a potent signifier of resistance and collective resilience. Living within the 1948 borders after the Nakba, the young artist Abed Abdi rendered a colourful, abstract painting entitled *Refugees* (1961), following an earlier painting in 1960 completed at the age of eighteen. Both works presented Palestinian refu-gees as a closely packed crowd (Figure 1.4). He developed his oeuvre by revisiting painful memories of the Nakba. A group of anonymous women and children, with

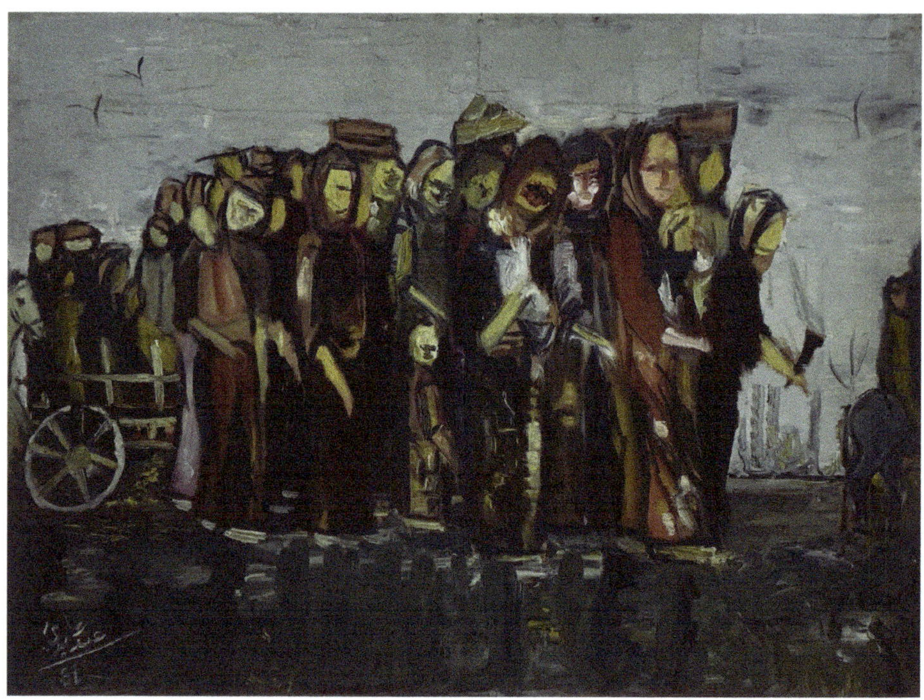

1.4 Abed Abdi, *Refugees* (1961). Oil on canvas. Courtesy of Barjeel Art Foundation, Sharjah.

the motif of a cartload of belongings, move in unison as one, though they also seem frozen in time. The painting alludes to both the mobility and stasis that characterised Palestinian displacement.[36] In other works, lines of refugees disappearing into the distance convey the sense of interminable departure.[37] Abdi's depictions of refugees in paintings and prints became central to the new Palestinian identity and its shared memory of the catastrophe.[38]

We have seen that displacement aesthetics traversed photography and visual art. Processional movement became central in symbolising urgent, forced departure, and exodus became a renovated visual narrative, its subsidiary parts gathered from the Bible and art history. These images had a remarkable power sustained across new decades. Today, according to Terence White, both Left- and Right-leaning media images of refugees still conform to these patterns.[39] Emma Cox refers to 'processional aesthetics' in the contemporary news media.[40] But we also see that this is historically rooted in the exodus imaginary, which was and still is the ubiquitous – both universalised and globalised – visual story of displacement.

Symbolising stasis

When refugees finally arrived at camps, they also arrived at tents, barbed wire, and fences, and these became potent symbols of the stasis they endured next. The advent of UNHCR-branded tents, so familiar today, emerged in 1950 with the organisation's foundation. Significantly, tent cities had a visual history preceding 1950. Before the First World War, military and humanitarian photography linked refugees with their emergency and temporary tent shelters. Picture news agencies (such as the George Bain News Service) and Christian relief committees widely distributed photographs of tent camps, such as of Armenian refugees in Gaziantep following the 1909 Adana massacre.[41] Over the ensuing decade, refugee camps rose in rapid response to the Ottoman Empire pogroms and deportations of Armenian, Greek, and Assyrian civilians. Camps were set up in Egypt, Syria, and Palestine. The British Army established encampments at Baqubah on the banks of the River Diyalah, in Iraq, for Assyrian refugees.[42] The Camp Commander described it as a 'tented city', hosting 40,000–50,000 refugees, structured into 'regularly laid out tented villages'.[43]

Early camp photographs highlight orderly rows of tents, as material evidence of effective organisation and administration. Increasingly, both military and humanitarian organisations such as the International Red Cross used wide-angle and aerial views to aestheticise the tent city, emphasising its expansive, geometric organisation, and indicating efficient management.[44] Devoid of people, the photos provided a clean perspective that obscured on-the-ground issues, such as poor sanitary facilities, unclean water, disease, and harsh environmental conditions. Such photos naturalised encampments as the condition of the modern refugee, dissociated from the daily realities of their hardship.

During the Second World War, tent camps administered by the Middle East Relief and Refugee Administration (MERRA), with others in East Africa, Palestine, and Mexico, emphasised human resilience. Photos of El Shatt refugee camp stand out for their depiction of healthy-looking Yugoslav refugees, appearing to overcome the challenges of the Sinai. Neat lines of tents housed 3,000 Yugoslavians, who were shown cooking, labouring, sewing clothes, and playing games. Images of both resilience and distance contrast with depictions of Palestinian tent camps in International Committee for the Red Cross (ICRC) photographs. Here, children are seen helping to build the camp on desert sands and rocky ground, documenting their collective hardship and struggle for existence.[45] The UN and the Quakers set up emergency tents after approximately 700,000 Palestinians were expelled during the Nakba.

The aesthetics of stasis was increasingly linked to the material deprivation of tent camps. Images of Khan Younis in Gaza, Jenin and Dheisheh camps in the West Bank, camps in the Jordan valley, and Nahr el-Bared in Lebanon, highlighted the deprived conditions of camp life. In the aftermath of the 1948 Nakba, tented expanses were photographed from above. Again, during the 1967 conflict, both tent and cinderblock cities came into aerial view, also capturing the magnitude of the disaster. For, now Palestinian civilians were doubly displaced. Aerial photographs such as of Jaramana camp on the outskirts of Damascus, emphasised scale with its expanse retreating into the background and a few children playing in the foreground. The aesthetic framing added a sense of protraction to their living conditions (Figure 1.5).[46] In other photographs, refugees appear at the edges of the frame. A face or body in the foreground establishes the scale of the tent city behind, implying that the camp lay at the edge of humanity.[47]

By 1959, the number of refugees housed in tents fell from 87 per cent to 37 per cent, because by the mid-1950s the United Nations Relief and Works Administration (UNRWA) started replacing emergency shelters with prefabricated concrete cinderblock buildings. Now families were crammed into dense spaces with shared sanitation. These new camps became permanent.[48] They have been described as ongoing 'spatial violence', a lasting imaginary of confinement.[49] The geometric configurations of the tent and the cinderblock cities underscored the paradox in refugee governance: the emergency had become permanent. Since 2023, with the Israel Defence Force's destruction of refugee cities such as Khan Younis in Gaza, and calls to

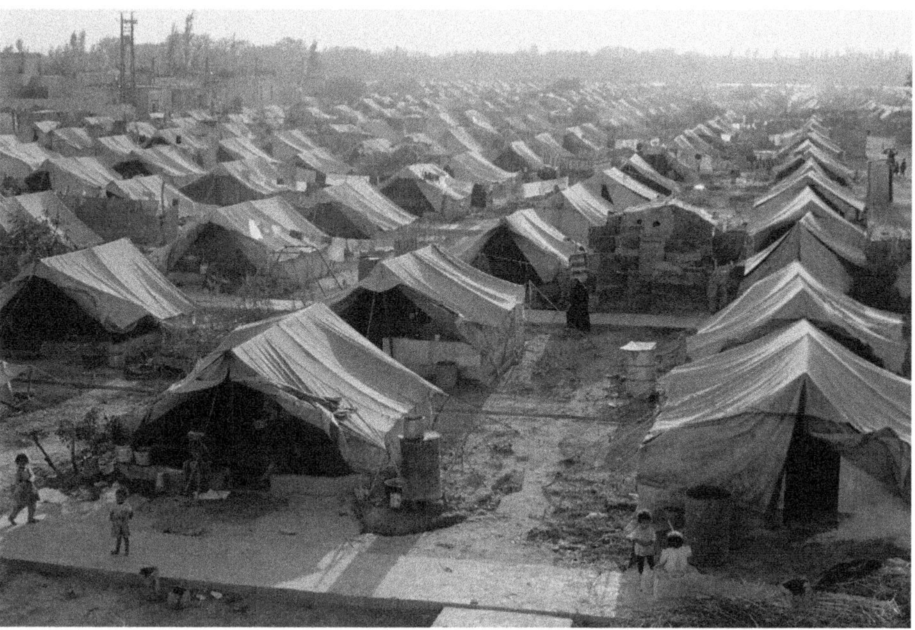

1.5 Aerial view of Jaramana camp, © 1970 UNRWA Archive. Photographer Unknown. https:// unrwa.photoshelter.com/search/result/I0000hCBf2V.gqys?terms=aerial%20view&.

relocate the Palestinian population elsewhere, the apparent condition of permanency is even more fragile.

From encampment to entrapment, a further symbol of immobility is the barbed wire fence. A tool of control used against Indigenous populations and in the Boer War, in Europe it had been associated with prisoner of war disease from 1918.[50] Visually, however, it was powerfully invoked in the Spanish Civil War. For instance, Robert Capa's photographs at Argelès-sur-Mer (*Picture Post*, 1939), accompanied the story of 120,000 civilians and soldiers fleeing the Fascist armies led by Franco.[51] Barbed wire camps also became a defining symbol of Franco's brutal victory. The spiked wire was a violent form of containment that was both dehumanising and agonising.[52] Following the German occupation of France, new camps detained unwanted foreigners (*indésirables*), including Jewish families behind barbed wire. Refugee camps led to concentration camps. Hannah Arendt was imprisoned at Gurs in 1940. She escaped on the *SS Sinaia* before Gurs became a transit camp for deportation to Auschwitz in 1943.[53]

Barbed wire featured in many artists' works in the first half of the twentieth century. The German and Austrian artists who fled to Britain, only to then be interned, took the material of their imprisonment into their own artistic hands. Fences, wire, and walls became sources of inspiration in artworks made for camp newsletters (Fred Uhlman, *People Behind the Barbed Wire*, 1940; Hugo Dachinger, *Internee*, 1940; Hermann Fechenbach, *Release*, 1940). Wire also featured on the poster for the now renowned exhibition, *Art Behind the Wire*, which internees created at the Isle of Man internment camp in 1941. Dachinger contributed a modernist watercolour of a yellow, red, and black human eye juxtaposed with grey-blue barbed wire. To a contemporary audience, the eye supplies an ambiguous impression of both being watched and looking out beyond the wire. It is a reminder of human fragility. In Australia, the internees shipped on a brutal 12,000 mile journey on the *Dunera* included Ludwig Hirschfeld Mack, whose harrowing works associated barbed wire with intense feelings of isolation, as expressed in *Desolation: Internment Camp, Orange* (1941).[54] These images are testament to the creativity of artists despite the hardships of 'internment life', and their resilience in using their talent and exhibition practice to ask the art world to lobby the government for their release. This important aspect of advocacy and cooperation will be discussed further in Chapter 5.[55]

Images of waiting were also central to portrayals of displacement. Waiting for transport at a train station or by the side of the road, waiting to arrive at a safe destination, all this was conveyed through facial expressions, and in bodily postures and gestures. Displaced bodies were at times treated in a formulaic manner, particularly as frozen in time and space in press photographs, such as those seen at this chapter's outset (Figure 1.1). As the Second World War came to an end, European displaced persons (DPs) and German expellees were often similarly depicted in paintings and photographs, waiting in queues on roads and railways, resting with exhausted children on their cases or baskets, or massed together in reception centres. They appeared, in such images, to be stuck, caught in the hiatus between going and coming, hoping for travel permits and Allied transports.[56] A painting by Ivor Bailey Rees-Roberts, *Displaced Persons* (1945), depicts an expelled German family waiting by the side of the road, presumably for a ride, as military trucks file past them. The mother stands upright, impassive, her child holding onto her for comfort. Perched on the proverbial suitcase, her elderly father sits in despair, head in hands. The nation's defeat is symbolised in masculine frailty and the material object of uncertainty.[57]

The British War Artists Advisory Committee sent artists to record the liberation in Europe. Official War Artist Mary Kessell travelled to Hanover, Hamburg, and Berlin where she was confronted by the plight of internally displaced civilians. She was one of only three women whose war artist appointment took her outside Britain. In Bergen-Belsen, after the Allied liberation, and as the full horror of the Holocaust was coming to light, she made many memorable drawings and paintings of the war's immediate aftermath. Documenting the defeat of Germany, she focused on displaced civilians. Blurry, scrawled figures appear as spirits more than human bodies, suggesting the unfathomable nature of the scenes to which she bore witness. In her charcoal drawings *Refugees at a Railway Station in Berlin, September* (1945) and *Refugees: Mother and Child* (1945), Kessell focused on waiting women and children, also sitting on their luggage (Figure 1.6).[58]

Akin to the wrapped bodies of Henry Moore's famous Blitz gouaches, Kessell presents the anonymity of displacement to which 'abject bundles of humanity' were reduced, as she described in her diary. Unlike Moore, however, she foregrounded displaced people's emaciation. Kessell described the refugees as 'utterly apathetic – just bundles' covered in lice, 'waiting for trains that come today or perhaps come tomorrow'. Interpreting the scenes around her, her mind delved into art history – to Goya's famous etchings, *The Disasters of War* (1810–20), which had 'come to life' for her in Germany. She wrote: 'I've never seen a more pitiable sight – such bits of humanity – with nothing to hope for – looking without seeing. God seemed so far away from them all'.[59] Haunted by their ghostly bodies, the fugitive images Kessell produced reflected her sense of the precarious humanity of displaced women and children. These works provide a unique interpretation of displacement aesthetics.

This was also quite unlike the aerial and humanitarian photographs of refugee camps. Official Artists like Kessell and internees like Dachinger conveyed the range of emotions arising in displaced people's uncertainty and their stasis. Both the urgency of forced departure and the hopelessness brought by its faltering were depicted in images of mobility and immobility. Displacement aesthetics would ascribe meaning

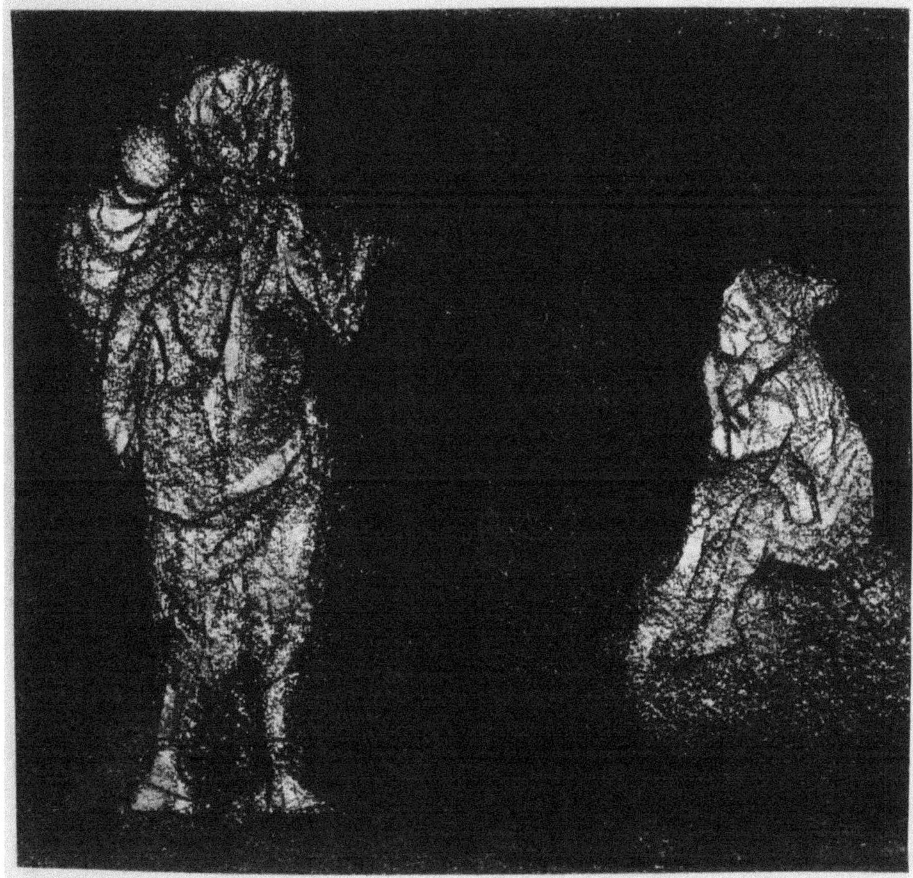

1.6 Mary Kessell, *Refugees: Mother and Child* (1945). © IWM Imperial War Museum.

to these signifiers according to the need for images, regardless of the intention of the maker or the positionality of the subject. The dialectic of the mobile and the static remain central in representing refugees in the present day.

The crowd and the portrait

Mobility and immobility are often synonymous with throngs of people. Whether travelling in convoy or gathered at the wire in camps, crowds became a prominent feature of displacement aesthetics. Columns of faceless, unidentifiable people moving together as one mass or, conversely, trapped in a confined space – both were ubiquitous in depictions of refugee crowds. Scholars have seen the crowd as a phenomenon of modernity, a political symbol of assembly, revolution, collective action, and a form of psycho-social behaviour. Its negative associations were madness, delusion, and mob violence.[60] In the twentieth century, the crowd became one of the standard images of modern war and refugee crisis. Surprisingly, the refugee crowd has garnered little academic attention.

The negative impression of crowds stems from the influential argument that crowds are hostile, irrational forces. Gustav Le Bon's *The Crowd: A Study of the Popular Mind* (1896) defined crowds as an 'inferior form of evolution – in women, children, and savages'. In its most negative interpretation, crowds were driven by mysterious forces and unconscious instincts, and were cast as threats to the security of society and civilisation.[61] To some extent, refugee crowds induced similar fears for security at the border, and should thus be confined in camps. They were – and often still are – regarded as burdens on the welfare, education, and health systems reserved for citizens. By the late twentieth century, the word, 'crowd' denoted 'crowding' at the borders, 'crowding into' trains, towns, and camps, 'crowding out' locals, and above all, crowding by refugees. The verb 'to crowd' is often used to stir negative reactions, implying an unfettered state of amassing, overrunning, and overwhelming. The visual trope of the refugee crowd added aesthetic potency to those long-held ideas. Groups of people were presented as anonymous, de-individualised, forces so that even depictions of emotional distress were politically ambiguous. Crowds could be staged in different ways, such as menacing hoards or defiant resistors. From 1914 through to the Spanish Civil War, photographs and films of crowds gathered at ports and train stations, piling onto boats and trains, arriving at borders, were widely circulated in the international press, to mixed effect.[62]

In settings of colonial rule, crowds were understood as threats to be dispersed by force. Laws of emergency were continually passed in British India to prevent people from gathering, and to quash political protest in the most brutal terms that martial laws could legitimise, such as those resulting in the Jallianwala Bagh massacre (1919). Colonial photos only documented empty streets and humiliating punishments exacted on the populace; the dispersed crowd was conspicuously absent.[63] From the 1930s, photos of marches for Home Rule, mass meetings, and civil disobedience involving crowds stoked imperial anxieties. By the time of the Partition of India (1947), the British Empire's political and racial prejudices that repelled crowds had taken on the new significance of mass, forced displacement.

While mainstream British media portrayed Indian Independence as a success that vindicated colonial rule, photographs could evidence the abdication of governance and care for the 25 million displaced.[64] Large populations of Muslims, Sikhs, and Hindus forced to relocate were visualised gathering at railways stations, waiting to leave, or streaming along roads to reach what would become their new homes. Displaced crowds represented this fearful flight from communal violence. The camera lens was often focused on aerial or extreme wide-angle perspectives, emphasising the scale of the emergency. It did not seem to matter to the visual narrative who was doing the fleeing. Photographs typified the displaced crowd, whether this was people gathered in Delhi after riots in the Pakistani portion of the state of Punjab or 50,000 Muslim families at the ancient fort of Purana Qila, turned into a refugee camp (September 1947).[65]

Challenging such stereotypes, however, was the perspective of Indian artists, who were witnesses to the intercommunal violence. Their approach was grounded in resistance to colonial visual frameworks. As Emilia Terracciano demonstrates, artists produced work that could 'stand up to power, negotiate, and even vociferously contest the limits of the state's emergency claims'.[66] Artists also presented a different perspective to that of humanitarian pity. Their emotions derived from close, personal insight into forced relocation and violent separation. A case in point is the Indian modernist Satish Gujral's *Partition series*, made in Delhi from 1948 through to the early 1950s. The anguish of displacement was visceral to him. In paintings, drawings, and lithographs, Gujral's figures swirl around with intense turbulence. In one drawing, *Mourning En Masse* (1948), he conveys desperate emotions and a sense of chaos through the refugees' bodies (Figure 1.7). Their mournful faces render the scar of Partition at an individual, sensory, level, and as the figures spin out of the frame viewer's emotions are directly impacted.

Another artist, S.L. Parasher, made sculptures while he was Commander of a refugee camp in Ambala, using its soil to make the terracotta figure, *Refugee Woman*. According to Geeta Patel this work evokes the 'slow dread' of his subject with 'extraordinary compassion'.[67] The figure covers her mouth in a gesture to soothe her shock, while her eyes stare directly at us. In the form of sculpture, affective emotions in clay are powerfully executed.[68] Portraiture thus clearly depicts the emotional suffering of first-hand experiences of displacement.

Artists who were more distant from the events also favoured portraiture and figuration. In Britain, European refugees were popular subjects and sitters, but the distance from emotional connection was palpable. During the First World War, the influx of Belgian refugees resulted in portraits of the elderly or of young, beautiful women, that emphasised their demure character. William Strang's *A Belgian Peasant Girl* (1915) highlights the young refugee's demure femininity in rosy cheeks and downcast eyes. During the Second World War, female refugees again proved a beguiling subject for portraitists. They were painted as beautiful, mysterious figures, with eyes expressing intensity and resignation or with postures and hand gestures conveying vulnerability. Arthur Todd's *Rita the Refugee* (1941) depicts a forlorn, young woman staring wistfully with hands crossed between her legs, protecting her modesty. Her rosy cheeks and facial expression bear an uncanny resemblance to Strang's portrait

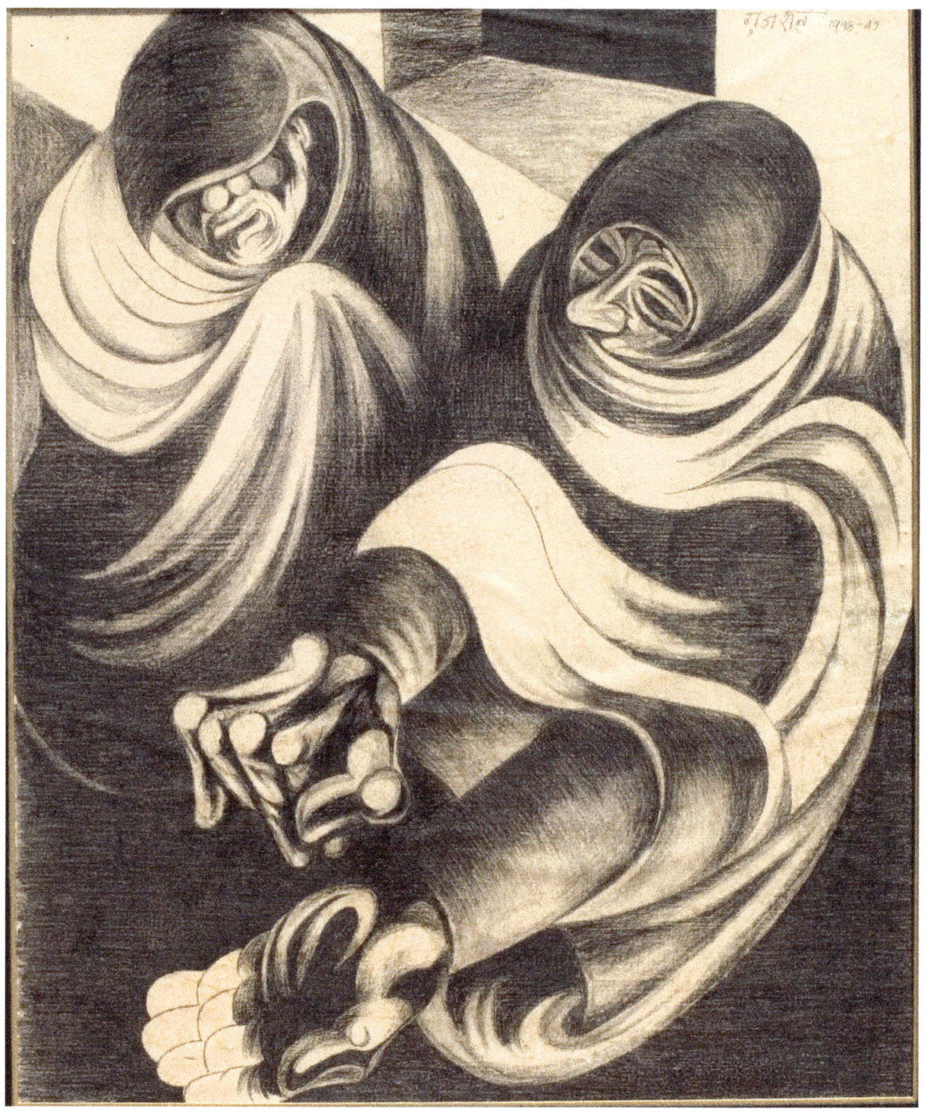

1.7 Satish Gujral, *Mourning En Masse* (1948). Oil pencil on paper. Partition series. Courtesy of The Gujral Foundation.

from twenty-five years earlier. By contrast, Kathleen Williams' *Refugee* (1943) and Victor Pasmore's *Portrait of a Jewish Woman* (1943–45) accentuate their dark hair, deep-set eyes, and resigned expressions. Alongside the mournfulness implied in their black dresses, these female refugees to Britain uphold their serene beauty.[69]

Exemplifying the image of the beautiful refugee woman was the society portrait painter David Jagger's *Jewish Refugee, Vienna* (1938). His idealising practice transformed

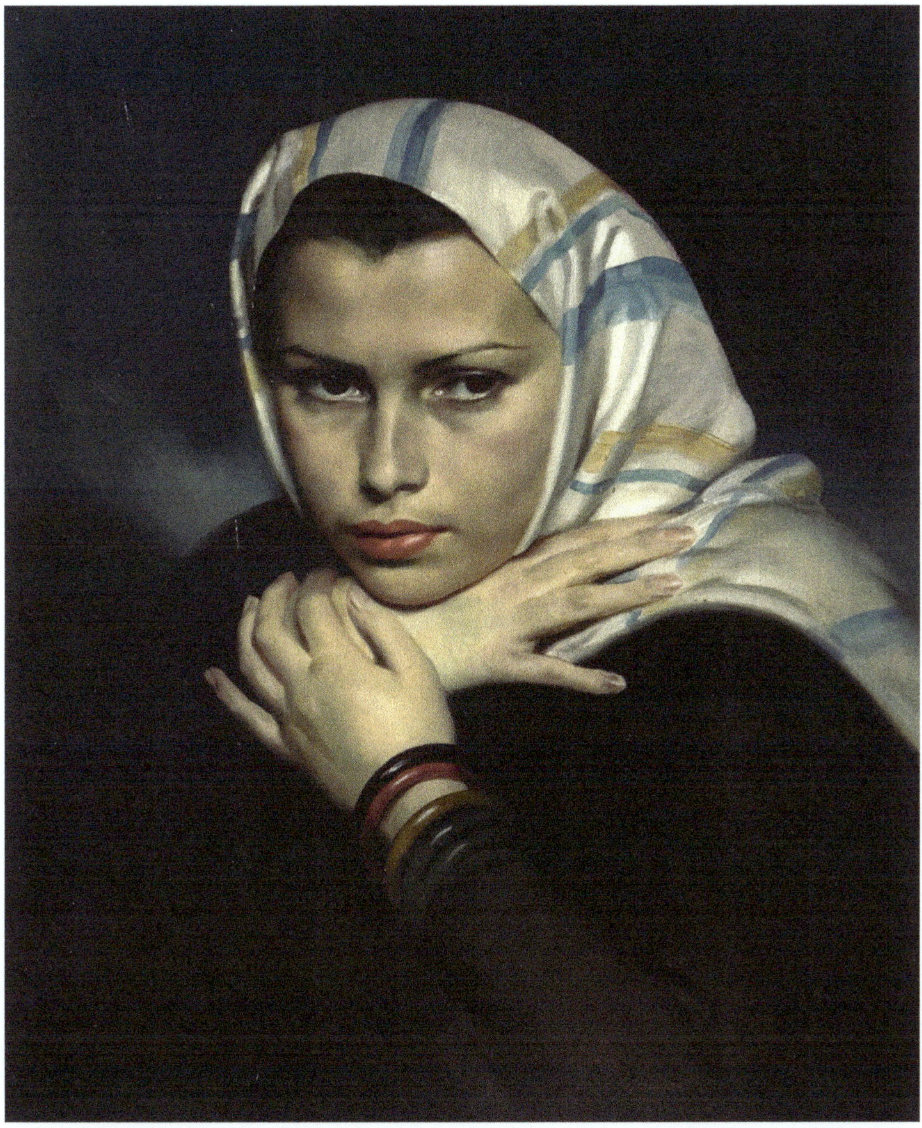

1.8 David Jagger, *Jewish Refugee, Vienna* (1938). © Nottingham City Museums & Galleries/ Bridgeman Images.

people into intense and captivating figures. Her head scarf and hand gesture suggest the woman is protecting her modesty, yet her painted red lips and side glance sexualise her beauty for the male gaze (Figure 1.8). The work is also noteworthy in that the artist included where the sitter was from in the title, giving the impression that he had travelled there or that her origins were a point of interest for the British public.

Beauty, therefore, was used as a point of contrast, to heighten the imagined violence from which female refugees fled. Violence was an invisible force lurking behind the portrait, which accentuated the woman's worth as an object of rescue. A few portraits made in Britain were of older men, and in these the sitter is marked by a dignified expression of both suffering and steadfastness (Nora Neilson Gray, *A Belgian Refugee* (1915–21); Ernest Townsend, *The Refugee* (1930s)). But mostly it was portraits of beautiful refugees, constructing women as passive, submissive, and alluring, with an exotic identity akin to orientalist conventions of eroticising female 'others'. This has had a lasting impact on humanitarian photography and photojournalism up to the present day, to an extent that it has become a normalised mode of feminising deservingness, and the sexualisation of young, female refugees goes unnoticed.[70]

During the Second World War, many artists sought sanctuary in Britain and also used portraiture to bring personal, less exotic qualities to their fellow refugees. Josef Herman's *Refugees* (1941) portrays a family escaping with children and a mattress roll in hand. The terrified eyes of the mother, father, and daughter haunt the image.[71] Lucian Freud was a ten-year-old boy when he arrived in Britain in 1933. Growing up with fellow Jewish refugee families, at the age of nineteen he painted a group portrait, *The Refugees* (1941). It is a diverse assembly of people: a man with a yellow hat, another wearing the dark glasses of a blind persons, a teenage boy, and several women both with and without headscarves. Bright colours and facial expressions provide diversity to refugee identity in contrast to the usual images of refugees.[72]

At this moment, Hannah Arendt was contemplating that Jews did not want to be labelled as refugees and thus stripped of their individual identity; they sought not to be defined by stereotypes or to be seen as an undifferentiated mass of victims. These portraits confirm her observation. Seeing refugees as anonymous crowds or, conversely, as unique individuals, were the poles by which photographers and artists envisioned displacement. It seems almost too obvious to state that displacement was both a collective and a personal experience, and that the aesthetics of displacement shaped each and every depiction.

'Womanandchild': gendering the aesthetics of compassion

As the above discussion indicates, gendered ideals of femininity, passivity, and humanity permeate the representation of female refugees. The conflation of the 'womanandchild' features in visual art, humanitarian imagery, and photojournalism. Its historical roots lay in Christian ideals of compassion and duty, coalescing in the sacred figures of Madonna and child, the 'universal mother', repeated over time in a wide range of visual cultures.[73] Since the First World War, images of civilians on the move feminised the representation of urgent departure in artworks, ranging from

Theophile Steinlen's coloured pencil drawing *L'exode Belge* (1915) and his *Flight* series (1916), to Josef Herman's *Mother and Child Fleeing* (1942), where a rush of blue represents the anguished flight from a pogrom, and to the now iconic black-and-white photographs of Lodz survivors traipsing over snow-covered train-tracks towards Berlin (Fred Ramage, *Berlin 1945).*[74]

The tropes through which refugee women were represented also reinforced conventional gender roles: alone without a male protector meant both their safety and honour was in peril. Political scientist Cynthia Enloe identified the idea of the 'womanandchild' as an enduring amalgamation, appearing again and again in international politics and humanitarian rhetoric.[75] The paternalistic notion of the 'deserving victim', according to Erica Burman, 'not only strips away agency but also pathologises those who do not appear so innocent'. Such slippages obscured both women's and children's rights which, when connected, were a shared infantilisation. Idealised models of motherhood and childhood underpinned patriarchal society.[76] Religious art of the Madonna and Child, Malkki argues, survived in 'perennial resonance' through contemporary photographs of refugees.[77] The problem was that this was the main way in which displaced women could be represented, regardless of their religion.

There was a double vulnerability to be found in depictions of nursing refugee mothers. In western artistic conventions, the Virgin Mary nursing the infant Christ represented both her compassion and the fragility of humanity. With the maternal breast also understood as a symbol of sustaining life, photographers working for UNRRA depicted women and their babies in this way. In Italy, an UNRRA photographer penned the words 'Madonna and Child' on the reverse of a photograph. However, far from the beatific Christian ideal, the mother is in a ragged dress sitting amongst ruins, with her baby in a makeshift basket. From her seated position, she looks up at the photographer with exhausted eyes.[78] The abiding reference to Christian symbolism in the context of the immediate postwar period framed women ambiguously. They were mothers who persisted in nurturing their children despite the war's devastation. However, such imagery also underscored that the ideals of motherhood were desperate for rehabilitation. For the UNRAA photographer this framing was a call to action to fund its relief programmes.

During the Cold War, the nursing mother trope was transferred to East Asia. A mother feeding her baby whilst fleeing danger, seen in earlier painting and photography, was now simply relocated to the Korean War context (Carl Mydans, *Life* magazine, 1951).[79] It is likely that Christian sentimentality appealed to American readers and funders alike. Thus, the mother's body under threat was a covert cipher for the state of the nation under Communism. When the 'womanandchild' is applied to displaced people, the removal from the patriarchal homestead implicates the nation's political and moral health. In 1999, *Time* magazine's cover of the war in Kosovo

(12 April), features a colour close-up of an Albanian mother nursing her infant while fleeing past the camera. Her identity, religion, and culture, are given over to the emotional aesthetics of the Christian convention, and the sentiments that inflect her double vulnerability.[80]

In 1952, many Korean modernist artists fled to the city of Pusan and staged exhibitions throughout the war. They, too, were witnesses, driven to depict massacres, refugees on the move, and women and children. The motif of a Korean woman with her child on her back underscored the absence of men. The fatherless family took on a symbolic role. Sim Suk-ja's painting *Mother and Two Children* (1953) depicts two siblings squabbling and their mother trying to separate them, an overt reference to the conflict between the north and south.[81] Both UNICEF and UNKRA (the United Nations Korean Reconstruction Agency) frequently used drawings and photographs to depict Korean women and children without husbands, as seen for example in drawings for its magazine cover, *UNKRA in Action* (1952).

Weeping refugees were also popular images. Polish artist Tamara de Lempicka was famous for her Art Deco depictions of luscious nudes, glamourous modern women, dashing gentleman, and flapper femininity. She had been a refugee twice in her life, leaving her life and possessions in St Petersburg in 1918, then once again in 1931, fleeing Paris for the US with her Jewish husband (portrayed in *Idylle, Le Depart*, 1931).[82] Affected by this experience, her paintings took a dramatic turn, addressing the bleak plight of women in wartime. Compared with her previous vibrancy, de Lempicka now adopted a sombre palette of brown and grey in order to register the disconsolate emotions of a mother and her teenage son in *The Refugees* (1937). The change in formal quality allowed her to dig deeper into her subject's forlorn expressions and gaunt features. Similarly in *The Flight* or *Somewhere in Europe* (1940), a mother, whose red eyes well-up with tears, nurses her baby (Figure 1.9). *The Flight* was the successor of an earlier, Spanish Civil War painting, *Mother Superior* (1935), where the motif of tears is equivalent to Picasso's many *Weeping Women* of the same period.[83]

De Lempicka's portraits were completed in the US. Though weeping figures drew on art historical conventions, it is possible that she was inspired by photographs of female refugees in the American press. At a time when Jewish refugees were being refused entry visas around the world, especially in the US, her paintings reveal her profound awareness of this precarity.

This was not the exception. Throughout the twentieth century, compassion was elicited through symbols that were repeated in images with remarkable consistency across visual forms – art reproduced in popular magazines, in humanitarian publications and mass media. The depiction of tears made women and children 'ideal victims' deserving of compassion.[84] This 'over-gendering' was also seen in photographs of

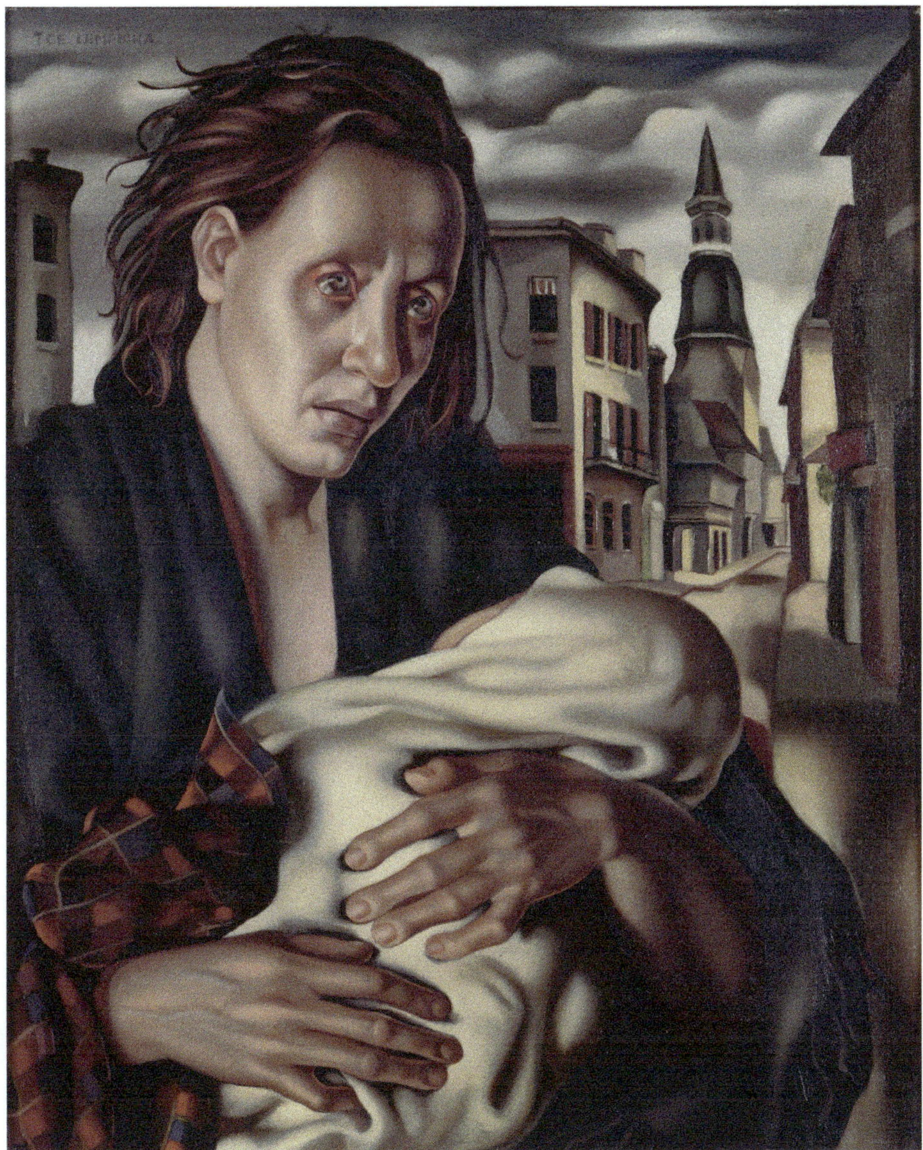

1.9 Tamara de Lempicka, *La Fuite ou Quelque part en Europe* (1940). © Tamara de Lempicka Estate, LCC/DACS 2024. © Musée d'arts de Nantes - Photographie: Cécile Clos.

Nazi camp liberations, which newspaper editors also favoured. Jewish women were depicted as fragile victims whose acts of resistance were erased.[85]

Although this was not the only way to depict women and children, the underlying paternalism of humanitarian sentiment meant that 'womenandchildren' were quintessentially seen as passive victims. As Lisa Malkkii writes, 'the need to help' was accompanied by benevolence and domesticity.[86] Gendered empathy and sincere sympathy for female refugees had its limits, however, and these can be seen in the patriarchal construction of the postwar family and conceptions of who would be ideal immigrants. Significantly, in the 1950s, it was much harder for unmarried displaced women than men to be selected for resettlement by the IRO, despite the aesthetics of compassion.

The lone father/motherless child

In addition to the images of 'womenandchildren', there were also compelling depictions of fathers as caregivers and men as emotional beings. This indicated a shift in the representation of displaced families. A scene emerged that would have been regarded as unnatural: a father as a sole carer and thus a motherless child. Josef Breitenbach, himself an Austrian Jewish exile, was an UNKRA Official Photographer whose Korean images were renowned. For instance, *Mendicant (War Refugee Father and Child, Pusan, Korea)* (1953) depicted a much-reduced father-figure nurturing a young child.[87] The father's exhausted but gentle expression heightened the pathos of the scene, while the mother's absence signified that Korea's loss was also one of patriarchal power in the units of both family and nation. This emergent representation suggested that the crisis of this wartime family was both national and universal, to which Breitenbach was personally attuned, having escaped Nazi Europe.

In 1954, Breitenbach wrote to Lieutenant General John B. Coulter (Agent General of UNKRA) in New York, outlining the extent of the dissemination of his UNKRA photos. He gave public lectures to the American-Korean Foundation and the Columbia University Institute of Arts and Sciences, and gave radio and TV interviews. His images were reproduced in yearbooks, magazines, the *New York Times Magazine* and *New York Times Sunday Magazine*. His exhibition attracted 1,500 visitors in the first two weeks and toured the country. Breitenbach praised the Lieutenant General's 'tireless and invaluable efforts' on behalf of the Korean (and for that matter of the American) people, of whose plight he hoped people had become aware through his photographs. The letter explains the afterlife of UN photography and the ongoing role that it would play in disseminating ideas about refugees.[88] Nora Hui-Jung Kim writes that, as South Korea entered the legal framework of the international refugee regime its neo-colonial relationship with the US reshaped refugeedom beyond Europe's borders.[89] Visual images were key to this reshaping.

The same year that Josef Breitenbach photographed *Mendicant (War Refugee Father and Child, Pusan, Korea)*, the Palestinian artist Ismail Shammout painted what was to become an iconic work. *Whereto?* (1953) depicts a lone father fleeing on foot with his three young sons. One, unable to walk, is carried on his father's shoulder whilst another boy looking up is guided by the paternal hand. The artist drew on his own memories to accentuate the ongoing uncertainty of finding safety. The painting encapsulates the longing for return, the key political issue for Palestinians after 1948. It was a powerful statement about the lost motherland, and within it, the fearful and exhausted grimaces of the all-male family upturns gendered expectations of stoic impassivity. Chrisoula Lionis argues that the landscape was conventionally a feminised trope in Palestinian art.[90] At the age of 22, Shammout's innovation in expressing male emotion was drawn from his own experience and was significant in light of the fact that Palestinians have been misrepresented by the dichotomous tropes of powerlessness and militancy.[91] A few years later, Shammout's *Here Sat My Father* (1957) returned to the traumatic longing of a lone child, a young boy staring at an empty, broken chair, mourning his absent father. In the background are two destroyed homes.[92]

The defining experiences of his teenage years transformed Shammout. At the age of 17 in 1948, his family was forced out of Lydda, and he witnessed the horror of massacres and the death of his brother by dehydration. By the age of 19, he was living in Khan Younis, a Quaker-run refugee camp in Gaza assisted by UNESCO and UNWRA. He began teaching art to displaced children. Shammout's family received token payments of $8–$12 USD a day, affording him 'a little time for painting and more recently sculpture', according to UNESCO's magazine, *Impetus* (1950). The magazine celebrated the young artist with an illustrated watercolour of a Palestinian woman carrying a vessel on her head, baby in arms, child by her side, and tents in the background. The work was auctioned by UNESCO. Praising the teenager, the story noted: 'Despite the fact that he has only three small, improvised tools to work with, Ismail's sculpture has been sufficiently interesting to inspire some of his pupils and fellow teachers to try their hand at the art'.[93] Shammout was fast becoming a young, cultural leader for whom the experience of his exiled community could be articulated as an aesthetics of displacement. He would attend art school, stage the first Palestinian art exhibition in Gaza, and become one of Palestine's most revered political artists, later heading the Palestinian Liberation Organisation (PLO) art department. The impact of displacement on women and children was likely to have been a daily reality that influenced his subject choice as a budding artist, but it was also relevant for UN agency communications at the time.

We have seen that there were exceptions to the gendered depiction of refugees, and to the essentialism of passive, feminine victimhood. Women did lead, and emotional, nurturing fathers followed. But for all that, it must be acknowledged that images of young men were less visible and less numerous at this time. The gendering of refugees continues to this day, with new inflections, for instance in mediatised representations of young men as less deserving or as threats to the host community and state.

Children alone

Images of children without adults emerged in the First World War and its aftermath, alongside humanitarian and international efforts to assist not just French and Belgian orphans but also child victims of the Armenian genocide and famine-affected children in Central Europe. In illustrated pamphlets, charcoal drawings, and colour posters that were mass circulated for international aid appeals, babies and female youngsters often featured. These were the most fragile, feminised refugees. Lone and crying children were seen in charity appeals aimed at assisting Armenian, Greek, and Syrian refugees who fled ethnic cleansing in Türkiye in 1915. In an American Near East Relief Fund (NER) poster, *Lest We Perish* (1915), designed by the children's book illustrator Ethel Franklin Betts Bains, a young girl pleads with her hands outstretched, with a bloodied head and teardrop running down her face. The poster's use of 'we' in the title implied that the fate of the lone refugee child was the shared fate of all Christians and all humanity (American Committee for Relief in the Near East 1915). The NER raised millions of dollars and took care of thousands of Armenian orphans from Christian families.[94] The same imagery was central in the Save the Children Fund publications. Its leader, Egglantyne Jebb, was to campaign for the Geneva Declaration of the Rights of the Child to be adopted by the League of Nations in 1924. The national branches of the Red Cross in the First World War had also canvassed support using images of lone children, sometimes protected by a nurse. They appealed for funds to care for 15,000 refugee and orphaned children. All these children meant one thing above all: that depicting frightened, scared innocents would cut through to parents, who would donate.[95] It is notable, however, that humanitarian images in the twentieth century did not take account of the militarisation of young people. Customs of 'militarised cuteness' saw families dress their very young children up in soldiers' and nurses' uniforms. Boys were recruited as buglers and drummers. Naval apprentices were heroised for dying in service. Many underaged youths fought in national and guerrilla armed forces.[96] The military and emotional labour young people performed in wartime, or their agency in leaving their family to join up underaged, was not yet part of the humanitarian story.

Across the twentieth century, the figure of the vulnerable, lone child was an iconic presence in humanitarianism's moral armoury: political campaigning, public education, and fundraising.[97] In 1938, Jewish children who arrived on the Kindertransport were featured in newspaper images. However, as Tony Kushner argues, their rescue was largely forgotten until the 1980s when it belatedly provided a backstory that might redeem an otherwise insular British national identity.[98] A 1938 *Picture Post* double-feature, 'Their First Day in England', told the story of a group of German-Jewish teenage boys at a holiday camp in Dovercourt Bay, Harwich. Close-ups of smiling teenagers playing football and table tennis, learning English, were accompanied by the words: 'they are in a land where they will not be despised on account of race!' Even so, the story expressed stereotypes that the children were from privileged families or were supported by 'a wealthy Jew'.[99] Increasingly, press photographs of Jewish teenagers shifted to more vulnerable images of children arriving exhausted, their 'lives broken by Nazi pogroms'.[100] Their rescue mattered as a way of reinforcing dominant political narratives. This self-congratulatory aspect of humanitarianism survives into the present, amplified by 'white saviourism'.

After 1945, international agencies including UNRRA, UNESCO, and UNICEF commissioned photographers to represent the millions of displaced European children in need of protection, food, clothing, and shelter. Whether these children had parents or not, images of lone children dominated their representation. Two types of photographic images were frequently published by these agencies' communications departments. Parental absence and material neglect were most often conveyed by ragged clothing and bare feet. The other collection of images, however, focused on the work of the UN agencies and showed happy children, smiling, eating, clothed, cared for by doctors, or learning in schools. Together, such depictions formed a 'before-and-after' picture of relief. The children's transition from a state of helplessness affirmed the UN's success in rescuing them from family destruction, poverty, and malnutrition, thereby transforming them into figures of hope. In a 1949 issue of UNESCO's magazine, *Courier*, the caption of the journal's cover puts words into young children's mouths: '"Help us, please!" Refugee children look to UNESCO – and to you'. Two small European girls are shown looking up at a benevolent adult just out of the picture frame. The accompanying story refers to the duties of the state.[101] These images emphasised that the UN was an agent of internationalism and efficiency, coordinating multi-national change, but, arguably, doing so in the guise of a universal parent.[102] On the ground in operations, UNRRA relief workers also became substitute parents, since in these images they were shown caring for displaced and orphaned children.

News media and UN photos did not, however, capture the children's anxiety or the lingering trauma of parental separation. Photographs of the Lingard children, for instance, helped to craft a story of a Jewish 'unaccompanied child refugee' who had been pathologically ill but had been swiftly returned to health and happiness, healed by a 'normal', middle-class childhood.[103] In French-occupied Germany, photographers focused on children, and this enhanced France's image among the Allies, erasing the Vichy regime's role in the mass murder of Jewish children.[104] Thus, the discourse of lost childhood was framed as a failure of adults, and the corollary was the need for democracy and for postwar reconstruction to invest in the next generation.[105] Child rescue advocates 'institutionalised a gender-specific vision of humanitarianism and human rights' centred on the family as much as the individual, as Tara Zahra states.[106] They did not do all this gratuitously or because of blind prejudices. The 'before-and-after' imaging of displaced and unaccompanied children sought to galvanise governments and humanitarians, and to instil optimism in potential adoptive parents.

Both UN and humanitarian agencies, along with the ICRC, planned to rehabilitate approximately 13 million children who had lost a parent during the war. Photobooks were useful fund-raising strategies. UNICEF and UNESCO commissioned photographers Thérèse Bonney (*Europe's Children*, 1943) and David 'Chim' Seymour (*Children of Europe*, 1949) to produce exemplary books for sale, and excerpts were reproduced in UN reports and magazines to demonstrate their mission. Films that focused on the plight of orphans were also made, including the US Army production, *Seeds of Destiny* (1946), and the Swiss-American co-production, *The Search* (1948). Young children in these books and films were represented as victims of appalling misery but also potential agents of the future. Simone Gigliotti concludes that historical depictions are the 'visual emissary for the displaced and refugee children of today, and tomorrow'.[107]

A rarely discussed motif that features in displacement aesthetics is young children taking care of other, even younger, children and siblings. The older child who carries a toddler or baby is seen as taking on adult responsibilities. In 1951, the UN mounted a global campaign for the six-year anniversary of the UN Charter. The front cover of an official pamphlet featured a Korean child carrying a baby as if she were its mother (Figure 1.10).[108] The aim of United Nations Day was to raise funds for orphaned and refugee children in Palestine, Korea, West Germany, Greece, and Yugoslavia. Although the UN had just voted that UNICEF should receive USD$1,000,000 more for its programmes, the purpose of United Nations Day was to collect yet more funds from the international public. Highlighting children without parents in need of a globalised network of help, was a means to that end.[109]

Depictions of child victims were ubiquitous across all visual forms and all methods of dissemination and have persisted into the present day.[110] Photographs would often show children alone even when they were not orphans. Such was the ubiquitous pattern of victim imagery, that displacements beyond Europe saw European photographers apply similar frames of reference. One fund-raising photobook on Palestinian children was particularly pertinent. Per Olow-Anderson's *They Are Human Too: A Photographic Essay on the Palestine Arab Refugees* (1957) was prepared in cooperation with UNRWA. Aiming to present the humanity of refugees through close-up portraits of children, it began with a story, told through images and captions, of a disabled teenager called Samieha, living in Gaza. The book sales would fund Samieha's treatment

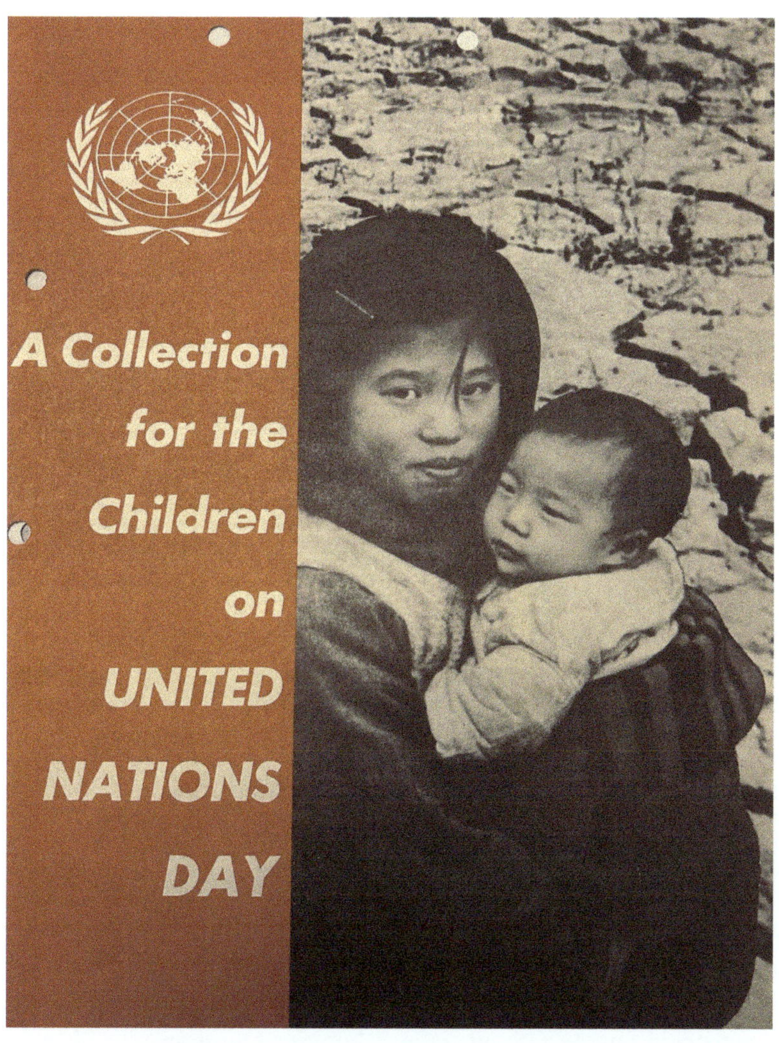

1.10 United Nations Day official pamphlet, 1951.

in the US.[111] Although she had a mother, this was mentioned only in passing and neither of her parents were depicted in the book. The impression that Samieha was alone, and implicitly an orphan, amplified her vulnerability. A decade later, during the immediate aftermath of the 1967 Arab–Israeli War, journalist Winifred Carr used her popular 'Family Forum' column in a British newspaper for a photographic story about the thousands of Palestinian children living in makeshift refugee camps in Jordan.[112] Images of lone children rather than children with mothers were chosen as the most powerful way to report on hunger and disease amongst the now twice displaced population.

Whether in camps, hospitals, or streets, lone refugee children became intimate cyphers evoking the whole of displacement aesthetics. They symbolised rupture from the domestic realm of home, alienation, and dispossession. A sweet, diminutive face in turmoil stood for lost contact with parents and that, in turn, denoted the demolition of the family system. Lone children shown crying required rescue, comfort, and – importantly – parental love. Foreign adults adopting orphaned children were responding, at least in part, to the universal ideal of humanitarianism wherein the bonds of familial love were thought to best assuage the suffering of the innocent. Thus, like their predecessors in earlier conflicts – Robert Capa's depiction of a child crying in a Spanish refugee camp, for example – aid organisations utilised images of tearful children.[113] Such motifs were part of the lexicon of communicating both humanitarian need *and* the kind of political injustice that makes children the prime sufferers.

The depiction of lone infants was particularly intense and parsed in emotional, visual language. Many artists over the century joined forces with humanitarian organisations, participating in 'cultural activism', through exhibitions on children's art as well as artists working with local and national charities directly on refugee campaigns.[114] In 1959 the UN sponsored the first truly global campaign – World Refugee Year (WRY), in alliance with numerous charities, to raise funds for the remaining unsettled European displaced persons, over 900,000 Palestinians, 700,000 Chinese fleeing Communist China to Hong Kong, and Russians in China.[115] The British artist (and cartoonist) Ronald Searle was commissioned to draw the illustrations for *Refugees 1960*. His drawing of a little girl eating an apple appeared on the cover. The text was written by the artist's wife, Kay Webb, who described 'hard core cases, the refugee rejects languishing in camps', and went on to detail the separation of families resettled in disparate locations, and newcomers born in the camp.[116] For a media campaign, Searle drew a baby from an Italian refugee camp, lying on its stomach, looking upwards, helpless. Webb wrote, 'forty million refugees in the world and over 100,000 are still in Europe without country, home or future' (Figure 1.11). A caption pleaded, 'Give him a chance'.[117] Fund-raising meant the capacity to feed, clothe, and give the baby a chance to survive.

Although the campaign began as the result of Conservative British politicians and journalists disturbed by the sprawling refugee camps they visited in Palestine, WRY's aim was to make the scale and urgency of refugee needs more comprehensible.[118] Despite the work of the UNHCR, the 1951 Refugee Convention and 1967 Protocol (which extended asylum rights beyond Europe), refugeedom was an ongoing reality not confined to the Second World War. The image of a White, European baby in Figure 1.11, therefore, was a powerful choice in communicating the message of hope for a future but one that needed nurturing and security. In an era before children's distinctive rights were recognised, the baby presented a universal image symbolising

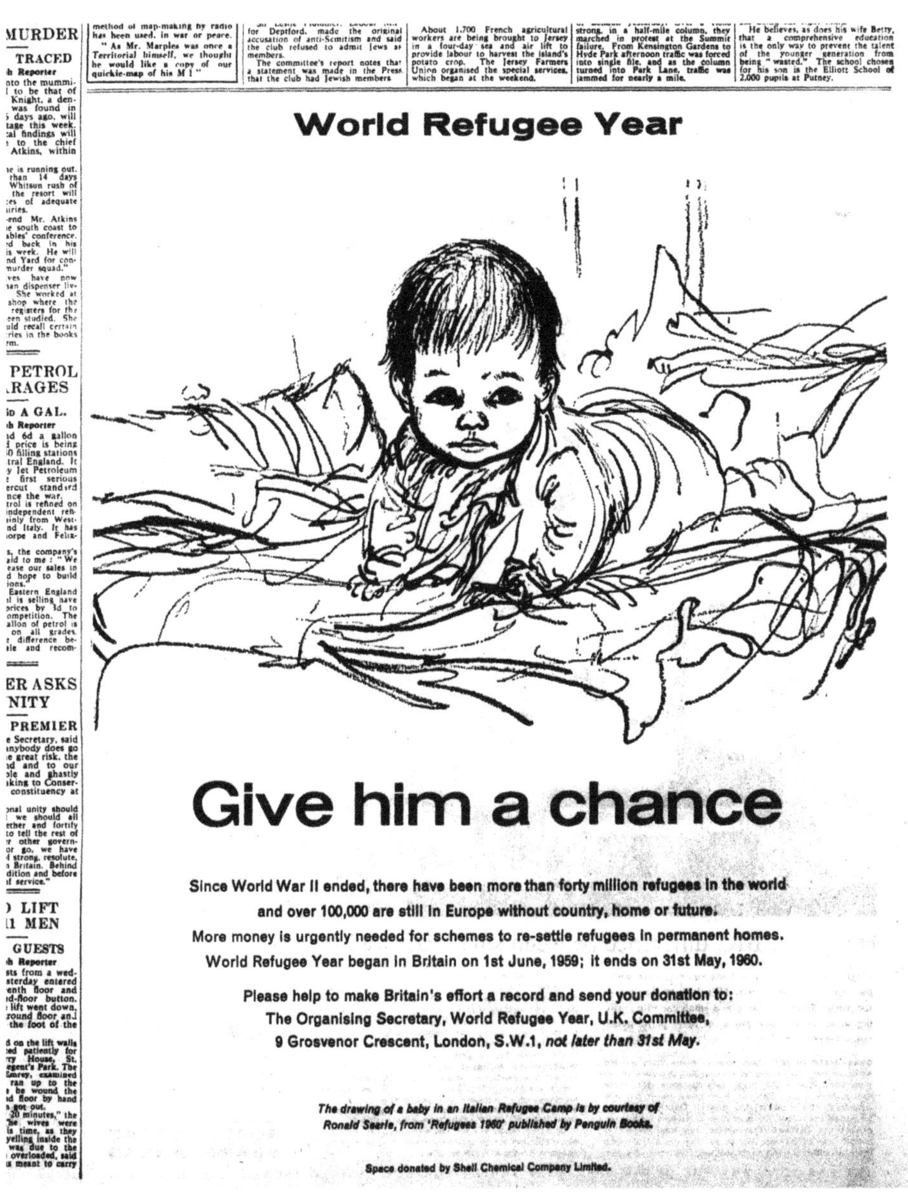

1.11 Ronald Searle drawing, advertisement for World Refugee Year, *Daily Telegraph* (May 1960).

the aspirations of the Universal Declaration of Human Rights (1949), and the ongoing concern to reconstruct an ideal of childhood interrupted by war and displacement.

In its desire to frame concerns about children and young people, WRY harkened back to postwar campaigns to resettle teenage Jewish survivor orphans in Canada. In order to be seen as innocent, vulnerable, and in need, their adolescence was downplayed. Girls had to appear pretty and innocuous, and boys had to fit the expectations of future citizens for the growing nation.[119] Hannah Arendt's observation that Jewish refugees hid their difference to be accepted in their new countries was even more pertinent for young people. In contrast to the dominant discourses that adults made about child refugees, the voices of children are obtuse.[120] Visual images that adults made to represent displaced children and youth had the best humanitarian intentions, but they also reflected the social values that young people were expected to embody. In the context of the power dynamics of visual representations, children's drawings take on immense importance. Through their own artwork, child and teenage DPs offered unique insights into their emotional world, one without siblings or parents, without their language and culture of birth, and one where they were often deprived of knowing their own origins.

This is especially pertinent when young people depicted each other. A case in point is that of thirteen-year-old Samuel Bak, who survived the Vilna ghetto with his mother, and turned to his love of drawing while at Landsberg DP camp in occupied Germany. In watercolour and ink, he drew the other children in the camp. One of these drawings, called *Children Alone* (1946), evoked the common experience of separation and isolation.[121] Two children, walking hand in hand, facing away from the viewer, gingerly approach a blurred horizon in the distance. It was a stark, solitary perspective emphasising young survivors' reliance on each other as they faced an uncertain future without parents. Bak's insight was, arguably, more profound in explaining what the bureaucratic designation of 'unaccompanied minor' really meant for them. It also underscores the shared work of all survivor children in making sense of who they are and what they had been through collectively. Thus, images of survivor children take on a very different meaning in this young artist's vision.

Bak's *Children Alone* can be compared with the drawings that teenage survivors of concentration camps made under the care of Viennese art therapist Marie Paneth at Lake Windermere in England. Their works never included people – neither adults nor children – but are populated by deserted villages, houses, roads, and landscapes. They are a testament to the trauma of loss and the catastrophe of their parents' annihilation. The bleak, powerful truthfulness of young people's art was entirely distinct from humanitarian portraits of child refugees – where they are almost always either mute or relentlessly positive – that adults made in seeking to rescue and rehabilitate them. The lexicon of humanitarian imagery thus sits within displacement aesthetics in its emphasis upon voicelessness, an absence that the visual insights of teenage displaced artists contradicted.

Objects of belonging: materiality and affective emotions

In response to the plethora of objects collected in museums and the material turn in historical research, the material culture of displacement has become a subject of academic interest. According to historians Leora Auslander and Tara Zahra, the fact that refugees and exiles have gone to great lengths to 'bring, make, find and pre-serve all kinds of things is evidence of their significance *to them*'.[122] Consequently, we expand our understanding of displacement aesthetics to include materiality and the embodied, affective qualities of objects. Recently, artists have created specific responses to the materiality of displacement. They bring tactile qualities to the surface in highly emotional encounters; objects associated with displacement are imbued with memories and are tangible triggers for storytelling.[123] Artists have sensed the affective power of objects to elevate humanity and fragility; sometimes the sensation of rupture can be best amplified by focusing on an isolated, humble artefact.

When thinking about displacement, we might consider that the English noun 'belongings' signifies personal possessions that 'belong' to a person. Conversely, used as a verb, belonging is associated with memories and feelings about home, but also that it is possible to be cut adrift from a place of security. The Dada artist Marcel Duchamp was acutely aware of this significance for the origin of art. His encyclopae-dic collection *Box in a Valise* (1941) was a portable gallery of miniature versions of his works of art, contained in a suitcase. Duchamp's double experience of exile in the world wars had resulted in his sustained meditation about art in emergency and about replicability in exile.[124] This can be contrasted with other artists' investment in objects that index their own subjectivity and can trigger the affective emotions of memories of home. Anthropologist Alisa Sopova has described how the Ukrainian language has a word that denotes the dual meanings of an 'emergency suitcase' or 'anxious suit-case'. It describes the container that a refugee will need to immediately escape with, carrying significant talismans like a photo album, a piece of wallpaper, a children's comforter, or more practical items.[125] Affective objects can be cyphers of security, comfort at home, or bridges to the past, catapulting one back into spaces of belonging. By contrast, other objects have come to represent refugee experiences and aestheticise displacement. These objects are often taken from modes of transportation – boats or trains – and have come to hold particular significance in the list of items that materialise forced mobility.

People flee, often clinging to a few material possessions. Emotions are inevitably attached to these belongings and objects, which surface in photographs and artworks. As we saw with the Spanish Civil War and the French exodus, people were depicted with belongings piled onto lorries, cars, and bicycles.[126] In particular, the suitcase was an emotive example of both a symbol and a synecdoche in representations of displacement aesthetics. Suitcases carried the stories and embodied meanings of, for instance, packing in an emergency or leaving for an uncertain destination, and thus the precarity of displacement. They act as containers of surviving memories defined by absence, the mnemonic objects left behind. As Orvar Lofgren argues, the 'throwntogetherness' of containment reminds that the past, present, and future can be organised, intertwined, and stored.[127] The suitcase resembles an archive that encloses a longing for home and the burden of memory and mourning.

During the Second World War, baskets, blankets, and suitcases signified the European refugees arriving at British railway stations. Frequently reproduced in newspapers, the refugee suitcase evoked transitoriness, homelessness, and contained anguish, emotions that were particularly fraught in the case of children. Individuals, their families, and their culture were crammed into one singular object. For Jewish refugees, suitcases would come to hold a darker symbolism of death and lost identity. Across the world, museums dedicated to the memory of the Holocaust use suitcases to refer to both European refugees and the Nazi genocide. The humble suitcase carries the intense emotional weight of traumatic memory and yet also the survivor's hopes for resettlement.[128]

The refugee on the move was a major way of representing the impact of war on the civilian population. This movement was often seen as a crowd, convoy, or column and identified displacement from war's violence with the mode of transport. In the First World War, loaded carts drawn by mules or horses featured in newsreels and illustrated newspapers. From the late 1930s, the Japanese bombing and occupation of China generated both a huge quantity of western photojournalism but also Chinese artistic responses. Jiang Zhaohe's epic painting, *Refugees* (1943), depicts people with a single suitcase strapped to a mule. The work was exceptional for its combination of European modernism and Chinese ink and brush techniques, which meant its depiction of civilian terror was novel.[129] Civilians are huddled together against the threat of bombs from the sky, ears covered against the din, and a woman carries her dead child. The method of their rushed transport alludes to the unseen violence outside the frame. Such was the power of this work that the occupying Japanese forces banned its exhibition. By contrast, western newspapers focused on movement. For instance, *Picture Post* described how: 'Tens of thousands of panic-stricken refugees began to pour out of the city. With their bits of furniture and bedding they streamed across the Yangtse bridges'.[130] A photo of an old rickshaw driver carrying a young, wealthy man through a crowded Chungking street presented a contrasting image of inequality and privilege in the midst of crisis.

During the Spanish Civil War, ships loaded with refugees were regularly photographed. These included the photographs of hundreds of Basque children, soon a media spectacle, arriving at Southampton Docks in England in May 1937.[131] The images of Jewish refugees sailing from Europe to Palestine also became an international media phenomenon, as Simone Gigliotti notes, though the press tied the anti-Semitic trope of Jews as 'wanderers' to the image. Boats also lent themselves to the message that seafaring was precarious, but also to what Gigliotti has called the 'home-seeking condition'.[132] By contrast, Lynda Mannik reveals how passengers on the *SS Walnut*, escaping to Palestine, took photos that focused on the mundane, daily life on board, images of a life in waiting that were a meaningful part of their journey.[133] For Vietnamese refugees, Thy Phu writes that families kept photographs 'because they reminded us not only of all we had lost but also of all we had survived'. Family photos were self-representations that eschewed victimhood and did not rely on spectators to recognise or reaffirm the humanity of the displaced.[134] Their personal, affective qualities contrast with the quite different emotions associated with the traces of displacement when those traces become synecdoches, standing in for a vast phenomenon.

The symbolism of refugee boats has often been debated. Depictions of shipwrecks and their survivors were frequent in the genre of eighteenth- and nineteenth-century marine painting, the most celebrated of which, Theodore Géricault's *The Raft of the Medusa* (1818–19), J.M.W. Turner's *Disaster at Sea* (1833–35), and Eugene Delacroix's *The Shipwreck of Don Juan* (1840), are recognised icons of Romantism. During the First World War, when Red Cross ships and ocean liners such as *The Lusitania* (1915) were torpedoed, the rescue of passengers was represented in lithographs for newspapers and illustrated journals, and they engaged with this art history to depict desperation, the fragility of life, and the hope of rescue.[135] The Viennese modernist Marie-Louise von Motesiczksy painted *The Travellers* (1940) (Figure 1.12), not long after she and her mother arrived as refugees in England.[136]

The allegory consisted of a group huddled in a rickety, wooden boat, tossed in rough seas. A female nude is seated in the middle, while another woman holds a mirror, perhaps looking at her former self. Behind them, an older woman (probably the artist's mother) crouches, staring out at the vast expanse of sea. The dark colours add to the depiction of being cut adrift. A man with one foot in the boat and one in the water may be her brother, Karl, who remained in Vienna to resist the Nazis but was arrested and later died in Auschwitz. The wooden lifeboat was a means of containing several narratives, exploring not just escape, but also the uncertainty of relocating to England.

During the Vietnam War, large freighters and small wooden fishing boats defined refugees as 'boat people' in the popular imagination. Photographers sold stories of boats in danger, for example Phil Eggman's photograph of refugee families on a fishing vessel being rescued by the *USS Blue Ridge* after eight days at sea.[137] Eddie Adams' famous 1977 photo-essay, 'The Boat of No Smiles', recorded in a series of photographs a boat that had drifted for five days in the Gulf of Siam, after the Thai coastguard pushed it back (1.13).[138] It is taken as a given that the fishing boat communicates

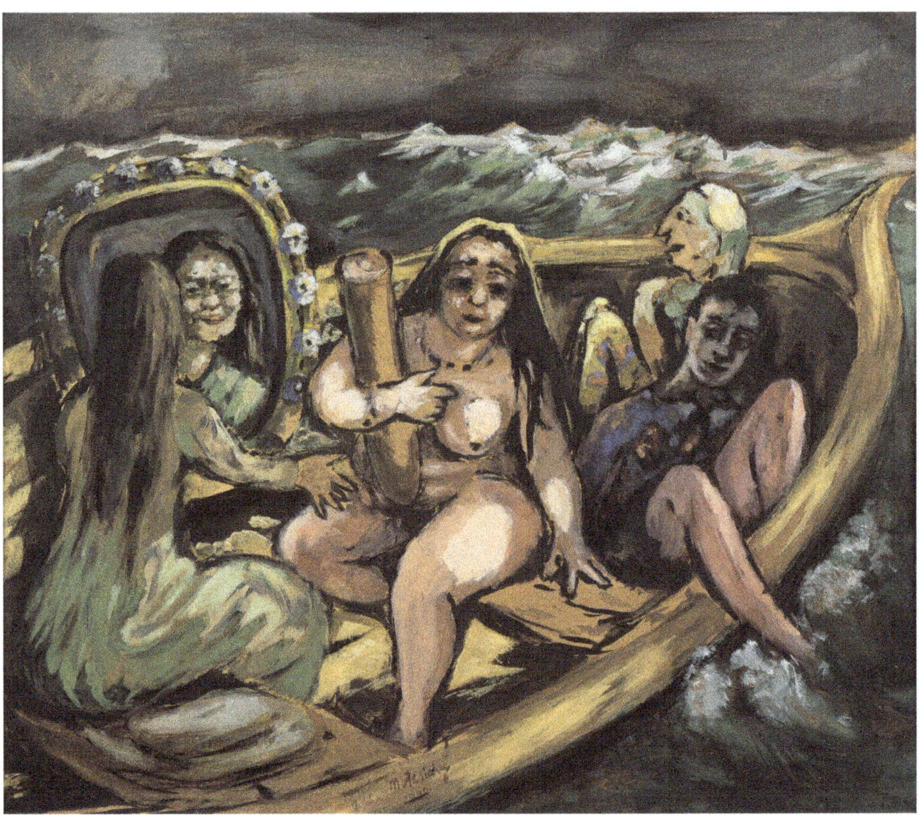

1.12 Marie-Louise von Motesiczksy, *The Travellers* (1940). © Marie-Louise von Motesiczky Charitable Trust 2024. Stanley Museum of Art, the University of Iowa.

the material conditions of the 'boat people'. However, this set of photos focuses on a mother and child perched on a pile of ropes trying to shelter from the heat.

In another picture, a named woman, Nguyen Thi Yen, cradles her unconscious child. These images reached international audiences. Adams recalled that the feature 'appeared Page One worldwide. The State Department asked for the photographs to be presented to Congress. As a result, America opened its doors to 200,000 Vietnamese. [President] Carter said it was the pictures that did it'.[139] The feminising of the boat as a vessel of poverty and otherness helped to humanise the journey that refugees undertook.

In later decades, similar images accompanied reports investigating the opposite response.

With repatriation policies in the ascendent, the *New York Times* referred to 'sad flotsam' and 'drift home' while deploring the abject approach of the British administration in Hong Kong of forced returns to Vietnam.[140] As a generally sympathetic paper,

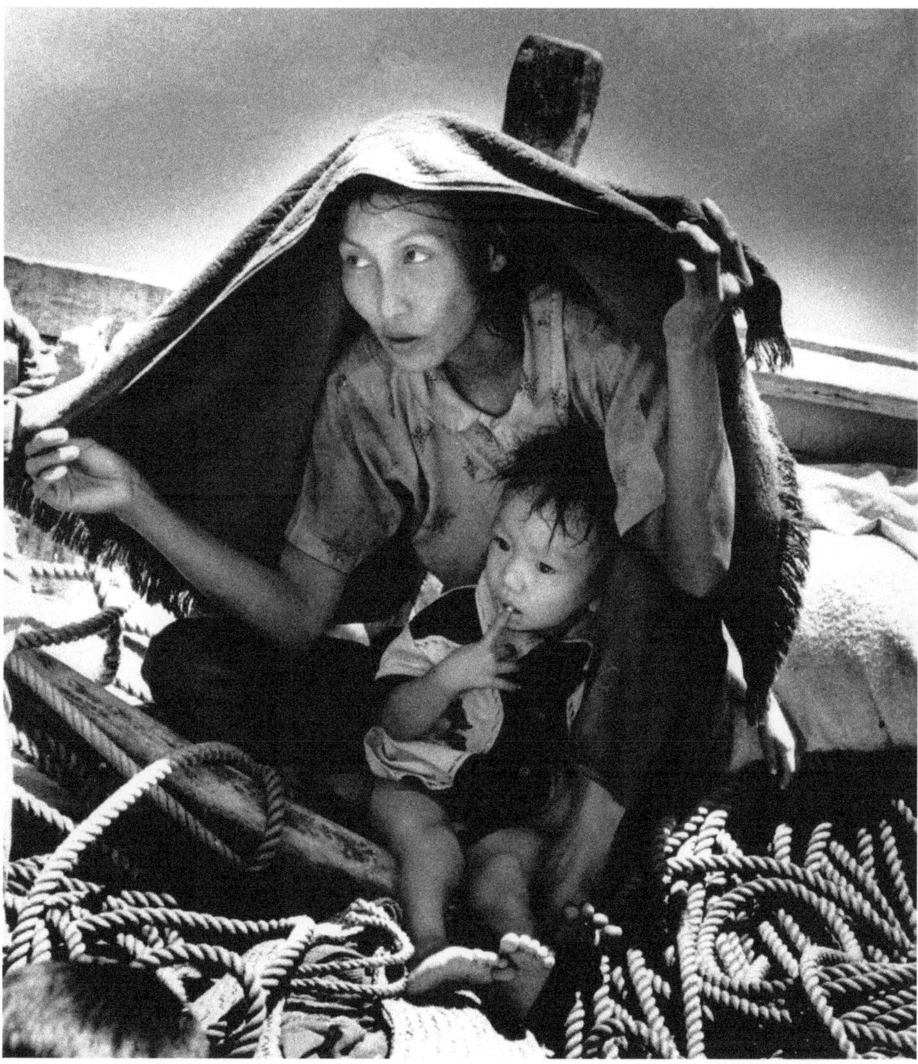

1.13 Eddie Adams, *The Boat of No Smiles* (1 November, 1977). Photo-essay. Courtesy of Associated Press/Alamy Stock.

it repeated the 'womanandchild' visual prevalent in humanitarian media. Indeed, this enabled Adams' photograph to have a significant political impact. By 1978, the UNHCR designated that all 'boat people' would gain refugee status and were eligible for special resettlement schemes.[141] Nevertheless, initial compassion for these refugees shifted in the 1990s to antipathy and stigmatisation as Right-wing politicians broke with previous bipartisan support for asylum seeker resettlement.[142] In recent times, the idea of boat arrivals as security threats became part of both Australian and British governments' rhetoric. Right-wing slogans of 'Stop the Boats' and 'Turn Back the Boats' associate refugees with waves and floods of so-called illegal migration. As we will see in Chapter 2, this in turn affected how artists engaged with forced displacement.

Earlier, we noted that refugee camps during the time of the First World War were photographed from the air. Row after row of tents or rudimentary buildings arranged in a vast aerial perspective emphasised the stasis associated with displacement experiences. Public interest in the material culture of displacement only increased in the decade after the Second World War. In 1959, London hosted Refugee Week as part of World Refugee Year, with the support of Brigadier G. Chatterton and the *Daily Telegraph*. Thirty thousand people came to see an exhibition showcasing European refugee camps at the Royal Exchange, which then toured Britain. Earl Clement Atlee, who had been the Labour Party Prime Minister between 1945 and 1951, visited the exhibit. Earlier, in 1939, when he was leader of the Opposition, Attlee had hosted a ten-year-old Jewish child refugee, Paul Willer, so this exhibition resonated with him personally. It included replicas of the furnished huts that Brigadier Chatterton had seen on his European tour, including a hut that a group of reporters and volunteers built and then lived in for a week. Photographs show a neat interior like a show home, with a dining table but no residents. Kitchen items and personal belongings made the temporary home appear comfortable and semi-permanent.[143] By contrast, living in deprivation, discomfort, and instability defined the reality for refugees living in camps, just as boats symbolised refugees and defined them by departure and arrival.

The tropes, motifs, and synecdoches discussed thus far come further into view when channelled into representations of India's Partition in 1947. This is a crucial point, for the focus on European refugees can easily erase the longer, global underpinnings of European empires and their decolonisation, which created so much of postwar history. The British policy of Partition underwrote the largest forced migration in modern history, with over 12 million people displaced. Muslims, Sikhs, and Hindus were forced to relocate, and to endure pogroms, rapes, and massacres. The mass circulation of images of Partition refugees included only scant information about the colonial policies underpinning the event and little about the enormity and multiplicity of the provinces affected. Photographs of Partition were to affect Indian and Pakistani national politics for decades afterwards.[144] Western photojournalism and humanitarian media often echoed the tropes of displacement aesthetics that we have already discussed, coalescing in what would become increasingly normalised during the later twentieth century: the racialised refugee.

American photographer Margaret Bourke-White, famous for her images of Buchenwald concentration camp, drew on all the familiar themes of mobility and exodus, the crowd, the camp, the nursing mother, and the lone child. Her photo-essay for *Life* magazine, 'The Great Migration: Five Million Indians Flee For Their

Lives' (1947), formed some of the most celebrated, iconic representations of Partition, and were reproduced over many decades. The photograph, 'Spindly but determined old Sikh, carrying his ailing wife, sets out on the dangerous journey to India's border', and people on foot carrying sacks on their heads, were yet another iteration of Exodus. *Life* journalist Lee Eitingon Frizell accompanied Bourke-White and penned the captions for her photos: 'Misery of the dispossessed reflected in the face of this Moslem boy, perched on the wall of the Purana Qila fortress in New Delhi. Below him thousands of his unhappy fellows, who have fled their homes in terror, are trying to survive until they can organise a convoy for the long march to Pakistan'.[145] Head in hands, the boy's despair signalled – as had other children in photographs, paintings, and prints across the twentieth century – the emotional consequence of the alone child.

In her later report, *Halfway to Freedom* (1949), Bourke-White's caption changed to 'The future, as always, belonged to the young. A fragment of the vast Muslim refugee camp at Delhi'.[146] She was alert to what she called 'the classic colonial pattern' of extracting resources and decimating local economies, and the sanitising of 'inhumanity' when termed 'an exchange of populations'.[147] Asma Naeem writes her 'sympathies were for the *individual* Indians struggling against colonial powers', though she understood Independence as a march of progress for the Indian nation.[148] Bourke-White saw herself as a humanitarian and yet has her critics. Even Eitingon Frizell baulked at her asking 'scared refugees to repeat their action of flight multiple times until she got the perfect photo'.[149] Nevertheless, these photographs are positioned by Indians at the centre of museums of Partition, for instance in Amritsar, and are held as important documents of a deeply scarring time.

The word refugee was sometimes equated with the deprivation of dignity, and hence displaced Indians often preferred words such as *udvastu* (uprooted) or *bastuhara* (one who lost one's homeland).[150] Notably, neither India nor Pakistan signed the 1951 Convention Relating to the Status of Refugees or the 1967 Protocol, which extended the right to seek asylum to non-Europeans but continued its focus on fear of persecution and departure from a home country, which excluded people displaced by famine or those who were internally displaced (IDPs).[151] It is only partly true to say, as does Heather Johnson, that by the late twentieth century, the racialisation of the refugee consolidated an 'undifferentiated victim, voiceless and without political agency', with national policies.[152] Particularly in western humanitarian images of misery, poverty, and aid-dependence, the visual codes were by now set, despite all good intentions.

Displacement aesthetics in later modern and contemporary art

The first half of the twentieth century was important because of the impact of the two world wars, and the dawn of both the international refugee regime and human rights law. However, we have been arguing throughout this chapter that it is also critical because artists used their creative power, their status, and their connections to organisations and cultural programmes to protest, to raise awareness, and to provoke debate, sometimes working with a humane or personal agenda or more directly with humanitarian agencies and grassroots organisations. Many artists took practical action to support refugee causes, well beyond making art about refugees. In the Second World War, much advocacy occurred through collaboration between artists and the art industry, a focus of discussion in Chapter 5. In 1964, the British sculptor Barbara Hepworth donated works for sale to the UNHCR in Paris.[153] Her modernist sculpture did not rely on the representation of refugee experiences. More recently, there was a tendency to fund-raise for refugees through representations of them, often reacting to media images with various degrees of sensitivity and success. Banksy's ironically titled sculpture *Dream Boat* (2015) – a boat full of African figures – repurposed from his temporary art project Dismaland, sold at Miami Art Week, with 50 per cent of the sale price donated to the charity *Choose Love*.

The visual tropes from the first half of the twentieth century have often continued into the present day. Every conflict, no matter where in the world, represents displaced people in these familiar forms, even when this creative energy is spurred on by urgency, compassion, and solidarity. This has coincided with the globalisation of art, the circulation of images on social media and, at least in theory, a greater degree of visual consumption, perhaps even literacy, among audiences and spectators. Heightened awareness of the ethics of representation and the questioning of the presence of refugee voices, and the seeking of agency and empowerment in collaborative art projects, have received a mixed response within academia and the public sphere. Artists, exhibitions, biennials, and festivals have, wrongly or rightly, sometimes been accused of insensitivity, elitism, and even outright exploitation. As mentioned in the Introduction, misrepresentations of displaced peoples can cause outrage, such as the Swiss-Icelandic artist Christoph Büchel's *Barca Nostra* (*Our Boat*, 2019).[154] We will also see in Chapter 2, that some artists who have suffered displacement feel deeply uncomfortable about the trope of the boats. Some artists, however, reclaim its potential.

Tropes are used and reused in producing a range of images about displacement that cannot simply be bifurcated into the normative and non-normative. Artists, as we have seen, engage with tropes for a range of reasons: sometimes because they are personally and culturally meaningful, sometimes to engage with the history of art, or finding in tropes the power of emotional resonance. Material culture is also important in embodying synecdoches that convey experiences and memories through objects. We see this in contemporary art about displacement. Mona Hatoum's *Exodus I* and *II* (2002) comprised two coloured rectangular suitcases connected by long strands of black, human hair. Hatoum transformed the suitcase – symbol of exodus and a trope in Palestinian art – into a deeply personal reflection on her Palestinian family's experience of exile during the Lebanese Civil War, linking her personal history of departure with the fragility of black, female hair. The work deliberately recalled Marcel Duchamp's *Boite en valise* (1935–41), with its own demonstration of exile as a portable museum; the suitcase that contained sixty-nine miniature reproductions of his artworks.

Similarly, Tiffany Chung, in *Reconstructing an Exodus History: Boat Trajectories from Vietnam and Flight Routes from Refugee Camps and of ODP Cases* (2020), used red threads to embroider the journeys of Vietnamese refugees across the world. The map reflects her own family's journey and a larger geography of mobility by boat and plane. Hew Locke's *The Wine Dark Sea* installation (2016) presents a suspended flotilla of sculpted vessels, including those used by Cuban refugees and in the Vietnam War film, *Apocalypse Now* (Dir: Coppola, 1979). Importantly, Locke links the material culture of forced mobility to displacements from slavery and colonialism. In the Palais de Tokyo's exhibition, *Dislocations* (Paris, 2024), Fati Khademi borrowed her father's travel bag, embroidering military weapons and explosions in a tribute to her family's displacement and the exile of Hazara people from Afghanistan (*Leaving is Longing*, 2022). Her work borrows from the iconography and the methods of War Rug weavers across Afghanistan and in refugee camps in Pakistan from the Russian invasion of Afghanistan onwards, a history we shall return to in Chapter 4. In these works, threads are used to connote mobility, layering personal meaning onto political events.

We saw earlier that tent cities were visualised as distant expanses. However, some contemporary artists had a closer focus. Emily Jacir's *Memorial to 418 Palestinian Villages Which Were Destroyed, Depopulated and Occupied by Israel in 1948* (2001) was an embroidered UNWRA refugee tent. Architects Sandi Hilal and Alessandro Petti's *Stateless Heritage* (2022) was a presentation of mural-sized colour photographs taken by Luca Capuano of the streets of Dheisheh refugee camp, first established in 1949. *Stateless Heritage* had a practical function, as part of a submission advocating for refugee camps to be designated UNESCO World Heritage Sites. Tania Bruguera's Tate Modern Turbine Hall Commission (2018) embedded a photographic portrait of a Syrian refugee, Yousef, in the Turbine Hall's floor. Visitors touched the 'mural', slowly revealing the portrait. Ben Quilty painted a series, *Life Vest, Lesbos* (2016), which depicted orange jackets as individual portraits differentiated by the names in each painting's title, for instance *Reza* (201), *Ali Jaffari* (2017), and *Fazel Chegini* (2017). Against stark, black backgrounds, the roughly-painted, impastoed orange vests were memorials to those who lost their lives seeking asylum, some by suicide while incarcerated in Australia's offshore detention system.[155]

In addition, social practice and participatory projects with refugee communities have navigated inequalities through remuneration and long-term engagement.[156] In *There's No Place* (2020–ongoing), Jakkai Siributr collaborated with Shan (Muslim) minority children who are currently stateless and living in the Koung Jor Shan refugee camp on the Thai/Myanmar border. He teaches young people to use embroidery to share their cultural heritage through story cloths, and to express their hopes and dreams. This project raises the global community's awareness of Shan children's lack of civil rights in the middle of a decades-long conflict that receives little global attention. Since 2010 the Sydney-based *Refugee Art Project* – a not-for-profit organisation – has worked with offshore and onshore asylum seeker detainees to make art and hold exhibitions. It is a collective voice against the brutal and deeply traumatising colonialism of Australia's detention system.[157]

One final example is an extraordinary story of the transformation of a displaced child artist into a major figure of international contemporary art. As a young Kosovar Albanian, Petrit Halilaj experienced the brutality of the war with Serbia, becoming a refugee in 1999. In an Albanian camp, he met Italian child psychiatrist Giacomo Poli, who encouraged children to draw. Halilaj produced thirty-eight drawings, which mixed threatening scenes of soldiers, guns, violence, death, and houses burning with fantastic, imaginary landscapes full of forests and birds. Non-governmental organisations (NGOs) noticed his artistic talent, and one of his drawings was presented to Kofi Annan, Secretary-General of the UN. These colourful drawings attracted attention as images of trauma, innocence, and hope. Remarkably, video footage exists of the young Petrit talking about his drawings of parrots, jungles, and peacocks. It is only after attending art school, and becoming an accomplished contemporary artist, that Halilaj has returned to his childhood drawings. They became the deeply resonant, personal source material for the large installations that have now travelled the world in acclaimed exhibitions.[158] *Very Volcanic Over This Green Feather (Papagall)* (2022) transformed details from the drawings into large cut-out banners, printed onto felt and suspended in a maze from ceilings (Figure 1.14). This is perhaps one of the most searing and affective reimaginings of displacement seen by gallery visitors this century. The artist has enlarged and intensified the fusion of a displaced child's reality and dreamworlds, a jungle full of terror and the hope of escape.

Thus, we have seen how contemporary artists can mobilise the most extraordinary suffering of war and displacement into a magical dream that inspires and reaffirms the value and meaning of making and looking at art.

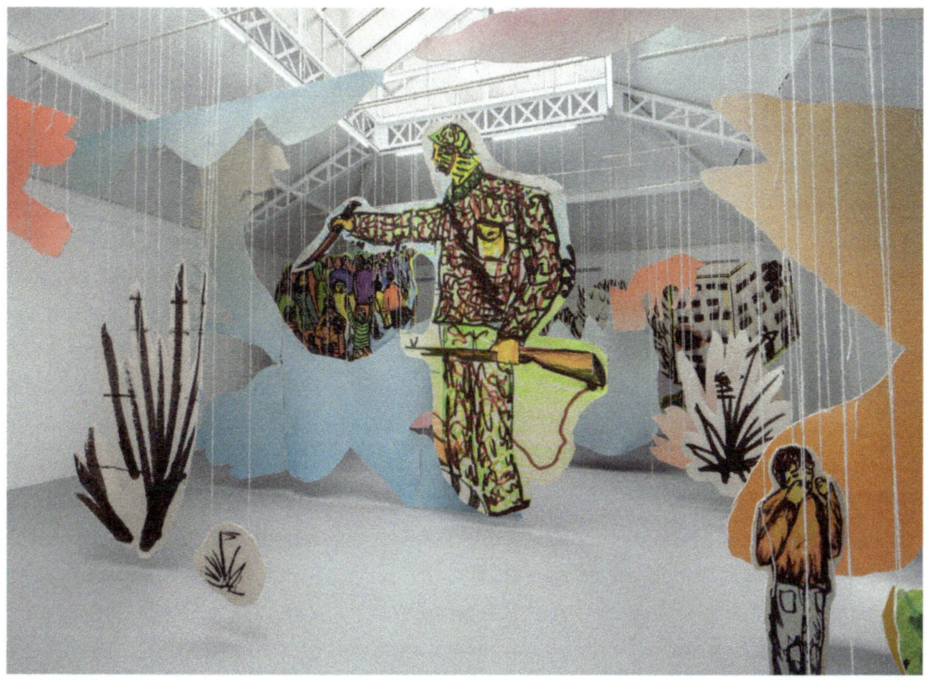

1.14 Exhibition view, Petrit Halilaj, *Very Volcanic Over This Green Feather* (Papagall), 2022. © Petrit Halilaj, Photo. Archives Mennour, Courtesy of the artist and Mennour, Paris.

Conclusion

The making of the cultural artefact that we have been considering – the figure of the modern refugee – emerged in Europe during two world wars and then in conflicts in Palestine, Korea, through Partition, and extending into the Cold War era. The era of internationalism and the formation of the UN resulted in both the aspirational Universal Declaration of Human Rights (1949) and the legal agreement of the 1951 Refugee Convention.[159] The political figure of the Cold War refugee legitimised the international legal order, while new legal regimes allowed nations to preserve their ability to decide their own citizenship and immigration policies.[160] Peter Gatrell explained that there were many ways to 'manufacture' the displaced, and this chapter has argued that visual representations were fundamental to this process.[161] Visual tropes crossed different cultural arenas, and traversed new conflicts, chronologies, and geographies, propelled all the while by their sustained and affective power. As we have seen, this was neither reductive nor did it inevitably silence refugee voices. Artists held a particularly important place in bringing their visions and experiences into understanding refugee experience. Visual metaphors that animate documentation, art, and media images alike could be sources of personal and cultural meanings that hold affective power for communities. This is the point that our book emphasises, and one which enables us to see how the past survives in the present.

Understanding the ubiquity of visual tropes of refugees has been a critical starting point for this book, since, as Valerie Holman observed, few books have concentrated on the visual aspect of forced migration. She argues that images contain and release the displaced in ordered frameworks, enabling the coincident representation of both the most abject and ideal types of 'refugee' identity. Images contain codes and embody artistic traditions that support particular understandings of experiences, even at the moment of observation and far more upon reflection.[162] Norms of belonging, good citizenship, and healthy, useful bodies were produced in images by the UN agencies for DP resettlement and labour migration. Yet humanitarian images often reinforced a view of refugees as both wretched and model victims, relentlessly on the move or permanently stuck. Over the century, the cultural figure of the refugee has reproduced an aesthetic vocabulary of displacement through mobility and other tropes, often dehistoricised and gendered. However, we also learned that artists' interactions can both contribute to norms and also differentiate from and challenge them. Artists were often witnesses to personal events and caught up in them, rather than distant observers; much of art was constitutive of aesthetic experience. There is a complex historical and contemporary relationship between witnessing and interpreting refugee experiences. Many artworks continue to have a sustained historic, cultural significance. Theorists of art, from Aby Warburg in the first decades of the twentieth century to Georges Didi-Huberman in its closing decades, have sought to explain the ability of lexicons of metaphor and gesture to capture creative imaginations and humanitarian emotions across time.

Our discussion of the visual motifs of displacement recognises the agency of the image, its afterlife, and, crucially, its returning power to elicit an intense emotional response. This does not imply that there are essential truths or singular readings in such images and that spectators are passive recipients of displacement aesthetics.[163] Displacement aesthetics is never a closed or completed system of the visual, seamlessly running from past to present, nor is it a cultural pathology or deficiency for which there are remedies. We argue that radically different meanings and purposes can be sustained by the same set of tropes and images. Certain narratives and emotions appear and reappear within a trajectory of displacement aesthetics, such as mobility, stasis, victimhood, and pity. But they, too, can remain ambiguous and paradoxical.

The common motifs and conventions of displacement aesthetics shaped how the refugee became a cultural figure in the first half of the twentieth century, but they do not necessarily communicate fixed meanings and were, ultimately, repurposed and reinterpreted over time and through different lived experiences. Common motifs have appeared to deepen the emotional resonance of war and to communicate how the experience of conflict forces people into extreme states of precarity and dispossession. Contemporary artists, all too aware of the pitfalls and visual archaeology of images, have sought to explore, engage, and transform metaphors that have become rigid.

Trinh T. Minh-ha wrote in 'The Image and the Void' that 'invisibility is built into each instance of visibility, and the very forms of invisibility generated within the visible are often what is at stake in a struggle'. Continuing, she states, that activism requires multiple modes of resistance through 'the seen, the barely seen, and the unseen; in the between, the margins, and the borders of visible reality; and through the power of blanks, holes, silences, and empty spaces'.[164] We know, as well, that there has been a rapidly increasing space for alternative global, feminist, post-national and decolonising histories of art. It is with this final point that Chapter 1 concludes: understanding displacement aesthetics alerts us to the questions of visibility and invisibility, to dominant formulas and silences, and to what is outside of the frame. Displaced artists are not, however, speechless emissaries, as they can be found struggling against the opacity of being inside and outside the art industry, which is considered in Chapters 2 and 5.

Displaced artists' works can be sold in the global art market and collected by museums. Yet the artists themselves frequently encounter travel restrictions. This is an old story. In November 1930, the Americans issued visas amounting to just 15 per cent of its total immigration quota. By 1933, only 1,450 visas were issued to German artists, musicians and scientists, victims of Nazi policies to Aryanise culture, to rid it of Jews, degenerates and Communists.[165] Doubts about whether or not artists were good citizens continued after 1945, with questions concerning their fitness for employment. In 1949, the IRO noted that artists and intellectuals were included in the 'hard-core group' of DPs, those difficult to resettle along with the sick, disabled, and elderly. Challenging this perception, IRO officials reported that they referred to this discrimination against artists and intellectuals as an 'embargo on brains'.[166] Arguably, that embargo continues today as displaced artists face complex intersectional barriers that restrict access to visas, networks, training, mentorship, career opportunities; a voice, and a space in national and international art industries.

Notes

1 Ilya Kliger, 'On "Genre Memory" in Bakhtin', in I. Kliger and B. Maslov (eds), *Persistent Forms: Explorations in Historical* Poetics (New York: Fordham University Press, 2016).

2 'The Symbolic Figure of Our Age', *Picture Post*, 7:1 (6 April 1940). Emphasis added.

3 Peter Gatrell, Anindita Ghoshal, Katarzyna Nowak, and Alex Dowdall, 'Reckoning with Refugeedom: Refugee Voices in Modern History', *Social History*, 46:1 (2021): 75.

4 Georges Didi-Huberman, Keynote address, 'The History of Art is a Story of Migrations', *Transporting Images Symposium*, Cogut Institution for the Humanities, Brown University, accessed 14 February 2025. January–November 2023. www.youtube.com/watch?v=A5 iBZbLVvgM

5 Lyndsay Stonebridge, 'Refugee Genealogies: Introduction', in E. Cox et al. (eds), *Refugee Imaginaries: Research Across the Humanities* (Edinburgh: Edinburgh University Press, 2020), pp. 15–16.

6 Marta Zarzycka and Martijn Kleppe, 'Awards, Archives and Affects: Tropes in the World Press Photo contest, 2009–11', *Media, Culture and Society*, 35:8 (2013): 925; Lilie Chouliaraki, *The Ironic Spectator: Solidarity in the Age of Post-Humanitarianism* (Cambridge: Polity Press, 2014), p. 50.

7 Stephen Eisenman, *The Abu Ghraib Effect* (London: Reaktion Books, 2007).

8 Karen Halttunnan, 'Humanitarianism and the Pornography of Pain in Anglo-American Culture', *American Historical Review*, 2:100 (1994): 330–334; Chouliaraki, *The Ironic Spectator*, p. 27.

9 Philippe-Alain Michaud (ed.), *Aby Warburg and the Image in Motion*, trans. Sophie Hawkes (New York: Zone Books, 2004); Georges Didi-Huberman, 'Foreword: Knowledge-Movement', in Michaud (ed.), *Aby Warburg and the Image in Motion*, pp. 7–19. Georges Didi-Huberman, *L'image survivante: histoire de l'art et temps des fantômes selon Aby Warburg* (Paris: Editions de Minuit, 2002).

10 K.W. Forster, 'Aby Warburg: His Study of Ritual and Art on Two Continents', *October*, 77 (1996): 5–24; K.W. Forster, 'Introduction', in Aby Warburg, *The Renewal of Pagan Antiquity* (Los Angeles: Getty Publications, 1999), pp. 1–75.

11 Aby Warburg cited in E.H. Gombrich, *Aby Warburg: An Intellectual Biography* (Oxford: Phaidon, 1986), p. 179. See Charles Green, 'The Memory Effect: Anachronism, Time and Motion', *Third Text*, 22/6, 95 (2008): 681–698; Charles Green, 'Robert Smithson's Ghost in 1920s Hamburg: Reading Aby Warburg's Mnemosyne Atlas as a Non-Site', *Visual Resources: An International Journal of Documentation*, 18/2 (2002): 167–181.

12 Dawn Chatty, *Displacement and Dispossession in the Modern Middle East* (Cambridge: Cambridge University Press, 2010).

13 Javier Rodrigo and David Alegre Lorenz, 'Before the Convention: The Spanish Civil War and Challenges for Research on Refugee History', *Refugee Survey Quarterly*, 41 (2022): 210.

14 Peter Gatrell, *The Making of the Modern Refugee* (Oxford: Oxford University Press, 2013).

15 Greg Burgess, *The League of Nations and the Refugees from Nazi Germany* (London: Bloomsbury, 2016), p. 48ff.

16 Sebastian Huhn, '"Plausible Enough": The IRO and the Negotiation of Refugee Status After the Second World War', *Journal of Contemporary History*, 58:3 (2023): 399, 405.

17 R. Hariman and J.L. Luciates, *No Caption Needed: Iconic Photographs, Public Culture and Liberal Democracy* (Chicago, IL: Chicago University Press, 2007).

18   Didi-Huberman, 'The History of Art is a Story of Migrations'.

19   David Farrier, 'Terms of Hospitality', *Postcolonial Asylum: Seeking Sanctuary Before the Law* (Liverpool: Liverpool University Press, 2011), pp. 154, 170.

20   Gatrell, *The Making of the Modern Refugee*; Peter Gatrell et al., 'Reckoning with Refugeedom: Refugee Voices in Modern History', *Social History*, 46:1 (2021): 75.

21   Pathé Gazette issue circa January 1915: 'Refugees on the Road, Fleeing from the Belgian Town Furnes Which is Under German Attack'. www.britishpathe.com/asset/100976/. Emphasis added.

22   www.bridgemanimages.com/en/gestel/exodus-chalk-pastel-on-paper/chalk-and-pastel-on-paper/asset/1547561. Emphasis added.

23   Liisa H. Malkki, 'Speechless Emissaries: Refugees, Humanitarianism, and Dehistoricisation', *Cultural Anthropology*, 11:3 (1996): 377–404; Prem Kumar Rajaram, 'Humanitarianism and Representations', *Journal of Refugee Studies*, 15:3 (2002): 248.

24   *La Domenica del Corriere* (Courier Sunday), 17–24 September (1922), front page illustration. www.bridgemanimages.com/en/beltrame/greeks-fleeing-smyrna-greek-turkish-war-1919-22-1922-colour-litho/colour-lithograph/asset/2809137

25   https://modernbritishartgallery.com/artwork/the-exodus/; https://www.bridgemanimages.com/en/brangwyn/exodus-study-c-1918/photo/asset/2649092?offline=1

26   Annette Hoffman (ed.), *Exodus: Border Crossings in Jewish, Christian and Islamic Texts and Images* (Berlin: De Gruyter, 2020).

27   Jo Labanyi, 'The Touch of the Image: Affect and Materiality in Photojournalism of the Spanish Civil War', in Brenda Lynn Edgar, Valérie Gorin, and Dolores Martín-Moruno (eds), *Making Humanitarian Crises* (Cham: Springer, 2022), pp. 79–100.

28   Caroline Brothers, *War and Photography: A Cultural History* (London: Routledge, 1997), p. 141. Valerie Holman, 'Representing Refugees: Migration in France 1940–44', *Journal of Romance Studies*, 2:2 (2002): 54ff.

29   Hanna Diamond, 'Representing Defeat: Photographic Images of the French Exodus of 1940, *War and Culture Studies*, 1:3 (2008): 17.

30   www.bridgemanimages.com/en/dupin/the-exodus-from-paris-1940-chalk-gouache-on-paper/chalk-and-gouache-on-paper/asset/219388

31   Fred Dallmayr, *Marc Chagall: The Artist as Peacemaker* (London: Routledge, 2020), p. 22.

32   It included work by Joan Miro and Andre Masson, Alexander Calder, Eugene Berman, Jacques Lipchitz, Adolph Gottlieb, Robert Motherwell, Edouard Pignon, Fritz Wotruba, Wilfredo Lam, and Vieira da Silva. It was Varian Fry's idea to raise funds and awareness of the International Rescue Committee. https://museum.oglethorpe.edu/exhibitions/international-rescue-committee-irc-flight-portfolio/

33   Elżbieta Kossewska, 'I work for the People Who Love … ': David Lazer, Marc Chagall and the Jewish State', *The Jewish Quarterly Review*, 111:1 (2021): 1–9.

34   'Spring Homeward Exodus Begins', *UNRRA Team News*, Germany (1 April 1946).

35 https://unrwa.photoshelter.com/galleries/C00009xWZSJER24M/G0000lHZxGn3mcC8/ I0000fwH7fe7hy3M/Historic-Milestones; https://unrwa.photoshelter.com/galleries/C00 009xWZSJER24M/G0000lHZxGn3mcC8/I0000ZBxQB3jJ4EY/Exodus

36 https://abedabdi.com/portfolio_tag/refugees/; www.barjeelartfoundation.org/collection/ refugees-abed-abedi/

37 See also Abdi's 1976 drawing, *Fleeing from the Massacre.* https://commons.wikimedia. org/wiki/Category:Abed_Abdi#/media/File:Fleeing..._from_the_Massacre,_Abed_ Abdi,_1976.jpg

38 Tal Ben-Zvi, '*Wa-ma Nasayna* ('We Have Not Forgotten): Palestinian Collective Memory and the Print Work of Abed Abdi', *Israel Studies* (Spring 2016):183–208.

39 Terence Wright, 'Moving Images: The Media Representation of Refugees', *Visual Studies*, 17:2 (2002): 53–66.

40 Emma Cox, 'Processional Aesthetics and Irregular Transit: Envisioning Refugees in Europe', *Theatre Journal*, 69:4 (2017): 477–496.

41 https://www.loc.gov/pictures/resource/ggbain.27084/

42 The National Archives, UK, Catalogue Ref: CN/5/2/37.

43 Brigadier-General H.H. Austin, C.B., C.M.G., D.S.O., *The Baqubah Refugee Camp: An Account on Behalf of the Persecuted Assyrian Christians* (London and Salford: The Faith Press), 1920.

44 ICRC images from 1948: Nabi-Yscoul (Ramallah). Aerial view. https://avarchives.icrc.org/ Picture/81614; https://avarchives.icrc.org/Picture/81643

45 ICRC photo, children clearing rocks in Jelazone camp, near Ramallah, 1949. https://avar chives.icrc.org/Picture/80979

46 https://unrwa.photoshelter.com/search/result/I00002q19qLalaXQ?terms=aerial%20 view&

47 www.bridgemanimages.com/en/noartistknown/israel-palestine-a-refugee-camp-in-the-jordan-valley-for-palestinians-driven-from-their-homes-by/nomedium/asset/26 35322

48 www.unrwa.org/content/replacing-tents-fabricated-shelters

49 Samar Maqusi, 'Acts of Spatial Violation: The Politics of Space-Making inside the Palestinian Refugee Camp', *Arena: Journal of Architectural Research*, 5:1 (2021). DOI: 10.5334/ajar.324.

50 Tabea Linhard, 'Barbed Wire: A History of Cruelty', in Mabel Moraña (ed.), *Liquid Borders: Migration as Resistance* (Abingdon: Routledge, 2021), p. 90.

51 'The Forgotten Army', *Picture Post*, 3:2 (15 April 1939).

52 Francie Cate-Arries, *Spanish Culture behind Barbed Wire: Memory and Representation of the French Concentration Camps, 1939–1945* (Lewisburg, PA: Bucknell University Press, 2004).

53 Christoph Jahr, 'The Life and Afterlife of a 20th Century French Camp: Gurs', in G. Anderl, L. Erker, and C. Reinprecht (eds), *Internment Refugee Camps: Historical and Contemporary Perspectives* (Bielefeld: Verlag, 2022, vol. 192), pp. 276, 280.

54 Stephen Coppel, 'Behind Barbed Wire: Printmaking in Australian Internment Camps by Erwin Fabian and Ludwig Hirschfeld Mack', *Art in Print*, 5:3 (2015): 16–21.

55 https://artuk.org/discover/artworks/art-behind-wire-internment-life-poster-313202

56 www.gettyimages.com/detail/news-photo/refugees-are-waiting-for-their-transport-in-berlin-1945-news-photo/1068938832?adppopup=true; www.bridgemanimages.com/en/noartistknown/german-displaced-persons-wait-in-berlin-s-anhalter-station-in-1945-refugees-are-carrying-their-few/black-and-white-photograph/asset/2945027; www.gettyimages.com/detail/news-photo/mother-and-child-in-the-waiting-hall-of-frankfurt-station-news-photo/2637179?adppopup=true; www.gettyimages.com/detail/news-photo/huddling-in-blankets-the-only-survivors-of-an-original-150-news-photo/3362692?adppopup=true

57 www.iwm.org.uk/collections/item/object/22542

58 www.iwm.org.uk/collections/item/object/15246

59 Private papers of Mary Kessell, 'German Diary 8 August–5 October 1945', Imperial War Museum.

60 Jeffrey T. Schnapp and Matthew Tiews (eds), *Crowds* (Stanford, CA: Stanford University Press, 2006).

61 Gustav Le Bon, *The Crowd: A Study of the Popular Mind* (Mineola, NY: Dover Publications, 2002).

62 Civil War refugees arriving at the French town of Argeles-Sur-Mer (photo by © Hulton-Deutsch Collection/CORBIS/Corbis via Getty Images). https://www.gettyimages.co.uk/detail/news-photo/civil-war-refugees-celebrate-crossing-the-franco-spanish-news-photo/613464920?adppopup=true

63 Nasser Hussain, *The Jurisprudence of Emergency: Colonialism and the Rule of Law* (Ann Arbor: University of Michigan Press, 2003); Christopher Pinney, *The Coming of Photography to India* (London: British Library 2008), p. 85.

64 Chandrika Kaul, '"At the Stroke of the Midnight Hour": Lord Mountbatten and the British Media at Indian Independence', *The Commonwealth Journal of International Affairs*, 97 (2008): 677.

65 www.gettyimages.co.uk/detail/news-photo/crowds-of-refugees-gathered-in-delhi-having-fled-the-punjab-news-photo/3378242

66 Emilia Terracciano, *Art and Emergency: Modernism in Twentieth Century India* (London: I.B. Taurus, 2018), p. 11.

67 Geeta Patel, 'Portraits of Unspeakable Anguish', *The Guftugu* Collection, accessed 14 February 2025. https://guftugu.in/2019/10/18/portraits-of-unspeakable-anguish/

68 https://artsandculture.google.com/asset/rufugee-woman-by-s-l-parasher/PAu-uY JcWa_pQ?hl=en

69 https://artuk.org/discover/artworks/refugee-64656/search/2024-works:refugee/page/1/ view_as/grid; https://www.tate-images.com/T00602-Portrait-of-a-Jewish-Woman.html

70 See Holly Edwards' discussion of Steve McCurry's green-eyed *Afghan Girl* (National Geographic, 1985). In 'Cover to Cover: The Life Cycle of an Image in Contemporary Visual Culture', in Mark Reinhardt, Holly Edwards, and Erina Dugganne (eds), *Beautiful Suffering: Photography and the Traffic in Pain* (Williams College Museum of Art and University of Chicago Press, 2007).

71 https://www.bridgemanimages.com/en/herman/refugees-c-1941-gouache-on-paper/ gouache-on-paper/asset/3612115

72 www.bridgemanimages.com/en/freud/the-refugees-1941-panel/oil-on-canvas/ass et/3250770

73 Terence Wright, 'Refugees on Screen', working paper, Refugee Studies Centre, 5 (2000): 1–28.

74 www.flowersgallery.com/artists/34-josef-herman/works/165074/ www.gettyimages.co.uk/ detail/news-photo/handful-of-survivors-from-the-150-refugees-who-left-lodz-in-ne ws-photo/2658548?adppopup=true

75 Cynthia Enloe, *Bananas, Beaches and Bases: Making Feminist Sense of International Politics* (Oakland, CA: University of California Press, 2014).

76 Erica Burman, 'Beyond "Women vs Children" or "WomenandChildren": Engendering Childhood and Reformulating Motherhood', *International Journal of Children's Rights*, 16 (2008): 180.

77 Liisa Malkki, *Purity and Exile: Violence, Memory, and National Cosmology among Hutu Refugees in Tanzania* (Chicago, IL: University of Chicago Press, 1995), p. 11.

78 UN archives, NYC, UNRRA/ 717. Italy, Madonna and Child. UNRRA s-0800-00 20-0015-00006.

79 https://www.getty.edu/art/collection/object/1098JS

80 Photo by Bosnian photographer Damir Sagolj. https://content.time.com/time/covers/ 0,16641,19990412,00.html

81 Roe Jae-ryung, 'The Korean War and the Visual Arts', in P. West, S. Ji-moon, and D. Gregg (eds), *Remembering the Forgotten War: The Korean War through Literature and Art* (London: Routledge, 2001), p. 58.

82 www.bridgemanimages.com/en/de-lempicka/idylle-or-le-depart-1931-oil-on-panel/ oil-on-panel/asset/1767835

83 Marta Zarzycka, 'Mourning Bodies: Photographs of Grief', in *Gendered Tropes in War Photography: Mothers, Mourners, Soldiers* (Routledge: New York, 2016), pp. 1–2.

84 Birgitta Höijer, 'The Discourse of Global Compassion: The Audience and Media Reporting of Human Suffering', *Media, Culture and Society*, 26 (2004): 517–520.

85 Barbie Zelizer, 'Gender and Atrocity: Women in Holocaust Photographs', *Visual Culture and the Holocaust* (London: Bloomsbury, 2001), p. 256.

86 Lisa Malkki, *The Need to Help: The Domestic Arts of International Humanitarianism* (Durham, NC: Duke University Press, 2015).

87 https://collections.lacma.org/node/205470

88 Letter from Josef Breitenbach to Lt. General Coulter, 1 May 1954. S-0526-0043-0007-0000, UN Archives, New York.

89 Nora Hui-Jung Kin, 'Cold War Refugees: South Korea's Entry into the International Refugee Regime, 1950–1992', *Journal of Refugee Studies*, 35:1 (2022): 435–453.

90 Chrisoula Lionis, *Laughter in Occupied Palestine: Comedy and Identity in Art and Film* (London: I.B. Taurus, 2016), p. 122.

91 In the 1990s, the artist converged biblical and classical themes in a nineteen-mural project (with Tamam Al-Akhal), *Palestine: The Exodus and the Odyssey* (1997–2000). Lionis, *Laughter in Occupied Palestine*, p. 20.

92 https://dafbeirut.org/en/ismail-shammout/works/1722-232995-here-sat-my-father-

93 *Impetus*, Monthly review of Reconstruction in Education, Science and Culture (March–April 1950): 18–19.

94 Ethel Franklin Betts Bains, 1917. www.iwm.org.uk/collections/item/object/2296

95 https://calisphere.org/item/ark:/28722/bk0007s1k2n/

96 Ana Carden-Coyne, 'Boy Mascots, Orphans and Heroes: The State, the Family and Cultural Heritage, 1914–1918, *Cultural and Social History*, 17:5 (2021): 1–30.

97 Heidi Fehrenbach, 'Children and Other Civilians: Photography and the Politics of Humanitarian Image-Making', in H. Fehrenbach and D. Rodogno (eds), *Humanitarian Photography: A History* (New York: Cambridge University Press, 2015), pp. 165–199.

98 Tony Kushner, 'Truly, Madly, Deeply … Nostalgically? Britain's On-Off Love Affair with Refugees Past and Present', *Patterns of Prejudice*, 52 (2018): 172–194.

99 'Their First Day in England', *Picture Post*, 1:12 (Saturday 17 December 1938).

100 'How History was Made in the Year 1938', *Picture Post*, 1:14 (Saturday 31 December 1938), p. 36.

101 *Courier*, 2:8 (September 1949).

102 Silvia Salvitici, 'UNRRA's Recipients Portrayed', in Fehrenbach and Rodogno (eds), *Humanitarian Photography*, pp. 202, 212, 218.

103 Rebecca Clifford, 'The Picture of (Mental) Health: Images of Jewish "Unaccompanied Children" in the Aftermath of the Second World War', *Journal of War and Culture Studies*, 15:2 (2022): 137.

104 Humbert, 'Picturing Displaced Persons', p. 227.

105 Tara Zahra, *The Lost Children: Reconstructing Europe's Families after World War II* (Cambridge, MA, London: Harvard University Press), 2011.

106 Zahra, *The Lost Children*, p. 117.

107 Simone Gigliotti, 'Displaced Children of Europe, Then and Now: Photographed, Itinerant and Obstructed Witnesses', *Patterns of Prejudice*, 52:2–3 (2018): 149–171.

108 United Nations Day official pamphlet, 1951.

109 UNICEF press release ICEF/319, 11 September 195. UN archives.

110 H. Fehrenbach and D. Rodogno, '"A Horrific Photo of a Drowned Syrian Child": Humanitarian Photography and NGO Media Strategies in Historical Perspective', *International Review of the Red* Cross, 97:900 (2015): 1123.

111 Per Olow-Anderson, *They Are Human Too: A Photographic Essay on the Palestine Arab Refugees* (Washington DC: Henry Regnery Co., 1957).

112 Winifred Carr, 'The Nightmare of Jordan's Refugee Women and Children', *Daily Telegraph* (14 July 1967), p. 15.

113 www.mutualart.com/Artwork/Refugee-Child-Crying-Refugee-Girl-on-Ba/61A749 BC513D5E38

114 Sîan Roberts, 'Education, Art and Exile: Cultural Activists and Exhibitions of Refugee Children's Art in the UK During the Second World War', *Pedagogica Historica: International Journal of the History of Education*, 53:3 (2017): 300–317.

115 Peter Gatrell, *Free World? The Campaign to Save the World's Refugees, 1956–1963* (Cambridge: Cambridge University Press, 2011), p. 13.

116 *Refugees 1960: A Report in Words and Drawings by Kaye Webb and Ronald Searle* (London: Penguin, 1960), p. 4.

117 Ronald Searle and Kay Webb, World Refugee Year appeal poster, *Daily Telegraph* (23 May 1960). Drawing by courtesy of Ronald Searle from *Refugees 1960* (Penguin Books).

118 Gatrell, *Free World?*

119 Antoine Burgard, 'Visualising Holocaust Child-Survivors in Canada: From Postwar Humanitarian Campaigns to National Memory', *Cultural and Social History*, 17:5 (2020): 731–754.

120 Rebecca Clifford, *Survivors: Children's Lives After the Holocaust* (New Haven, CT: Yale University Press, 2020), p. 12.

121 www.yadvashem.org/yv/en/exhibitions/art-liberation/bak.asp

122 Leora Auslander and Tara Zahra, *Objects of War: The Material Culture of Conflict and Displacement* (Ithaca, NY: Cornell University Press, 2018), p. 4. Emphasis in original.

123 Zuzanna Dziuban and Ewa Stanczyk, 'The Surviving Thing: Personal Objects in the Aftermath of Violence', *Journal of Material Culture*, 25:4 (2020): 381.

124 Dalia Judovitz, 'Duchamp's "Luggage Physics": Art on the Move', *Postmodern Culture*, 16, 1 (2005), accessed 14 February 2025. https://pmc.iath.virginia.edu/issue.905/16.1judo vitz.html

125 Alisa Sopova, 'Anxious Suitcases and their Contents: Experience of the War in Ukraine through a Material Lens', *American Ethnologist*, 50, September (2022): 54–64.

126 Hanna Diamond, 'Representing Defeat: Photographic Images of the French Exodus of 1940', *Journal of War and Culture Studies*, 1:3 (2013): 284.

127 Orvar Lofgren, 'Containing the Past, the Present and the Future: Packing a Suitcase', *Narodna umjetnost*, 53:1 (2016): 59–74, Article 59.

128 Joachim Schlor, *Jewish Culture and History*, 15:1–2 (2014): 76–92.

129 https://www.namoc.org/zgmsgen/ChinesePainting/201306/9cd203052ef245d4afc0c6e ec324d367.shtml

130 'The War Goes on', *Picture Post*, 3:11 (17 June 1939).

131 Photograph by Edward G Malindine (photo by Daily Herald Archive/National Science & Media Museum/SSPL via Getty Images). www.gettyimages.co.uk/detail/news-photo/span ish-refugees-may-1937-child-refugees-from-the-basque-news-photo/1360176488?adp popup=true

132 Simone Gigliotti, *Restless Archive: The Holocaust and the Cinema of the Displaced* (Bloomington, IN: Indiana University Press, 2024), accessed 14 February 2025. https:// doi.org/10.2979/RestlessArchive.0.0.02

133 Lynda Mannik, *Photography, Memory and Refugee Identity: The Voyage of the SS Walnut, 1948* (Vancouver: UBC Press, 2013).

134 Thy Phu, 'Refugee Photography and the Subject of Human Interest', in Tanya Sheehan (ed.), *Photography and Migration* (London: Routledge, 2018), pp. 139–140.

135 Frauke V. Josenhans, *Artists in Exile: Expressions of Loss and Hope* (New Haven, CT: Yale University Art Gallery, 2017).

136 The painting is in the collection of the Stanley Museum of Art, University of Iowa.

137 Associated Press, 30 November 1977. https://commons.wikimedia.org/wiki/Category: Vietnamese_boat_people#/media/File:35_Vietnamese_boat_people_2.JPEG

138 https://commons.wikimedia.org/wiki/File:Boat_of_No_Smiles,_blanket_shelter.jpg

139 Eddie Adams in 'A Photo Can Change Society', *Chicago Tribune* (18 May 2004): 5.1.

140 Barbara Basler, 'Sad Flotsam, the Boat People Must Drift Home', *New York Times*, 4 December (1989).

141 Michael Pugh, 'Drowning not Waving: Boat People and Humanitarianism at Sea', *Journal of Refugee Studies*, 17:1 (2004): 51.

142 John Van Kooy, Liam Magee, and Shanthi Robertson, '"Boat People" and Discursive Bordering: Australian Parliamentary Discourses on Asylum Seekers, 1977–2013', *Refuge*, 37:1 (2021): 16.

143 'Refugee Week Opens in the City', *Daily Telegraph* (1 December 1959); '30,000 People See Refugee Exhibition', *Daily Telegraph* (12 December 1959).

144 M.D. Mahbubar Rahman and Willem Van Schendel, 'I am Not a Refugee': Rethinking Partition Migration', *Modern Asian Studies*, 37:3 (2003): 551–584.

145 Original caption from *Life*, 1947. Patrick French, 'The Brutal "Great Migration" that followed India's Independence and Partition', accessed 12 December 2024. www.life.com/history/margaret-bourke-white-great-migration/

146 Margaret Bourke-White, *Halfway to Freedom: A Report on the New India in the Words and Photographs of Margaret Bourke White* (Simon and Schuster: New York, 1949), pp. 18, p. 20.

147 Bourke-White, *Halfway to Freedom*, p. 232.

148 Asma Naeem, 'Partition and the Mobilities of Margaret Bourke White and Zarina', *American Art*, 31:2 (2017): 84. Emphasis in original.

149 Anna Deem, 'Halfway to Freedom: A Report on the New India', in Thomas Riggs (ed.), *The Literature of Propaganda*, vol. 1 (Detroit, MI: St. James Press, 2013), p. 168.

150 Pallavi Chakravarty Ghosal, 'Redefining the Partition Refugee', *Proceedings of the Indian History Congress*, 75 (2014): 546–554.

151 James Hathaway, 'Food Deprivation: A Basis for Refugee Status?', *Social Research*, 81:2 (2014): 327–339.

152 Johnson, 'Click to Donate', p. 1016.

153 Tate Gallery Archives, TGA 965/2/4/3.

154 Balca Arda, 'Contemporary Art on the Current Refugee Crisis: The Problematic of Aesthetics Versus Ethics', *British Journal of Middle Eastern Studies*, 46:2 (2019): 310–327.

155 Australian War Memorial collection. www.awm.gov.au/collection/C2478469I

156 Suzana Milevska, 'Solidarity and the Aporia of "We": Representation and Participation of Refugees in Contemporary Art', in K. Lynes, T. Morgenstern, and I. Paul (eds), *Moving Images: Mediating Migration as Crisis* (Bielefeld: Verlag, 2020), pp. 245–262.

157 https://therefugeeartproject.com/home/

158 Tate St Ives interview with Petrit Halilaj, 2022. www.tate.org.uk/whats-on/tate-st-ives/petrit-halilaj-very-volcanic-over-green-feather

159 Gatrell, *The Making of the Modern Refugee*.

160 Paul A. Kramer, 'Unsettled Subjects: Inventing the Refugee in North American History', *Journal of American Ethnic History*, 39 (2020): 3.

161 Gatrell, *The Making of the Modern Refugee*, p. 13.

162 Valerie Holman, 'Representing Refugees: Migration in France 1940–44', *Journal of Romance Studies*, 2:2 (2002): 68.

163 See Chari Larsson, *Didi-Huberman and the Image* (Manchester: Manchester University Press, 2020).

164 Trinh T. Minh-ha, 'The Image and the Void', *Journal of Visual Culture*, 15:1 (2016): 1.

165 Greg Burgess, *The League of Nations and the Refugees from Nazi Germany* (London: Bloomsbury, 2016), pp. 13–28.

166 Josephine Ripley, 'Placing Displaced Persons', *Forbes Advocate* (9 December 1949), p. 9. Reprinted from the *Christian Science Monitor*.

2 From representation to lived experience: displaced artists and intersectional barriers

This chapter begins with a creative dialogue on the trope of refugees fleeing in boats, which was recorded as a conversation between Mahboobeh Rajabi (an artist and cultural producer) and Ambrose Musiyiwa (a poet and journalist) in March 2023. The recording was installed in the *Traces of Displacement* exhibition at the Whitworth Art Gallery (2023–24). The artists discuss a set of drawings by Cecily Brown *Untitled (Shipwreck)*, which were painted in 2016 in response to media images of the Syrian 'refugee crisis'. Reminding us of how art history is continually repurposed in response to contemporary political crises, Brown's works draw upon iconic paintings including Theodore Gericault's *The Raft of Medusa* (1818–19) and Eugene Delacroix's *The Shipwreck of Don Juan* (1840). Featuring densely layered human forms which create a sense of claustrophobia and urgency, the works appear as rapidly executed sketches of people in a moment of great distress and vulnerability. Executed in watercolour, gouache, and charcoal, Brown's works do not depict specific contemporary media images. Instead, they remain politically ambiguous, neither condemning nor endorsing tropes of refugees in flight.

The creative dialogue between Musiyiwa and Rajabi was installed next to Brown's artworks. It enabled visitors to listen to two different perspectives on the power of the boat trope – on the one hand to elicit solidarity, and on the other to promote damaging stereotypes of refugees. Musiyiwa recalls that: 'I actively took to poetry as a way of processing the images I was seeing. I was seeing exactly the same images [as Cecily Brown] of people making these impossible journeys through the Mediterranean, trying to get to places that they thought would be safe. The shipwrecks, the children who were drowning, hundreds of them … this is what I was seeing'. For Musiyiwa, the Brown paintings 'remain relevant' due to the small boat journeys people were making between 2011 and 2023, and because there are still 'no safe routes to Britain for people seeking refuge'.

By contrast, artist Mahboobeh Rajabi said:

> I straight away don't like the image of the boat because it has been repeated a lot, a lot and a lot that it became like a symbol … For me, the people, and their background, and their stories are more important. So not only is it important to reflect on what are the boats and what is happening but, actually, the identity of the people who are on the boats: their careers, their professions, their likes. They are human beings. So, the reason, and all the layers behind them getting into the boats, for me, is something that needs to be progressed … That identity gets lost … people who are tired crossing the roads, mountains, taking the boat. But who are these people? They are doctors, nurses. They are artists. They are mothers, fathers, who had a normal life like anybody else … For me, the element of the boat became like a box to categorise people that it is very hard to come out of … [and] you had to stay with that box in order to describe yourself, which is not healthy.

By working directly with creative people who have gone through the asylum process, and publishing their poetry, Musiyiwa's practice aims to provide 'spaces for counter-narratives' to stereotypical images of displacement.[1]

In the collaborative process of designing the exhibition, the authors and co-curators held extensive discussions, which revealed how visual tropes weigh heavily – and lastingly – on those with personal experiences of forced migration and displacement. Yet there are many different perspectives on the usefulness of art in addressing these themes. Some artists see the aestheticisation of displacement in images as necessary for genuine political change, but others see this as akin to building social barriers that are difficult to overcome.

In the previous chapter, representations of displacement centred on a set of visual tropes in tandem with the emergence of the international refugee regime. Displacement aesthetics, we argue, are representational and affective but also bound to lived experience. But as the above dialogue demonstrates, artists have different responses to what they witness and experience and how they respond to the history of art-making. This chapter shifts the discussion from representation to lived experience, focusing on contemporary artists who have experienced forced migration and displacement.

Here, we concentrate on a group of contemporary artists from backgrounds of forced migration and displacement and the barriers they face in Britain. All of the artists, apart from one, are at an early or emerging point in their career. Their testimony is important because it reveals the specific issues that impact displaced artists trying to forge careers in the art industry. This question of representation, experience, and presence in the art world underpins our understanding of the impact of displacement aesthetics, and hence it will be returned to throughout this book. The chapter explores how displacement aesthetics underwrites the experiences of displaced artists, casting a long shadow over their lives and presenting a set of profound challenges to their careers, which require exploration through intersectional analysis. Understanding this lived experience will also assist scholars in writing cultural and art history, and curators in preparing exhibitions, especially as displaced artists often act as representatives of particular communities.

The creative industries (and scholars too) can gain greater awareness of the potential and limits of displaced artists' 'cultural capital'. By this we mean the capital that an artist with a background of displacement can hold due to their personal experience, formal and informal knowledge, social networks, and language, which extend beyond their economic position. Cultural capital is a marker of the continually renegotiated dynamics of social and cultural inclusion and exclusion.[2] Inviting such artists into the gallery institution, or writing about displaced artists, is an imbalanced exercise at best, even while attempting to share in the power of culture. To echo Nicole Fleetwood's analysis of 'carceral aesthetics', while artists strive to make work in the most extraordinary circumstances of urgency and exclusion, art institutions are not designed to reflect the scope of the talents of displaced artists outside of a trauma perspective or an activity convened around the limited role of 'refugee week'.[3]

The chapter arises from a long association between the authors and the artists through collaborative projects, co-curation, and art-making. This colloboration sought to provide career enhancement for artists, while also allowing researchers to learn from artists' individual experiences and our collective projects. Understanding the barriers that artists face is crucial in grasping how the specific experience of seeking asylum and acquiring refugee status, as opposed to other forms of migration, affects the career of newcomer artists. The chapter examines the different structural barriers that shape artists' capacities to develop careers, mediate cultural institutions, and get ahead in the local and international art world. It first considers the foundations of the refugee regime and its processes as it impacts upon artists. It discusses the thorny issue of legal travel to work opportunities and explores the 'burden of proof'. It reflects on the social and economic barriers peculiar to displaced artists, and their intersection with gender barriers. The final part considers barriers to professional recognition. Throughout this chapter, close visual analysis of contemporary art will reveal how displacement aesthetics operates in encounters between representation and lived experience. This provides a fresh art historical interpretation in relation to the overlooked aspects of lived experiences of refugeedom.

Background context and method

This chapter is based on data derived from interviews with a small group of creative practitioners who undertook a Creative and Social Entrepreneur (CASE) training programme during 2021 with In Place of War, an international non-governmental organisation (NGO) based in Manchester. The aim of the interviews was to learn more about their individual artistic practices and what they needed to advance their careers. We sought to understand the barriers they faced, their experiences on the CASE programme, and how the UK arts industry could improve to serve them better. The interviews were semi-structured and took place over an hour of recorded conversation conducted in English but with two artists using Arabic or French translators. The interviews have been anonymised, and artists are referred to only through their country of origin and their artform (digital artist, visual artist, performing artist, and painter).

The project team went on to collaborate on an artistic and co-curated intervention at Manchester Art Gallery, entitled *Rethinking the Grand Tour* (2022–ongoing), and a temporary exhibition at the Whitworth Art Gallery, *Traces of Displacement* (2023–24). This led to reflection on the positionality, cultural power, and authority of academics, curators, and art institutions, in comparison with displaced artists. The research team and co-authors are a group of (racially, culturally, and linguistically) privileged researchers (and three of us are White migrants to Britain). We have not had direct experiences of displacement. As scholars committed to understanding the challenges, rights, and interests of displaced artists, we agree with migration scholar Elena Fiddian-Qasmiyeh that academic research must be 'grounded in a recognition of the inequalities and structural barriers that characterize and frame encounters in displacement situations'.[4] But we also have to acknowledge that our institutional status and power can be less visible to us, despite all our best intentions of anti-racist principles. Collaboration is an ongoing learning curve that requires acknowledgement, humility, and reflection.

It has also been fundamental to pay special attention to how representations underpin our assumptions about displacement, but also to come to understand the differences in socio-economic backgrounds, ethnicities and origins, and art practices.[5] One of the outcomes of this thinking was to ponder how to fully realise the value of working with a small group of artists over several projects and over a longer time period, which produces different relations to understanding compared to short-term projects. Due to the size of the sample group, the evidence presented in this chapter, therefore, does not claim to be representative of all creative artists' experiences nor does it reflect the huge range of varied experiences and arts policies in other countries. We argue, however, that in order to understand the barriers facing artists in the UK, the depth and detail presented in these interviews provides a rich understanding of encounters between discourses, institutions, and lived experiences (modes 2 and 3 of displacement aesthetics).

This chapter complements the body of art historical scholarship focused on issues of refugeedom and forced migration in contemporary art. However, studies of internationally established artists do not tend to explore lived conditions and professional barriers that displaced artists regularly face or the impact of political and economic challenges on their practice.[6] This chapter seeks to bolster research in museum and curatorial studies which identifies the need to move beyond representation, and to avoid exacerbating structural inequalities imposed on refugees.[7] Consideration of the barriers is not the only way of understanding their work. Nevertheless, understanding lived experience of professional barriers will provide more insight into contemporary art practice and will have practical consequences for how institutions can work with artists and vice versa. Overarchingly, to understand displacement aesthetics as lived experiences entwined with representations, this chapter draws on conversations with artists as well as relevant artworks. Focusing on the barriers artists face, it will consider immigration policies and invisible forces such as gender, work, and education, which shape the living conditions of displacement aesthetics, providing a foundation for future research into this field.

'Unfull time': waiting for status

Nations around the world have developed hostile policies towards refugees and migrants, frustrating and delaying legitimate asylum-seeking processes, detaining applicants in appalling conditions, carrying out often-unlawful deportations, while also hardening borders and subjecting refugees to bureaucratically masked criminalisation, including forced deportation to a so-called safe third country.[8] In Britain, the application of criminal justice rhetoric to immigration and asylum policy has eroded the democratic freedoms that Britons supposedly hold dear. This suggests that borders are a fragile and porous construction, and that the presence of refugees exposes each state's ethical and legal borderlands. The border, Mary Bosworth argues, is a 'figment of our imagination or perhaps an unrealizable dream'.[9] By contrast, refugees are a commonplace media spectacle, propelled onto screens in homes and across the newspapers each day. In turn, this 'hyper-visibility', Fiddian-Qasmiyeh observes, affects both media and humanitarian discourse. It renders refugees either as security threats or as suffering victims, passive though grateful recipients of sympathy and aid.[10]

The hyper-visibility of fleeing and arriving people, as we saw in Chapter 1, contrasts with the invisibility of asylum seekers in detention, a subject taken up by many artists and discussed in Chapter 5. To apprehend the meaning and impact of displacement aesthetics is to recognise 'seeking refuge as a process' rather than fixating on the cultural figure of the 'refugee'.[11] Taking this into account, here we turn our attention to the drawn-out processes facing artists who seek and then gain asylum in the UK. Waiting to gain official refugee status while unable to legally work has a lasting impact. In 2021, the UK Refugee Council reported on processing delays leading to 'years of uncertainty, poverty, and de-skilling'.[12] Asylum seekers must be deemed destitute in order to be eligible for accommodation and a paltry weekly allowance well below the living wage. The system was not designed to ensure a duty of care. Instead, it is fundamentally punitive. This was affirmed in the first-hand experiences of the artists we interviewed. One artist and producer waited four years to gain her refugee status, in which time she witnessed the detention of pregnant women in British holding facilities, a practice that has been unlawful since the 1916 Immigration Act.

The time delays built into the asylum process and the aftermath of its decisions are felt particularly by younger artists, as these suspensions impact their ability to study, to work, to build networks, and to advance their careers as artists in their new country. While there is some data on refugees in the professions of teaching and medicine, the creative industries have not been systematically studied. A digital artist described the length of time, the strain of waiting and worrying about being deported, and the subsequent impact on their career:

> I'm a refugee from Iran, and I came here when I was 21. Even starting to think, 'Can I be an artist?' was a big question ... What is often forgotten is that in order for people to become refugees, they need to go through the asylum process, which means facing hardships and going through the Home Office. Until your asylum application is approved, you don't have permission to work. It took me, for example, five and a half years to get my refugee status and so that was a huge barrier... I was always worrying what's going to happen to me.[13]

She explains the bureaucratic mechanics of arriving as a refugee in the UK, being first held in detention and then released into the community under restrictive conditions, going on to describe the profound emotional effect of having to constantly worry about being deported to Iran where she would face near certain persecution. Fear certainly adds to the trauma of asylum seeking, and is amplified by the drawn-out processes of waiting and worrying. This worry is felt by all asylum seekers, who are left in limbo, often in a precarious living situation, without security but with the dread of impending deportation hanging over their heads. Scholars have noted how the state deploys temporality to instill a state of 'protracted liminality' in precarious living, housing, and economic survival.[14] Writing about contemporary Palestinian art focused on refugeedom and statelessness, Chrisoula Lionis has observed that drawn-out processes of waiting are a form of 'banal evil', a widespread form of violence imposed upon Palestinians that often fails to arrest attention, eliciting apathy rather than moral condemnation.[15]

The Scottish artist Caroline Walker has brought to light women's particular experiences of waiting for refugee status, drawing empathy from her feminist perspective. She collaborated with the charity *Women for Refugee Women*, and a small group of asylum-seeking women who had been applying, waiting, and reapplying for their status over many years. The women wanted their stories to be told through visual art, which was seen as a far cry from the testimonies they are forced to narrate to the Home Office. Art enables a more collaborative and shared visuality, one that avoids the tropes and negative stereotypes of displacement aesthetics. Against the temporal injustice of UK policy, Walker depicts the quiet spaces where women attempt to carve out even a temporary space of self-care while being a non-citizen, an invisible human. In *Abi, Midday Brixton* (2017), the sitter is lying on a mattress in her Brixton church basement, having not only endured the trauma of displacement but now, as many people experience, having become homeless during the long period of waiting for status. Abi forged a makeshift home among piled-up boxes in a Church basement. Pinned to the wall, as though it is a proper bedroom, is a gallery wall of drawings Abi made while waiting. Here we have the non-displaced artist engaging with the displaced artist's work; both reflect and connect as forms of relief in this context of temporal and domestic injustice. In an interview, however, Abi shared that she had to move as she was being harassed; even her meagre sanctuary became unsafe and temporary.[16]

In *Joy, 11.30am, Hackney* (2017), the sitter is relaxing on her own bed, with a bright-red floral bedspread, suggesting something akin to her name and to feminist hope: the joy of a room of one's own, and the powerful emotions associated with the right to privacy and to the safety that a woman who must flee also yearns for. It is also an ambiguous, even tenuous space, however: the bedroom door is ajar and the viewer peers into her dignified privacy, suggesting that a woman's right to independence and personal freedom is fragile (Figure 2.1). Feminist art historian Griselda Pollock describes Walker's practice of conveying a 'world glimpsed in passing, seen by chance'; a glimpse of women's lives in limbo while waiting for status.[17] Joy, the sitter, also spoke of the temporariness of refugee status for which she had to reapply; time is against the vulnerable.[18] Joy seems to embody the isolation and slowness of 'unfull time'.

For artists who are displaced, the reality of unfull time has a dramatic professional impact. Firstly, the stop-start-stop of establishing an art career in a new country as a refugee means facing an industry where ageing and delay are viewed

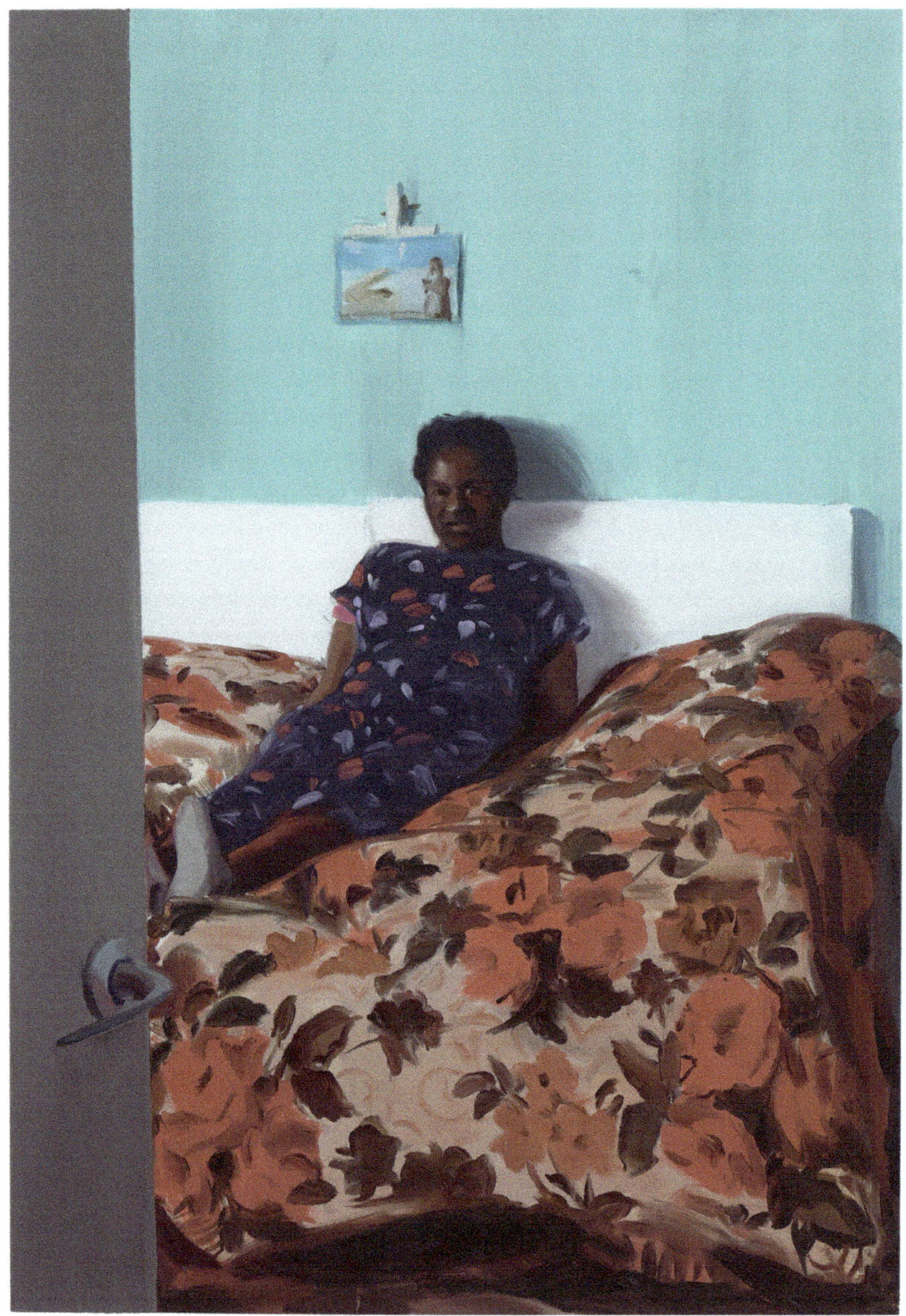

2.1 Caroline Walker, *Joy, 11.30am, Hackney* (2017). © Caroline Walker. Courtesy of the artist; Stephen Friedman Gallery, London; GRIMM, New York/Amsterdam/London, and Ingleby, Edinburgh. All rights reserved, DACS 2024.

negatively. Artists must overcome language barriers whilst being held back from the networking that cements relationships and leads to the very professional opportunities where the artist's practice becomes known (see Chapter 3). Only then are the exhibition prospects and commissions which forge reputation and patronage likely to follow.

For artists, losing time is doubly serious because artistic careers take a long time to develop and consolidate. In interviews, this loss of time was frequently commented upon. The digital artist recalled her feeling that: 'I'm losing my youth. That was my nightmare for me … I was thinking: I'm losing my 20s, who would give me back [the year] when I was 24? Who would give me back my 20s? It's something impossible'.[19] When after five years this artist eventually secured her refugee status, she worked doubly hard to establish her career by whatever means were at her disposal. Her immediate opportunities came from working with community arts organisations: the experience was, in her words, 'great' because they were 'supporting me to understand this city, and Manchester has a great community of people who would care: small organizations like CAN (Community Arts North West) and Commonword'.[20]

Positive opportunities, however, can sometimes produce less-positive outcomes. Amy K. Levin has noted the danger of perpetuating a troubling dichotomy even as the creative industries seeks to empower refugee communities and assist hosts to 'gain respect for new populations'.[21] In the UK, community arts projects may only offer short-term funding, and they often do not lead to opportunities with mainstream galleries or art museums. It is therefore difficult for artists to exhibit their work independent of the community arts context, which exists in a separate ecosystem to the mainstream art gallery sector and is sometimes regarded as less impactful and professional. To be sure, it is the global arena of biennials where curators seem more ambitious in providing a platform for marginalised artists, but for the most part, mainstream galleries, both commercial and public, are the gatekeepers of professional opportunity, of networks and resources, and of the mentoring that enhances an artist's reputation. These domestic institutions have the power to clear the crowded path to funding, curated shows, exhibition sales, and collector sales, which is particularly important for artists whose immigration status restricts their travel. The gallery system complements the top-end mentoring that aspiring artists gain from graduate-level study in the pressure-cooker, hyper-competitive environments of art schools in the Global North.

Waiting in limbo, with limited access to formal study or professional opportunity, contrasts with the contemporary art world, which often speaks for displaced artists without aligning with or mentoring them. These challenges are compounded by another key barrier that is fundamental to forging a successful career: the freedom to travel to one's own exhibitions and to attend artist residencies. The art industry relies upon not just the international circulation of artworks but also the international circulation of art practitioners, including artists, curators, art writers, collectors, administrators, critics, and more.

The politics of passports

Movement is the cornerstone of both creativity and economy in the arts, but it has also been enshrined in the Universal Declaration of Human Rights since 1949 (Article 13). Waiting, and living without freedom of movement is a lived condition that is an important aspect of displacement aesthetics. For artists, travel is part of the process of becoming not just internationally recognised but also acclimatised to the expectations and issues of contemporary art. For instance, artists are expected to participate in public programmes and roundtables, give artist talks and interviews, attend media events, and engage with social media platforms. In addition, the increasing number of arts festivals and biennials that survey the global field of art with selections of artists from around the world place great demand on their physical presence. Artists waiting for official status or the right to travel cannot always accompany their own exhibitions to meet potential patrons, or attend events, or be included in public programmes that profile their own art. Not surprisingly, the value of their art in the marketplace is therefore diminished or becomes less visible. The great irony is that while displaced artists' works can travel freely across borders and be purchased for international collections and museums, the artists themselves cannot travel. Restrictions on visas and passport access are highly politicised and designed to restrain and contain. Arguably, it is an unofficial form of tacit detention, one which robs artists of privileged access to citizenship and passports.

In the UK, refugee status is required to access the right to a passport that will enable travel, and there are distinct limitations and zealous surveillance at airports. Indeed, as one of the artists with UK residency stated, travel to their own exhibitions is habitually hampered by problems gaining a visa to enter another country.[22] Place of birth and refugee status cast a definite shadow over what Hannah Arendt called 'the right to have rights', particularly when the visa system of another country is contingent on unseen variables that impact the artist's access to the international arts industry.[23]

One visual artist we interviewed, who arrived in the UK with a respected practice, described the pressures of measuring short-term involvements with art projects and collaborations against the permanent right to stay in the UK. She explained:

> The visa issue! … I think that's the biggest problem for us as artists … If we have been invited to be in an exhibition in the UK that's fine, though it is really difficult to do

that. But if you have another exhibition somewhere else outside the UK, it's really difficult to be there, to get a visa … and for other artists to come to the UK.[24]

As a solution, the artist had the compelling idea of an International Artist's Visa made possible through a dedicated partnership with the Home Office. Currently, the main way artists can visit the UK is via a standard Business Visa, but it is well documented that while there is a high rejection rate, the Home Office retains the processing fees. The irony here is that while many artists are making images about refugee crises, and touring the world to participate in biennials and key gallery exhibitions, displaced artists are frequently stymied from following similar paths.

In the UK, the Global Talent Visa is one tool that artists can try to use to enter the country and reside for up to five years. They must demonstrate their financial security, exceptional talent, and creative leadership, which must be proven and recognised. The Home Office relies on endorsements from an officially accredited body, such as the British Academy, which only serves the humanities and social sciences. There is simply no comparable body recognising or celebrating practising artists. Further, the Global Talent Visa processing times are long, costs are very high, and of course rejected applications are not refunded.[25]

Artists who encounter the Home Office must therefore navigate a disorienting hall-of-mirrors of restrictive barriers. Invitations to artists abroad have become impractical and logistically labyrinthine. Across the first three decades of the twenty-first century, Home Office policies negatively impacted museums, galleries, universities, and industry workshop events. The inability of a whole class of prominent and emerging artists to speak about their works in person, in turn, affected the reception and understanding of art. For example, in 2020, Manchester Art Gallery and the University of Manchester attempted in vain to obtain a visa for the Syrian-born artist Azza Abo Rebieh to attend a workshop in London. The artist had been imprisoned by the Assad regime and was now a refugee in Beirut. Even so, her art attracts considerable international attention and is in significant UK collections such as that of the British Museum, as well as many others on the international stage. Abo Rebieh has been able to attend artist residencies in France, but she could not come to speak about her work in Britain.

On the day she was to speak remotely, with a hundred people in London waiting for her to talk, the internet connection failed. The artist missed the opportunity to talk about her work and a committed audience of experts and artists were disappointed due to the continuing inadequacies of remote conferencing. The frustrating background, of course, was that the UK Home Office retains an extremely hostile and skeptical attitude to artists from the Global South, especially those who have refugee status, and at that time Syrian artists were regarded with the utmost suspicion, so much so that Western Union refused to process a payment to the artist. The Home Office charged an exorbitant visa processing fee and did not refund the rejected application, a situation that many people in the cultural industries have encountered. The UK seem particularly hostile in this respect, since Abo Rebieh had no problem travelling to France to participate in her exhibition there.

Manchester Art Gallery, like many museums in the UK, comes up against similar obstacles. In 2017, the gallery invited the Tentative Collective to participate in the exhibition programme of the New North and South network, an initiative to commemorate Partition and 70 years of independence supported by the British Council. However, the Home Office rejected their visa on spurious grounds – including that they did not have children; the assumption being perhaps that a person without children is more mobile and less attached to their home country. Drawing attention to the artists' absence, the gallery installed on its walls the official visa rejection letter of the Karachi-based group. This was placed next to a poster with the words 'Artists Missing' and that the North and South are 'still divided' (Figure 2.2). Together, the artwork and the gallery suggest how much British audiences lose due to hostile policies towards artists from the global South. The gallery's ambitious programme to connect with South Asian artists, in a city that has a large South Asian community, was thwarted.

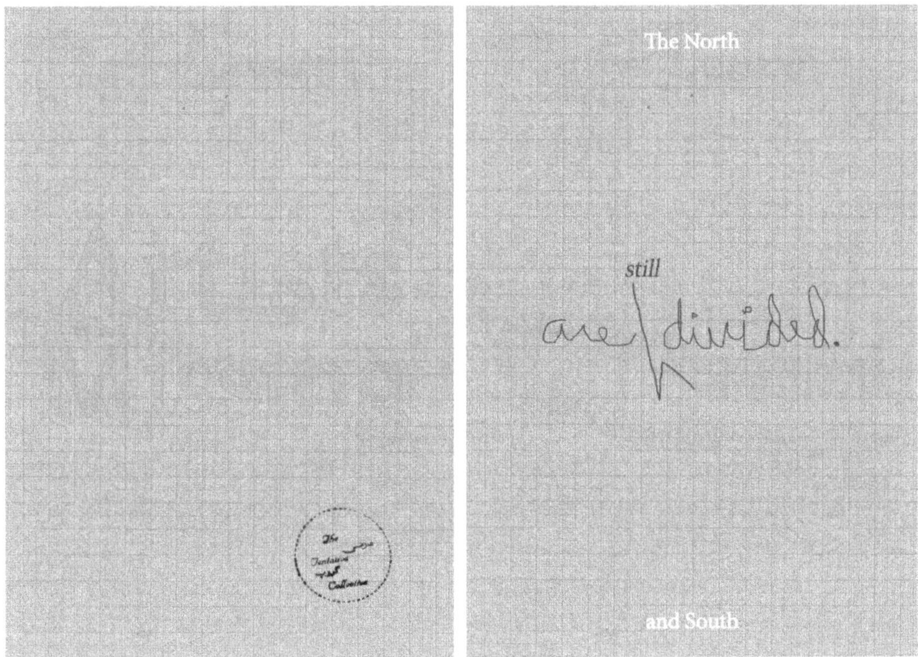

2.2 Tentative Collective, *Untitled* (2017) (detail). Courtesy of the artists and Manchester Art Gallery.

But as the artists themselves noted, 'the legacy of colonization haunts us 70 years later as we increasingly inhabit suspicious islands surrounded by walls'.[26] It is no glib statement, observing just how much the North and the South are divided; how artists are penalised, and audiences are missing out. This was the purpose of the so-called hostile environment, which punishes 'outsiders', underwrites a very narrow definition of belonging to the nation if not to humanity, and disengages museum visitors from learning about the perspectives, lives, and histories of other people in the world.

The hostile visa environment was pioneered by Conservative Party politician, later Prime Minister, Theresa May, who was the UK Home Secretary between 2010 and 2016. The policies impacted displaced artists almost immediately. The first ever exhibition of Iraqi contemporary art in 2010, for instance, was thwarted by the Home Office, who decided that bank statements provided for the visiting artists were inadequate. In March 2010, a Manifesto Club Dossier entitled *Deported: Artists Barred from the UK* was signed by eminent artists and cultural leaders across Britain. The signatories wrote:

> Home Office restrictions that discriminate against our overseas colleagues on the grounds of their nationality and financial resources and will be particularly detrimental to artists from developing countries, and those with low income. Such restrictions will damage the vital contribution made by global artists and scholars to cultural, intellectual and civic life in the UK.

The dossier cited a plethora of artists and musicians unable to attend their own openings, performances, and artist residencies. It recounted the case of renowned American artist, Cristina Winsor, who was held in immigration detention by UK Border Force before being officially barred from entering the country and immediately deported.[27] Significant though the dossier is, our research examines how artists with refugee status in the UK further their careers whilst navigating the resettlement process. What we have found as a result of our interviews is an initial step towards understanding the wider implications of restrictions for artists from backgrounds of forced displacement who are currently living in the UK.

To put this in further context, politicians have expressed very little concern that the UK's vaunted soft power, gained from the international prestige of its national cultural sector, had frayed due to the expansion of hostile visa policies. This is despite the fact that the media often notes cultural workers' concerns about the impact of Brexit, and senior arts workers, as well as scientists, have pleaded for more open borders with easier movement in and out of the country. Twelve years on from the official hostile policy, the 'hostility rather than hospitality', accorded to artists from the Global South and from areas of war and conflict, continues to create near-impossible conditions, especially for refugee communities. The great loss is not just to individual artists, but to art museums, to academic knowledge, and most of all to the British public itself, especially in the light of ongoing hostility to migrants and refugees, and the hardening positions of almost all political parties.

Restricted travel is, arguably, part of a tacit continuance of hostility, in this case towards displaced artists. It prevents them from having a platform, having a voice, and making a career that works and that will contribute to the culture sector. For one performing artist, a recent refugee who had not yet established any arts networks in the UK, the problem of travel to Europe to pursue a critical career opportunity is telling if not exemplary. They said:

> For example, last month. I should have been in Denmark for a few concerts and festivals. I organised everything all the tickets and everything. But I didn't manage to get the visa. Everything was prepared and then everything had to be cancelled, and there are so many difficulties I experience being here … Sometimes you're working, you prepare everything. And in the end, it [the problem of travel restrictions] has made us nearly lose everything.[28]

For this artist, the lengthy process of gaining refugee status while trying to maintain any performance schedule, despite the networks they already had, led ultimately to great disappointment. They were met with financial losses, loss of faith, and many brick walls. We will return in Chapter 5 to the topic of artists' resilience, despite all the pain and trauma that continues as an undercurrent of their past and present. One of the ironies of displacement aesthetics is that while the creative work of displaced artists may achieve international attention, they face continual barriers when trying to mobilise or monetise this activity.

The paradox of proof

When artists seek asylum, like all applicants, they must prove that they have a 'well-founded fear of persecution', so as not to be returned to the place of persecution. This is the cornerstone of Article 33 of the UN Convention Relating to the Status of Refugees (1951). This principle is called *non-refoulement*, and it continues to discern a wide range of national government and judicial interpretations across the world, since its first drafting.[29] Sheona York's important work describes the operating construction of the 'bogus' versus 'genuine' refugee, which shapes both policy and its exercise in applicant interviews, and places the 'burden of proof' on the applicant, rendering 'credibility' the over-riding legal issue in asylum determinations. York observes that the 'well-founded fear' is 'conflated with their motives and methods of escape'. The subsequent development of a 'refusal culture' or 'culture of disbelief' has led to the 'over-burdening of proof' akin to the criminal standard of 'beyond all reasonable doubt', despite the fact that the UNHCR *Handbook on Procedures and Criteria* allows for the exercise of 'benefit of the doubt' when 'the applicant's account appears credible'.[30] This slipperiness in the hands of officials, who consistently misapply the law, underpins the adversarial encounters of asylum processes. Thus, in Britain, the Home Office requires claimants to produce evidence and to repeatedly testify to their persecution through official interviews, narrating to authorities their personal, often traumatic experiences. They must tell their stories to gain refugee status by proving that they meet the Home Office's interpretation of international law. It is the findings of our interviews and research that the burden of proof and the associated signs that demonstrate the authenticity of proof are inadvertently but not completely harmlessly replayed in the well-meaning humanitarian operations of activities such as Refugee Week and, closer to home, for the arts community in artistic opportunities siloed around refugeedom.

There is a crucial further element at play in ameliorating the burden of proving persecution. The UNHCR *Handbook* states that 'While the burden of proof in principle *rests* on the [asylum] applicant, the duty to ascertain and evaluate all the relevant facts is shared between the applicant and the examiner' (para 196).[31] Even though the burden of proving the veracity of a claim to asylum is meant to be shared between applicant and host, in practice the process is combative, adversarial, intimidating, and unsympathetic. The brutality, and indeed absurdity, of this adversarial process is poignantly represented in Kurdish Iraqi artist Hiwa K's film *View From Above* (2017). An experimental video produced for *documenta* 14, the film chronicles the story of a character called 'M', who fled from the northern, Kurdish part of Iraq and applied for asylum 'in one of the Schengen countries'. In the film, 'M' explains that the UN considered Kurdistan a safe zone and in order to be deemed a refugee one has to come from the 'unsafe zone', or at least prove to an official that this is the case.

After waiting five years for asylum to be granted in one Schengen country (described as country 'X') the work's protagonist receives a rejection and notification that he will be deported back to his country of origin. A deserter from the army and fearful for his life, 'M' decides instead to cross the border into another Schengen country (described as 'XX'), where he reapplies for refugee status. This time, aware that the interview would require him to produce proof of familiarity with a region that both he and the interviewer had never experienced first-hand, 'M' spent weeks in advance of his interview with people from a town in the unsafe zone. Interviewing them and studying every corner of the town, he was able to draw a map of the town and to be intricately familiar with a place he had never visited. In his interview with an official from country XX, 'M' demonstrated cartographic knowledge of the city, impressing the decision-maker and ultimately leading to acceptance of his asylum application.

It is unclear if *View From Above* is a true story, autobiographical, or a composite of multiple experiences. The ambiguity of the film, which relies on the voice of the artist to narrate the story of M, highlights how understandings of truth and fiction are manipulated in the asylum process, and how definitions of 'safe' and 'unsafe' zones are arbitrary. The impact of the work rests on its ability to show how combative forms of interviewing play a key role in hostile immigration policies. Over the first two decades of the twentieth century, the criminalisation of migration and asylum has gained unprecedented focus in scholarship across the fields of migration, criminology, and socio-legal studies.[32] Importantly, *View From Above* visualises the embodiment of these policies in affective terms, astutely expressing the anxiety induced by the assumption of not being believed, or indeed believable. As film theorist Anja Sunhyun Michaelsen points out, the work draws attention to the assumption that telling one's own story is a form of empowerment. Instead, the film suggests the significance of mastery over obscuring the distinction between fiction and truth, and that 'telling one's story requires a form of narrative mastery unavailable for most'.[33]

As border policies harden internationally, the combative form of interviewing has become more pronounced. Since the 2007 UK Border Act was passed, those who have suffered persecution, torture, and rape have been subjected to government policy that conflates immigration and criminal processes and creates categories of 'belongers' and 'non-belongers'.[34] This goes back further than 2007. It is consistent with fallout from the 2012 Home Office hostile environment policy that resulted in the Windrush scandal. Commonwealth citizens had come to the UK, often as children with their parents. Under new conservative policies they were suddenly dubbed 'illegal immigrants' and expected to 'prove' their residency, even though the Home Office had not retained the very documentation that would prove their legal right to remain. Dubbed the 'Windrush Generation', they were dismissed from work, denied access to public health, bank accounts, and driving licences, were made homeless, and deported. One hundred and twelve British residents of Caribbean origin were detained and thirty-one people were deported.[35] This exposure of a 'hostile environment' policy brought to light the Home Office's weaponising of the burden of proof. It exposed the racism that underpinned the rewriting of the rights of citizenship, including the right to work and lead a healthy life. Black Commonwealth communities were suddenly and falsely designated as 'illegal immigrants'.

Despite judicial findings that the policy was illegal, Minister Sajid Javed's apology in 2019 did not lead to a decline in deportation rates. In 2019, 5,203 people were forcibly removed from the UK.[36] Thus, the burden of proof, coupled with the culture of disbelief practised by immigration officials, government solicitors, and judges-has deeply undermined the institution of asylum.[37] This was underpinned by the politically driven, populist hostility that has reshaped the twenty-first-century refugee regime in Britain, across Europe, and elsewhere. The UK government's attempt in 2022 to deport asylum seekers to Rwanda, a state with its own human rights issues, is an expression of this hostility. While UK refugee policy shifted in 2024, with a change of government, nevertheless both the UK and European states continue to explore policies of offshore detention.

How, then, does the burden of proof within the public administration of asylum law impact artists in the UK culture sector? Making art does not free artists from the burden of proof. The personal narratives that evidence persecution and refugee experience have become intrinsic to exhibitions and collection displays in contemporary art exhibitions and historical museums. As discussed in Chapter 1, displacement aesthetics has been forged by and in the spaces of art institutions on a globalised scale, in museums, galleries, biennials, and festivals that focus on 'refugee arts'. In the UK, over the first two decades of the twenty-first century, museums have made passionate public commitments to working with refugee communities. This has taken the form of participatory art projects, often led by an artist who is not from a background of forced displacement, working with refugee communities to provide art classes and other services, or working with settled communities as project consultants.[38] Art galleries have done this both to communicate the refugee experience and to learn from displaced artists; they have also commissioned works of art by displaced artists and toured shows that proudly feature displaced artists.[39] Across European and Anglo-American museums, curators have attempted to welcome refugees through so-called joint enterprise, which is to say in projects that ostensibly share power.[40] This means jointly deciding on themes for exhibitions and choosing objects and artworks for display. It also means shifting from objectifying refugees as figures of representation to commencing genuine involvement, collaboration, and shared decision-making (see Chapter 5).

As argued throughout this book, displacement aesthetics is a historical, cultural, and institutional phenomenon, but it is also a generator of change. Museums and arts sector advocates wish to resist the negative representation of refugees, as Domenico Sergo has argued.[41] But, they also need to rely less on famous artists who engage with the refugee and migration discourse. Instead, they must begin to provide professional opportunities for displaced artists to work directly with influential curators in museums and to be mentored by them. However, if their presence in the gallery system overly relies on the expectation that their work must inflect the trauma of being forced to leave families, homes, communities, then this can be too deterministic. Moreover, it suggests that there is a further burden of proof that the belonging of the artist depends on the authenticity of experience.

The entwined paradox for artists from backgrounds of forced displacement is three-fold. First, they must have documentation that supports their claims. Second, when they finally gain refugee status, these artists tend to make connections with community groups and community arts organisations that are often but not always linked by nationality or ethnic identity. These connections usually hinge on festivals and events directly planned to present refugee experiences. Once again, the artist must often re-narrate their trauma, making art or performances that represent the journey, the suffering, the plight, the identity of what it is to be a refugee. More on this point later, but it seems that the same obligation is not forced to the same degree on non-displaced artists. Third, artistic networks and opportunities often come through community art networks, which do not tend to break the gatekeeping barrier of the mainstream art institutions. For some artists, the period of life in which they were a refugee feels like a painful shadow that was walked with, a 'deeply held within burden', and should not continue to determine their career path.[42]

These factors shape the critical paradox of refugeedom as it plays out in the arts sector: while there are many well-intentioned arts organisations that attempt to collaborate with displaced artists and not just pay lip service to them, some artists feel they need to resist making art about being a refugee in order to avoid being forever branded by a former experience. Displaced artists are not necessarily interested in 'the cultural figure of the refugee' informing the focus of their work. Ultimately, the 'paradox of proof' underscores the precarity of the displaced artist. We might here point to Judith Butler's notion of precarity as a politically-induced condition that, as Mette Louise Berg explains, involves a precarity produced by structural inequalities and exclusionary legal frameworks.[43] For forcibly displaced artists, the result is that the tangible burden of proof – proof of persecution, refugee criteria, and prior national citizenship – extends to mandating an intangible proof that is authenticated by continually re-representing the trauma that lies at the heart of the very aestheticisation of displacement, which museums also seek to disrupt. Finally, the on-going 'burden of proof' produces an individual's passport to creative legitimacy within the Global North arts industry and museum sectors. The passport, ultimately a validator of national belonging, is without doubt our most important personal document, impacting not only our ability to move and to access state resources, but also, vitally, our ability to access labour markets and employment opportunities.

Economic precarity and the impacts of gender: welfare, housing, and the right to work

There is a growing field of research in the social sciences that acknowledges the impacts of economic precarity on displaced populations.[44] Running parallel to this, art historical scholarship, particularly in the wake of the global financial crisis, has focused on the impacts of economic barriers upon artistic practice and the livelihoods of artists. To date, the points of convergence between these lines of enquiry are yet to be adequately analysed and understood.

Economic barriers, uncertainty around income, and exploitative or casualised employment conditions are experienced by the majority of arts sector workers.[45] Artists usually supplement their art practice with paid work and also undertake free work to gain exposure and forge networks. Gregory Sholette describes the infinite mass of workers as 'dark matter', people who spend decades in unrelated and poorly paid jobs.[46] In the UK, employees within the creative industries tend to come from the middle classes, and those with working-class backgrounds are substantially fewer than in other sectors.[47] Thus, the ability to supplement a creative practice within these conditions impacts acutely upon those with working-class backgrounds who cannot fall back on generational wealth or familial support. Due to its short-term and elite character, public arts funding (such as Arts Council England) is not a reliable route to fill this precarious economic gap. Instead, artists develop informal and formal work networks of peers and mentors over many years.

For artists from backgrounds of forced displacement, specific factors arise that are additionally deleterious. Recent research that focused on the UK arts sector suggests that economic barriers may be more encompassing than those linked to ethnicity and gender, since economic barriers operate as roadblocks to the change required to alleviate or eradicate other disadvantages.[48] Our research considers the economic precarity faced by artists from asylum seeking and refugee backgrounds as a central professional barrier, one that adds to numerous other obstacles that are not as easily captured by Arts Council data.

The asylum system is responsible for creating a distinct experience of precarity in the areas of housing and financial provision. During the asylum support period, until an application has been assessed and approved, asylum seekers in the UK are offered government accommodation and a basic living allowance. Applicants are not permitted to choose either the location or the type of accommodation (e.g. apartment, shared house, hostel, or bed and breakfast); these are designated by government authorities based on a compulsory 'dispersal policy'.[49] While the policy aims at proportionate resource allocation across the UK, regions with more affordable housing tend to lack employment opportunities or other structures of support. If asylum seekers have their applications approved, they are granted refugee status. This gives them either long-term or indefinite leave to remain in the UK, as well as the right to work, though employment problems tend to persist. As Nuria Targarona Rifa and Giorgia Donà suggest, previous debt linked to displacement (including trafficking networks in border crossing) makes it difficult for some refugees to avoid 'informal' or 'undocumented' employment networks, even after gaining the right to work.[50]

Although refugees can now apply for standard welfare benefits such as Universal Credit (UK government-paid unemployment benefits), being granted refugee status also means that people are no longer offered a place to live. So, while universal credit is typically higher than the asylum support allowance, it is also supposed to cover housing costs. A painter from Syria described the difficult decision she faced when receiving Universal Credit payment:

> I'm looking and searching for some work that is stable. I don't want to always be on Universal Credit, waiting for work. I need something … For all these difficulties, I have a plan to work as a teaching assistant or to get a part time job. Maybe next year, or the year after that, I want to get a job for myself. I can't live and ignore my art, you know. I will always think about how I can make art and exhibit my work.[51]

One of the primary economic challenges faced by artists is finding the time and resources required to create work. This continues to be the case when artists are selected for high-status residencies in art museums or universities that increasingly emphasise diversity and inclusion in their selection criteria. Artists' experiences are especially painful when they had an already established career in the countries from which they fled.

Questions around precarious labour and migration are not new; for example, they constitute a long-standing part of feminist art history and practice. Angela McRobbie notes how women artists in service-based and 'immaterial labour' economies attract precarious supplementary work and financial debt.[52] Artists and art historians have exposed how this precarity has been reproduced by sidelining the conditions in which women artists work. Griselda Pollock identified the 'invisibility of women as creators' in contrast to the 'visibility of the feminine' in artistic figuration.[53] Maura Reilly notes the patriarchal basis underpinning the art world's 'master narratives', as art museums and private markets fail to collect art by women.[54]

The work of New York-based artist Mierle Laderman Ukeles is seminal in this regard. Since 1969 she has instigated a feminist critique through what she called 'maintenance art'. In 'Manifesto for Maintenance Art 1969! Proposal for an Exhibition "Care"', Ukeles juxtaposed maintenance labour, such as cleaning, with artistic labour and the care and conservation of art in art institutions. Her performances and sculptural installations in the 1970s collaborated with the Department of Sanitation in New York (DSNY), working closely with 500 city street cleaners and sanitation workers, many of whom were migrant men and were, according to Ukeles, upset that they were unappreciated and invisible to the majority of people living in the city.[55] Significantly, while feminist scholars often describe this work as pioneering in terms of artistic labour, its relevance to migration is often overlooked. The same oversight exists in discussion of contemporary feminist artistic collaborations involving migrant women. For displaced artists, who also feel invisible to the wider arts industry of the host country, a huge amount of 'maintenance work' is taken up in dealings with the Home Office and immigration authorities, which is not just 'a drag' that takes 'all the time', as Ukeles writes, but is far more sinister in that it is always shadowed by trauma, not being believed, and the threat of deportation.

The Los Angeles-based artist Suzanne Lacy has worked with Manchester Art Gallery and local organisations towards *Uncertain Futures + 100 Women* (2020–ongoing), an art and research collaborative work which analyses the intersectional inequalities facing women over fifty around work (Figure 2.3). As part of this project, Lacy released a new film *Cleaning Conditions*, a two-week performance that she staged in the gallery in 2013, as part of Hans Ulrich Obrist's *do it* exhibition in the

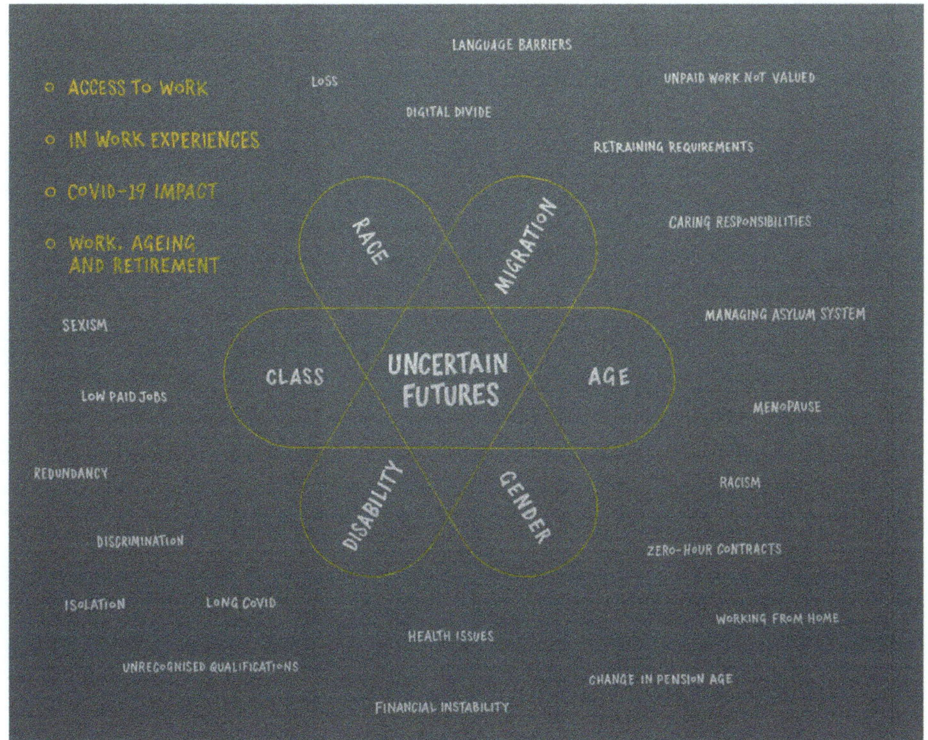

2.3 Uncertain Futures Research Matrix diagram. Courtesy of Manchester Art Gallery. Dr Sarah Campbell, Manchester Metropolitan University; Dr Elaine Dewhurst, University of Manchester with Suzanne Lacy, artist; Ruth Edson, Manchester Art Gallery, and the Uncertain Futures Advisory Group: Akhter Azabany, Erinma Bell, Sally Casey, Atiha Chaudry, Rohina Ghafoor, Marie Greenhalgh, Teodora Ilieva, Tendayi Madzunzu, Jila Mozoun, Elayne Redford, Nadia Siddiqui, Circle Steele, Patricia Williams, and Louise Wong. Graphic design: Source Creative.

context of Manchester International Festival. The performance was made in collaboration with a team of volunteers described as 'sweepers' from labour, living wage, and immigration organisations, who swept the gallery floors every day and conversed on current working conditions throughout England. In one of the aesthetic productions of the installation, a diagram of uncertain futures marks out key words that condition the women's personal and working lives, some of whom are migrants and refugees. 'Managing the asylum system' is specifically mentioned here in the text, although it is a bit hidden among a list of other experiences such as caring responsibilities, racism, discrimination, ageing, and menopause.

Women artists who have been through the asylum system face specific and pronounced economic barriers, including gender-specific marginalisation and exclusion. Health and social care researchers demonstrate that regulations hindering asylum seekers' access to work or benefits is harmful to women's mental and physical health, exacerbating destitution and dependence.[56] This hostile environment in the UK has affected artists we have worked with in numerous ways that have impacted their lives and their practices. The performing/digital artist has made such issues the subject of her practice, which is often characterised by solidarity with forcibly displaced women and the problems they encounter as asylum seekers. Together with CAN Refugee Women's Project, and the BOAZ Trust, she was involved in a participatory, immersive performance *Rule 35* (2015). Based on the testimonies of female refugees placed in detention centres in Britain, the artist recalled:

> I've done a few theatre projects where we worked with refugees and asylum-seekers and we created performances, raising awareness. [...] One of them was *Rule 35*, talking about the UK Rule 35 [Detention Centre Rules], which states that no pregnant woman, and no woman with an illness, should be placed in a detention centre. I was in a detention centre with a pregnant woman.[57]

This performance arose directly out of her lived experience of the law being broken, and her experience of mothers and pregnant women. Moreover, women in the asylum system face limited access to free maternity care, which has been linked to several deaths. Facing an under-recognised form of economic precarity, these women are made financially responsible for servicing their care. As a result of 'draconian NHS charging policies', they avoid care or suffer a debt burden.[58] Finally, the ambitions of women artists with caring duties are disproportionately hindered by freelance or casualised paid work, which does not include parental leave, since childcare and domestic labour remain by and large the domain and responsibility of women.

While some of these barriers may cut across economic demographics or social identities, backgrounds of forced displacement are, as we have seen, also layered by unfull time, which diffuses and exacerbates other divisions of productive time. The lived experiences of economic precarity for displaced artists are often as understated and opaque as the intersectional barriers concealed in both asylum system regulations and art-institutional perceptions. At the same time, displaced artists often reflect strategically on such experiences through their practice, as they seek to intervene in the processes of identification that affect them. Displacement aesthetics unpacks the interconnectedness of experiences and identifications and highlights the indispensability of a focus on artists' lives.

Understanding the barriers to professional recognition

In addition to the issues of refugee identity, wasted time, travel restrictions, and the burden of proof, a further disadvantage faced by artists with backgrounds of forced displacement is proficiency with language and professional discourse within the art world. This will be further explored in Chapter 3, as lack of mastery over language and what is often called 'artspeak' compounds existing inequalities within the arts sector.

Research demonstrates the challenges arts industries in the UK face in terms of the diversity of the creative workforce. There are particularly low numbers of people of colour and global majority workers across museum, gallery, music, film/television, and visual arts sectors.[59] The arts and cultural industries in the UK are also strongly stratified by ethnicity, age, and class. Little has changed since a 2010 study of UK art schools, which noted the 'colonisation' by middle-class applicants of various creative industry jobs, from volunteer positions to prestigious, continuing appointments.[60] This has become more pronounced, not less, as the number of people with tertiary qualifications has increased, mirroring growth in the creative economy, within which art schools are incubators for wider creative industries.[61] While there is a prevailing sense that both universities and the creative industries in the UK are amongst the best in the world, access to them is marked by pre-existing privilege; creative industry jobs are often awarded to graduates from elite universities.[62]

This impacts acutely upon artists from backgrounds of forced displacement. They have already faced significant barriers, compounded by structural racism within creative industries.[63] According to Roaa Ali, damaging attitudes and misconceptions about minoritised ethnic communities have a negative impact on how culture is represented and produced, and it impacts decision-making within institutions.[64] For displaced minorities, education is also a critical area of inequality. Interruptions to artists' education and careers are exacerbated by the systemic failure to recognise their prior qualifications and industry experience. Those deficiencies reflect what Liisa Malkki describes as the 'sedentarist principles' that underpin societal conceptualisations of education.[65] That is to say, the undetected assumptions that children and young adults sail relatively smoothly through national educational systems. Within Malkki's sedentarist frame, refugees are outsiders because their educational profiles cannot be easily standardised, their experiences are unpredictable and unplanned, and they frequently present without certifications or with qualifications that are not recognised.[66]

Education for refugees is considered a stopgap measure, with life-long (and tertiary level) learning not a prime focus for either government or NGO policy on refugees.[67] While UNHCR guidelines for three decades aimed for a 'ladder of education opportunity', refugee access to education remains a critical challenge. The older individual refugees are, the more restricted their education opportunities are. An indication of this, according to the UNHCR, is that only 3 per cent of refugees are enrolled at university level, compared with 37 per cent of non-refugee populations. Only 63 per cent of refugee children are enrolled in primary education, and only 24 per cent in secondary schooling. This indicates the attainment gap that refugees experience in trying to create a pathway from education to an established career.[68] Moreover, it suggests that the educational opportunities so far offered to displaced people have operated much like an educational pyramid, focused on primary and secondary education, and largely overlooking higher education.[69]

This limiting outcome has meant that the UNHCR and its partners now strive for what is known as the '15by30' roadmap. With an eye toward changing the educational profile of refugee populations, this goal is a commitment to 15 per cent of young refugees having access to higher education by 2030.[70] In the UK over 70 universities offer refugee and asylum-seeking student scholarships. These awards are a recognition that people seeking asylum in the UK are often effectively locked out of university education. This is in large part because they are mostly ineligible for university loans as they are classed as international students and charged higher fees than those with residency or citizenship.[71]

The impact of these higher education policies toward refugees in the UK was discussed with us at length by one creative practitioner we interviewed who fled Iran as the result of her student activism. Her Iranian qualifications consisted of a nearly completed Associate Diploma, but that progress was not recognised in the British higher education system. Classed as an international student and ineligible for a student loan, the cost of continuing higher education was impossible, particularly while she was living on the asylum support cash allowance. The failure to recognise her qualifications directly impacted on her employment prospects. She recalled:

> I started basically to look for work, which was absolutely not possible because I didn't go to university here, I didn't go to school here, and all my other experience prevented me from a career. So, I took an administration part-time job and then I became

> self-employed in order to get an [art] commission. Then I started [my artistic career] because I had previous [community arts] voluntary work.[72]

What her experience demonstrates is on the one hand the lack of access to tertiary education in the UK and the failure to recognise prior qualifications, and on the other, a reshaping of the specific training and employment prospects that are open to artists with backgrounds of displacement. These opportunities are in large part connected to the community not-for-profit arts sector. This artist explained further that while her training in Iran was focused on performance, in the UK she was forced to take whatever training was available. In her case, this was in digital arts, offered through a Manchester-based community arts organisation. She expanded: 'they provided courses for young people who couldn't go to university … . I was an asylum seeker so I couldn't go to university. I couldn't get work, so they said that you can take this course'.[73] What this means is that while this artist did find access to free arts training, she was not afforded the agency to decide on the type of training that would build on her existing expertise or her professional interests. Now working with a range of organisations, from homeless charities to women's groups and migration NGOs, this artist did take up the entry-level digital production course but continued to independently hone her performance skills. In addition, the developed self-taught animation skills are now also part of her creative practice.

This artist's tenacity is striking. Her experience demonstrates that the range and level of educational and training choices open to refugees (and to migrants) are less open than those available to the general UK population. The limited palette of choices offered to those who have already spent years attempting to gain permanent residence, and the rights equivalent to their neighbours, deprives displaced artists of the agency to develop art in the direction they wish to pursue. It limits their choices far more than their British citizen peers ever experience. Having said this, being ranked in the typically highly competitive selection process for art school degrees is far less bruising than being shut out altogether.[74]

A possible pathway for a few displaced creative artists is to apply to PhD programmes in universities. Three of the artists we interviewed had decided that this unexpected pathway would result in better prospects for their ultimate aim of a career of exhibitions in art galleries, and even of making a living in the visual art industry. There are indications that the university sector in the UK is occasionally willing to provide special access provisions and ranking mechanisms that cater to the challenges faced by individuals with backgrounds of displacement. For example, the University of Manchester is exploring a special route for displaced artists within the 'practice-based' model of PhD research that does not require an MA as a pre-requisite. One of the artists interviewed for this project is applying for this route, as her studies in Iran were interrupted by her flight from the country. However, this will be self-funded since public funding is extraordinarily competitive and requires first-class undergraduate degrees and distinction-level MAs as a basic starting point.

Access to higher education is not just central to developing creative practice, it is key to the establishment of professional networks. As one visual artist explains: 'we are using the [UK higher] education system. We put ourselves in the institutions to have these connections, to know more people, you know, because it is a bit easier if you know a few people'.[75] Access to networks through art schools is vital to initiating contact with peers outside and beyond the community arts sector. This means contact with the mid-career and established artists who teach in UK institutions, as well as with their intake of peers, who become powerfully bonded in each course intake, especially in graduate-level programmes such as creative art PhDs. This process is not without substantial challenges: for example, not all displaced artists are young, and ageism within the higher education system generates a reduced capacity to assist the careers of mature students, who do not meet the categories of 'early career artist' or 'emerging artist' as straight-forwardly as the peers.

More than just the conduit to training and networks, higher education holds further promises and can be key to escaping persecution. Unlike artists with refugee status who have gone through the asylum process, others apply from their country of origin to postgraduate programmes as a means of obtaining a student visa, and residency in the Global North. As Ane Marie Ørbø Kirkegaard and Sisse Mari-Louise Wulff Nat-George argue, the globalisation of higher education needs to be understood beyond its importance to career advancement, the boost to national and local economies, or its role in disseminating knowledge systems. It can also be a unique avenue of escape for people fleeing persecution.[76] Kirkegaard and Nat-George demonstrated that one in five students had escaped from armed conflict, and one in three from social conflicts related to politics, ethnicity, religion, and LGBTQI issues. Although similar figures for tertiary students in the UK do not exist, the study does correspond anecdotally with PhD applicant queries from conflict-torn countries.

Higher education is a significant but easily overlooked migration avenue for forcibly displaced artists. Once accepted into higher education programmes, student migrants can then traverse previously closed national borders and can travel to areas that their friends and family from the same countries and regions cannot.[77] Access to these very desirable student visas remains contingent on multiple factors, including official transcripts of qualifications from an artist's home country translated into English, letters of support from recognised experts and senior artists, and socio-economic factors that include the ability to cover often-considerable international student fees and the cost of living. Overcoming these barriers is fundamentally important for artists to gain professional recognition, to expand the networks from which they have been displaced and to acquire a new language, and to have their training deemed equal to that of the host country.

Creative interventions and alternative pathways

Drawing attention to the impacts of economic precarity, lack of access to educational opportunity, and restrictions on movement, this chapter has thus far demonstrated the diverse and intersectional barriers that face displaced artists in post-migrant contexts. At the same time, it has also aimed to highlight the ways in which artists have themselves navigated these barriers to develop their careers and to establish professional networks. Here, we turn our attention to international initiatives which both recognise and directly respond to the barriers and dangers facing artists with backgrounds of displacement. More specifically, we focus on two examples: the first an initiative of a major international institution, and the second a smaller-scale, artist-run network. We explore these examples not to suggest that they are a panacea for the challenges faced by displaced artists, but rather that they signal alternative and creative models for directly responding to two of the major challenges facing them – the need to secure safety from persecution, and the need to advance professional networks and training in the face of restrictions on movement.

As outlined at the outset of this chapter, a primary challenge facing artists is that of restrictions upon movement. This restriction continues well after an artist has achieved refugee status, but inevitably begins with 'initial' displacement, when one is being forced to flee. While images of people fleeing from persecution have proliferated across modern and contemporary art, increasingly, arts organisations are moving beyond the representation of displacement to raise public awareness or to garner support for people forced to flee. Instead, they are using their capacity and capital as cultural organisations to provide material assistance to artists who have been forcibly displaced. An example of this came in the wake of the Russian invasion of Ukraine when several international initiatives emerged to focus on artistic residences as a means for facilitating movement and safety for Ukrainian and Belarusian artists. Listed as opportunities for 'Creatives at Risk' on the worldwide network of artistic residencies, *ResArtis*, these international programmes include the Emergency Residency in Tbilisi Georgia, Emergency Studios in Sweden, or Artists at Risk in Finland.

These programmes, which are largely facilitated by small or medium-sized organisations, complement efforts by large organisations such as non-profit PEN America and the Artists at Risk Connection (ARC) project. Founded in 2017, ARC serves artists of all disciplines, including cultural professionals who face persecution. In the first seven years of their operation, they assisted over 500 artists (more than half of these being visual artists) to access emergency funds, legal assistance, fellowships, and temporary relocation programmes through ARC's international network of over 70 partners. Focusing on the needs of artists, but also the organisations that host and work with them, ARC develops practical tool kits such as the freely accessible *Safety Guide for Artists*. Developed from strategies collected from artists who have directly experienced persecution, including visual artists such as the Cuban Tania Bruguera, the guide provides practical tips for artists on issues such as how to document persecution, prepare for threats, understand risk, and find assistance.

Importantly, the guidance and training offered by ARC, targeting organisations, also focuses on practical strategies for working with artists at risk. This guidance takes the form of online training sessions provided without charge for organisations around the world. First taking place in 2021, these sessions tackle issues such as digital safety training, security planning processes, cultural rights, mitigation of surveillance and harassment by state and non-state actors, self-care, and mental health support. These activities aim to minimise the risks that arise for cultural workers (artists as well as museum professionals) who are actively engaged with political issues that may garner censorship, surveillance, harassment, or prosecution. In so doing, this array of ARC training activity points both to a recognition of the threat faced by cultural workers in a globalised art economy, as well as a growing sense of responsibility for cultural organisations to directly intervene.

While ARC works to secure the safety of artists at risk, there are also a growing number of artist-run initiatives which directly respond to the intersectional barriers faced by displaced artists. Directly scrutinising and challenging the barriers to professional recognition, artists are developing new organisational structures for providing art education and access to professional networks beyond institutional settings.

One such example is the Artists for Artists (AfA) masterclass, an experimental pedagogical platform that brings leading international artists directly together with early career artists for mentorship. Founded in mid-2020 during international COVID lockdowns, AfA now counts alumni from over 40 countries among its community. Currently operating as an art project (that is without not-for-profit status), AfA's primary activity takes the shape of online thematic 'editions', a series of lectures, small-scale workshops, and mentorship activities. These editions, which take place twice annually, are curated according to themes which have included 'institutional collapse', the 'politics of sharing', 'states in states', 'radical care', and 'language is never on the ground'. Each edition is centred around concepts and artistic practices that reflect those of AfA mentors. These artists, including, for example, Tania Bruguera, Richard Bell, Gregory Sholette, and Ahmet Öğüt, lead the programme and the intensive workshop for early career artists who are chosen through an international open call process.

Significantly, AfA's activity is peer-to-peer, both in its pedagogical structure, but also in its approach to payment. For participation of early career artists AfA does not require financial payment. On the contrary, each edition generates seed funding for the practice of participating artists through a system of peer-to-peer funding achieved through enrolment donations. Once an application is accepted, the Participating Artist is asked to provide a donation that is pooled into a traceable online Group Fund. This fund is then redistributed to a participating AfA artist selected by their peers through a voting system. Offering mentorship and access to professional networks, and circumventing the need for travel or payment for participation, the structure of AfA thus demonstrates the ways in which new and experimental platforms might challenge the barriers facing artists with backgrounds of displacement.

The relevance of AfA's working model to artists with backgrounds of displacement was an issue taken up directly in the AfA edition entitled *Language is Never on the Ground* in 2022.[78] Led by artists Katarina Zdjelar, Hiwa K, Lydia Ourahmane, and the Palestinian collective Radio Alhara, the edition focused on artistic practices connected to the issue of language, exploring themes such as voice as survival, acoustics as somatic memory, and sound as a measure of displacement. *Language is Never on the Ground* reflected an issue that will be taken up at length in Chapter 3, which explores the 'problem of language' in displacement aesthetics. Examining contemporary art practice and the linguistic challenges experienced by displaced artists, it highlights how the issue of displacement is overlooked in understandings or analysis of contemporary art practice.

To be sure, there is a need for further research, targeted policy, and funding which address the specific challenges faced by displaced artists. Importantly, international initiatives such as AfA, or indeed New York-based ARC, recognise these challenges.[79] They demonstrate the kinds of strategies that may be implemented to alleviate the impact of forced displacement on creative practitioners. Focusing on barriers to mobility and education, these initiatives suggest how artistic and institutional networks can be harnessed in new ways, offering practical interventions to the barriers that have been described here.

Conclusion

Conversations with artists in this chapter have provided useful insights that complement studies into refugee populations at large, not just artists. The artists reflected on their experiences and the predicaments they encountered inside a regressive system of bureaucratic intervention. This chapter has argued that in order to fully grasp the consequences of displacement aesthetics in the contemporary art world and in creative industries, the lived experience of artists must be taken into account, and this should also implicate how we write about art and cultural history. Understanding the intersectional nature of the barriers that these artists face as they move from asylum seeker to refugee and later to UK residents and citizens, is a critical journey that could inform knowledge of art practice and culture, as well as the artistic eco-system. Displaced artists, we find, encounter barriers that are specific to their experiences. This generates particular forms of inequality that, in turn, impact their career trajectories. These aspects range from time that cannot be reclaimed, travel restrictions, language and education interruptions, and multiple layers of social and economic precarity. A fuller appreciation of these intersectional barriers as entwined and mutually reinforcing should enable institutions, funding schemes, and artist residencies to avoid hindering or even humiliating refugees, as has sometimes been the unfortunate case. Displaced artists are often stalled in gaining a professional profile that generates opportunities to speak from a position of cultural authority, which can counter negative representations of refugees. Although the experience of refugeedom may be short-lived in one person's lifetime, the perceived identity of being 'a refugee' sticks.

Finally, it is important to reflect upon how representation and lived experience in displacement aesthetics have points of departure and convergence. Artists' depictions of these intersectional challenges will be taken up in later chapters. As the book continues, the panorama of displacement aesthetics will be seen in its four modes: visual tropes; language and identity; art institutions; labour. This analysis implicates issues of labour and museum practice that will be taken up in ensuing chapters.

Notes

1 Monica Manolachi and Ambrose Musiyiwa, 'Literary Translation as a Form of Social and Pedagogical Activism', *Érudit*, 35:1 (2022): 8. See also the global network: https://forcedmigrationandthearts.blogspot.com/

2 Michele Lamont and Annette Lareau, 'Cultural Capital: Allusions, Gaps, Glissandos in Recent Theoretical Developments', *Sociological Theory*, 6:2 (1988): 153–168.

3 Nicole Fleetwood, *Marking Time: Art in the Age of Mass Incarceration* (Cambridge, MA: Harvard University Press, 2020).

4 Elena Fiddian-Qasmiyeh (ed.), *Refuge in a Moving World: Tracing Refugee and Migrant Journeys Across Disciplines* (London: UCL Press, 2020), p. 17.

5 On positionality, see Chrisoula Lionis, *Praxes of Displacement: Contemporary Art and Methods for Cultural Resilience* (London: Routledge, 2025.

6 T.J. Demos, *The Migrant Image: The Art and Politics of Documentary during Global Crisis* (Durham, NC: Duke University Press, 2013); Anne Ring Petersen, *Migration into Art: Transcultural Identities and Art-Making in a Globalised World* (Manchester: Manchester

University Press, 2017); Christine Ross, *Art for Coexistence: Unlearning the Way We See Migration* (Cambridge, MA: MIT Press, 2022).

7 Domenico Sergi, *Museums, Refugees and Communities* (New York: Routledge, 2021), p. 55.

8 Bimal Jhosh, *Refugees and Asylum-Seekers: Managing a Looming Humanitarian and Economic Crisis* (Cham: Springer, 2018).

9 Mary Bosworth, 'Border Control and the Limits of the Sovereign State', *Social and Legal Studies*, 17:2 (2008): 199–215.

10 Fiddian-Qasmiyeh, *Refuge in a Moving World*, p. 2.

11 Brett Shadle, 'Refugees in African History', in William H. Worger, Charles Ambler, and Nwado Achebe (eds), *A Companion to African History* (Hoboken New Jersey: Wiley Blackwell, 2018).

12 *Living in Limbo: A Decade of Delays in the UK Asylum System*. www.refugeecouncil.org.uk/wp-content/uploads/2021/07/Living-in-Limbo-A-decade-of-delays-in-the-UK-Asylum-system-July-2021.pdf

13 Anonymous interview with artist, 2021.

14 Senyo Dotsey and Audrey Lumley-Sapanski, 'Temporality, Refugees, and Housing: The Effects of Temporary Assistance on Refugee Housing Outcomes in Italy', *Cities*, 111 (2021): 3.

15 Chrisoula Lionis, *Laughter in Occupied Palestine: Comedy and Identity in Art and Film* (London: I.B. Tauris, 2016), p. 155.

16 Interviewed by Liz Jobey, 'Lives Interrupted: Caroline Walker's Paintings of Female Asylum Seekers in London', *Finanical Times* (2 February 2018), p. 4.

17 Griselda Pollock, 'Glimpsing the Work of the World or What Painting Invites us to Notice', in *Caroline Walker: Women's Work*, Midlands Art Centre catalogue (Birmingham: Midlands Art Centre, 2021): 20.

18 Pollock, 'Glimpsing the Work of the World'.

19 Anonymous interview with digital artist, 2021.

20 Anonymous interview with digital artist, 2021.

21 Amy K. Levin, 'Conclusion: Tomorrow's Heritage of Migration', in Amy K. Levin (ed.), *Global Mobilities: Refugees, Exiles and Immigrants in Museums and Archives* (London: Routledge, 2017), p. 473.

22 Jesper Gulddal and Charlton Payne, 'Passports: On the Politics and Cultural Impact of Modern Movement Control', *Symploke*, 25:1 (2017): pp. 9–23.

23 Hannah Arendt, 1968, cited in Gulddal and Payne, 'Passports', p. 14.

24 Anonymous interview with visual artist, 2021.

25 'Apply for the Global Talent visa', *gov.uk*, accessed 24 January 2023. www.gov.uk/global-talent

26 *The Tentative Collective*, tentativecollective.com, accessed 24 February 2023. www.facebook.com/TentativeCollective

27 www.liveartuk.org/uploads/documents/Manifesto_Deported.pdf

28 Anonymous interview with performing artist, 2021.

29 Gilad Ben-Nun, 'The British-Jewish Roots of Non-Refoulement and its True Meaning for the Drafters of the 1951 Refugee Convention', *Journal of Refugee Studies*, 28:1(2014): 93.

30 Sheona York, *The Impact of UK Immigration Law: Declining Standards of Public Administration, Legal Probity and Democratic Accountability* (Cham: Springer, 2022), pp. 59–60, 62, 71–72; UNHCR: The UN Refugee Agency, *Handbook on Procedures and Criteria for Determining Refugee Status and Guidelines on International Protection under the 1951 Convention and the 1967 Protocol Relating to the Status of Refugees* (Geneva: UNHCR, 2019): 43.

31 UNHCR, *Handbook on Procedures and Criteria*: 43.

32 Agnieszka Kubal, 'Struggles against Subjection. Implications of Criminalization of Migration for Migrants' Everyday Lives in Europe', *Crime, Law and Social Change*, 62 (2014): 91–111.

33 Anja Sunhyun Michaelsen, '"Locked Out in Nature": Films on the European Asylum System, Latent Violence, and Ghosts', in Christoph F.E. Holzhey and Arnd Wedemeyer (eds), *Weathering: Ecologies of Exposure, Cultural Inquiry*, 17 (Berlin: ICI Berlin Press, 2020), pp. 207–225.

34 Gina Clayton and Georgina Firth, *Immigration and Asylum Law (9th edition)* (Oxford: Oxford University Press, 2021), pp. 390–391, 563.

35 Amelia Gentleman, *The Windrush Betrayal: Exposing the Hostile Environment* (London: Guardian Books, 2019); Clayton and Firth, *Immigration and Asylum Law*, p. 557.

36 Clayton and Firth, *Immigration and Asylum Law*, p. 560.

37 Jessica Anderson, Jeannine Hollaus, Annelisa Lindsay, and Colin Williamson, 'The Culture of Disbelief: An Ethnographic Approach to an Under-Theorised Concept in the UK Asylum System', *Oxford University Refugee Studies Centre Working Paper*, series no. 102, 31/7/14.

38 Kate Rodenhurst, *Engaging Refugees and Asylum Seekers Project Review and Social Outcome Evaluation*, October 2005–2007 included four commissions and peer mentoring schemes (2007: 13, 15, 16). https://archive-media.museumsassociation.org/16122013-engaging-ref ugees-and-asylum-seekers-report-2007.pdf

39 Sergi, *Museums, Refugees and Communities*, p. 1.

40 Sharon Macdonald, 'Conclusion: Refugee Futures and the Politics of Difference', in J. Bock and S. Macdonald (eds), *Refugees Welcome? Difference and Diversity in a Changing Germany* (New York, Oxford: Berghahn Books, 2019), p. 323.

41 Sergi, *Museums, Refugee and Communities*, p. 2.

42 Anonymous interview with digital artist, 2021.

43 Mette Louise Berg, 'Producing Precarity: The "Hostile Environment" and Austerity for Latin Americans in London', in Elena Fiddian-Qasmiyeh (ed.), *Refuge in a Moving World: Tracing Refugee and Migrant Journeys across Disciplines* (London: UCL Press, 2020), p. 479.

44 Catherine Sue Ramírez, et al. (eds), *Precarity and Belonging: Labor, Migration, and Noncitizenship* (New Brunswick, N.J.: Rutgers University Press, 2021).

45 Hans Abbing. *The Changing Social Economy of Art: Are the Arts Becoming Less Exclusive?* (Cham: Palgrave Macmillan, 2019), p. 186.

46 Gregory Sholette, *Dark Matter: Art and Politics in the Age of Enterprise Culture* (London: Pluto Press, 2010), p. 5.

47 Heather Carey, Dave O'Brien, and Olivia Gable, 'Social Mobility in the Creative Economy: Rebuilding and Levelling Up?', Multiple: Creative Industries Policy and Evidence Centre and Work Advance, 2021. https://pec.ac.uk/research-reports/social-mobility-in-the-creative-economy-rebuilding-and-levelling-up., 2. This report concludes phase 2 of the PEC's 'Class in the Creative Industries' programme. Led by PEC researchers at Work Advance, the University of Edinburgh, and the Work Foundation, and co-funded by the Arts and Humanities Research Council and the Department for Digital, Culture, Media and Sport.

48 Kristina Kolbe, Chris Upton-Hansen, Mike Savage, Nicola Lacey, and Sarah Cant, 'The Art World's Response to the Challenge of Inequality', Working Paper 40, International Inequalities Institute, London School of Economics, January 2020, accessed 22 October 2022. http://eprints.lse.ac.uk/id/eprint/103146

49 The dispersal policy was introduced with the Immigration and Asylum Act in 1999.

50 Nuria Targarona Rifa and Giorgia Donà, 'Forced Unemployment or Undocumented Work: The Burden of the Prohibition to Work for Asylum Seekers in the UK', *Journal of Refugee Studies*, 34:2 (2021): 2055.

51 Anonymous interview with painter, 2021.

52 Angela McRobbie, 'The Gender of Post-Fordism: "Passionate Work", "Risk Class" and "A Life of One's Own"', in Angela McRobbie, *Be Creative: Making a Living in the New Culture Industries* (Chichester: Wiley, 2016), pp. 57–58.

53 Griselda Pollock, 'Women Who are Artists/ Artists Who are Women', *Critique d'Art*, 31 (2008): 1.

54 Maura Reilly, *Curatorial Activism: Towards an Ethics of Curating* (London: Thames & Hudson, 2018), pp. 19–21. Ana Munoz-Munoz and M. Barbano Gonzalez-Moreno, 'The Presence of Women Photographers in the Permanent Collection of Ten European Museums', *Curator*, 60:2 (2017): 205–215.

55 Toby Perl Freilich, 'Blazing Epiphany: Maintenance Art Manifesto 1969! An Interview with Mierle Laderman Ukeles', *Cultural Politics*, 16:1 (2020): 22.

56 Rayah A. Feldman, Susan Bewley, Rosalind Bragg, and Miriam Beeks, 'Hostile Environment Prevents Women from Accessing Maternal Care', *BMJ (Online)*, 368 (2020): 968.

57 Anonymous Interview with digital artist, 2021.

58 Feldman, Bewley, Bragg, and Beeks, 'Hostile Environment Prevents Women from Accessing Maternal Care', p. 968.

59 Andrew Pinnock, 'The Menace of Meritocracy: Unmasking Inequality in the Creative and Cultural Industries', *Cultural Trends* 28:2–3 (2019): 254.

60 Also see Sherice Clarke, 'Language Learning for Migrants, Refugees and Asylum Seekers', in Nicola Abery et al., *The New Museum Community: Audiences, Challenges, Benefits* (Edinburgh: Museums Etc, 2010), pp. 138–167.

61 Mark Banks and Kate Oakley, 'The Dance Goes on Forever? Art Schools, Class, and Higher Education', *International Journal of Cultural Policy*, 22:1 (2015): 50–52.

62 Banks and Oakley, 'The Dance Goes on Forever?', p. 52.

63 www.ethnicity.ac.uk/research/projects/diversity-in-creative-industries/

64 Roaa Ali, *How to Approach Anti-Racist Audience and Community Research*, 2023. www.culturehive.co.uk/CVIresources/how-to-approach-anti-racist-audience-and-community-research/

65 Liisa Malkki, 'National Geographic: The Rooting of Peoples and the Territorialization of National Identity among Scholars and Refugees', *Cultural Anthropology*, 7:1 (1992): 31.

66 Maalki cited in Linda Morrice, 'The Promise of Refugee Lifelong Education: A Critical Review in the Field', *International Review of Education*, 67 (2021): 859.

67 Linda Morrice, 'The Promise of Refugee Lifelong Education: A Critical Review in the Field', *International Review of Education*, 67 (2021): 861.

68 Morrice, 'The Promise of Refugee Lifelong Education', p. 852.

69 Morrice, 'The Promise of Refugee Lifelong Education, p. 861, and Sarah Dryden-Peterson, 'The Politics of Higher Education for Refugees in a Global Movement for Primary Education', *Refuge: Canada's Journal on Refugees*, 27:2 (2012): 10–18.

70 '15by30 Roadmap', *UNHCR*, accessed 28 June 2022. www.unhcr.org/605a0fb3b.pdf

71 'UK University Scholarships for Refugees and Asylum Seekers, UCAS, 21 June 2022, accessed 28 June 2022. www.ucas.com/connect/blogs/uk-university-scholarships-refugees-and-asylum-seekers

72 Anonymous interview with digital artist, 2021.

73 Anonymous interview with digital artist, 2021.

74 Johan Galtung and Dietrich Fischer, *Violence: Direct, Structural and Cultural* (Berlin and Heidelberg: Springer Briefs on Pioneers in Science and Practice, 2013), pp. 35–40.

75 Anonymous Interview with visual artist, 2021.

76 Ane Marie Ørbø Kirkegaard and Sisse Mari-Louise Wulff Nat-George, 'Fleeing through the Globalised Education System: The Role of Violence and Conflict in International Student Migration, Globalisation', *Societies and Education*, 14:3 (2016): 391–394. The study investigated conflict-induced student migration – a field which until recently was overlooked in Education and Migration Studies. It explored how increasing globalised student migration is linked to both violent conflict and to changes to the internationalisation of education. Using mixed methods design (including interviews with University of Malmo students),

it found that 1 in 5 students used education as a pathway through which to escape conflict and persecution.

77 Kirkegaard and Wulff Nat-George, 'Fleeing through the Globalised Education System', p. 391.
78 www.afamasterclass.org/artists
79 https://artistsatriskconnection.org/

3 The 'problem' of language: identifications, definitions, and translations

Aesthetics plays a key role in positioning refugees as figures of crisis. Refugees are stereotyped and the condition of refugeedom is compartmentalised, distinct from other forms of displacement. This is deeply rooted in the history of empires, settler colonialism, forced population exchange, and environmental disaster. As discussed in Chapter 1, the construction of the refugee regime was accompanied and interwoven with visual tropes common to humanitarian photography, the media, UN agencies, and visual art, creating a mutually reinforcing but limited discussion of displaced persons and refugeedom as a problem to be solved.

Crucially, understandings and manifestations of the so-called refugee problem, as represented in visual tropes, are also fundamentally shaped by the 'problem' of language. This problem emanates from the language used in discourse to describe refugees, asylum seekers, and displacement, but also from who is speaking for, and on behalf of, whom. In the decades following the Second World War, there was an increasingly standardised way of talking about those forcibly displaced, amongst humanitarian agencies, non-governmental organisations (NGOs), and governments. Anthropologist Liisa Malkki astutely describes the consequence of this, explaining that '[r]efugees suffer from a particular kind of speechlessness in the face of national and international organisations whose object of care and control they are'. For Malkki, this speechlessness is directly linked to contemporary forms of humanitarianism which prioritise the language of 'development', policy science, and relief, over the accounts of refugees themselves.[1]

From the twentieth century to the present day, the issue of refugee voices has continued to be central to a grounded understanding of forced displacement, since representation is so often taken up by government agencies and NGOs rather than communities themselves. While there is growing social recognition of the ethical issues of speaking on behalf of 'others', this has not been adequately applied to refugee populations.[2] This might, in part, come as a consequence of viewing displacement as a temporary condition, rather than as a permanent or 'fixed' form of marginality (such as those pertaining to gender, race, sexual orientation, or disability); nonetheless, speaking on behalf of others remains an important political question. The issue of voice – that is the ability to speak and to be heard – is inherently political.

Both the failure to question who speaks for displaced populations, and a possible implicit understanding of displacement as a temporary condition are things, we suggest, that should be met with profound unease. Indeed, if we are to move from an understanding of refugees as objects of knowledge towards an understanding of them as 'knowing agents' with the capacity for political agency, language is a vital place to start.[3] Language is acknowledged in the social sciences as the primary barrier for refugees and displaced populations, one that directly impacts everything, including access to healthcare, employment, education, and social relationships, particularly in processes of resettlement. However, this understanding of the significance of language has not yet been adequately applied in understandings or analysis of contemporary art practice that engages with forced displacement.

This chapter contends that language is a critical iteration of displacement aesthetics, which is of paramount importance in visual art discourse and art industry practice.[4] Focusing on the nexus between language, political discourse, and the lived experience of forced displacement in artistic production, as well as the role of institutions in shaping, constituting, and reproducing forms of displacement, this chapter explores both mode 2 (language and identities) and mode 3 (institutions) of displacement aesthetics. It builds upon analysis of visual tropes and representations of refugees and displacement presented in Chapter 1 and the intersectional barriers explored in Chapter 2, in order to examine how language intersects with experiences, understandings, and representations of displacement in contemporary art. In so doing it contends that while many scholars have analysed visual representations of displacement in contemporary art, questions of language and voice remain a vital but overlooked aspect of art practice that communicates knowledge of displacement.

In addition to the discussion of art and institutions, the chapter also brings in data gathered from interviews with artists whose backgrounds include forced migration and displacement. These testimonies allow close analysis of the impact that language and systems of identification can have. This ranges from the discursive category of 'refugee artist' and where this framing fits within a typology of art-making, to the (often-problematic) language and terminology employed in art discourse and curatorial practice for describing displacement. Finally, discussion concludes with an analysis of how language operates as a distinct and yet unrecognised barrier for artists with backgrounds of displacement.

This chapter has a twofold aim: first, it seeks to demonstrate the relationship between contemporary art practice, language, and processes of identification and experiences of displacement. Second, it aims to investigate who it is that speaks, translates, and performs experiences of displacement in contemporary art spaces and discourse. These two factors are key to understanding the linguistic grounding of displacement aesthetics, and its relationship to increasingly globalised art worlds, markets, and art historical discourse. When considered together, these two key lines of enquiry demonstrate the representational *and* operational nature of displacement aesthetics. This is traceable in artistic representation but also across the invisible forces which impact displaced people's everyday lives to produce aesthetic outcomes.

Language, participatory museums, and the importance of (self) identification

Across art worlds (international systems that link practices, networks, institutions, and economies), the issue of language, voice, and the narrativisation of displacement is one of growing concern. This is perhaps nowhere more apparent than in public art museums and galleries, institutions which have, since the early 1990s in particular, harnessed participatory practices to integrate community experience in their collections research, exhibitions, and public programming.[5] Indeed, this shift is reflected in the International Council of Museums decision in 2022, after wide consultation, to define the museum as 'open to the public, accessible, and inclusive', and asserting that 'museums foster diversity and sustainability'.[6]

In Europe the 'participatory turn' in museum practice has also coincided with the European refugee crisis. Numerous projects have emerged which have brought the stories and active presence of refugees and asylum seekers into the museum on a scale not seen previously.[7] Of these initiatives, *Multaka: Museum as Meeting Point* is a now celebrated example of refugee-led change in museum participation. Beginning in 2015 as a joint initiative of the Museum of Islamic Art and several institutions in Berlin (including the Pergamon Museum, the Bode Museum, and the German Historical Museum), the Multaka project offered training to people displaced to Germany from Syria and Iraq to work as tour guides within museums. With the initial aim of drawing in Arabic-speaking visitors to the museum, Multaka guides were understood as a 'connecting link' between the museum, 'host' communities, and new community' constituents – the main instrument of connection being that of language.[8] The group soon realised its capacity to engender transcultural learning experiences for local visitors, and to harness the potential of museums as spaces of mutual dialogue for host and displaced or migrant communities.

While Multaka began with the expectation that guides would provide tours in their native Arabic, by 2018 this approach shifted to also include other languages, such as Farsi. Additionally, Multaka guides shifted the focus of their tours away from museum objects from their countries of birth, toward those in which they had a personal and professional interest. This was crucial as the training of guides was across diverse fields, including lawyers, educators, artists, and students. The project, operating now as the Multaka International Network, has at the time of writing partnered with over twenty-nine museums around Europe, including in Switzerland, Italy, Greece, and the UK. What is significant about these changes is that on the one hand they signal a desire for cultural mediation of displacement through museum practice and public programming, while on the other, they demonstrate a need for museums (and by implication curators, arts administrators, and audiences) to shift understandings of refugee communities' contribution to knowledge as extending beyond the lived experience of refugeedom. That is to say that the museum is capable of providing spaces and tools for displaced communities and participants to be acknowledged as 'knowing agents'.

Multaka is also an example of the expectations often placed on displaced communities by curatorial and educational administrators when invited to speak or to take on a position of leadership in art institutional settings. There remains an expectation that they should speak to the experience of refugeedom or demonstrate expertise only in relation to the country or culture of their birth or heritage. The eventual change to Multaka's approach reflects an issue of paramount importance for arts institutions that work with communities and artists with backgrounds of forced displacement – that of self-identification. Collaborative institutions should include the provision for communities and artists to choose the language in which they participate, and indeed the language and terminology with which their backgrounds are described. This is particularly significant in a period when language around displacement has become increasingly blurred and instrumentalised, and refugees are exposed to political and public opprobrium.

This was an issue experienced first-hand by the authors during the collaborative process of curating two exhibitions, *Traces of Displacement* (Whitworth Art Gallery) and *Rethinking the Grand Tour* (Manchester Art Gallery) in Manchester in the UK (discussed in more detail in Chapter 5). In the long development phase of these projects (2022–23), groups of creative advisors and co-curators with backgrounds of displacement and forced migration worked with gallery staff and academic researchers to curate exhibitions using their collections. They were also invited to design a public programme and to contribute their own art works to exhibitions. Throughout the development phase of these projects a recurring subject of negotiation emerged: the language with which to describe experiences of displacement and the terminology with which artists themselves wished to be identified. While experiences and understanding of migration and displacement were fundamentally understood by the collaborative team as valuable forms of knowledge and expertise that no-one else on the project team possessed, and for which they were remunerated, the co-curators and artists had to decide how they would be described publicly, in wall texts and communications materials. In the case of the project *Rethinking the Grand Tour*, at Manchester Art Gallery, almost all the artists decided to disavow references to refugeedom, migration, or displacement in relation their personal identities, and simply took the name of their profession: artist.

This disavowal was, in the case of Manchester Art Gallery, instructive. The co-curators did not want to be typecast as 'refugee artists' (an issue taken up later in this chapter and also discussed in Chapter 2). Moreover, they were concerned about this label in a period of intense political hostility and heated public debate regarding the right to seek asylum in the UK. Like many countries in Europe, and elsewhere, the UK has seen a spike in discriminatory rhetoric on immigration and integration policies. Recent studies in the social sciences and linguistics have demonstrated the lived consequences of malevolent language used to describe migrants and refugees, documenting violent outcomes and hate crimes.[9] This rhetoric has relied on the criminalisation of refugees, with rhetoric based on terminology such as 'queue jumping', 'illegal migration', 'criminal gangs', and linguistic dichotomies of worthiness and unworthiness. In this context, the reluctance of creative practitioners to identify with forced displacement was not only a matter of safeguarding, it was also a matter of avoiding the professional pigeonholing that occurs in the art world when artists are labelled 'refugee artists'.

The challenge for art institutions and the discipline of art history is to balance the needs of creative practitioners towards the language of displacement, whilst also fostering space for public discussion, exchange of knowledge, and intercultural dialogue which counters antagonistic political rhetoric. Crucially, a key instrument for countering this political rhetoric is language itself, and the use of specific terminology around displacement. For instance, the artists in this project just wanted to be called artists from Manchester, identifying their practice as one grounded and interwoven with the local region. Nevertheless, a primary challenge to working out the right terminology is the fact that the wider culture of language used in the public sphere to describe people forced to flee is constantly in a state of transition.[10] In the UK, for example, since the so-called European refugee 'crisis' in 2015, these categorisations in the media have ranged from 'refugee crisis' to 'Mediterranean migrant crisis', 'Calais migrant crisis', and 'European migrant crisis', with the media shifting between humanitarian narratives of victimhood to associations with criminality and terrorist attacks, as well as Islamophobic and racist discourses.[11]

In this environment of hostility and danger, precise terminology and carefully considered language is crucial to describe communities, countries, collections, and histories impacted by displacement. Otherwise, there is a serious risk of contributing to damaging political rhetoric that emboldens and normalises the abuse of vulnerable communities. For those working in art galleries and the cultural industries this is fraught territory. Consideration and implementation of appropriate terminologies, however, will offset any confusion or distress to those who seek to work harmoniously with hard-to-reach communities. Indeed, current museological debate and practice recognises these risks, particularly in light of the decolonial turn, which interrogates the relationship between museum collections and colonial histories of violence, and their ongoing legacies for communities in the present day. Importantly, as suggested at the outset, displacement is too often considered separate from these decolonial efforts, despite rising scholarly interest in analysing the relationship between forced displacement and colonialism.

The decolonial turn in museums and galleries has been characterised by attempts to critically engage with terminologies that carry colonial legacies and cause offense to communities in the present day. One example is the deliberate shift in practice in the Netherlands, where since 2019 the term 'Dutch Golden Age', used to describe seventeenth-century advances in the Netherlands in the fields of art, science, and trade, is increasingly debarred, or vetoed, for its failure to highlight the relationship between that history and those of slavery and colonialism. The substantial public and industry debate that followed this change in the Netherlands demonstrates how integral language is to decolonial efforts. As museologist Csilla E. Ariese argues, language is crucial to decentring (that is shifting understandings of cultural norms) because it provides acknowledgement, inclusion, and positive effects for those whose histories are sublimated, culturally marginalised, or are frequently spoken for by others.[12]

Language takes on particular significance in artistic production and cultural institutions within so-called 'postmigrant' societies (e.g. the UK, Canada, and Germany), and those whose national identities, participation, and opportunities are negotiated in a 'postmigrant state'. Cultural theorist Sten Pultz Moslund and art historian Anne Ring Petersen argue that postmigration is both a perspective and a condition, a 'pervasive realisation, in the population and among politicians, that an irreversible change, affecting all members of society, has already taken place and is taking place, and that this change will spur, and necessitate, further change'.[13] Within such a state, language is, as Mirjam Gebaur argues, more than a means of communication; it is also central to the construction of subjectivities and marking social and cultural belonging.[14]

Responsive to the global impact of the *Black Lives Matter* and *MeToo* movements, as well as the demands for decolonising and climate justice, art institutions have sharpened their attention on questions of diversity in programming, leadership, and collections management. Indeed, many organisations working with, against, or alongside art institutions (including MuseumDetox in the UK; Decolonise the Museum and MuseumHue in the US) have gained increased international visibility.

These organisations, whilst often collaborating with museums, may also take on more ambivalent or antagonistic roles toward art institutions – critically engaging with museum policy and protocols. These include, for example, diversity programming and recruitment, investigation into museum benefactors, and terminology and language used within art institutions. This push is particularly apparent in post-migrant societies where diversity work in museums is often understood as socially beneficial. Indeed, a recent blueprint for museum educators convincingly demonstrates that language is essential to diversity work since it is central to positionality and allyship for museum workers engaging with culturally marginalised histories.[15]

Significantly, diversity and inclusion work (and associated staff training) in museums does not always home in on the specificity of displacement, conflating it with other experiences of migration or racial difference. This is important because a background of displacement often entails experiences of intersectional forms of discrimination (including racialisation), and barriers faced are often particular to the experience of being forced to flee. While these intersectional barriers as they impact artists' careers are analysed at length in Chapter 2, here, it is sufficient to say that diversity and inclusion work within museums must also address the issue of language and terminology related to displacement. As public 'contact zones', art museums and galleries are uniquely placed to foster informed public debate and critical thinking.[16] In terms of engagement with displacement, this requires museums and galleries to take a responsible, informed, and consistent approach to the use of key terms relating to people forced to migrate. For example, the three key terms relating to displacement – asylum seeker, refugee, and migrant – are often used interchangeably. It is important to distinguish these terms not only because there is an essential legal difference between them, but also because their conflation is often deliberately used in political rhetoric as a means of maligning the forcibly displaced within public discourse.[17] A free and publicly available lexicon of terms (something discussed later in this chapter), drawn for example from the UNHCR's glossary of terms, would be particularly useful in this regard.[18]

Terminology and language are thus as an integral part of what refugee historian Peter Gatrell defines as 'refugeedom'. That is, the political, social, and cultural worlds of refugees and 'the distinctive domain or sphere of practice in relation to a category of humanity defined by displacement'.[19] Language underpins refugeedom because it is an essential element of the social and cultural worlds of the forcibly displaced, as well as the refugee regime to which they are subject. It is important to understand that language and visual representations and reflections on displacement are not mutually exclusive. Rather, they exist in a symbiotic relationship, revealed in how contemporary art engages with experiences of displacement. We turn, here, to examples of contemporary art that demonstrates the aesthetic function of language as it relates to experiences of displacement. Attuned to the importance of 'mastery' over language, these works demonstrate how issues of identification, voice, translation, and narration of experience are key to displacement aesthetics.

Mother tongues and performances of 'mastery'. Who speaks? Who translates? Who performs?

In 2020 UNICEF released a research report which identified language as the primary barrier facing refugee children's access to services and education in Greece; a nation which was at the forefront of the European refugee crisis, taking in over 850,000 refugees in a single year at its peak in 2015. Identifying the challenges faced by teachers in learning environments, the UNICEF report refers to the Common European Framework of References for Language, which provides guidelines for describing learning achievement throughout Europe. This European framework designates six levels of language learning, ranging from beginner (A1), and intermediate (B1) through to mastery (C2).[20] The Common European Framework of References for Languages is not alone in using the term 'mastery' to describe fluency and ease with language proficiency; the term connotes what Julietta Singh describes as the use of language to exert control and dominance over others.[21]

Mastery inflects intertwined political, gendered, colonial, and enslaving discourses. Julietta Singh argues that the concept of mastery is rooted in histories of violence and the wielding of power over others. Drawing on examples of anticolonial thinkers such as Frantz Fanon and Mahatma Gandhi, Singh juxtaposes the destructive uses of mastery (such as colonial domination) with more celebrated or seemingly innocuous forms of mastery (such as the intellectual or linguistic) to demonstrate how the concept tacitly reinforces colonial logics. For Singh, the issue of language is of central importance for the imagining of decolonial futures. As she explains, 'the intimate political nexus of language, mastery, and colonisation always summons the problem of what language is'. Thus, in understanding displacement aesthetics and its impact on artists and art gallery practices, language is a powerful tool, denoting both oppression and the possibility of change.

Interestingly, the political nexus described by Singh is one echoed some four decades earlier by philosopher Jacques Derrida, who noted that the foreigner is first of all foreign to the language of the law, including that pertaining to the right of asylum. Reflecting that a person who seeks asylum 'must ask for hospitality in a language, which, by definition, is not [their] own', Derrida argues that this barrier of language is the first act of violence the foreigner undergoes, claiming their rights in a language they either cannot speak or are not proficient in.[22] Put differently, mastery (linguistic as much as political) is in the hands of others. Drawing attention to this first act of violence, Derrida points out that the suspension of this violence is nearly impossible, or at any rate interminable.

This sense of an apparent endless violence, or 'foreignness', manifested through language, is reflected in Iranian-Greek artist Stefanos Tsivopoulos' video work, *Land* (2006). Described by the artist as a tragic comedy, the 8-minute film begins with a view of three men, who seem to be asylum seekers or migrants, from diverse cultural backgrounds, waking up on a rocky beach (Figure 3.1). The work proceeds to show each man speaking aloud in his own langauge, wondering about the land in which they find themselves: 'what is the name of this place?'; 'who owns this place?'; 'can it be defined topographically, or is it like a vacuum?'. However, as the work progresses, it becomes clear that not only are these men lost, but they are also unable to communicate with each other, to find a way to safety, and to navigate territory they can only describe as 'this place'.

Characterised by the slow movement of the camera tracing the landscape, the film concludes with an unexpected zoom out, which reveals to the viewer that the men are in fact on an uninhabitable desert island. Without a common language,

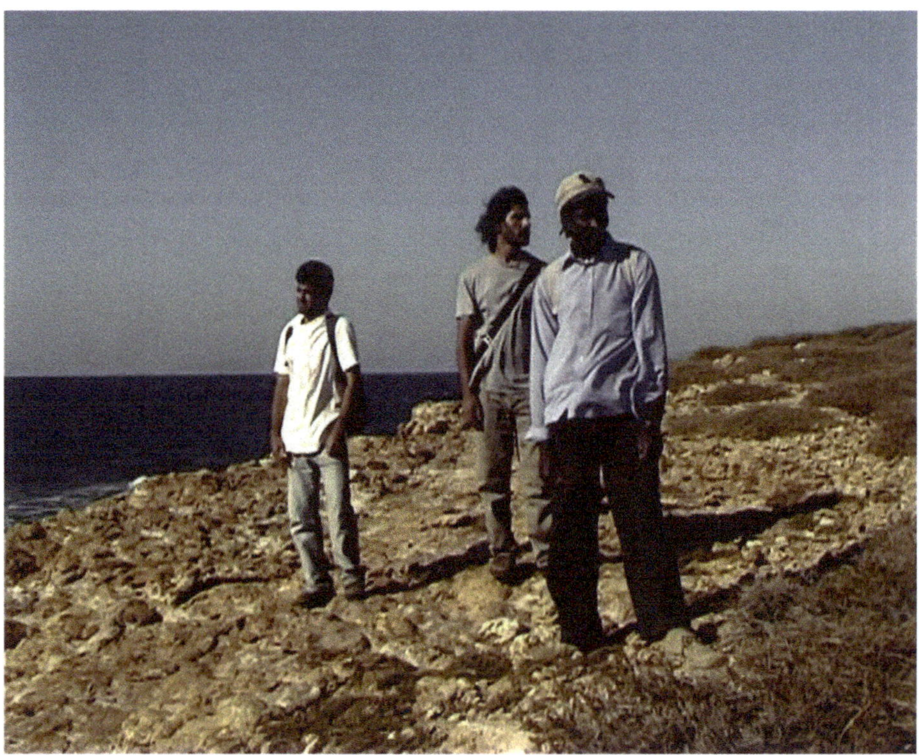

3.1 Stefanos Tsivopoulos, *Land* (2006). Video (still). Courtesy of the artist.

the three protagonists in *Land* are in effect condemned to a hopeless future, a perpetual limbo of foreignness that reminds us of Derrida's assertion that the violence of language inflicted on foreigners is interminable. Adding to this is the fact that audiences are provided with an aerial view of the island (and the three men) that might be described as a 'god's eye view', placing them in a position of privilege and power. This privilege is not just topographic, it is also linguistic. Audiences are afforded linguistic privilege because they can follow all languages and dialogue presented in the work through the use of subtitles which reflect the dominant language of where the work is exhibited (e.g. Dutch in the Netherlands, Greek in Greece, English in the UK, and so on). The narration, storytelling, and indeed comprehension of the story of displacement represented in the film are thus afforded to the communities which host the work. In contrast, the men depicted on screen are, literally, lost in translation.

Produced in 2006, *Land* reflects the artist's long-standing concern with issues of displacement and migration, demonstrated in works such as *Nemesis* (2022) and *The Cardinal* (2023), which consider the relationship between refugee populations and other 'host' communities in Greece. Importantly, however, *Land* predates the 2015 European refugee crisis and Greece's association with refugee flows by almost a decade, thus demonstrating an understanding of Greece as being a place with an arguably long-standing association to transition for populations forced to flee, rather than a final destination. For example, unlike other European states, Greece received few asylum seekers until the early 1990s, remaining a transit country, even during the Yugoslav wars of the 1990s.[23] Today, the work is part of the National Museum of Contemporary Art Athens' (EMST) permanent collection, one which centres Greece's position at the southeastern edge of Europe and maintains a focus on border tensions, geopolitical relations, and marginalised narratives. The collection consists largely of artists from neighbouring countries, such as Türkiye, the Balkans, and the MENA region.[24]

Much like the other works in EMST, *Land* is not only a reflection of the geopolitical placement of Greece and the precarious conditions created by borders and exclusionary politics, it also mirrors the impact of displacement and forced migration on populations in the region. Filmed in Greece after the artist had migrated to the Netherlands, the film reflects Tsivopoulos' own personal heritage of displacement. He was born in Prague to an Iranian mother and a Greek father, who were both unable to return to their home countries due to political unrest and fear of incarceration due to Communist family ties. In the wake of the Greek Civil War (1946–49), thousands of members and supporters of Communist forces fled Greece, becoming refugees in Former Yugoslavia, and the Eastern Bloc. In the case of Czechoslovakia (which accepted thousands of Greek refugee children), the Greek population was declared a national minority. The multilingual family and places of growing made a deep impression on the artist's sense of belonging and the significance of language in these processes.

The emphasis on the relationship to language, and collective and personal experiences of displacement is also reflected in another video work in EMST's collection, *Measures of Distance* (1988) by Palestinian artist Mona Hatoum. Where Tsivopoulos' *Land* can be seen as a reflection of mastery over language in terms of who is permitted, or indeed able, to speak, *Measures of Distance* considers the capacity of language to translate experiences of displacement. Created at a time when the artist was reflecting on her exile and displacement from her family due to the Lebanese Civil War, the work has attracted critical attention for its ability to reflect a multitude of distances – linguistic, geographic, temporal, and generational – created through experiences of war and forced displacement.[25]

Comprised of several visual layers, *Measures of Distance* is a video work that focuses on a series of letters written by Hatoum's mother in Beirut, addressing her daughter who was living in London.[26] Superimposed over background images of the artist's mother naked in the shower, the scrolling Arabic text of these letters is accompanied by taped conversations in Arabic between the two women. Hatoum's mother speaks openly about her sexuality, her feelings, and her husband's objections to their daughter's intimate observation. This soundtrack is frequently interlaced with the artist's own voice reading the letters in English. The year of the video's production (1988) is particularly poignant, as it was also the time of the first Palestinian intifada against the Israeli occupation. The work thus operates as a record of the personal impact of conflict and forced displacement on both mother and daughter, utilising language as a means of reflecting, and indeed mediating, the impact of displacement across multiple generations.

Born in Beirut to Palestinian parents, Hatoum became an exile whilst she was a student in Britain when Civil War broke out in Lebanon in 1975. The intergenerational experience of exile experienced by Hatoum (her parents forced to flee to Lebanon following the Nakba, and she unable to return to Beirut following the outbreak of the Civil War) has been described by Chrisoula Lionis as a form of Palestinian 'double exile'.[27] For Lionis, the experience of double exile is argued to have been experienced by the generation of Palestinian artists (and filmmakers, including, for example, director Michel Khleifi) that came of age during the events of the Lebanese Civil War, who like Hatoum, experienced the destruction of Beirut, a city which had become a surrogate Palestinian capital.

For many Palestinian artists, their experiences of displacement compounds the trauma of exile experienced by their parents.[28] In the case of Hatoum, one can find traces of what Marianne Hirsch defines as 'post-memory' when subsequent generations inflect past traumatic histories that are not their own through visual cues such as photos and material objects. Here, the artist references in opaque terms Palestinian experiences of displacement and dominant memories of the Nakba (the 1948 catastrophe or occupation of historical Palestine).[29]

On the surface, *Measures of Distance* stands apart from the artist's wider oeuvre for its storytelling elements, and its reference to specific geographies and conflicts. However, it is also a work of narrative opacity; language operates simultaneously as point of access and as instrument of obstruction. While the use of Arabic and English opens the work to a wider range of audiences, the artist's decision to read letters in English at an almost equal volume to the tape recordings of her mother in Arabic means that audiences may struggle to grasp all the details of the women's narratives. This reflects Hatoum's deliberate decision to alienate both Arabic speaking, and non-Arabic speaking audiences of the work.[30] The constant negotiation between Arabic and English, in spoken and textual forms of storytelling forces an audience to experience linguistic gaps, and thus partial understanding. As Mehre Khan argues, this struggle between hearing and seeing, reading and viewing, is akin to experiences of those who belong to diasporic communities that negotiate which cultural motifs to merge, leave behind, or reject.[31]

The exploration of linguistic form and intergenerational memory in *Measures of Distance* are central points of focus in critical evaluations of her art. The popularity of the work (particularly since its acquisition by the Tate in 2000) reflects not only the global profile of Mona Hatoum, but also a growing international focus on contemporary Arab artists since the turn of the century. The renewed global interest in contemporary Middle Eastern art following 9/11 marked a major turning point for Arab artists whose work proliferated at art fairs and exhibitions both in the region and abroad. However, this focus on contemporary art practice often sidelined modern art histories of the Arab world. As art historian Nada Shabout notes, the historiography of Arab modern art suffers both from colonial legacies, which effectively excluded the Middle East from modernity and contemporaneity, and from restrictions on language. As she points out, teaching the history of art from the Middle East at any university in 1999 was an almost unimaginable task due to the lack of translated art histories from Arabic to the international languages of English or French.[32]

In this way, *Measures of Distance* can be understood as a work that not only engages the role of language and translation in representations of displacement and intergenerational memory, but also as a work that foreshadows the problems relating to language and understandings of contemporary Arab art, which has seen an extraordinary growth in its international profile since 2000.[33] Of particular interest is the way in which the work negotiates displacement, art-making and the issue of a 'mother tongue' in two main ways: addressing the intimacy of languages spoken in childhood and with family members; and the role of the artist in translating language and experience in English, the common language of the contemporary art world.

The mother tongue, or *lingua materna* in Latin, is a vernacular term referring to linguistic socialisation that was first used in the context of social and political transformations of the Middle Ages and the Early Modern period, which produced new concepts of family, nation, and the state.[34] Significantly, the concept of the mother tongue is at the centre of what is described as the 'monolingual paradigm', a key social structuring principle. As Yasemin Yildiz points out, it organises modern social life everywhere, from imagined collectives such as cultures or nations, to individual subjectivities and the formation of disciplines and institutions. The monolingual paradigm has focused on social engineering of monolingual populations, particularly through education. Displaced artists have engaged with this issue, demonstrating the challenges of navigating the dominance of the English language in the international art world. They also highlight the lived conditions of being 'in-between' language as a result of displacement.

For instance, Lebanese-Dutch artist Mounira Al Solh tracks microhistories of people on the move, and bears witness to impacts of displacement and protracted conflict. Working across diverse mediums of video, installation, textiles, performance, painting, and drawing, Al Solh integrates oral testimonies, word play, and experiments with language in her practice. She uses social practice methods to consider concepts of transience and the (often ironic) gaps, convergences, and idiosyncrasies of language for migrant communities. Her work is inflected by her own personal history of migration, and the experience of living in multilingual communities. Born in Lebanon in 1989, Al Solh's family fled Beirut and emigrated to Damascus, cities which both, as a result of their colonial histories, use French, English, and Arabic in everyday language. As an adult, Al Solh migrated again to the Netherlands, where English proficiency is the highest in the world outside the Anglosphere.

Currently residing between Beirut and Amsterdam, the artist's work has, since her migration to the Netherlands as an adult, focused on the sense of loss and confusion, as well as the tragicomic results of moving between languages. An example of this work is *All Mother Tongues are Difficult*, a visual essay originally commissioned for art platform *Ibraaz* in 2015 (Figure 3.2).[35] Springing from a research project about language, *All Mother Tongues are Difficult* was developed when Al Solh was applying for Dutch citizenship, which required language proficiency. Ironically, in order to learn Dutch, the artist travelled to Belgium where she found that studying Flemish was more helpful for proficiency, for in the Netherlands her social circle preferred to communicate in English. In Antwerp, however, Al Solh set about learning Flemish both through a language centre and through a series of workshops with people residing in a home supporting mental illness.[36] In this setting, the artist worked with

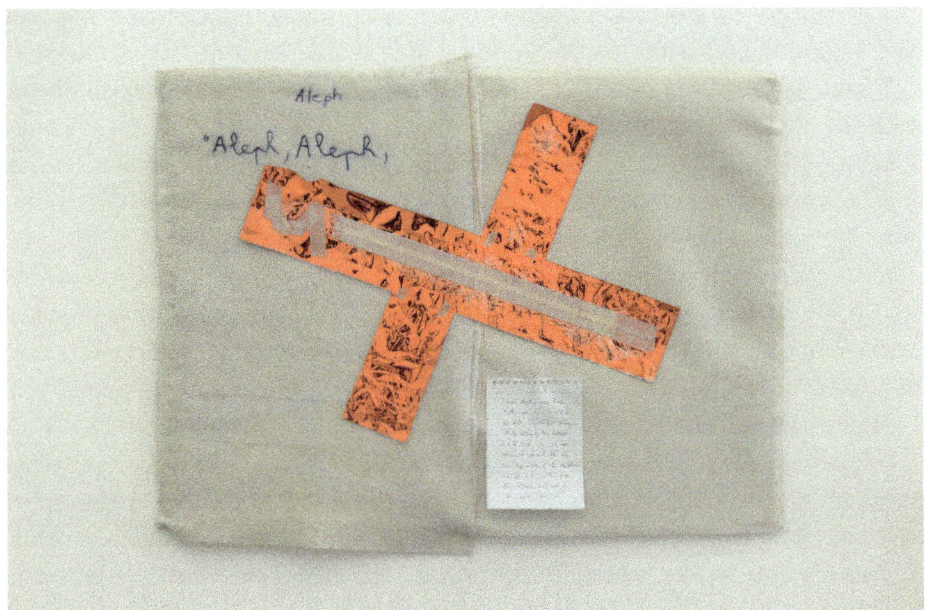

3.2 Mounira Al Solh, *Aleph, Aleph (After Eight series)* (2014). Mixed media, hand-stitched embroidery on textile, 64 × 78 cm. Courtesy of the artist and Sfeir-Semler Gallery Beirut/Hamburg.

patients of varying cultural and linguistic backgrounds to write letters about love. In her *Ibraaz* visual essay, *All Mother Tongues are Difficult* (2015), the artist draws together her research on language, her own hand-stitched media, and the letters produced in Antwerp to create an alphabet of 'findings'. Grouped in alphabetical order, Al Solh presents hand-stitched media, each focused on a particular Arabic letter, accompanied by a brief, poetic text that considers the letter's significance in culture, history, and in specific words or phrases. 'Aleph', for example, the Arabic letter 'A' (Figure 3.2), is described as 'the silent support for the vowel it bears … the interruption in articulation, it is a thought to have once expressed'.

For Al Solh, the concept of the mother tongue is seen as integral to what she described as 'visual luggage', an approach that can be seen across multiple works dealing with language, ranging from *Samaa/Maas* (2014), to the artist's *NOA (Not Only Arabic) Magazine* (2008–ongoing), and her now celebrated series *I Strongly Believe in Our Right to Be Frivolous* (2012–20). 'Visual luggage' is cultural, social, and indeed political. She explains that the process of language learning for the purposes of obtaining a passport led her to understand that 'sometimes a language can be a threat, a weapon, an entrance ticket, a tool of torture, of prejudice'.[37] Thus, the artist reminds us that 'mastery' over language is about dominance, as much as it is for access and understanding.

Al Solh's body of work focusing on research into language was created in response to the European refugee crisis. At the outset of the crisis, when Al Solh was living in Lebanon, she witnessed first-hand what she describes as the reversal of her childhood, when she fled Beirut to her mother's country of origin, Syria. Now, it was the artist witnessing Syrians fleeing to Lebanon. The sense of repeated history, and the blurred line between personal and collective memory is palpably sensed in Al Solh's works from this time, which were featured in her solo exhibition *All Mother Tongues are Difficult* at Gallery Sfeir Semler in Beirut. One such example is the video *Eat My Script* (2014), which takes as its starting point the exchange of goods and food between Al Solh's mother's family in both Syria and Lebanon during periods of conflict. The movement of both goods and families translates as a way of questioning our ability to communicate the trauma of conflict and displacement.

Situating herself in the geographical and cultural spaces where history and biography overlap, Al Solh's practice often uses language as a means of bringing together disparate yet interconnected temporalities and personal histories. This experimental approach to storytelling underpins the ongoing drawing series *I Strongly Believe in Our Right to Be Frivolous*, which documents over 500 personal encounters between the artist and displaced people in Lebanon, Europe, the US, and beyond. The series chronicles testimonies, life stories, and impressions of each of the individuals the artist meets. Drawn on yellow-lined 'legal pads', suggestive of notes taken during an official interview, each portrait includes a brief text in Arabic. Seen together, the drawings can be understood as a dossier of testimonies of displacement, operating as a geopolitical snapshot of life in the wake of the European refugee crisis.

While *I Strongly Believe in Our Right to Be Frivolous* might be interpreted as an archive of displacement, it reminds the viewer of both the capacity and the limitations of archives in narrating experiences of forced migration, and the fragmentary, disembodied, and incoherent nature of refugee voices that are only partially rendered in a legalistic framework. Al Solh's decision to use yellow legal paper is particularly significant in this regard, reminding us of the burden of proof (discussed in detail in Chapter 2) placed upon forcibly displaced people to recall *particular* stories of forced migration in order to secure asylum. Presenting snapshots of people's experience, and often refusing to recount narratives of how or why portrait subjects were displaced, *I Strongly Believe in Our Right to Be Frivolous* reminds us of the fragility of testimony, and therefore the fault lines of the burden of proof as the cornerstone of international refugee law. This is particularly palpable for non-Arabic speaking audiences, who can see the portraits and archive on display but are unable to access the stories presented therein.

The focus on the limitations of archives, sublimated histories of displacement, and the role of artist as translator of experiences of forced migration is also witnessed in the work of London-based artist Kani Kamil. Born in Sulaymaniyah in the Kurdistan Region of Iraq, Kamil's practice, which ranges from video, sound, and photography to embroidery, focuses on the reclamation of sublimated female histories. Often using her own body and hair as primary material, Kamil's work draws particular attention to issues of gender and social equality in the Iraqi Kurdistan Region. A subject long excluded from public discourse, gender-based violence in Iraqi Kurdistan is an issue which has only moved into the mainstream since 2010, as a result of Kurdish transnational women's rights networks. These networks span Iraq, Syria, and Türkiye, with the Rojava revolution (2012) of northern Syria having the most globally recognised impact on women's rights. While in the early 1990s (the childhood years of Kani Kamil), gender-based violence was rarely discussed, its entry into the forefront of public debates in the region inspired Kamil's art practice.[38]

This approach is explored in *Reflection on Archival Material* (2020–ongoing), a series of hair embroideries which Kamil has based on images she has seen by watching an unreleased audio-visual archive from northern Iraq (Figure 3.3). Due to the sensitive nature of the topics relating to women's testimony, these opaque, ephemeral pieces of sewn calico, a fabric suggestive of virginity and marriage rituals, evoke the fragility of both the documentary and the testimonial image. The postcard-sized pieces

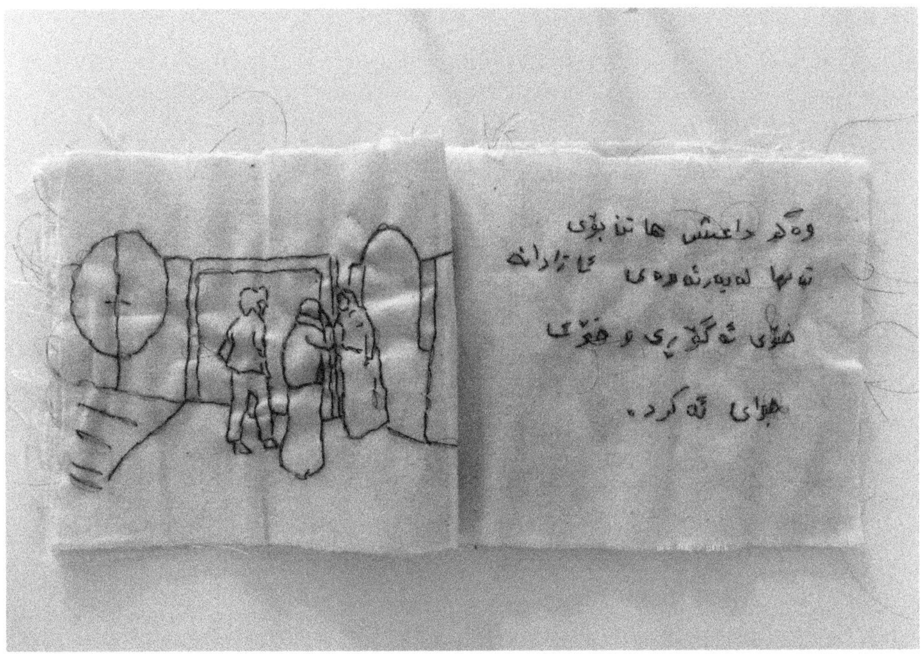

3.3 Kani Kamil, *Reflection on Archival Material* (2020–ongoing). Human hair stitched on canvas. Courtesy of the artist.

of embroidery each recreate a still image drawn from a secret VHS archive in Iraqi Kurdistan, made in the early 1990s during a period of intense upheaval in the region. Kamil's series thus draws together oral testimonies during the aftermath of Kurdish displacement resulting from Iraq during the Iraq–Iran war (1980–88). Importantly, this archive remains hidden today, since the gender-based violence it documents lingers as a traumatic issue for the women involved, the female archivist, and Kurdish Iraqi society more broadly. Using her own hair to embroider traces of the video stills, Kamil draws attention to her positionality as holder of memory. Entangling traces of her own body with the archival images, she collapses personal and collective memory, embodying a complex history and heritage rather than attempting to narrate the women's stories.

Significantly, Kamil's privileged access to the video archive sees her become something of a visual translator of the material, transmitting testimony into new visual forms on the one hand, but also translating between Kurdish dialects, and then into English for international art audiences. For Kamil, the unavailability of Kurdish Sorani (central Kurdish) translations online presents a frequent problem, as she is often unable to understand specific meanings of words and proverbs. This problem was alleviated only recently, when in 2022 a crowdsourcing effort led by one man (Bokan Hassan) took the initiative to add half a million pieces of Sorani language data to Google Translate. For Kamil, her role in this challenging artistic process is seen as one that is focused on listening, whereas a simultaneous visual and linguistic translator seeks to understand and transfer the meaning of particular expressions and proverbs. Moreover, she operates as a filter of testimony, and is acutely aware of the sensitivity of the archive's subjects and its documented personal histories.

Similarly to Al Solh and Hatoum, Kamil emphasises the role of artist as both conduit and interpreter of displacement, and as an agent of its obstruction. This approach to power relations can be traced across the practice of several contemporary artists working in this area, with notable examples including Hiwa K and his 2017 work *A View From Above* (discussed in Chapter 2) and Candice Breitz. Where Hiwa K's *A View From Above* presents the story of 'M' and his experiences undergoing interrogation in order to gain asylum, which question the validity of a system that requires high-stakes performances of stories of displacement to ensure safety, Candice Breitz's video work *Love Story* (2017) challenges viewers to consider whose stories of displacement they are willing to listen to in a media-saturated landscape that privileges particular tropes and narratives of refugees, asylum seekers, and their reasons for fleeing different forms of persecution.

Bretiz' *Love Story* premiered at the 2017 Venice Biennale, where it was one of the most talked-about works shown within a Biennale, focusing on issues relating to

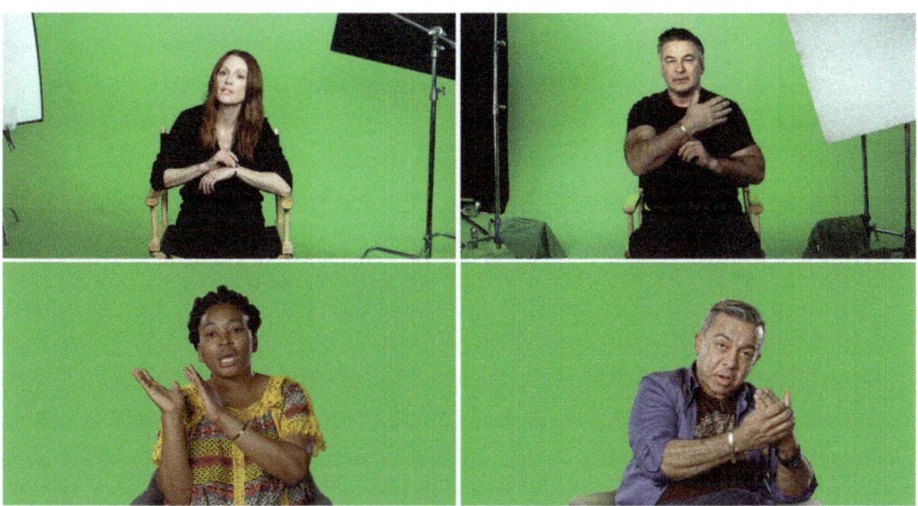

3.4 Candice Breitz, Stills from *Love Story* (2016). Featuring Julianne Moore and Alec Baldwin. Interviewees: Mamy Maloba Langa and Luis Ernesto Nava Molero. Seven-Channel Video Installation, Commissioned by the National Gallery of Victoria, Outset Germany + Medienboard Berlin-Brandenburg. Image Courtesy of the Artist.

refugeedom, exile, migration, and national identity. The two-channel video is based on interviews with six people, each forcibly displaced from different parts of the world: Angola, Syria, Somalia, Venezuela, and the Democratic Republic of Congo (Figure 3.4). *Love Story* is typically installed across two rooms. The first video features Hollywood actors Julianne Moore and Alec Baldwin seated in a sound-studio setting, performing fragments of interviews, imitating the gestures and voices of the refugees Breitz has also interviewed, but whose videos are installed in a separate room or are made available online. As actors, they are compelling in their capacity to inhabit the characters of the people Breitz interviewed in Berlin, New York, and Cape Town. The diverse group of refugees include the now famous Syrian swimmer Sarah Ezzat Mardini; a former child soldier from Angola, José Maria João; Mamy Maloba Langa, a survivor from the Democratic Republic of Congo; Shabeena Francis Saveri, a transgender activist from India; Luis Ernesto Nava Molero, a political dissident from Venezuela; and Farah Abdi Mohamed, a persecuted atheist from Somalia. The viewer connects the subjects across both videos through idiosyncratic gestures performed by Baldwin and Moore, as well as singular items of clothing (such as sunglasses) worn in both videos.

On its surface, *Love Story* reflects upon a media environment where celebrity stories are prioritised over real-life stories of adversity and resilience. With deep irony, the work shares the strategies of celebrity-led humanitarian campaigns, designed to elicit sympathy and raise awareness; these campaigns rarely afford the opportunity for those directly affected to tell their own stories in their own voices. More than this, today's refugee regime and the contemporary western celebrity system may be more closely linked than we first imagine. As artist Chris Campanioni argues, both figures are similar in the ways they are represented to the public as 'a sight and site of state power and a social-structuring apparatus'. Moreover, contemporary phenomena such as celebrity charity and humanitarian interventions have intersected to simultaneously valorise and dehumanise refugees.[39]

Importantly, it is not just Julianne Moore and Alec Baldwin who represent power based on notoriety and professional status, or indeed racial and cultural backgrounds. The same might also be said of Breitz herself, who is today one of South Africa's most renowned artists, with a strong international following and profile. The artist is clearly aware of her positionality (as a White South African), having grappled with issues of Whiteness over the last three decades of her practice. For Breitz, the issues of who can speak for whom, and which kind of stories audiences are willing to hear are concerns that can be traced across her oeuvre and her approach to social practice (for example in works such as *TLDR*, 2017).[40] The pertinence of Breitz's *Love Story* is found in its capacity to raise questions about the power of translation, the right to self-narration, and the politics of positionality in providing 'voice' for those who are spoken for and about.

Questions regarding who speaks for whom, and in what language or form, return us to Julietta Singh's argument that mastery over language is central to political discourse, both postcolonial and anticolonial. Yet, in a contemporary art world grappling with the entwined (yet unacknowledged) issues of colonial legacies and unprecedented waves of forced migration, the issue of language remains oddly overlooked. Considered together, the works of Stefanos Tsivopoulos, Mona Hatoum, Mounira Al Solh, Kani Kami, and Candice Breitz make evident that there is an urgent need to think through the significance of language in representations of forced displacement, as outlined above, but also to re-evaluate the significance of language as a political and social instrument in arts administration, curatorship, and art writing. In so doing it demonstrates that displacement aesthetics is both representational and operational; that is, it is felt in artistic reproduction but also traceable in the invisible forces which impact the everyday lives of artists with backgrounds of displacement.

Mastery, brokerage, and positionality for artists with backgrounds of displacement

For cultural historians, cultural producers, and art writers, especially those working in the Global North, the nexus between language and displacement remains under-appreciated. In part this is perhaps because our current model of global art history is, as James Elkins argued, essentially flawed. For Elkins, it is the conditions under which global art histories are studied that are key to the problem. Arguing that the least theorised problem in art history is the lack of diversity of writing, Elkins has convincingly demonstrated that this results both from the reliance on English as the language of art history and the dominance of conceptual models (focused on leading terms such as 'master narrative', 'peripheral', 'regional', etc.) in art education, and accordingly curatorship and art criticism.[41]

Critical engagement with what can be described as a particular kind of monolingualism in the art world is something that has increasingly concerned theorists in recent decades. This is in large part shaped by the spread of internationalised art markets, the establishment and proliferation of major exhibitions (biennials, triennials), and increased access to objects of art and art history as a result of the internet. For Elkins, it is of particular significance that acknowledgement of the homogenisation of language in the art world resulting from the globalisation of art is often conflated with the globalisation of art history. This, in effect, means that while we acknowledge the impact of globalisation on the art objects and practices discussed and analysed in art history, we are often remiss in acknowledging the impact of globalisation on the way we learn art history. That is, the role of globalisation on the institutions where we are educated in art history, and the impact of globalisation on the methods and indeed languages we use within art historical disciplines, including curatorship and museum studies.

It is important to consider how this homogenisation of language impacts artists themselves, particularly those who come from backgrounds of forced displacement. To assess this impact, our discussion here focuses on research drawn from the creative industries as well as refugee studies, and on interviews with artists from backgrounds of displacement, now living in the UK. Analysis of their experience will reveal the direct, and often under-acknowledged, impact of 'mastery' over language on their career trajectories and professional relationships.

While on the surface it might seem that the needs of artists with backgrounds of displacement are similar to other global majority groups in the UK, there are key points of divergence. The most critical need, arguably, is language. Refugees are significantly less likely to speak English than other global majority populations. Moreover, their languages are different to the main ethnic languages spoken in the UK.[42] In contrast to the waves of postwar immigration to the UK from Commonwealth countries (such as Caribbean nations or from South Asia), the origins of recent refugees are much more diverse, and English is frequently not their first, second, or even third language.[43] For artists, language competence impacts directly on their professional opportunities since artistic careers are not just public-facing, but also demand eloquence in professional vernacular for publicity, media, gallery presentation, and networking.

This should come as no surprise. There is a long-standing body of scholarship that demonstrates the importance of language proficiency for social integration, and its significance as a 'pillar of survival'.[44] These studies highlight that language is key to self-sufficiency and to integration into education, health, and employment. It therefore stands to reason that language proficiency is at the core of the UK government's refugee integration strategies.[45] It is also central in NGO and community agency policies and outreach activities to support refugees and asylum seekers.[46] Although language is appreciated in numerous government agendas as a key facilitator in social integration, there remains a poor understanding of scale and need. There is, for example, no national strategy in the UK and there is little evidence of any joint approach that links policy makers.[47]

Recent research which focused on refugees resettled in the UK demonstrates that higher language proficiency results in more contact, and more positive relationships, with the majority population, leading in turn to better well-being.[48] Conversely, low language proficiency leads to the risk of long-term dependency, exclusion, and poor emotional and physical health.[49] There are many challenges in gaining access to English language training in the UK. These challenges range from travel costs, childcare, costs of classes, waiting lists, and lack of information about where to access classes. The barriers are compounded by long-running cuts to funding for language classes, with a reduction in government funding for ESOL (English for Speakers of Other Languages) classes in England. Funding dropped from 203 million pounds in 2009–10 to just 131,000 during 2014–15.[50] Lack of ESOL training creates lasting employment barriers for refugees in the labour market and forces people into precarious forms of work. In 2022, the Ukrainian refugee influx increased that demand and there was a widely reported paucity of services available to new arrivals.[51] A number of art museums, including Manchester Art Gallery, began to host ESOL classes, working with agencies to contribute spaces for classes that Ukrainian and Afghan families could attend.

Lack of English-language mastery produces deep anxiety for artists with backgrounds of displacement, something reported to us repeatedly by artist collaborators based in Manchester. For them, language proficiency was identified as a psychological and social barrier as well as a professional hindrance. The key role of language was summarised, for example, by a musician from the Democratic Republic of Congo recently arrived to the UK. With the assistance of a French translator, she explained to us that: '[S]ince I've been living in England, I don't speak very good English, although I can understand some. I tried to integrate. I try to be like everyone else, but I can see some barriers'.[52] This artist was by no means alone in identifying this challenge. In all our interviews, artists with backgrounds of forced displacement were unambiguous in emphasising that language competence limits access to art networks, funding calls, and training. An additional challenge was the capacity to make use of contemporary art's industry-specific dialect of English, characterised by specialist art terminologies and jargon. Artists generally become familiar with this dialect via graduate art programmes, art literature, and art discourse, and it is essential for funding applications where professional artists describe their practice using this language. Problematically, this grasp of English becomes a metric of expertise, professionalism, and position within the industry.

Proficiency in language shapes an artist's capacity to describe themselves and their identity with sensitivity and nuance. This point was made in discussions with a painter, formerly a Syrian journalist with superior language skills in Arabic. By devastating contrast, she testified to her lack of English proficiency, which soon led to complications when she began collaborative artistic work. She explained:

> There are many difficulties. So, for example when we talk about religion [it is] very difficult to understand which is their religion, and to be able to communicate what my religion is. Sometimes, I just take a step back and don't talk about these kinds of issues because I can't communicate what I want 100%.[53]

Thus, lack of language proficiency compounds the feeling of isolation and alienation that many refugees feel when they try to speak. In addition, for artists, who need to contemplate the labyrinthine, highly competitive mechanics of the cultural scene that they seek to enter, this also impacts their capacity for access. This artist offered a solution:

> I would be happy to give £1,000 for a person who can support me in the industry and is able to organise and negotiate for me – because having my work exhibited is a big deal for me. I need this not just because of language challenges, but also because of not knowing the cultural scene and networking circles.[54]

What her comments indicate is the need for cultural brokers (particularly for artists who do not yet have a representative gallery) to act as intermediaries (linguistically, socially, and professionally) between artists and the local art industry, as well as with arts funding agencies. Successful cultural brokerage could operate in the service of artists and the creative sector more broadly. It would, however, require an appreciation that language and integration are two-way processes. This is to say that while the lack of English proficiency might acutely hinder artists, it also impedes arts institutions from searching for neglected communities. This same artist explains:

> There are particular communities that don't engage with museums. Like for example, [galleries] do welcome Syrian communities, but even within the community there are some people who have no interest, or don't know how to engage.[55]

Underlying this artist's statement is recognition that refugee integration in the cultural sector is a two-way process, requiring change by institutions as well as adaptation by refugees.[56] While language is key to these two-way processes of integration, it remains a challenge, even for the most well-meaning of institutional programmes.

This was apparent during the In Place of War (IPOW) Cultural and Social Entrepreneur Programme (CASE), which was delivered in English in Manchester (see Chapter 2). The CASE programme delivered an array of training modules and resources focused on content ranging from funding applications, alternative economic models, and examples of social engagement. The programme, delivered to artists with backgrounds of forced displacement, provided content that was new to all artist participants. However, it did so in English, a language in which the artists had variable proficiency. With the best intentions from both sides of the lectern, the challenge of learning new information and engaging with novel social and entrepreneurial models was sizeable. As this same artist-participant explained, English language fluency was, for her: 'yet another thing that was difficult for me … This whole process [of setting up a creative enterprise] is difficult for me. It would be even in Arabic'.[57]

A lesser problem (though one not exclusive to forcibly displaced artists), is what commentators of contemporary art derisively refer to as 'artspeak', by which they mean the specialised jargon used in contemporary art criticism and art curatorship and deployed by young artists, curators, and critics around the world. The most extreme versions have been caricatured as 'International Art English', a term invented satirically by David Levine and Alix Rule. In other words, one's inclusion in the contemporary art industry is often signalled by deploying an assumed common knowledge of difficult to comprehend jargon and theory.[58] At its conception, 'International Art English' was coined as a tongue-in-cheek satire, but in recent years there has been an acknowledgement that difficult jargon and cryptic theory increases political exclusion.[59] A lack of fluency both in English and in 'artspeak' directly impacts on artists' exchanges with curators and wider circles of younger artists, and both may well affect success with funding applications and pitches to curators.

While arts funding guidelines encourage diversity, they do not adequately recognise the challenges faced by ethnically and linguistically diverse artists who have migrated, whether as refugees or otherwise, to the UK. For example, displaced artists are at a considerable disadvantage compared with their peers as they try to access public arts funding. Artists who do not speak English as a first or second language need to acquire fluency in industry-specific language and grant writing terminology. Even worse, artists with backgrounds of displacement are often locked out of funding, for they are ineligible to receive money from government agencies or arts organisations. The consequences of being ineligible for funding were described to us by a spoken word artist originally from Nigeria:

> They [EU and UK arts funding agencies] have … funding they put out there, but people can't have access to it. There is a door that has been locked and we don't talk about it. Those people don't talk because they already feel let down by the system. People are excluded, [and] they already feel mentally that they have been excluded.[60]

This artist succinctly described key social barriers that actively exclude asylum seekers from arts funding. For him, the key way around these barriers was access to mentorship, networks, and alternative resources. This view is reflected in IPOW's development of its CASE programme, and its first rollout in the UK. Participants' feedback on the IPOW programme focused on the importance of how to develop a business and financial plan, as well as the key steps in accessing arts funding in the UK.

Refugees' lack of professional networks, mentors, or cultural brokers results in a critical absence of communication and support, which leads to both material and psychological exclusion from the arts industry and professional opportunities. This is also felt as a loss of personal agency and purpose in life. The CASE interviewees insisted that the very process of realising that available artistic and institutional networks are not accessible, or that institutions and funding mechanisms operate in ways they do not understand or are very different in their home countries, is psychologically arduous and frustrating. They may feel hopeless, and one of their solutions was to imagine they could outsource the administrative side of their art practice to someone who they believed would be 'in the know', a person we have described as a cultural broker.

Considered together, what these narrations demonstrate is that artists with refugee backgrounds experience particular forms of exclusion in extreme and repeated forms, something expounded upon in the forthcoming chapter, which focuses on the question of labour. These artists also face a more intense version of the same barriers that beset all artists across the UK cultural sector, particularly those with global majority backgrounds. This is reflected, for example, in professional employment opportunities. Arts and cultural employers in the UK recruit talent mainly from a White, middle- and-upper-class pool. Even when this is not intentional, discrimination remains – something taken up directly in Human Resources equal opportunity manuals which define the practice of hiring people who look like oneself as 'confirmation bias'.[61] These barriers, we argue, are central to the operation of displacement aesthetics, often underlying creative projects and practices engaged with the issue of displacement, but in need of more substantial analysis in art history and curatorial studies.

It is important to acknowledge that while creative practitioners with backgrounds of forced displacement face unique *and* shared barriers compared to artists with global majority backgrounds, the terminology that frames and limits these artists is of vital significance. Put differently, while an artist with a background of displacement might face specific challenges as a result of this experience (which do often differ from that of a 'migrant' or 'global majority' artist), this does not mean that it is appropriate or indeed helpful for institutions (for example museums or funders) to describe artists within these terms of explicit identification with their citizenship status. To do so is not only to draw a power differential, but also to pre-determine the frame with which a creative practitioner's work is interpreted and understood.

Language protocols, key terminologies, and future tool kits

Flattening and homogenising difference and multiple, often intersectional and fluid, identities, the label 'refugee artist' proliferates humanitarian and NGO projects, community arts circles and (albeit to a lesser degree) social practice art projects around the world. However, the absence of this term in the international contemporary art industry (that is, in major gallery, museum, and exhibition contexts), is a sign that curators and arts administrators recognise that this characterisation cannot be easily, or indeed appropriately, applied from humanitarian discourse across to the art industry. What this might also suggest is an implicit recognition that this label is suggestive of a 'discursive identity' which is applied to an artist rather than the result of an artist's *own* identification. This is significant because, as linguist Jan Blommaert reminds us, identity is discursive insofar as it is constructed through language and communication. A 'discursive identity', then, is dependent on context, purpose, and occasion, a semiotic process of symbols and narratives. Thus, language does not merely describe or communicate, because discourses *do things*. As Blommaert explains, language positions people as powerful or powerless, dominant or dominated.[62]

While artists with backgrounds of displacement do face specific and often pronounced barriers, we might understand the absence of the 'refugee artist' discursive identity in contemporary curatorial and exhibition practices as recognition that this flattening category does not suffice within a typology of artist types. Although today there is an enormous breadth of artist types, ranging, for example, from 'war artist' and 'humanitarian witness' to 'antiwar artist' and 'protest artist', generally speaking, artists are defined and differentiated in the art industry by a standard group of five parameters. These are medium (painting, performance, video, etc.), career status (e.g. emerging, mid-career, established), adherence to various art movements (conceptualism, surrealism, etc.), style (e.g. street artist, figurative artist, etc.), and genre (portrait artist, landscape artist, etc.).[63] The discursive identities are each predicated on what an artist does, rather than who they are. Moreover, the identification of the 'refugee artist' stands apart from categories of ethnic diversity used in the UK, or terms such as CALD (Culturally and Linguistically Diverse) used in Australia. This is because the condition of refugeedom is based on a sense of temporariness, rather than a fixed cultural, racial, or ethnic identity.

As UK-based artist and researcher Alex Rotas notes, while the terms 'refugee' or 'refugee artist' initially appear as synonyms to those of 'emigre' or 'exile', they have developed a distinctly different meaning. The latter carry a historical tone which signifies a certain romanticism toward experiences of displacement. Associated with modernist artists such Piet Mondrian, Andre Breton, and Marc Chagall, these terms signify a particular kind of suffering (one that is distinctly European) and, as Rotas argues, suggest a 'boundary with the host culture [that] is more permeable, less guarded, and less dangerous, than "refugee" and his or her host'.[64] Significantly, Alex Rotas' reflections on whether 'refugee art' is possible or indeed desirable, took place around two decades ago, in 2006, when she was advising an exhibition in Britain by artists who were or had been previously refugees or asylum seekers. Thus, well before the 2015 European refugee crisis, Rotas' research was questioning how the 'lexical minefield' for asylum seekers and displaced artists in Britain would change over time, and whether artists would choose to identify with the label of 'refugee artist', or whether the art world would engage with them.[65] Since then, the issue of language and displacement in contemporary art context has remained a serious, yet often unacknowledged, challenge, and the art industry still struggles with collaboration and professional protocols relating to displacement.

The 'lexical minefield' has become an important area of critical enquiry in museum practice. Here one might consider as an example the 2018 *Words Matter: An Unfinished Guide to Word Choices in the Cultural Centre* research publication, composed by the National Museum for World Cultures in the Netherlands and led by Director of Content Wayne Modest and General Director Stijn Schoonderwoerd. This project identities the need for art professionals and museum staff to understand the sensitivity of language, explaining in its introduction that

> it has become a necessity to be self-critical about the types of narratives we develop and the words we use … we have had to think about the words or phrases that are sensitive to particular groups that can cause offense, that elide important context, and that are understood as derogatory.

A blend of lexicon and tool kit aimed at curators, marketers, and educators, *Words Matter* consists of a list of words alongside an explanation of their sensitivity, providing alternative words that might be used in their place. Framed as an ongoing project, *Words Matter* signals a shift in professional practice where language is understood as deeply embedded in contemporary political debate, identity formation, and colonial legacies.

Political rhetoric surrounding forced migration, refugeedom, and displacement are today in constant rotation within news headlines around the world. Places such as museums offer a space through which to critically evaluate the language that circulates, and to consider new ways of working, which acknowledge how language affects a sense of belonging both in the art world/creative industries, and society more broadly. Thus, the need for practical 'tool kits' and re-evaluated guides in the creative industries that address the issue of displacement is more urgent than ever. This is a concern also shared by curator Domenico Sergi, who argues that museums have an ethical responsibility to critically reflect on how language constructs are produced, and how they can affect refugees and asylum seekers. He suggests museums should 'develop more nuanced approaches to the language they use in the context of programmes, exhibitions and community engagement projects concerned with forced displacement'.[66]

The re-evaluation of language must extend beyond wall texts and object labels, which although central to exhibition practice are not the only area where the understanding and the communication of knowledge and perception is crucial. Re-evaluation should, for instance, extend to the description of works in museum catalogues and databases, which is often mired in misinformation, lack of information, and colonial terminologies that have remained unchallenged for decades. Also, serious consideration by museum staff and collaborators must be given to the choice of language used in community outreach projects, education programming, and community co-curation. More than this, in order for museums to be both inclusive *and* safe spaces, equality, diversity, and inclusion practices must hone in on the issue of language, and provide, for example, greater linguistic diversity by way of translators for events, linguistically diverse public programming, and diverse labelling beyond the host country language. This approach reflects an understanding of social cohesion and integration as being shared; that is, beneficial to communities and practitioners with backgrounds of displacement as well as to art institutions and arts professionals.

Conclusion

The theme of the 2024 Venice Biennale, *Foreigners Everywhere*, is but one measure of the international art world's sustained focus on the issue of displacement. Yet the controversy that followed the 2024 Biennale and the aftermath of major international art events, such as the 2017 Venice Biennale and *documenta* exhibitions, underscores that greater sensitivity to issues of language in regard to forced migration and displacement remains urgent.[67]

To demonstrate this point, public responses to Olu Oguibe's 2017 work *Monument for Strangers and Refugees* in Kassel's Königsplatz is instructive. Erected as part of the documenta 14 exhibition (2017), the 16-metre-tall memorial was sought to rebuke xenophobia and express gratitude for the hospitality and care that Germany had undertaken during the Syrian refugee crisis. Oguibe's obelisk monument bears the biblical inscription 'I was a stranger and you took me in' (Matthew 25:35) in Arabic, English, German, and Turkish. Despite the artist's motivation, the work was perceived as controversial by conservative lawmakers and Kassel constituents, who were also highly critical of the so-called open-door policy adopted by German Chancellor Angela Merkel in 2015 (later restricted in 2017). As a result, and as is now well known and documented, Oguibe's work was removed from the *documenta* exhibition after pressure from Right-wing politicians, only to be reinstalled permanently in 2019 in a nearby square which occupies a distinctly more discrete position.[68]

Both in its original location and its now permanent home, the obelisk became a meeting point as well as a 'selfie backdrop' for Turkish, Eritrean, Syrian, and other migrant communities in Kassel. It is useful here to ask whether Oguibe's monument would have stirred the same anger were it inscribed only in German, or indeed only in English. For it is the inscription in Arabic and in Turkish that is situated at the nexus of how the work mediates hospitality, inviting, on the one hand, migrant communities in Kassel to feel connected and represented in the city, while on the other reinforcing a sense of xenophobia for those who could not read foreign language texts. This is particularly pronounced as the texts appear on a large memorial that takes up public space and insists by its very monumentality that the language of the other belongs in the civic spaces of the city.

As Anne Ring Petersen explains, artworks provide 'communities and nations with important collective points of orientation and identification, or with points of counter identification'. Thus, when works produce controversy, they operate as expressions of the cultural and historical circumstances and context.[69] It is precisely the attention, representation, and mediation of language in Oguibe's work that charges it with power to operate, as Petersen notes, as a sign of 'orientation and identification'.[70] It is the multilingualism of the work that is at the centre of its controversy; demarcating a sense of insiderness and outsiderness, the languages in the work simultaneously draw people in, whilst potentially provoking a sense of alienation in others.

The reception to Oguibe's work also reinforces a central argument posited at the outset of this chapter; namely, that language is a primary barrier for displaced populations, which should be critically assessed in art practices, in art discourses, or in the creative industries. Exploring both mode 2 (language) and mode 3 (institutions) of displacement aesthetics, this chapter has aimed to demonstrate the inextricable links between language, political discourse, and the lived experience of forced displacement in artistic production, as well as the role of institutions in shaping, constituting, and reproducing forms of displacement. The significance of art institutions and their relationship to displacement aesthetics will be taken up at length in the following chapter, which focuses attention on the intersection between artistic labour, participation, authorship, and institutional care.

Notes

1 Liisa H. Malkki, 'Speechless Emissaries: Refugees, Humanitarianism, and Dehistoricization', *Cultural Anthropology*, 11:3 (1996): 386.

2 Linda Alcoff, 'The Problem of Speaking for Others', *Cultural Critique*, 20 (1991): 5–32.

3 Malkki, 'Speechless Emissaries', pp. 377–404; Heather L. Johnson, 'Click to Donate: Visual Images, Constructing Victims, and Imagining the Female Refugee, *Third World Quarterly*, 32 (2011): 1015–1037.

4 Feng Hou and Morton Beiser 'Learning the Language of a New Country: A Ten-year Study of English Acquisition by South-East Asian Refugees in Canada', *International Migration* 44.1 (2006): 135–165; Megan D. Morris et al., 'Healthcare Barriers of Refugees Post-Resettlement', *Journal of Community Health*, 34 (2009): 529–538; Paula G. Watkins, Husna Razee, and Juliet Richters, 'I'm Telling You … The Language Barrier is the Most, the Biggest Challenge': Barriers to Education among Karen Refugee Women in Australia', *Australian Journal of Education*, 56:2 (2012): 126–141.

5 Throughout this book we use the term 'participatory practice' to describe art practice which foregrounds the role of social collaboration as vital to artwork and art-making. Alternatively described as 'social practice' or 'relational aesthetics', these participatory practices move away from an understanding of the artist as sole creator of the work, instead focusing on the social bonds, activities, and communal experiences created through art practice.

6 'Museum Definition', International Council of Museums, 24 August 2022, accessed 8 June 2022. https://icom.museum/en/resources/standards-guidelines/museum-definition/

7 Nuala Morse, *The Museum as Space of Social Care* (Taylor & Francis, 2020); Susanne Boersma, 'Facilitators of Integration? The Potential Role of Museums in Integration as a Two-Way Process', *Museological Review*, 24 (2020): 114–115.

8 Annette Loseke, 'From Transcultural Entanglements to Integrated Learning Experiences? Transcultural Museum Education at Berlin's Museum of Islamic Art', *Journal of Elementary Education*, 15 (2022): 119.

9 Kristina Boreus, *Migrants and Natives – 'Them' and 'Us': Mainstream and Radical Right Political Rhetoric in Europe* (London: Sage, 2020).

10 Michelle Foster, *International Refugee Law and Socio-Economic Rights: Refuge from Deprivation* (Cambridge: Cambridge University Press, 2007), pp. 1–7.

11 Ala Sirriyeh and Simon McMahon, 'The Evolving (Re)Categorisations of Refugees throughout the "Refugee/Migrant Crisis"', *Journal of Community & Applied Social Psychology*, 27:2 (2017): 105–114.

12 Csilla E. Ariese 'Decentering', in Csiila E. Ariese and Magdalena Wroblewska (eds), *Practicing Decoloniality in Museums: A Guide with Global Examples* (Amsterdam: Amsterdam University Press, 2021), pp. 53–54.

13 Sten Pultz Moslund and Anne Ring Petersen, 'Introduction: Towards a Post Migrant Frame of Reading', in Moritz Schramm (ed.), *Reframing Migration, Diversity and the Arts: The Postmigrant Condition* (New York: Routledge, 2019), p. 67.

14 Mirjam Gebaur, 'Postmonolingual Struggles and the Poetry of Uljana Wolf', in Moritz Schramm (ed.), *Reframing Migration, Diversity and the Arts: The Postmigrant Condition* (New York: Routledge, 2019), pp. 170–192.

15 Wendy Ng, Syrus Marcs Ware, and Alyssa Greenberg, 'Activating Diversity and Inclusion: A Blueprint for Museum Educators as Allies and Change Makers', *Journal of Museum Education*, 42:2 (2017): 143.

16 James Clifford, 'Museums as Contact Zones', in James Clifford, *Routes: Travel and Translation in the Late Twentieth Century* (Cambridge, MA, London: Harvard University Press, 1999), pp. 188–219.

17 Eleanor Paynter, 'Border Crises and Migrant Deservingness: How the Refugee/Economic Migrant Binary Racializes Asylum and Affects Migrants' Navigation of Reception', *Journal of Immigrant & Refugee Studies* 20.2 (2022): 293–306.

18 'UNHCR Glossary', *UNHCR*, accessed 20 June 2023. www.unhcr.org/glossary/#a

19 Peter Gatrell, Anindita Ghoshal, Katarzyna Nowak, and Alex Dowdall, 'Reckoning with Refugeedom: Refugee Voices in Modern History', *Social History*, 46:1 (2021): 75.

20 Despina Karamperidou et al., 'Unlocking Learning: The Co-Creation and Effectiveness of a Digital Language Learning Course for Refugees and Migrants in Greece', UNICEF, December 2020, accessed 25 June 2023. www.unicef-irc.org/publications/pdf/AKELIUS.pdf

21 Julietta Singh, *Unthinking Mastery: Dehumanism and Decolonial Entanglements* (Durham, NC: Duke University Press, 2018), p. 69.

22 Jacques Derrida, 'The Principle of Hospitality', *Parallax*, 11:1 (2005): 7.

23 Panayiotis Papadimitriou and Ioannis Papageorgiou, 'The New "Dubliners": Implementation of European Council Regulation 343/2003 (Dublin-II) by the Greek Authorities', *Journal of Refugee Studies*, 18:3 (2005): 301–302.

24 'EMST: Collection Exhibition', *EMST*, accessed 20 June 2023. https://www.emst.gr/en/exhibitions-en/collection-exhibition

25 Joanne Morra, 'Daughter's Tongue: The Intimate Distance of Translation', *Journal of Visual Culture* 6.1 (2007): 91–108; Gabrielle A. Hezekiah, 'Intuition and Excess: Mona Hatoum's Measures of Distance and the Saturated Phenomenon', *Paragraph*, 43:2 (2020): 197–211.

26 www.tate.org.uk/art/artworks/hatoum-measures-of-distance-t07538

27 Chrisoula Lionis, *Laughter in Occupied Palestine: Comedy and Identity in Art and Film* (London: I.B Tauris, 2016), pp. 48–73.

28 Lionis, *Laughter in Occupied Palestine*, pp. 48–73.

29 Chrisoula Lionis, 'A Past Not Yet Passed: Postmemory in the Work of Mona Hatoum', *Social Text*, 32:2 (2014): 77–93.

30 Claudia Spinelli, 'Interview with Mona Hatoum' in G. Brett, M. Archer, C. de Zegher, and P. Manzoni (eds), *Mona Hatoum* (London: Phaidon Press, 1996), p. 140.

31 Mehre Y. Khan, '"Shaking up" Vision: The Video Diary as Personal and Pedagogical Intervention in Mona Hatoum's Measures of Distance', *Intercultural Education*, 18:4 (2007): 325.

32 Nada Shabout, 'Framing the Discipline of Contemporary Art of the Arab World through the Press', in Hamid Keshmirshekan (ed.), *Contemporary Art from the Middle East: Regional Interactions with Global Art* (London: I.B. Tauris, 2015).

33 Anthony Downey, *Dissonant Archives: Contemporary Visual Culture and Contested Narratives in the Middle East* (London: Bloomsbury, 2015).

34 Yasemin Yildiz, *Beyond the Mother Tongue: The Postmonolingual Condition* (New York: Fordham University Press, 2012), p. 10.

35 Mounira al Solh, 'Projects: My Dick in my Dick, Kiss Me Again, After Eight, All Mother Tongues are Difficult and their sisters', *Ibraaz*, 22 January 2015, accessed 20 June 2023. www.ibraaz.org/projects/99/

36 Eva Hesler, 'Mounira Al Solh, *Mother Tongues*', *Asymptote*, accessed 20 June 2023. www.asymptotejournal.com/visual/eva-heisler-mounira-al-solh-mother-tongues/

37 Hesler, 'Mounira Al Solh, *Mother Tongues*'.

38 Yaniv Voller, 'Countering Violence Against Women in Iraqi Kurdistan: State-Building and Transnational Advocacy', *International Journal of Middle Eastern Studies*, 46 (2014): 351.

39 Chris Campanioni, 'The Right to a Dignified Image: The Fashioning and Effacement of the Refugee within the Celebrity System', *Journal of Cinema and Media Studies*, 61:1 (2021): 28.

40 Breitz's work *TLDR* (2017) focuses on a community of sex workers who live and work in Cape Town, South Africa. A three-channel video installation that maps out ideological points of difference between feminist groups, Amnesty International and sex-work abolitionists, *TDLR* focuses on the struggle for sex workers' essential human rights. Featuring intimate documentary interviews, the work directly asks how, why, and whether artists living and working with privilege can meaningfully represent the lives of those belonging to marginalised communities.

41 James Elkins, *The End of Diversity in Art Historical Writing: North Atlantic Art History and Its Alternatives* (Berlin: De Gruyter, 2021).

42 Jacqueline Stevenson and John Willott, 'The Aspiration and Access to Higher Education of Teenage Refugees in the UK', *Compare*, 37:5 (2007): 673.

43 Bharti Patel and Nancy Kelley, *The Social Care Needs of Refugees and Asylum Seekers* (Bristol: Social Care Institute for Excellence, 2006).

44 Anne J. Kershen (ed.), *Language, Labour and Migration* (New York: Taylor & Francis, 2017), p. 1.

45 Linda Morrice, Linda K. Tip, Michael Collyer, and Rupert Brown, '"You Can't have a Good Integration When you don't Have a Good Communication": English-language Learning Among Resettled Refugees in England', *Journal of Refugee Studies*, 34:1 (2021): 683.

46 Stevenson and Willott, 'The Aspiration and Access to Higher Education of Teenage Refugees in the UK', p. 673.

47 Morrice, Tip, Collyer, and Brown, '"You Can't have a Good Integration When you don't Have a Good Communication"', p. 694.

48 Linda Tip, Rupert Brown, Linda Morrice, Michael Collyer, and Matthew J. Easterbrook 'Improving Refugee Well-Being With Better Language Skills and More Intergroup Contact', *Social Psychological and Personality Science*, 10:2 (2019): 144–151.

49 Morrice, Tip, Collyer, and Brown, '"You Can't have a Good Integration When you don't Have a Good Communication"', p. 694.

50 Morrice, Tip, Collyer, Brown, '"You Can't have a Good Integration When you don't Have a Good Communication"', pp. 683–684.

51 Miranda Bryant, 'Calls for more Funding for English Classes for Ukrainian Refugees', *The Guardian* (30 June 2022).

52 Anonymous interview with performing artist, 2021.

53 Anonymous interview with painter, 2021.

54 Anonymous interview with painter, 2021.

55 Anonymous interview with painter, 2021.

56 Alison Strang and Alastair Ager, 'Refugee Integration: Emerging Trends and Remaining Agendas', *Journal of Refugee Studies*, 23:4 (2010): 589–607.

57 Anonymous interview with painter, 2021.

58 David Levine and Alix Rule, International Art English, *Canopy*. www.canopycanopycanopy.com/contents/international_art_english

59 Mostafa Heddaya, 'When Artspeak Masks Oppression', *Hyperallergic*, 6 March 2013, accessed 22 June 2022. https://hyperallergic.com/66348/when-artspeak-masks-oppression/

60 Anonymous interview with spoken word artist, 2021.

61 See Roaa Ali, 'How to Approach Anti-Racist Audience and Community Research' (2023), accessed 23 June 2025. www.culturehive.co.uk/CVIresources/how-to-approach-anti-racist-audience-and-community-research/

62 Jan Blommaert, *Discourse: A Critical Introduction, Key Topics in Sociolinguistics* (Cambridge: Cambridge University Press, 2005) pp. 75, 204.

63 Sylvia Walker, 'What are the Different Kinds of Artists? A Complete Overview', *Contemporary Art Issue* (16 October 2021), accessed 20 June 2023. www.contemporaryar tissue.com/what-are-the-different-types-of-artists/

64 Alex Rotas, 'Is 'Refugee Art' Possible?', *Third Text*, 18:1 (2004): 51–60.

65 Rotas, 'Is 'Refugee Art' Possible?', pp. 51–60.

66 Domenico Sergi, *Museums, Refugees and Communities* (London: Routledge 2021), p. 55.

67 Henry Broome 'Thousands of Art Workers Call for Israel's Exclusion From the Venice Biennale', *Hyperallergic* (26 February 2024), accessed 13 September 2024. https://hyperaller gic.com/873858/4000-art-workers-call-for-israel-exclusion-from-the-venice-biennale/

68 Bonaventure Soh Bejeng Ndikung, 'The Curious Case of Olu Oguibe's Monument for Strangers and Refugees', *Frieze* (22 March 2021), accessed 6 September 2023. www.frieze. com/article/olu-oguibe-monument-strangers-refugees-controversy

69 Anne Ring Petersen, 'The Square, the Monument and the Re-Configurative Power of Art', in Anna Meera Gaonkar et al., (eds), *Postmigration: Art, Culture, and Politics in Contemporary Europe* (Bielefeld: Transcript Verlag, 2021), p. 239.

70 Petersen, 'The Square, the Monument and the Re-Configurative Power of Art', p. 239.

4 Displacement aesthetics and artistic labour: the care of workers

The art world is both an art *and* a labour market. Artists are workers with entrepreneurial and contractor status and are also sometimes employers. The art world is also, fundamentally, a capitalist industry that depends on myriads of art workers whose labour sustains art institutions, agencies, galleries, their products, and their public programmes. The industry owes a duty of care to the people who labour to produce, maintain, interpret, and exhibit art – including artists. This covers the art museums and public art spaces, as well as points of sale (such as commercial galleries), even though regulated or contracted employment does not necessarily fit what all artists do or how they work.

Unfortunately, displaced artists do not fit easily into this system, even when it works well, and it often does not. Displaced people face barriers that other workers don't experience, not just in gaining work – always a hurdle for migrants – but also barriers in simply gaining the right to work because of regulations or the lack thereof. They face extra problems with art institutions and even in collaborations with other artists, with setbacks despite galleries, museums, and other artists wishing to work with them. Displaced artists do not, or are by inattention not allowed to, fit in.

This chapter begins to explain some of the key employment regulations, legal barriers, and so-called normal expectations about both paid and unpaid artistic work that affects displaced people, given their constrained opportunities for work. To understand this cruel aspect of displacement aesthetics, we must remember the second truth about working in the visual arts: for most in the art world, artist labour and expertise are usually not remunerated or rewarded. The exceptions are sales of art and artist fees. Both are one-off payments (the latter are quite small) and neither provides a steady income for the vast majority. Sales of art are, for most artists, negligible or non-existent. Artist fees are paid by art museums or public-funded art spaces to artists when they exhibit. They might be likened to small slices of very pleasant cake handed out a few times, but they are certainly not an artist's bread and butter.

The small stream of these fees dries up as an artist ceases to be emerging and enters the desert of mid-career. Most artists have day jobs as picture-framers, installers, waiters, in supermarkets, or – very rarely because such positions are so few – as tutors or lecturers in art colleges. Their day jobs pay for rent and art materials. The exceptions to this are the celebrated labours of a handful who are remunerated very well. One of the most distinctive and spectacular tropes about contemporary art concerns the work of these very few, the 1 per cent or less of artists, and the idea that artists' work makes them peripatetic, mobile, glamorous, and even postnational figures. Many displaced artists, hindered by legal barriers, precarity, and invisibility, are disqualified from participating in the spectacle but are not permitted to have day jobs until they gain the correct legal status as refugees and residents (as discussed in detail in Chapter 2).

Within the range of the art industry's dealings with its workers, it is tricky to pinpoint work and remuneration that might be properly available to displaced artists, just as it is hard to imagine the broad shape of an art world that might place principled limits on free artistic self-expression when that artistic liberty seems to negatively affect others. This is partly because the art world is a marketplace and partly because unbridled self-expression is so valued. However, ethical protocols such as anonymity and anonymisation are familiar from academia and funded research and there may be situations, for instance where the identity of assistants and participants should be protected in social practice art and in performances, where these are needed. It is also obvious that there may be tensions between artists and their assistants, some of whom may have backgrounds of displacement and exclusion, especially if they are non-artists or are exploited.

It might also be thought that new forms of social practice art and participatory art which take community and conviviality as their themes are exempt from these tensions or have opened pathways for displaced artists. This does not seem to have necessarily been the case, for instance in the abject roles for displaced people in works by major artists such as Christoph Schlingensief or Santiago Sierra. The opposite, however, has equally been true of carefully planned art projects, for example by international knowledge exchange platform, The Silent University (2012–ongoing), who have faced their own obstacles. Finally, and unexpectedly, both artists and critics remain extremely intolerant of incursions by those who are apparently non-artists – amateurs, outsider artists, community members – into public art spaces such as art museums. The mainstream art world is not at all accepting of their presence except for the academics and scholars who speak for them.

This chapter considers how displaced artists collaborate with visual art institutions and the market, pinpointing the issue that artists' labour is almost always unremunerated. On the few occasions where artist fees are paid for exhibiting in publicly funded art spaces, the fees are very low because of the assumption that artists are always aspiring for the trajectory of the entrepreneurial, peripatetic, postnational artist that is so dominant in the art market. By the term 'art market' we refer on the one hand to the primary market of commercial art galleries representing a stable of artists and presenting their latest art in exhibitions of new work, and on the other to the secondary market, where art is re-sold, most obviously at auction by specialist art auction houses. Within the secondary market, artists receive no recompense for the re-sale of their works unless there is legislation that *droit de suite* royalties be passed on to the artist – and in the majority of jurisdictions, including the UK, this is not the case. Artist Union England in the UK and the National Association for the Visual Arts in Australia ask that artistic relationships proceed through clearly defined, contracted agreements but their use is extremely rare. There have been some demands from artists and art worker representatives for more stable remuneration for artists, not as a replacement of the art market but as a supplement to it; however, these voices are small in comparison with the mercantile status quo. There is of course an enthusiastic but delimited discourse in the arts sector around the idea of a Universal Basic Income, one that aligns with concerns in the arts for sustainability and care. This wider call for care is a subject returned to later in this chapter; it implies less reliance upon sales-based remunerations, which are in any case relatively rare in proportion to the wide field of artists. Over decades, many nations, from the Netherlands to France, have tentatively experimented with such schemes for artists, though their limited appeal to laissez-faire economists has meant governments are increasingly reluctant to take such ideas seriously.

In the Global North, cultural and educational institutions have increasingly developed equality, diversity, and inclusion policies and programmes of activity. In the cultural sector such as art museums, there is also a strong discourse around institutional care and hospitality when working with communities. These policies and discourses have also become main tenets of contemporary art institutional practices; however, displaced artists continue to report experiencing barriers when collaborating with art institutions. Many institutions are content to maintain support for the professionalised model of art school graduate programmes which feed into art dealer galleries and publicly funded experimental art spaces. Yet sustained poverty and exclusion challenge the art industry's assumptions about its own generosity, hospitality, and care.

The presence of displaced artists exposes extraordinary tensions within the art industry – in art-making, exhibition-making, biennial-making and for audiences of art, including casual visitors. Displaced artists spark multivalent stresses that were there well before the present, stretching back to the early 1970s and before. This is because pressures inevitably erupt whenever curators or museum directors or artists employing assistants attempt a triple act. This firstly stretches the definition of the contemporary artist so that new groups within society, including displaced people, are selected and anointed as contemporary artists. It secondly claims that definitions of contemporary art are pushed so that genuinely new and innovative art is supposedly exhibited but without care for participants or subjects. Thirdly, this triple act overextends the definition of contemporaneity. Art is bracketed as part of a wider field of cultural evidence defining the contemporary period by including forced displacement and ignoring the long cultural history of refugeedom pre-dating the last couple of decades and also leveraging contemporaneity's stress-points for wider society, including the fear of refugees. We shall look at these one by one but, first, a little background.

Art, labour, and migrancy

Since the late 1960s, contemporary artists have attacked preconceptions about work and artistic labour. Feminist artists, for instance, led discussions about work and its undervaluation. Mierle Laderman Ukeles wrote her Maintenance Art Manifesto in 1969, in which she proposed an exhibition to be titled *Care*.[1] A couple of years later, in a landmark article, Linda Nochlin, then a professor of art history at Vassar, the famous women's liberal arts college, argued that there had been no great women artists because of, first, the prevalent but flawed notion that great art was a result of innate individual artistic genius and, second, the social and institutional factors that oppressed and discouraged 'all those – women among them – who did not have the good fortune to be born White, preferably middle class, and, above all, male'.[2] Her argument, which of course applies to refugees as well, was that the notion of genius failed to take into account the long, privileged periods of study and experimentation that precede the making of great art. Domestic work and care meant that women – and we extend her observation to refugees, and in particular women refugees – did not have the necessary time to devote to art, and that institutional restrictions denied them equal access to art classes (her particular example was the unavailability of the nude model in life-drawing classes to 'lady' students). Her conclusion – and, once more, we might substitute women with refugees – was that 'it was *institutionally* made impossible for women to achieve excellence or success on the same footing as men, *no matter what* the potency of their so-called talent, or genius'.[3] The widely read article was immensely significant in the formation of the women's art movement because it articulated an entirely new perspective based on the recognition of barriers in art that disenfranchised all artists other than White men. In the UK, Silvia Federici, amongst others, was exploring the grassroots women's network, Wages for Housework (founded in 1972), and the gendered violence surrounding domestic and care labour.[4]

In 1977 Ukeles became the first and only artist-in-residence of the Sanitation Department of the City of New York (but unsalaried and unremunerated). During this time she made *Touch Sanitation Performance* (1978–80), which included her *Handshake and Thanking Ritual*, a monumental performance over eleven months of early morning shifts in which Ukeles travelled across New York's five boroughs to personally meet every single sanitation worker, shake their hand and say, 'Thank you for keeping New York City alive'.[5] Slightly later, Suzanne Lacy would use the phrase 'New Genre Public Art' to identify activist art usually made outside art galleries or art museums that brought artists into direct contact with the wider public.[6] Pointing to increased racial discrimination and violence, the attempt to circumscribe the gains women had made during previous decades, the censorship efforts of politicians in league with conservative fundamentalists, and deepening health and ecological crises, Lacy argued that social issues should determine the form of new genre public art and that the general public must be engaged. She often argued that experimental forms of art would bridge the gap between artist and public: 'installations, performances, conceptual art, and mixed-media art, for example, fall into the new genre category, a catchall term for experimentation in both form and content'.[7] Yet, despite the historical radicalism of this practice, feminism was dominated by White western women's perspectives. This point was underscored by African American theorist bell hooks, whose renowned 1984 argument stated that differences created by class and race could not be simply transcended by recognising gender.[8]

Little seemed to change. In the Introduction, we identified the 1993 edition of New York's Whitney Biennial as one of the first activist exhibitions aggressively seeking social justice on behalf of minorities whose long history was grounded in slavery's forced displacement of (Black) peoples. Even before that, there were constant artist protests against the Whitney Biennial's lopsided gender balance; in 1987 the Guerilla Girls, an activist collective, staged a show at the downtown Clocktower gallery, in which they presented the exact numbers and proportions of women and artists of colour in the uptown Whitney Biennial.

All these issues surfaced with even greater force after the end of the Cold War in 1989, as artists explored the expanding outsourcing of work in neo-liberal economies, and as they pointed to the continuing, dramatic undervaluation of artists' work. In their separate examinations of the politics of work and labour in art, most writers bracket postmodernism as a period that ended around 1989, with a new generation of art historians rediscovering the older generation of pioneering activist artists.[9] Almost ten years after their 1987 Clocktower show, the Guerilla Girls presented a new poster, *Traditional Values Return to the Whitney* (1995), a graph depicting a statistical breakdown by gender and race of the artists in the 1991, 1993, and 1995 Biennials that highlighted the fragility of any advances in the art world's gender equity: 60.3 per cent

White males were included in the 1991 exhibition; 36.4 per cent in 1993; then back up to 55.5 per cent in 1995, displacing minorities once again.[10]

Meanwhile, the relation between artistic labour and social inequality was explained at length across multiple fields: in the discourses of social justice, in the decolonisation of museological practices, and in sociologically oriented studies on inequality in art galleries and museums.[11] Labour in art was not a neutral given, to artists or to art historians, and it became a pivotal part of art history's discourses about globalisation in the post-1989 period of expansive capitalism.

A new documentary realism indexed the shift from postmodernism to globalised contemporaneity, highlighting that in both industrial and post-industrial societies labour had become increasingly outsourced, precarious, and poorly paid. Photography-based investigations, in particular, documented postindustrial labour and deindustrialisation, such as: Berndt and Hilla Becher's deliberately repetitive, black-and-white photographic grids of decommissioned German steel mills and cooling towers; Mitch Epstein's colour photographs of power plants; Edward Burtynsky's aerial views of mining operations or monumental figure compositions of itinerant labourers breaking up ships in Bangladesh.

The Los Angeles-based conceptual photographer Allan Sekula's documentary series, *Fish Story* (1989–95), a multi-decade catalogue of the international shipping industry, its routes and oceanic vistas, and its workers' devastation by neo-liberal capitalism, became a touchstone for this approach. The wide turn to realist depictions of labour was based on reviving and adapting documentary forms that were drawn from much earlier photography and cinema. This was clear in Sekula's choice of the photographic essay and the photobook, both familiar genres from their heyday in the 1950s as opposed to the huge, mural-sized colour photographs of artists like Thomas Struth and Andreas Gursky, prominent at the same time. *Fish Story* had little to do with the postmodern tropes of simulacra, textuality, and immateriality that were so integral for Sekula's CalArts, postmodernist colleagues (he taught at the Los Angeles art school from 1985 until his death in 2013). Instead, he constructed an apparently humble, patient realism with a minimum of dramatic rhetoric or human gesture, describing a mosaic of disparate but interconnected production processes. *Fish Story* charted the networks of postindustrial, service-based labour with images of vast, anonymous container ships traversing the world's oceans, and deindustrialised and deserted harbours and shipyards across the Global North. Commentators found that Sekula's small, colour photographs were images of interconnected, geo-economic 'enforced migrancy'.[12]

Fish Story was modified, tweaked, and displayed in multiple iterations (for example, at the 'political' Whitney Biennial in 1993 mentioned above and in the Introduction) before its completion. Finally, it featured prominently (and uncannily, right next to a very dissimilar, highly expressive, vast array of drawings by veteran sculptor Louise Bourgeois) at Okwui Enwezor's groundbreaking *documenta 11* in 2002, one of the exhibitions that we noted placed stories of migration and forced displacement at the heart of contemporaneity.

Fish Story was a precursor of a wider tendency in the early 2000s to create representations of labour that refrained from foregrounding the labourers' identities, by which we mean a refraining from portraiture. Steve McQueen's *Western Deep* (2002), also exhibited at *documenta 11*, depicted migrant miners working deep underground in post-Apartheid South Africa. Although his focus on labour was sharper than Sekula, Epstein, or Burtynsky, McQueen still did not depict his miners as distinct, individually portrayed workers. In his discussion of his idea of the 'migrant image', T.J. Demos explained that even though it consisted of actual footage of miners and their place of labour, deep underground, *Western Deep* was not a documentary about labour conditions.[13] Rather, McQueen was choosing to subvert classic documentary expectations through his elaborate and idiosyncratic video editing, emphasising near-total darkness that was sometimes interrupted by flashing, blinding lights. Instead of reifying identity, Demos argued that *Western Deep*'s depiction of identity was also a reimagination of those identities.[14] Even though the figures of migrant workers were recognisable as such, their faces and bodies were submerged in a play of light and shadow, thereby unsettling recognition by means similar to the sixteenth-century artist of chiaroscuro painting, Caravaggio, whose deliberate erasure of the contours of his subjects' bodies and faces, as briefly noted in the Introduction, has been recently observed by theorists.

According to Demos, McQueen was refusing to delimit and overdetermine identity by blurring the contours that might otherwise contain a migrant worker's body. Demos, in turn, owed much to theorists like Giorgio Agamben with his concept of 'bare life'. For Agamben, bare life was existence stripped of political rights, left at the mercy of the law, severed from residence and national citizenship.[15] The places that host this condition are what Agamben called 'spaces of exception': gulags, places of incarceration, and, for the miners in *Western Deep*, migrant labour camps.[16] Demos endorsed Agamben's aspiration for a thoroughly reimagined future of rights based on residence rather than citizenship, pointing to a future where the boundary between citizens and displaced people might be dissolved.[17] For Agamben this must be a matter of empathy rather than just compassion; however, he did not reveal how equality for those outside national citizenship could be achieved, institutionally, politically, or administratively.

Empathising with the lived experience of forced displacement under capitalism, and imagining a paradigm of enforced migrancy, does not solve the obduracy of distinct disadvantage where there is a need not only for rights, but also for a situation wherein the collective and democratic mechanisms guaranteeing these rights would be transnationally accountable. As was made clear in the Introduction, such discussions in critical theory are intended to explain how the figures of migrants and refugees can create new visions of postnational and cosmopolitan existence, but this gap in Agamben's thinking was displacement aesthetics second mode in action, just as calling for justice is performative when it is oblivious to the unyielding, structural barriers that constituted the lived experience of forced displacement. The many barriers demarcating displacement from migrancy require continual acknowledgement. *Fish Story* and *Western Deep* documented labour's migrancy amidst both de-industrialisation in the Global North and extractive industries across the Global South, but the conditions of labour that displaced people experience exceeded these depictions of migrancy, both politically and aesthetically. Emphasising their exclusion and need neither ignored migrant labour's heterogeneity and suffering, nor claimed a unified, single cultural identity for displaced people.

Imagining this paradigm of enforced migrancy goes hand in hand with the trope of artists and curators constantly travelling and talking to each other around the world. We have already noted, as have many critics, that the international experiences of itinerancy and movement available to the very few artists and curators with international careers were conflated into the experience of migrants and displaced people, whose mobility was restricted.

Referring to the often-observed proliferation and expansion of art biennials in the global period, many writers, including Angela Dimitrakaki, postulated a cosmopolitan, 'art-world citizenship' that encompassed artists, curators, art dealers, critics, and theorists.[18] This cosmopolitanism often meant that curators, museums, or arts agencies commissioned artists to travel and then produce art about their experiences within often complex social and political situations, which the artists had little prior knowledge of or, sometimes, commitment to. The clearest, though very different, instances of this were artist residencies and war artist commissions, which are art projects made in war and peacekeeping zones. There is considerable literature about both, agonising over the ethics of transcultural representation and about representation without participation, proposing instead that there should be collaboration, diplomacy, and community usefulness built into the design of such commissions.[19] Beyond such very rarely available and privileged projects, obtained by only a few, Dimitrakaki also suggested that globalisation had made travel an indispensable part of artistic work despite (and even because of) the persisting restrictions and financial obstacles that travel involves. Her argument was that women artists were now appropriating this 'will to travel' instilled by late capitalism, recasting the *gendered* experience of travel, which had long been a predominantly male domain.[20] One of Dimitrakaki's examples was the collaborative three-artist research project,

Transcultural Geographies (2003–2004), which investigated the shifting geography of the Balkans, Türkiye, and the Caucasus after 1991.[21] The artists led participatory 'work sessions' attended mainly by women, out of which they developed their documentary films and video installations.

A couple of years earlier, *documenta 11* had presented the example of roving workshops, touching down at different locations. Director Okwui Enwezor had convened five connected forums, or 'Platforms' as he called them, in different locations worldwide. He dispersed curatorial responsibility for *documenta 11* between himself and his close-knit group of six co-curators, Carlos Basualdo, Ute Meta Bauer, Susanne Ghez, Sarat Maharaj, Mark Nash, and Octavio Zaya and then consulted even further with local experts and artists at each workshop ahead of the exhibition at Kassel in 2002. A decade or more later, Anne Ring Petersen would once again recapitulate the identification of migrant workers with artists who move countries to establish studios in their chosen cities, like Berlin, or whose families sent them to elite art school graduate programmes in the US, like Yale.[22] Her idea of artist migrant workers included those privileged few able to take advantage of the economic and institutional reality – the star system – of the global art system. These rare 'migrant workers' were in fact very privileged players, almost but not always from well-off or highly educated families whose relative wealth or family networks, even if hard won, distinguished them from refugees fleeing persecution and living in camps. Identifying the celebration of a very few, fortunate, cosmopolitan escapees with the incarceration embedded in most refugees' experiences of displacement, imagining a pathway from the latter to the former, was of a kind with the frivolous utopian world that Demos had skeptically reviewed.

Unrecognised labour and the right to work

Alongside restrictions on their ability to travel, asylum seekers across the European Union (EU) the UK, and the US face legal limits on their ability to work. At the time of writing, in the UK the Immigration, Asylum and Nationality Act (1996) has continued to circumscribe asylum seekers' right to work, and has been criticised for being more restrictive than in other European countries.[23] In the period after the UK left the EU, its post-Brexit immigration policies welcomed immigrants with recognised formal qualifications for high-skilled jobs, discouraging everyone else.[24] At the same time, the UK retained long processing times for asylum seeker applications – twelve months or more, instead of the six months or less which was standard in Europe. In Sweden, by contrast, asylum applicants were immediately allowed to work as long as they had proof of identity. That also created many intractable problems, however, for the system to obtain that proof – often lost and irreplaceable, or unclear and confusing. All these policies remained in place despite employers pointing out that lifting restrictions on work would benefit the wider economy of Europe where aging populations and low birth rates have meant that immigration is indispensable, not just for economic growth but also to fill vacancies in the burgeoning, low-paid service sector.

Work restrictions posed significant challenges for artists from backgrounds of forced displacement because they were compelled to remain dependent on the minimal support granted by the state and to spend 'unfull time' coping with bureaucratic barriers, remaining unable to study and unable to begin or re-establish careers in a new place. Artists often found themselves, at best, undertaking voluntary work or precarious, often illegal and undocumented labour. Sometimes, charitable organisations supported community arts projects that displaced artists could enter as volunteers and exit as paid employees. Community arts organisations have often provided welcome professional development opportunities for displaced artists. For instance, when the digital artist interviewed at length in Chapter 2 entered the UK as an asylum seeker, aged twenty-one, she was a graduate with a theatre director degree in Shiraz. She participated in a women's theatre programme organised by Community Arts North West (CAN) for the project called *Rule 35* (2015), in which displaced women re-enact their detention experiences. Once she gained refugee status, she also won artist residencies and, eventually, paid work with CAN which led to artist collaborations in Manchester and the Netherlands. Voluntary participation was beneficial for her, as it introduced her to key figures and mentors in the arts scene in Manchester. The issue of degrees of participation and free labour remains a thorny one across the cultural sector, which often relies on interns and volunteers. Once someone gains refugee status, they are often still bound to the voluntarism from which their main networks derive. One performing artist was granted refugee status, which meant she was able to be employed, but she still felt a powerful obligation to keep teaching music classes voluntarily:

> I am not paid and often I play my music in places like churches. And after, you sometimes have children or parents who come and see you because they're interested. They come and see you, because music is something that you share with other people. And when you have people approaching you, sometimes it is people with no finances and they don't have money, and some who do have money and they'll give you something. But if they don't have money, I can't force them to pay or say you need to pay me.[25]

On the one hand, creative work in the popular imagination and usually in cold reality, is simply a labour of love, undertaken without financial reward, but on the other, artistic work, like domestic labour, involves substantial emotional skill and creative intelligence, and is unpaid, precarious, and highly informal precisely because it is not recognised as work and because it is substantially carried out by women.

This was an issue that feminist artists and writers took up early on, pinpointing the gender gap between undervalued domestic work and art world success. While art history has gradually addressed these conditions in relation to feminist art, it has hardly been concerned with art made by displaced people. Unrecognised or invisible, gendered labour is, in fact, a large part of most displaced artists' experiences. Brickell and Speer postulated the 'unique labour' of 'managing displacement'.[26] According to them, this involved coping with precarious housing, terrible living conditions, planning for further forced relocations, managing everyone's loss of home, and recreating a more familiar environment. Even though further displacement is always possible, it is wrong to imagine that the involuntary stasis, hemming refugees in and preventing travel, even when it is offered and paid for, is temporary. It can go on for years.

Thus, with very few rights and little leverage, migrant workers and refugees self-organise. The Voice of Domestic Workers (VODW, established in 2009 but known as Justice for Domestic Workers up to 2017) has collaborated with artists and arts institutions, campaigning for the rights of migrant domestic workers in the UK.[27] Since 2016, the workers have been allowed to change employers within this six-month period, although their visa still expires at the end of it. The workers in VODW usually live with their employers and families in private households and are allowed to remain on a special visa for a fixed duration. In 2012, dependence on employers was increased, as a maximum duration of six months was imposed on the visa, and workers could no longer change employers in this period. Since 2016, workers can change employers, although the visa still expires after six months, and options to renew are only allowed to those officially identified as trafficked.[28] As VODW's membership expanded, quadrupling between 2010 and 2017, so too did its collaborations with arts organisations. These included the artist-run gallery Cubitt Artists, not-for-profit Showroom in London, and the People's History Museum in Manchester. VODW hosted creative workshops where biographies were shared with filmmakers and artists. VODW's work is a testament to the close interdependence between self-organised campaigning, collective deliberation on self-identification, and creative practice fostered by artistic sectors.

This was echoed at the 2003 London exhibition, *Leave to Remain*, curated by a former Bosnian asylum seeker, the artist Margareta Kern, who foregrounded the labels 'refugee' and 'asylum seeker' in the exhibition.[29] Displaced people who wish to become professional artists do not usually have access to the formal training that would equip them to decode the working processes of galleries and curators, which is to say to effectively and publicly identify themselves as working artists. This is also true for displaced artists who had significant careers in their home countries and for whom re-establishing themselves, when their training and professional experience is ignored, is just as hard. For example, almost all prominent commercial art galleries across the world have a strict policy of binning unsolicited artist submissions. State art museums use pre-prepared, pro forma letters thanking applicants but politely declining further meetings, or else they agree to meet while evading everything except the vaguest smiles. After a gallery declined to show her art, refusing her submission without clarification or feedback, one of the artists (a painter) was unsure whether her background of displacement was the cause of her knockback: 'They ask you a lot of questions about where you are from, how long you have been here. Maybe they need someone more famous or someone who knows more about the culture here'.[30]

It may not have been the problem at all, and she may even have excited some interest, but she would never know because no-one was mentoring her, and no-one told her exactly what they thought. For an artist with language barriers, unfamiliar with curators' and gallerists' expectations and covert behaviours, outsider status is reinforced; the art world proceeds slowly and cautiously, not by open submissions but by relationships and networks based on mutually reinforcing group approval. Labour relations are inscribed onto the art world's professional processes, which are marked by asymmetries and hierarchies cemented with shared training, sifting and culling of artists, and shared travel to biennials and peers' exhibitions. It is a cosy but ever shifting world, one in which anyone is allowed to produce art if they have the means, but hardly anyone gains recognition, and whatever acclaim may occasionally be gained evaporates over time. Verónica Tello identifies collaboration, defined in an unusually wide sense as a collective form of time-sharing (her word is 'co-presence'), as the key to situating contemporary art's 'international division of labour'.[31] Both symbolic and economic processes are integral in this economy, creating varying degrees of legitimisation that are both not immediately obvious and are often inconsistent.

Recognising displaced artists' labour

All artistic collaboration involves a division of labour.[32] Sometimes, but not always, collaboration means shared authorship. At other times, the word collaboration is stretched to its limit to include studio assistants, contractors, or fabricators as collaborators, but they have jobs delegated by the artist-in-charge and are usually paid for their labour in the production and display of artworks; in short, they are participants not co-authors.[33] Then, there are performances and so-called social practice art, in which communities, non-artists, assistants, and other artists may participate in a maze of convivial relationships which can be indexed by archives that the artists place on display; these archival records may include video installations and performances. This art hinges upon the active participation of the audience with the performers.[34] Participatory art involves collaboration and collective experience, not just blurring the boundaries between artist and spectator but also breaking the third wall between audience and performance, described in the Introduction.

Breaking the third wall relocates displacement aesthetics from invisibility into plain view. Often but not necessarily, everyone involved is credited, though the initiating artist is given headline status. In some notable works of art, established artists have worked with displaced people who were assistants and not credited as co-authors. There is an emerging literature about this. Zhe Jiang and Marek Korczynski have discussed VODW's labour-organising tool kit, within which creative practices are particularly grounded in collective storytelling.[35] In other words, VODW's programme resembled the forms and methods of community art created by activist organisers, artists, and non-artists, usually but not always outside the purview of the professional art world (though many art museums created discrete spaces for community art projects) from the 1970s onwards across Europe, the UK, North America, and Australia. Did the art world learn the lessons of many decades of community art practice? Has there been a shift in how professional artists collaborated with displaced people since Margareta Kern's *Leave to Remain* in 2003 and VODW's workshops, but also in light of more confrontational instances?

In 2000, the famous German theatre director and artist Christoph Schlingensief, who died in 2010, created an immensely provocative work, *Please Love Austria – First Austrian Coalition Week*, for the Vienna International Festival.[36] He commissioned twelve asylum seekers living in a detention centre on the outskirts of Vienna to live for a week in a shipping container that he placed beside the city's Opera House. On top of the container, a large banner spelt out the slogan 'Auslander Raus' ('Foreigners Out') (Figure 4.1).

Simulating *Big Brother*, the online television station, webfreetv.com, broadcast CCTV putatively from inside the container. The participants' faces were covered or disguised, hinting at the legal restrictions around identification that conditioned the work. Audiences were invited to vote each day to deport the least favourite asylum seeker. The winner would be given a cash prize and Austrian citizenship through marriage to a willing Austrian volunteer. There was a winner, losers were evicted from the container, but their deportation was part of the fiction of Schlingensief's reality show. Even then, the winner would have merely been on a path to full Austrian citizenship, but at least *Please Love Austria* preceded the Alien Law Act (2005, implemented January 2006) which closed off such marriages of convenience.[37]

Schlingensief was enacting the xenophobic rhetoric of the newly elected government, a coalition that included far-right politician Jorg Haider's People's Freedom Party. The artist had long simulated television reality shows in his work, and his intentions were the opposite of condoning the Austrian Right, but this was lost on furious, righteous Left-wing demonstrators who stormed the container. Celebrated after the

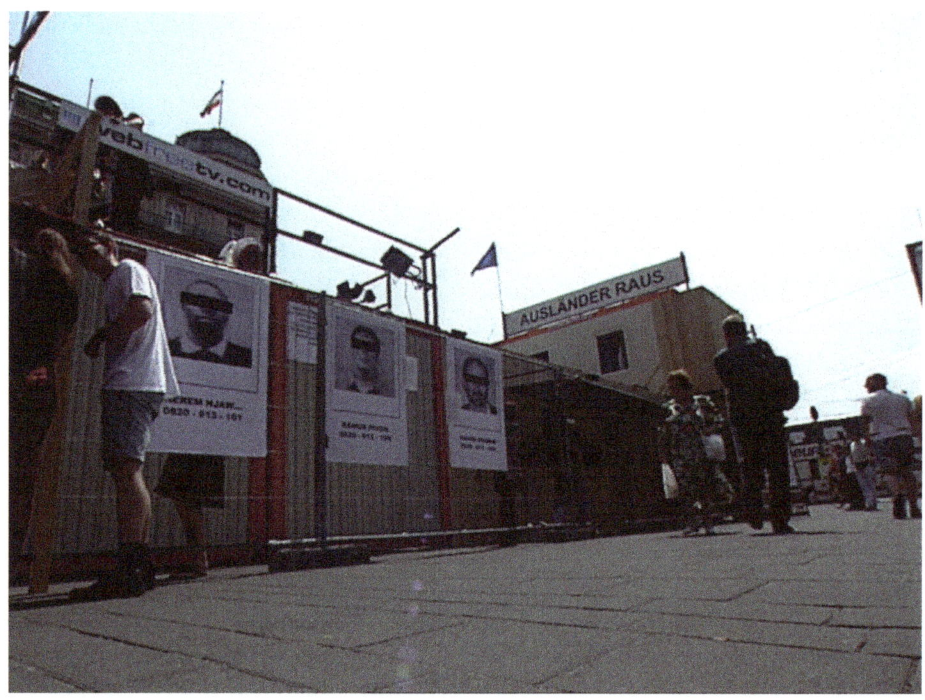

4.1 Christoph Schlingensief, *Please Love Austria* (2000). Video still from Paul Poet's film *Ausländer Raus!* (2002). Courtesy of Filmgalerie 451.

event, in Paul Poet's documentary, *Auslander Raus! Schlingensief's Container* (2002), the actual event polarised public discourse and elicited the kind of lunatic audience reactions that Schlingensief anticipated. While the right was delighted to corroborate the hate speech, blissfully oblivious to all irony, Leftists tried to free the participants and were angry at the artist's provocation. Claire Bishop argued that Schlingensief's artistic representation of detention managed to steer public attention toward asylum seeking to a degree that the state deportation centre, a few kilometres away, never did. Astutely, she also observed the reverse point, that participation in art does not have an intrinsic relationship to social or political participation; in other words, these are qualitatively different realms.[38]

Schlingensief did not task public art with usefully resolving political participation, and his work should not have been mistaken for direct democracy in action, still less was it meant to be the successor to Joseph Beuys' direct democracy activism during the 1970s. Instead Schlingensief drew great attention to the demonisation of asylum seekers by demonising asylum seekers himself. He was caricaturing both popular media and mainstream politics and was eager to antagonise his audiences. *Please Love Austria* should not have been evaluated based on its usefulness, its proposal of solutions, or its lack of care for audiences and participants. Indeed, lack of care was only partly true of Schlingensief's methods, for he sustained a deeply loyal troupe of assistants in his project. Moreover, *Please Love Austria* was not a collaboration with asylum seekers, nor with the detention centre, though it was realised with their assistance and participation. It was, instead, an intensely accurate embodiment of the contradictions of de-sublimated violence; in other words, it was an obvious instance of the dangerous triple act that we described at the start of this chapter. In this instance of participatory art, the participants may have been recompensed but they were put at risk. Their employment was short-term and they had little or no creative input.

The same year, Spanish artist Santiago Sierra, whose equally provocative art also featured abject labour within the context of late capitalism, presented *Workers Who Cannot Be Paid, Remunerated to Remain Inside Cardboard Boxes* (2000) in the main hall of the KW Institute for Contemporary Art at Berlin as part of an exhibition surveying his work.[39] He hired and paid six asylum seekers under the shadow of deportation and living in a local asylum seekers' housing facility to sit in cardboard boxes for four hours each day for the six-week duration of the show. Sierra declared that their financial remuneration must be secret because German law forbade paid work for asylum seekers, thus penalising them with potential deportation, so he and KW could not be open about payments. The participants were Chechen refugees who willingly volunteered for the work. Visitors were made aware of their presence in the installation before entering the show. The workers were only partially visible through small holes on the boxes and could be clearly heard when they coughed. *Workers Who Cannot Be Paid* was first staged in Guatemala City (1999) and then New York (2000), where Sierra employed migrants and undocumented workers. Unlike in Berlin, payments could be legally made to those participants.

Workers Who Cannot Be Paid was simply and brutally direct about the labour conditions and laws that shaped it; these cruel restrictions were the central focus of the work. Sierra's choreography had the asylum seekers – the performers – sit still in boxes while visitors, aware of the workers' presence, moved freely but self-consciously around the gallery space. This had multiple consequences. For example, Friederike Sigler argued that the workers' restricted physical movement, contrasted with the visitors' freedom to roam, was the intersection of a hierarchy of gazes between the visitors (the self-aware subjects) and the hidden workers (the hidden objects of the gaze).[40] Thus, the invisible participant-workers were objectified and their labour was reduced to something similar to Agamben's concept of bare life, though Sigler signalled that it was Judith Butler's definition of precariousness as a bodily state of interdependency and vulnerability that informed the work.[41] The intentional invisibility of Sierra's asylum seekers meant it was only by induction that the visitor knew they were present, and their precariousness was dependent on a potentially exploitative but certainly dependent labour contract. Sierra's delegation of labour to his participants highlighted the contradiction between the precarious labour of working people (and especially that of undocumented workers) versus the artistic labour (Sierra's) of a successful, globetrotting, freelancing art star.[42] On the one hand, *Workers Who Cannot be Paid* embodied the inequalities within artistic participation that reflected the more general conditions of labour versus capital. Even the artist's reparative gesture of remuneration entailed legal risk for his workers. On the other hand, Sierra's work deliberately replicated exploitative labour conditions even as it critiqued them, but this was a provocation, and the desire for provocation was consistent across all his art. In this instance of participatory art, the participants were recompensed and put directly at risk, but they could not exercise any creative labour of their own. Their employment was short term and payment covert, and there was no consultation with the participants as to their representation.

Foregrounding the division of labour between participants and the artist employer, *Workers Who Cannot be Paid* was indeed substantially different to *Please Love Austria*, but neither work allowed the workers much agency, which is to say that neither work was useful to the participants beyond its duration and payment. Both performances were scripted by the artist and in both, the workers were invisible, except that in *Please Love Austria* they were potentially humiliated. It is almost too obvious to point out, but in contrast with VODW's migrant-led work and consultations with artists, there was no self-identification built into either artist's division of labour.

To sum up, both performances were deliberately designed to spectacularly deprive their participants of a voice and, as a result, only the artists were credited with making a point in favour of the participants. In the period after 2000, as we shall see, artists would begin to experiment with greater recognition for their employees, inventing more aleatoric choreography and handing over greater authority to their participants with successful results. The question now is, of course, whether *Please Love Austria* or *Workers Who Cannot Be Paid* enabled genuine catharsis and for whom, and whether events since 2015, the year that Europe's so-called refugee crisis really erupted, have altered our assessment of the artists' approaches. If staged now, would their reception be even more inflamed?

First, it is doubtful that *Please Love Austria*'s sheer shock value would have remained as potent, given the social licence by populist politicians to demonise displaced peoples. This was enabled by sensational and saturated media coverage of border-crossings and refugee encampments so that openly xenophobic border and asylum seeker policies have desensitised audiences. Commenting on *Please Love Austria*, T.J. Demos noted that Schlingensief was encouraging Austrian audiences to 'get in touch with their "inner Nazi"', but it is doubtful that they need that licence from an artist anymore.[43] Schlingensief's acidic mimicry of talk shows and of the far-Right has been diminished by the excesses of real reality, just as one might wish to be more cautious now because the stakes of offending have become so artistically, publicly, and institutionally high.

This brings us to the second point: there would now be more intense blowback against both *Please Love Austria* and *Workers Who Cannot Be Paid* from the art world, which would no doubt refuse the high stakes of shattering the third wall between public and artist if there is not sufficient care for the disadvantaged people represented in, or participating in a work of art. There have been many proofs of this heightened sensitivity to representation. In 2021, Santiago Sierra's commission for the Hobart-based, mid-winter Dark Mofo Festival was abruptly cancelled. Dark Mofo, a festival founded by the irascible art collector David Walsh, also the founder of the Museum of Old and New Art (MoNA), announced that Sierra would create a new work, *Union Flag* by calling for donations of blood by 'First Nations peoples from countries claimed by the British Empire at some point in history'. The intention was to soak a Union Jack flag, the flag of Tasmania's eighteenth-century coloniser, Great Britain, in Indigenous blood.[44] The backlash was instant and furious. Sierra was accused of mining and reproducing Indigenous trauma. Aboriginal artist and activist Jamie Graham Blair (a Trawlwulwuy and Plangermaireener man) wrote in an Instagram post, 'Indigenous bodies are not tools to be used by colonisers. We are not props for your White guilt art'. Sierra had proposed representation and participation without collaboration and consultation, and the response was clear: nothing about us without us.

Dark Mofo's defence was to appeal to the idea that free artistic self-expression, no matter the offence it caused, is 'a fundamental human right, and we support artists to make and present work regardless of their nationality or cultural background'.[45] But Walsh's own curators at MoNA wrote an open letter to him decrying the commission as completely tone-deaf and opining that it would damage patronage of his own institution. Within a day, the commission was abandoned. In this instance of participatory art, the participants were to be volunteers and not personally put at risk, but they would not exercise any creative labour of their own, their pro bono employment would be very short term, and they were to be put in a situation that they, as it turned out, found deeply offensive. Indigenous peoples are survivors of genocide, which was systemic across Australia, and they live with ongoing incarcerations and deaths in police custody. Without consultation with the participants as to their representation, Sierra's work would have been little more than a spectacle of trauma and an appropriation of Indigenous culture.

Participatory artists in the decades after 2000 became increasingly sensitive to the issues of collaboration and to who would be allowed to initiate ideas for artworks. The Silent University (SU) was started in 2012 by Kurdish artist Ahmet Öğüt, born in

Türkiye but then based in Amsterdam and Berlin. SU had been inspired by the Society to Encourage Studies at Home, a Boston women's network founded in 1878 by Anna Eliot Ticknor for learning transmitted through the mail service, a 'silent' method that defined both the Society and SU, and which developed into a platform for exchanging knowledge among refugees. The 'faculty' (the professors) were asylum seekers deprived of the right to work, and whose formal qualifications and expertise were not recognised in their new host countries. Silence was SU's claim for a quiet pedagogical network, circumventing linguistic and disciplinary barriers and producing lectures, discussions, publications, and archival research. Course teaching was open to anyone who wished to share their professional and academic knowledge, and their lived experience of displacement (Figure 4.2). SU quickly became legendary, collaborating with prestigious art institutions, starting with a one-year residency for Öğüt at Tate Modern with the Delfina Foundation, branching out into long-term partnership with the Showroom in London, Tensta Konsthall and ABF Stockholm in Sweden, and Stadtkurator in Hamburg.

SU was challenging one of the pathologies of displacement aesthetics, that institutions and art projects sometimes welcome marginal groups like asylum seekers but almost always in one-sided, short-term relationships and with little input into decisions, as part of an ever-changing exhibition or public programme roster.

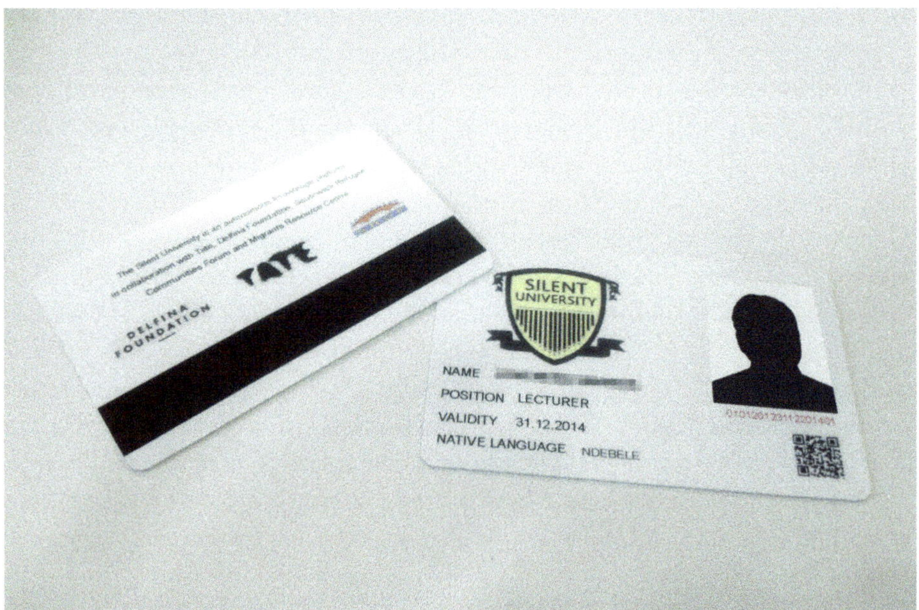

4.2 Ahmet Öğüt, *The Silent University* [Silent University Identification Cards] (2012–ongoing). Courtesy of the artist.

SU remunerated its participants where possible, but unlike either *Workers Who Cannot Be Paid* or *Please Love Austria*, it sought more enduring relationships, as seen in Öğüt's self-identification as SU's initiator and not its owner.[46] Nonetheless, Verónica Tello has suggested that the Silent University could have gone further in subverting sole authorship, given Öğüt's prominence in its public activities, in interviews, and social media.[47] The Silent University was intensely aware, however, of its dependence on the image of its founder, and for good reason – its members sometimes faced problems if they were identified, so this dictated anonymity and covering of faces to protect people in their undocumented status, appeals processes, difficulties with travel, or opening of bank accounts. It was therefore useful to SU to push one person forward in order to preserve the anonymity of others.[48] Over time, as the legal status of SU's faculty became less precarious, others took on more public roles, and SU was sensitive to crediting asylum seekers by name wherever it could but protecting their anonymity whenever necessary.

It has always been difficult for art museums and the art market to let go of its desire to foreground one person over a group. Since the 1970s, married artist collaborations like Christo and Jeanne-Claude or Ed and Nancy Keinholz, or family collaborations like the Boyle Family instead of Mark Boyle, found it difficult to exhibit their art unless one of them – always the man – was credited as the artist. This situation has persisted. As noted above, displaced people in participatory art projects sometimes preferred to remain anonymous for a variety of reasons, and pseudonyms are a way of featuring participants without compromising them. One instance is Nana Varveropoulou's *No Man's Land* (2012–14), in which she conducted photography workshops with displaced detainees over two years, exploring their indefinite detention at Colnbrook Immigration Removal Centre near London's Heathrow Airport. Varveropoulou was granted permission to access the centre to conduct photography workshops for the detainees. She included their photographs in *No Man's Land*, and some were credited by pseudonyms or aliases to protect their identity, especially as they were incarcerated, vulnerable, and waiting to be deported. For a curator, librarian, or archivist, the question of who to credit as the photograph's maker remains pertinent, but pseudonyms are sometimes preferable to anonymity and an archivist's problems remain of secondary concern.

The dividing line between sharing authorship and reproducing inequitable hierarchies by not crediting co-authors is not always obvious. Close attention to labour, expertise, and responsibility is required without the impulse to rush well-meant but uninformed criticism. A participant is not always a collaborator, as we have seen. This complexity was always part of Italian conceptualist artist Alighiero Boetti's embroideries, which the artist designed, and which Afghan women executed with their distinctive skill. From 1971 until his death in 1994, Boetti commissioned teams of women to embroider large cloth maps (the Mappe), shapes and patterns juxtaposed together (the Tutto), or collections of phrases that he designed and over which he happily encouraged and accepted the women's inventions and deviations from instructions. In the 1970s he spent considerable portions of each year in Kabul; one of the present book's co-authors even encountered him back then on Kabul's famous Chicken Street. This labour was abruptly interrupted by the Soviet invasion of Afghanistan on 24 December 1979, and the terrible wars that expelled the Russians only in 1989 with millions of refugees fleeing the country into Pakistan and Iran.

Once Boetti re-established contact with the women embroiderers, he continued to employ them, by necessity through male middlemen, at their camps in Peshawar. Though he never visited them in person again, he did travel to Pakistan and Afghanistan, including to highly dangerous conflict zones. At all times, contact with the displaced women was mediated through two trusted contacts, Peshawar woven rug dealers Shawalil and Jalil, who distributed the cloth, carefully designed and marked out by Boetti and ready for embroidering, to the women's male relatives, brothers, and husbands, so they could pass the works on to the women embroiderers, in what was an intensely regulated, traditional, and patriarchal culture. Everyone carefully checked the finished embroideries for defects and quality. Over a considerable period of time, Boetti was paying many women and their families more than average wages and, in the desperately poor Peshawar refugee camps, the embroideries were consistent, steady, dependable work, of which they were proud.

Boetti has recently been criticised for not crediting the displaced embroiderers by name as his collaborators.[49] It might instead be asserted that, although the women were not named and credited (a common denunciation where studio assistants or fabricators make very substantial aesthetic decisions), the real issues revolve around both positionality and intention. Boetti was not representing or depicting either refugeedom or displacement, nor was he speaking on behalf of his displaced employees. Rather, he was an employer using female refugees from an intensely patriarchal culture as labour to make his art; he did consciously and eagerly seek the women's modifications and elaborations. It is also important to remember that the embroideries did not incorporate any Afghan motifs or iconography. They are radically different to the new tradition of War Rugs that appeared after the Russian invasion, in which weavers introduced contemporary iconography that included tanks, rockets, and helicopters. In his detailed account of Boetti's connection with Afghanistan and then with the refugees after the Russian invasion (1979), Tate Modern curator Mark Godfrey turned to postcolonial theory to understand the fraught and blurry difference between Edward Said's concept of Orientalism, his indictment of western representations of the so-called Middle East, and early twentieth-century ethnographer Victor Segalen's concept of Exoticism – identification with a culture that one is not born into. This was an idea expressed by postmodern philosopher Paul Ricoeur, who wrote extensively on seeing oneself as another.[50] Segalen wrote about the evil effects of colonisation and European culture upon colonised populations. Drawing on Segalen, postcolonial poet Edouard Glissant, a Martinique philosopher, argued that 'encountering the Other super-activates poetic imagination and understanding … . The first edict of a real poetics of Relation'.[51] Seeing oneself as another, however, certainly requires an understanding of decolonisation and positionality.

In this instance of participatory art, the participants were recompensed and were not put at risk. They observed the severely patriarchal family structures of their society which contributed to their anonymisation, and they exercised considerable creativity in return for regular pay stretching over many years. The women were not individually credited by name, but they were also not represented in the works of art themselves, which did not appropriate Afghan motifs and are not identifiably orientalist in nature. Further, the women's creative labour was prominent and became internationally celebrated, and a book on their work was published.[52]

Boetti's model of workshop invention, dispersing execution of the art to participants whilst encouraging their aleatoric reinvention of his designs, was repeated decades later in Olafur Eliasson's workshop, *Green Light* (2016), commissioned by the Thyssen-Bornemisza Foundation for the 2017 Venice Biennale.[53] *Green Light* was a busy, open workshop, staffed by displaced people making lamps designed by Eliasson and visited by scores of biennale visitors throughout opening hours. Unlike Boetti, however, *Green Light* centralises the performativity of the physical labour of displaced bodies, encountered also in artworks such as *Please Love Austria* and *Workers Who Cannot Be Paid*. This returns us to Edward Said's observation from the Introduction, that nineteenth- and twentieth-century western culture was largely the work of exiles, emigrés, and refugees. We are no closer to a guidebook for participatory art except for the loose rule that seems to have evolved over time: artistic self-expression should not harm those that it represents, and participatory art should not harm but rather benefit its participants. While Grant Kester is right to argue that participatory artworks such as Sierra's are 'speculative' and 'quasi-philosophical', they are nevertheless underscored by real labour conditions which often fly under the radar in the art world.[54] Participatory art from the 2010s onwards increasingly shifted from critiquing the hostile treatment of refugees through performances of harm to actual reparation instead, in the form of direct social work to aid communities, which in turn endorses more reparative aesthetics. Conscious of the distinct labour challenges that artists with backgrounds of displacement face, it has sought to set both a visual and an actual example of participation as collaboration.

Caring for workers

The various forms of participation described above often take place in art museums working with curators. In this context, short-term connections are built which do not allow curators to support displaced artists in negotiating a future career path. While this is not the job that most art museums set out to fulfil, it is precisely the job that most commercial art galleries representing artists do offer. One exception might be that of Arte Útil ('useful art'), in which curating seeks to deepen art's connections with neglected communities. This was a prominent part of Manchester Art Gallery and the Whitworth Art Gallery's ethos in the late 2010s and early 2020s. Arte Útil places social connection above other museum tasks such as collecting and conserving heritage and works of art. Instead, arts agencies and non-governmental organisations (NGOs) usually aim to fulfil those useful roles.

While inclusion in training programmes is welcome, some global majority artists are wary of the box-ticking exercise for diversity initiatives, which, in turn, can create 'forever participants' rather than advance a career path in the industry. Entering short-term programmes is often highly competitive and intense but, after finishing, it is difficult to translate the insights into meaningful and lasting networks or connections. A digital artist we interviewed discussed the experience of being a statistic for others to use, to congratulate themselves with, and she gained little confidence from the project.[55] And a displaced painter felt that galleries were interested in their work when they needed 'another event', such as Refugee Week, but they did not establish ongoing relationships or attempt to place her outside of the category they defined for her. The artist felt that to break from the loop of her participation in temporary events, and to enter the art world marketplace, she would need to 'run' and 'hustle' within a milieu that she already knew was highly sensitive to her gaps, as she identified them, which were her 'linguistic and social communication'.[56] Even when strategies are put in place in contemporary art (which is to say art's wide marketplace of ideas and artworks), artists find their available options limited. Far more constricted than elite art school graduates, they might feel pressured to perform their refugee background so as to not miss out on opportunities that might partly compensate for a lack of networks.

Attempts at inclusion through curated exhibitions or short-term public programmes are a necessary part of the museum's palette of activities. However, they cannot have the same impact of longer-term collaborations. Also, with limited and stretched resources, it is difficult for museums to offer generous, ongoing mentoring for the kind of careers that displaced artists seek, and which dedicated arts agencies wish they could provide. Museums may overestimate the unquantifiable soft benefits that they provide through the exposure they offer.[57] Ad hoc inclusion can also be felt as underappreciation. As for the permanent displays of art museum collections, the representation of migrancy and refugees' displacement runs the risk of being formulaic unless this deeper engagement can be fostered. Displaced artists are rarely afforded the opportunity to intervene in the display of their own cultures. However, as will be discussed in Chapter 5, we did develop a long-term and collaborative project that sought to make changes in the system and to advance the careers of artists. Similar issues are experienced by most artists except for a very few, privileged stars in the international art system, but the insights of displaced artists point to deep disadvantage and exclusion, as we also explained in Chapter 2.

The questions of the temporary and the permanent, the exhibited and the collected, are profound ones that continue to impact all minority artists in the industry. Leaders of art museums and commercial art galleries are unlikely to assert that sheer merit underlies the racial and gendered imbalances in their collections, programming, and purchases, but the aura of inclusiveness may hide myopia, not least of which is the notion that things have significantly improved. The low percentage of art entering permanent collections made by global majority or women artists has barely improved since 2010. This is despite the fact that the number of temporary exhibitions by such artists has increased. It is well known that museum collections do not yet reflect the diverse publics that they serve. Arts Council England's 2021/22 diversity report reveals that in 806 organisations, only 24 per cent of executive roles were occupied by Black, Asian, and ethnically diverse people.[58] The problem of diversity reaches from representation to leadership and thus decision-making about what and who will constitute the future collection.

In the US, the respected Burns Halperin Report identified that 11 per cent of acquisitions and 14.9 per cent of exhibitions at thirty-one museums between 2008 and 2020, were of art by female-identifying artists. There was little racial diversity (just 2.2 per cent were Black). Seventeen of the top twenty artists were White (the only three non-White female artists were Yayoi Kusama, Julie Mehretu, and Frida Kahlo). Burns and Halperin reported that: 'These totals are around a fifth of what they would be if collections actually represented the population of the US'.[59] They found that though women gained more attention in museum exhibition programmes, acquisitions of art by women peaked in 2009 and declined after that.

Back across the Atlantic, *Rethinking the Grand Tour* (2022–25) was planned as a major reinstallation of Manchester Art Gallery's permanent collection. Artists with backgrounds of displacement were recruited for their expertise and were key to the new selection and interpretation of the collection. The artists decided they would be publicly credited and named as artists rather than as displaced from their nations of origin. The reason was that they wanted their work and knowledge to be appreciated long-term, beyond what they felt was an identity-based typecasting of their practices. Highlighting their own personal histories may have strayed into the toxic debates around immigration of that time, since putting one's head above the cultural parapet as 'displaced' could also put one at risk, and art galleries are committed to being spaces of safety, welcome, and empathy.

Domenico Sergi stressed that the recognition of displacement also requires a degree of redistributing resources.[60] His example is 'Multaka: Treffpunkt Museums' (Multaka: Museums as Meeting Point), a multi-museum programme that involved funding and resources. Multaka started in four museums in Berlin in 2015, with a training programme in which displaced people developed and then conducted gallery tours for visitors. They were paid, which was possible because they registered with the Freunde des Museums für Islamische Kunst (Friends of the Museum for Islamic Art), a membership that circumvented German asylum-seeker work restrictions. Multaka offered mentoring, which led to further employment for some of the guides. Acknowledging the artists' displacement was a step in the right direction, however, as Sergi argues, this was different to simply recognising displacement, since for asylum seekers or refugees with work permits, social and economic precarity persists even when the right to residence is recognised. Multaka was later rolled out at the Pitt Rivers Museum in Cambridge, as well as the Tyne & Wear Archives & Museums in Newcastle (Multaka North East England), funded by the Esme Fairburn Foundation. The guides gave tours, not just about objects from familiar cultures but also reinterpreting British history, archaeology, and heritage sites, including Hadrian's Wall. They explained national and local histories specific to the area in German, Arabic, and Cantonese.[61]

In the UK and elsewhere, asylum seekers need care and welfare. They are sometimes provided with accommodation and allowances but are not permitted to work for pay. As soon as they have a job, however, refugees are deprived of this crucial aid. Thus, the recognition of labour goes hand in hand with autonomy and the more refugees can work, the more they dispel the myth that goes with care – that displaced people are victims. The apparent opposition between care (which involves dependency) and agency (which means self-determination), has recently been debated widely. Artists' labour, and particularly displaced artists' work, came into focus when discourses about care emerged, and so we will briefly review some of these ideas and attempt to see which, if any, apply to the art world and its institutions.

For a start, care must be distinguished emphatically from making images of care. Elke Krasny and Lara Perry wrote that care should be embedded within art institutions and art museums through policy changes within curating.[62] They distinguished between the practice of care and 'care washing', which does not involve change, but which may involve presenting declarations of care. For displaced artists, care means caring for them while they collaborate with art institutions. The question remains, does reframing labour through the lens of care reproduce victimhood? From the arts to healthcare, James Thompson asserted that we need to move beyond the 'denial of dependency' fuelled by 'neoliberal narratives of self-sufficiency', acknowledging instead that we are all enmeshed in webs of interdependency whereby care always sustains agency.[63] Christine Ross drew similar conclusions, that the success of a relationship between care-givers and care-receivers did not imply a hierarchy and is always reciprocal.[64] Care should not be abandoned, therefore, on the assumption that it detracts from autonomy.

Identifying the permutations in collaborations and participations means finding nuances that matter. This is crucial in understanding care in the arts. Some writers, including Sergi, suggest that personal testimonies in exhibition-making diminish the risk of painting displaced people as heroic or exceptional and, conversely, of portraying them as victims by focusing on suffering.[65] Testimonies, he argued, promote empathy and dissolve stereotypes. Other writers suggested that when displaced people continually recounted their stories, they were retraumatised. Resolving these ambiguities was the mission of Danish art space, CAMP, working with the adjacent, displaced people-led community space, Trampoline House, in Copenhagen. According to CAMP's curators, Frederikke Hansen and Tone Olaf Nielsen, its policy was that collaborations between academic researchers or external artists and Trampoline House must last for a minimum of six months and include voluntary work.[66] Guidelines included avoiding research interviews with asylum seekers during the first month of the collaboration. After that time, it was deemed that the relationship between researchers and asylum seekers would have had time to develop or, if not, the research was cancelled. Even if re-traumatisation did not occur, collaboration with displaced people often involves them performing and re-performing painful experiences, or confining them to the box of their displacement. This is extractive curatorship.

There are ways this was avoided, first and most obviously through hospitality, though this has itself been scrutinised for the assumption that it is a counterpoint to hostility and the remedy for exclusive ownership and national sovereignty. Philosopher Jacques Derrida spoke about a possibility of unconditional hospitality that exceeds the realm of the law in which the guest would be fully accepted.[67] However, Christine Ross had suggested that because Derrida framed hospitality as an encounter, the transformative effects that come with long-term living with the foreigner – with the displaced person or asylum seeker – might be ignored. The long duration involved in hosting displaced people was key, and she warned against the ease with which hospitality was never really offered. Nonetheless, Marsha Meskimmon and other authors continue to theorise the significant role of art in reimagining citizenship as a vehicle for intersectional subjects to participate equally in shaping their positionality in the world.[68]

Al-Madhafah/The Living Room (2016–ongoing) was a participatory art project based directly on the connection between hosts and displaced people. It was started by Decolonizing Architecture Art Residency (DAAR), which consisted of architects Sandi Hilal and Alessandro Petti, the latter had been, with Eyal Weizman, a co-founder of the investigative collective Forensic Architecture. Sandi Hilal is Palestinian, with extensive NGO experience. DAAR was joined by Syrian couple Yasmeen Mahmoud and Ibrahim Muhammad Haj Abdulla, who were resident in Sweden, and by Palestinian activist and artist Ayat Al-Turshan, working from Fawwar Refugee Camp. In form, *Al-Madhafah/The Living Room* resembled many well-known works of relational aesthetics and participatory art. It comprised experiences of conversations and meetings hosted by DAAR and its collaborators in domestic spaces. At first, the living rooms were in DAAR's own apartments in Stockholm and Boden, and in Palestinian camps, but later versions were hosted in art galleries. The project's iterations around the world, in Boden, Stockholm, the West Bank, Eindhoven, Abu Dhabi, and Paris, reversed what might have been expected. Those whose assigned roles were as guests, deprived of their ability to host on account of displacement, were ever-generous hosts welcoming others into intimate rooms with conversation and tea. *Al-Madhafah/The Living Room* subtly mimicked the ethics and the efficiency of so-called welcoming initiatives by governments or agencies seen in welcome spaces or designated zones of asylum. DAAR pointed us back to the apparent opposition between care and agency. The host–guest reversal not only inverted the relation between citizen and guest, it also involved work. The displaced guest-turned-host was making art and educating others, and not as an actor-participant following a script.

DAAR's living rooms lead us to the next questions of how art galleries and art museums might withdraw from their role of hosting visitors and move toward making room for displaced people to be hosts. When would they welcome the labour and knowledge of displaced artists? When *Al-Madhafah/The Living Room* ventured into art institutions beyond Sweden, it struggled to identify willing hosts. On the project's website, Sandi Hilal narrates the story of restaging *Al-Madhafah/The Living Room* in Paris to be part of an exhibition, 'Public Luxury'. She explained that she hesitated to host yet another iteration of the project if it was to be simply transferred from location to location. Her unease reflected the difficulty of identifying a truly appropriate host, and was resolved only when she formed an unexpected friendship with the Public Luxury curator, who wanted to bring the project to Paris. Hilal also recalled that Van Abbemuseum in Eindhoven hosted *Al-Madhafah/The Living Room* as part of a series of exhibitions, 'Positions', which it held during 2018 and 2019. She met Shafiq Omar Kakar, an Afghan security guard who fled Afghanistan in the 1990s and had been working for many years at the museum but was also an artist, a painter. She recalled:

[Kakar] introduced himself to me, and as soon as I began telling him about the Living Room, he instantly understood the project. I told him that the only condition for this project to exist was for a host to come forward, and he replied, with no hesitation: 'I'm the host'.[69]

The encounter with Kakar convinced both Van Abbemuseum and Hilal that they must go forward with the project, and they invited asylum seekers in danger of deportation from a community space in Eindhoven to be hosts in the living room. Kakar helped Hilal to determine the living room's location in the museum's entry area, neither off-site nor nestled deep inside a gallery. The living room's furnishings, carpet, and teapots became Afghan rather than Palestinian. Although the two stories had a happy ending, the awkward formality of normal curatorial transactions did not sit easily with DAAR. It is not a common occurrence, but conversational processes at the first stages of curators' collaborations, built on shared, lived experiences, and can work well with artists who have no confidence in the transactional recycling typical of the art market and curatorship. DAAR completely understood the back-office complexity of delegating work: it involves emotional labour that is often incorrectly assumed to be trivial or perfunctory. Hilal's reservations about replicating yet another work of relational aesthetics, decades after that genre of art-making had commenced, pointed to the always potential aestheticisation of displacement of which she was aware, even though her project already had such cultural capital that she could be selective.

The challenge of hospitality is that it is double-edged and that it has what Christine Ross described as a dark side.[70] This is a long way from a hasty, superficial reading of Derrida. Hospitality may involve real agency as much as it may simply reproduce hierarchies by merely representing hospitality and by depicting kindness. Kakar's crucial role in bringing *Al-Madhafah/The Living Room* to the Van Abbemuseum at first seems unlikely, since programme decisions and negotiations with artists and other museums are usually the domain of curators and the museum director. Were these simply unexpected, unpredictable encounters? Or was this less about pure chance and more about the result of connections that are hard to kindle without hospitality, warmth, and generosity? During a lecture in Sweden in 2019, Charles Esche, Van Abbemuseum's director, was prompted by Hilal to consider whether the encounter had been simply fortuitous. Esche made it clear that Kakar had in fact been more active in museum partnerships than his job title suggested. Years earlier, he had been the link connecting Van Abbemuseum with an informal knowledge exchange, the 'Skype Academy', linking the museum with artists in six Afghan cities.[71] By 2023, the Skype Academy had grown into a permanent community space at Van Abbemuseum, with Shafiq Omar Kakar as the project coordinator. Van Abbemuseum had made a clever long-term investment in the professional development of at least one displaced artist working in the museum. Working out how to care for workers in the art industry is an important crucial step in recognising and addressing how displacement aesthetics operates in art institutions.

Conclusion

We have explored participatory art involving displaced people and seen a range of relationships between employer and employed, which demonstrate how working in the arts involves labour issues that impact on displaced artists and severely affect their practice. Work for artists is often short-term and uncredited, and restrictions on the right to work, as well as precarity, coincide with the almost universal lack of specific, identified care for displaced people in the art world.

Hierarchies of authorship and assistance are inevitable, and sometimes an assistant's or a participant's anonymity may even be unescapable or necessary. Concerns with hierarchies of labour and authorship are highlighted in antagonistic forms of participatory practice, such as those of Santiago Sierra. These projects often result in heated debates about ethics and raise questions about the duty of care that artists and institutions owe to the participants. Some participatory methods lost their credibility because they did not sufficiently care for or support the dignity of the volunteers enlisted as assistants. Antagonistic participatory projects, while they may be a small proportion in the panorama of contemporary art, sought to make unfair power relationships more visible. However, as this chapter has demonstrated, more recent art practice has sought to move beyond the visibility of injustice to focus instead on mobilising care as the purpose of participation. This move toward care requires a considered approach to institutional collaboration. For example, working with displaced artists must mean fair pay, sometimes through innovations like the Multaka project.

Importantly, not all displaced artists want to be defined by their identity, even though, as we have seen, that identity may also have considerable cultural capital and attract invitations to biennials and purchases by art museums. As discussed in Chapter 3, displaced artists are well qualified to decide for themselves how they wish to identify. Alongside recognition of expertise and appropriate renumeration of labour, this issue of identification is key to both ensuring the creation of safe working spaces for artists and art workers, and the terms for ethical participation and collaboration. This chapter has demonstrated that caring for displaced artists involves both increasing agency within collaborations, as well as recognising less visible forms of labour that artists are often asked to bring to projects. Moreover, this chapter has highlighted the complexity and intersectionality of labour challenges that artists with backgrounds of displacement encounter in art markets and institutions.

Notes

1 Mierle Laderman Ukeles, *Manifesto! Maintenance Art* (1969), accessed 10 June 2024. https://queensmuseum.org/wp-content/uploads/2016/04/Ukeles-Manifesto-for-Maintenance-Art-1969.pdf

2 Linda Nochlin, 'Why Have There Been No Great Women Artists?', *ARTnews*, 69:9 (January 1971): 22–39, 67–71, 25; reprinted in Linda Nochlin, *Women, Art and Power and Other Essays* (New York: Harper & Row, 1988), p. 70.

3 Nochlin, 'Why Have There Been No Great Women Artists?', p. 70. Emphasis in original.

4 Silvia Federici, *Wages Against Housework* (Bristol: Falling Wall Press and the Power of Women Collective, 1975).

5 For the New York City Sanitation Department's own celebration of Ukeles, see Eleanor White, 'Portrait of an Artist: Mierle Laderman Ukeles', *Sanitation Foundation* (17 August 2020). www.sanitationfoundation.org/blog/portrait-of-an-artist-mierle-laderman-ukeles, acccessed 1 June 2024. Also see Sharron Jackson's chapter, 'High Maintenance: The Sanitation Aesthetics of Mierle Laderman Ukeles', in her *Social Works: Performing Art, Supporting Publics* (New York: Routledge, 2011), pp. 75–103; Patricia C. Phillips, 'Maintenance Activity: Creating a Climate for Change', in Nina Felshin (ed.), *But Is It Art? The Spirit of Art as Activism* (Seattle: Bay Press, 1995), pp. 165–193; also see Helen Molesworth. 'House Work and Art Work', *October*, 92 (2000): 71–97.

6 Suzanne Lacy, 'Cultural Pilgrimages and Metaphoric Journeys', in Suzanne Lacy (ed.), *Mapping the Terrain: New Genre Public Art* (Seattle: Bay Press, 1994), pp. 19–48; for Lacy's argument a decade later that New Genre Public Art was not a prescription for experimental art forms, see Suzanne Lacy, 'Time in Place: New Genre Public Art a Decade Later', in Cameron Cartiere and Shelly Willis (eds), *The Practice of Public Art*' (New York: Routledge, 2008), pp. 18–33.

7 Lacy, 'Cultural Pilgrimages and Metaphoric Journeys', p. 20.

8 See the arguments in bell hooks, *Feminist Theory from Margin to Center* (Boston: South End Press, 1984).

9 See Bill Roberts, 'Production in View: Allan Sekula's *Fish Story* and the Thawing of Postmodernism', *Tate Papers*, no 18 (Autumn 2012), accessed 14 September 2023. www.tate.org.uk/research/tate-papers/18/production-in-view-allan-sekulas-fish-story-and-the-thawing-of-postmodernism; on understanding gender in the economy of contemporary art, see Angela Dimitrakaki, *Gender, artWork, and the Global Imperative: A Materialist Feminist Critique* (Manchester: Manchester University Press, 2013). More recently, see those arguments extended to the gendered labour of craftspeople: Dave Beech, *Art and Labour: On the Hostility to Handicraft, Aesthetic Labour and the Politics of Work in Art* (Leiden: Brill, 2020); Danielle Child, *Working Aesthetics: Labour, Art and Capitalism* (London: Bloomsbury, 2019); for these ideas extended to the Global South, see Jennifer

Way, *The Politics of Vietnamese Craft: American Diplomacy and Domestication* (London: Bloomsbury, 2020).

10 For this poster, see Guerilla Girls, *Traditional Values and Quality Return to the Whitney Museum* (1995), accessed 4 June 2024. www.guerrillagirls.com/portfolio-com pleat-19852021/mq6yrjd3tbyaowhpd5lm4bc4xnmso3

11 Andrew Ross, 'Decolonizing the Cultural Workplace: A New Organizing Front', *New Labor Forum*, 31:1 (2021): 18–26; also see Orian Brook, Dave O'Brien, and Mark Taylor, *Culture Is Bad for You: Inequality in the Cultural and Creative Industries* (Manchester: Manchester University Press, 2020).

12 Roberts, 'Production in View: Allan Sekula's *Fish Story* and the Thawing of Postmodernism'.

13 T.J. Demos, *The Migrant Image: The Art and Politics of Documentary During Global Crisis* (Durham, NC: Duke University Press, 2013), p. 37.

14 Demos, *The Migrant Image*, p. 50.

15 Giorgio Agamben. *Homo Sacer: Sovereign Power and Bare Life*, trans. Daniel Heller-Roazen (Stanford, CA: Stanford University Press, 1998), pp. 127–128.

16 Agamben, *Homo Sacer*, p. 134.

17 Demos, *The Migrant Image*, p. 19.

18 Dimitrakaki, *Gender, artWork, and the Global Imperative*, p. 117; for the proliferation of biennials and globalist claims for their cosmopolitanism, see Charles Green and Anthony Gardner, *Biennials, Triennials and documenta: The Exhibitions That Created Contemporary Art* (Boston: Wiley-Blackwell, 2016).

19 On decolonising international artist residencies, see Miriam La Rosa, 'Hosts, Guests, Ghosts. The Art Residency as Site of Hospitality: Interrogating the Ontology of Art Residencies through Cross-Cultural Gift Exchange', PhD dissertation, School of Culture and Communication, University of Melbourne, 2022. On reconsidering national war artist commissions from the perspective of understanding displacement aesthetics, see Kit Messham-Muir and Uroš Čvoro (eds), *Art in Conflict: The Politics of Artists in War Zones* (London: Bloomsbury, 2023), and Charles Green, 'The War at Home', in Messham-Muir and Čvoro (eds), *Art in Conflict*, pp. 119–135.

20 Dimitrakaki, *Gender, artWork, and the Global Imperative*, pp. 117, 119.

21 See the artists' website: Ursula Biemann, Lisa Parks and Angela Melitopoulos, *Transcultural Geographies* (2004), accessed 10 June 2024.

22 Anne Ring Petersen, *Migration into Art: Transcultural Identities and Art-Making in a Globalised World* (Manchester: Manchester University Press, 2017), p. 96.

23 Emily Cunniffe, 'Non-Economic Migrants as Workers: Securing the Right to Work for Asylum Applicants in the EU', *European Journal of Migration and Law*, 24:1 (2022): 112–150.

24 Madeleine Sumption. 'Shortages, High-Demand Occupations, and the Post-Brexit UK Immigration System', *Oxford Review of Economic Policy*, 38:1 (2022): 98.

25 Anonymous interview with performing artist, 2021.

26 Katherine Brickell and Jessie Speer. 'Gendered and Feminist Approaches to Displacement', in Peter Adey, et al. (eds), *The Handbook of Displacement* (London: Palgrave Macmillan, 2020), p. 137.

27 For VODW, see its website, *Domestic Workers Are Workers. The Voice of Domestic Workers: A Support Network and Campaign Organisation*, accessed 10 June 2024. www.thevoiceof domesticworkers.com/

28 Kate Roberts, 'Rights Not Rescue: Lessons from Migrant Domestic Workers in the UK and their Struggle for Systems Change', *Anti-Trafficking Review*, 15 (2020): 167–170.

29 Alex Rotas, 'Is "Refugee Art" Possible?', *Third Text*, 18:1 (2004): 51–60.

30 Anonymous interview with painter, 2021.

31 Verónica Tello, 'What is Contemporary About Institutional Critique?', *Third Text*, 34, 6 (2020): 638.

32 For a detailed typology of artist collaborations in contemporary art, see Charles Green, *The Third Hand: Artist Collaborations from Conceptualism to Postmodernism* (Minneapolis: University of Minnesota Press, 2001).

33 Dave Beech summarises this well, writing that, unlike participants, collaborators 'share authorial rights over the artwork that permit them ... to make fundamental decisions about the key structural features of the work' (Dave Beech, 'Include Me Out! Dave Beech on Participation in Art', *Art Monthly*, 315 (April 2008): 3.

34 For a concise explanation, see Claire Bishop, 'Introduction: Viewers as Producers', in Claire Bishop (ed.), *Participation* (Boston, MA: MIT Press, 2006), pp. 10–17.

35 Zhe Jiang and Marek Korczynski, 'The Art of Labour Organizing: Participatory Art and Migrant Domestic Workers' Self-Organizing in London', *Human Relations*, 74:6 (2021): 865

36 Christoph Schlingensief, *Please Love Austria – First Austrian Coalition Week* (2004), accessed 26 March 2022. https://www.schlingensief.com/projekt_eng.php?id=t033 [schlin gensief.com]. The key English-language source on Schlingensief with an encyclopedic catalogue is Klaus Biesenbach, Anna-Catharina Gebbers, and Susanne Pfeffer (curators and eds), *Christoph Schlingensief* (New York and Berlin: MoMA PS1 and KW Institute for Contemporary Art, 2013).

37 Irene Messinger, 'There is Something about Marrying ... The Case of Human Rights *vs.* Migration Regimes using the Example of Austria', *Laws*, 2:4 (2013): 378.

38 See Claire Bishop's discussion of *Please Love Austria* in her *Artificial Hells: Participatory Art and the Politics of Spectatorship* (London: Verso, 2012), pp. 279–283; also see Carl Hegemann, 'Christoph Schlingensief: Art on the Edge of Reality', *ArtReview*, 1 May 2019, accessed 10 June 2024. https://artreview.com/christoph-schlingensief-art-on-the-edge-of-reality/

39 https://www.santiago-sierra.com/20009_1024.php?key=2

40 Friederike Sigler, 'Santiago Sierra's *Workers Who Cannot Be Paid*: Precarious Labour in Contemporary Art', in A. Halsema, K. Kwastek, and R van den Oever (eds), *Bodies That*

Still Matter: Resonances of the Work of Judith Butler (Amsterdam: Amsterdam University Press, 2021), p. 130.

41 Judith Butler, *Precarious Life: The Powers of Mourning and Violence* (London: Verso Books, 2004).

42 Sigler, 'Santiago Sierra's *Workers*', p. 132.

43 Demos, *The Migrant Image*, p. 15.

44 Dee Jefferson, 'Dark Mofo festival weathered the backlash against Union Flag and a First Nations boycott, but the impact will be lasting', *ABC Arts* (6 July 2021); the quote from Jamie Graham Blair is from this article, accessed 10 June 2024. www.abc.net.au/news/2021-07-06/dark-mofo-tasmania-arts-festival-impact-backlash/100252542

45 Dark Mofo creative director Leigh Carmichael, quoted by Sarah Cascone, 'An Australian Arts Festival Has Cancelled Artist Santiago Sierra's Plans to Douse the British Flag in the Blood of Indigenous People: The Dark Mofo Festival Pulled the Work after Outcry from Indigenous Groups', *Artnet* (23 March 2021), accessed 10 June 2024. https://news.artnet.com/art-world/santiago-sierra-dark-mofo-cancelled-1954026

46 Tello, 'What is Contemporary About Institutional Critique?', p. 646.

47 Tello, 'What is Contemporary About Institutional Critique?', p. 648.

48 See brut Wien, interview with Ahmet Öğüt, 'The Art of Assembly XVII: Ahmet Öğüt – The Silent University' (2022), accessed 12 June 2024. https://vimeo.com/716802627

49 The principal publication on Boetti is Lynne Cooke, Mark Godfrey, and Christian Rattemeyer (curators and eds), *Alighiero Boetti: Game Plan*, exhibition catalogue (New York: Museum of Modern Art, 2012); for a detailed photographic record of the displaced women embroiderers and their families, see Randi Malkin Steinberger, *Boetti by Afghan People* (Santa Monica: RAM Publications, 2011); also see Tim Bonyhady, *Two Afternoons in the Kabul Stadium: A History of Afghanistan Through Clothes, Carpets and the Camera* (Melbourne: Text, 2021), and in particular, see Bonyhady's chapter, 'The Artist Who Did Nothing', pp. 93–102, for a critique of Boetti's employment of the displaced embroiderers; for a pioneering, detailed account of Afghan displaced people's War Rugs, see Tim Bonyhady and Nigel Lendon, *I Weave What I Have Seen: The War Rugs of Afghanistan*, exhibition catalogue (Canberra: Australian National University School of Art Gallery, 2003).

50 Paul Ricoeur, *Oneself as Another*, trans. Kathleen Blamey (Chicago, IL: University of Chicago Press, 1994).

51 Mark Godfrey, 'Boetti and Afghanistan', in Lynne Cooke et al., *Alighiero Boetti: Game Plan*, pp. 154–175; for a differentiation between Orientalism and Exoticism, see Victor Segalen, *Essays on Exoticism* (Durham, NC: Duke University Press, 2002), p. 20; and Edouard Glissant, *Poetics of Relation* (Ann Arbor: University of Michigan Press, 2007), p. 29.

52 Christoper G. Bennett, *Order and Disorder: Alighiero Boetti by Afghan Women* (Los Angeles: Fowler Museum of Cultural History, 2012).

53 For Eliasson's account of this project, see Eliasson Studio, 'Green Light: An Artistic Workshop' (2017), accessed 10 June 2024. https://olafureliasson.net/greenlight

54 Grant Kester, 'The Device Laid Bare: On Some Limitations in Current Art Criticism', *e-flux* #50, December 2013. http://worker01.e-flux.com/pdf/article_8976479.pdf, p. 7.

55 Anonymous interview with digital artist, 2021.

56 Anonymous interview with painter, 2021.

57 Rachael Minott, 'The Past is Now: Confronting Museums' Complicity in Imperial Celebration', *Third Text*, 33:4–5 (2019): 573.

58 Arts Council England, *Equality, Diversity and Inclusion: A Data Report, 2021–2022*.

59 Charlotte Burns and Julia Halperin, 'Perceptions of Progress in the Art World Are Largely a Myth. Here Are the Facts', *The Burns Halperin Report* (New York: Studio Burns, 2024), accessed 10 June 2024. https://studioburns.media/perceptions-of-progress-in-the-art-world-are-largely-a-myth-here-are-the-facts/

60 Domenico Sergi, *Museums, Refugees and Communities: Communities, Collections and Representations* (London: Routledge, 2021), p. 51.

61 www.twmuseums.org.uk/volunteers/multaka

62 Elke Krasny and Lara Perry, 'Introduction', in Elke Krasny and Lara Perry (eds), *Curating with Care* (London: Routledge, 2023), pp. 3, 8.

63 James Thompson, *Care Aesthetics: For Artful Care and Careful Art* (London: Routledge, 2022), p. 61.

64 Christine Ross, *Art for Coexistence: Unlearning the Way We See Migration* (Cambridge, MA: MIT Press, 2022), pp. 17, 19.

65 Sergi, *Museums, Refugees and Communities*, p. 51.

66 CAMP and Nora El Qadim, 'On CAMP, Copenhagen: The Politics of Curating Art on Migration. A Conversation between Frederikke Hansen, Tone Olaf Nielsen and Nora El Qadim', *Parse*, no. 10 (Spring 2020): 1–8, accessed 20 June 2024. https://parsejournal.com/article/on-camp-copenhagen-the-politics-of-curating-art-on-migration/

67 Jacques Derrida and Anne Dufourmantelle, *Of Hospitality*, trans. Rachel Bowlby (Stanford, CA: Stanford University Press, 2000), p. 77.

68 Marsha Meskimmon, *Transnational Feminisms, Transversal Politics and Art: Entanglements and Intersections* (London: Routledge, Taylor & Francis Group, 2020), p. 62.

69 Decolonizing Architecture Art Residency (DAAR), 'Van Abbemuseum, Eindhoven', accessed 20 June 2024. www.decolonizing.ps/site/eindhoven/

70 Ross, *Art for Coexistence*, p. 292.

71 Charles van Esche in 'Conversation between Sandi Hilal and Charles Esche about the Living Room at the Vanabbe [sic] Museum at IASPIS on September 4, 2019', accessed 24 June 2024. https://www.decolonizing.ps/site/eindhoven/

5 Displacement aesthetics: collaboration, co-curation, and collections

Throughout this book, displacement aesthetics has been examined through four modes that reveal how representation is entangled with lived experience. This final chapter considers institutional efforts that directly address this entanglement in collaborative work and co-curation with art collections. First, we return to the foundational period of refugeedom to explore the collaboration between grassroots organisations and leading art institutions in advocating for refugees during the Second World War. Next, intentionally shifting across decades, the chapter examines a set of recent collaborations between academics, art institutions, and displaced artists in a co-curated temporary art exhibition and redisplay of a public collection. Finally, the chapter considers contemporary artists' attempts to reinterpret displacement across art museums' collections.

These are three illustrations of the operational dimension of displacement aesthetics, which shifts the focus from the visual representations of refugees and displacement to institutional actions that take account of displaced people. This work is connected to activities such as writing on behalf of artists for visa applications or negotiating with state agencies, and even carefully considering processes of cultural work on behalf of voiceless others, as Stuart Hall pointed out in his critique of representation.[1]

The overarching aim of this final chapter is to explore the progressive and inclusive activities of art museums through collaborations and collections. What is encountered in the gallery or art museum is made visible often through invisible or partial processes of revealing and uncovering. When we consider the displaced artists who have been selected for personal and professional support, ask what is selected for collections and exhibitions, and see what ends up on the walls of art museums, the long histories of the visible and invisible processes continue with an enduring legacy.

This chapter will explain the challenges that contemporary curators and galleries face by changing the focus from the representation of displaced artists, or the display of art that visualises the themes of forced migration and displacement, to an inclusive and collaborative approach with diverse communities and their art-making. Moreover, the chapter considers the ways in which displacement aesthetics impacts contemporary museological debates, including those focused on decolonial issues such as repatriation, patronage, and object loans.

Collaboration and advocacy in Britain's wartime art industry

The Second World War was a defining era during which a range of art organisations endeavoured to assist artists, curators, and dealers escape Nazi-occupied Europe, and also lobbied to have interned artists and cultural workers released. Much has been written about the exiled artists who emigrated to New York, with the support of Alfred Barr, Director of the Museum of Modern Art, and his wife, art historian Margaret Scolari. Scolari was instrumental in Varian Fry's daring efforts (and that of the Emergency Rescue Committee) to bring European artists to safety. Less analysis of the British experience is available, especially in terms of humanitarian advocacy in the art industry. Yet this history is important for understanding how, in the present day, institutional operations shape displacement aesthetics, which is distinct from art that is made about displacement. A prime historical example is how grassroots artist circles collaborated with Britain's foremost art institution, the National Gallery in London, mobilising its capacity to make representations to the British government on behalf of foreign, often unacquainted, artists in fear of their lives.

This new urgency was different to the diplomatic context of the Spanish Civil War, when many British artists engaged in antifascist humanitarian activities, against the official government stance of neutrality. The Left-wing Artists International Association (AIA) organised exhibitions and print sales to raise funds for food and medical supplies for the Republican cause. Members of the AIA included eminent artist Sir Muirhead Bone and a wide circle of artists and friends, such as Misha Black and Helen Roeder who felt compelled to respond to the rise of Fascism and Nazism. Due to government policy, however, there were few art institutional efforts in this period. Manchester Art Gallery famously refused to display Picasso's mural *Guernica* (1937) due to British foreign policy. It was left to local Communists to stage the exhibition instead, not in a gallery but in a commercial showroom.

With the triumph of Nazism, after Hitler's election as Chancellor in 1933, the political situation in Britain changed to permit more direct action. The Artists' Refugee Committee (ARC) was formed in response to an appeal that a group of Berlin-based artists made to British art luminaries, including Paul Nash, Augustus John, Herbert Read, Roland Penrose, and Margaret Gardiner. The artists had escaped Berlin only to find themselves threatened in Prague. The ARC supported artists in Czechoslovakia, Austria, and Germany and helped to organise visas.[2] This practical assistance involved dangerous and clandestine operations. Money was secretly passed though fake art dealers to galleries in Prague to assist with escapes.[3] Many artists received help, both well-known artists such as John Heartfield, Kurt Schwitters, Ludwig Meidner, and Oscar Kokoschka, and lesser known ones.[4] Assistance was not based on prominence but rather on a common plight, although the artist's eminent status was useful in making the case with the British authorities. Some artists were completely unknown to the loose coalition working behind the scenes. Nevertheless, support for their fellow artists spurred extraordinary actions. The motivations of both antifascism and compassion united most of the international art industry across linguistic, class, and artistic barriers and formed a contrast to the nervous vacillation of governments.

The growing refugee crisis after the 1938 *Anschluss* also altered the political context in which liaising directly with government bodies was possible. Artistic communities reacted to the rising awareness of anti-Jewish laws and antisemitism, along with around 200 humanitarian aid charities (Christian, Quaker, Jewish, and Left-wing) that rose to assist political and Jewish refugees from 1933, including finding guarantors for visas and submitting paperwork.[5] Public and media attention was also useful and hence art exhibitions advocated on behalf of European refugees. The AIA's 1941 exhibition, *War Pictures*, was its most popular, with around 150,000 visitors in three weeks and publicity lauding the 'common struggle against Fascist aggression'.[6] The AIA, alongside the Free German League of Culture (FGLC), united artists against the Nazis, and engaged in a wide range of broadly humanitarian activities, representing between 1,000 and 3,000 members. Co-founders Oscar Kokoschka and Fred Uhlman, and Uhlman's German-speaking English wife, Diana Uhlman, initially hosted meetings in their home, the first port of call for many refugees. As well as exhibitions, practical activities included lobbying, fund-raising, locating housing, supplying art materials, feeding, and physically caring for artists who had fled and were living in precarity.[7]

Linked communities of British and European artists forged this extraordinary effort with the support of small, commercial galleries such as the Whitechapel, New Burlington, and Ben Uri, the Modern Art Gallery (established in 1941 by dealer Jack Bilbo after his release from internment), as well as galleries in Ireland.[8] However, the question remains: what were the most powerful British art institutions of the period doing to assist refugees?

The answer lay in networks operating in parallel towards a common goal. Remarkably, a loose set of informal partnerships between Left-wing and Establishment cultural figures, and small and major art institutions, and the direct action of the collectives (including refugee-led ones such as the FGLC), underpinned the operation's success. It may be an unexpected paradox that the very uncertainty of international and national refugee law at this time allowed for a certain degree of operative flexibility when engaging with government. These actors cooperated behind the scenes at a time when government policies were developing and enforced arbitrarily, reacting to the changing political situation.

Wartime events changed rapidly. The urgency of cooperation was intensified once British policy turned against European refugees. In 1939, the British government assumed that Nazi sympathisers were among the refugees and thus a threat to national security. Sweeping powers of Regulation 18B (Emergency Powers Defence Act) concentrated in the Home Secretary the power to intern people indefinitely without charges or a trial process. This followed earlier repressive laws to quash dissent, free speech, and public disorder.[9] Hundreds of artists were now deemed 'enemy aliens' in the country where they had sought refuge and were subject to policies of internment or deportation to Australia and Canada. Notably, MI5 already had the German-speaking political refugees (amongst whom were trade unionists, socialists, Communists) who were regarded as 'undesirables' under surveillance.[10] Although the rescue of the Kindertransport children in 1938 met with political and public approval, attitudes to around 68,000 adult German, Austrian, and Czech refugees hardened during the *Blitzkrieg* and fears of invasion, with the media amplifying the sense of danger. While internment attracted some critics, it largely had public support. While it cannot be compared to Nazi concentration camps, the victims of Nazi persecution bore the scourge of being politically vilified as enemy aliens.

The Artists' Refugee Committee lobbied a wide range of government, charities, and businesses, as well as influential cultural leaders, on two main lines. Firstly, they sought guarantees that:

> camp conditions are tolerable both in England and the Dominions and that internees are in no way confused with prisoners of war, to arouse sympathy in the Dominions for interned refugees by contacting private people, cultural bodies and the universities, to supply artists' materials, comforts, and to give encouragement to interned artists; to encourage English people in every walk of life to do the same; to make known as widely as possible what are the real conditions in the camps and to rouse all sections of the public to press for immediate action.[11]

The ARC's second action was 'to get the whole principle of the present policy changed so that a man's innocence and that alone shall secure his release'.[12] They wrote to charities, unions, academics, learning and medical associations, and journalists, and called on eminent members of the artistic establishment, such as the eminent war memorial architect, Sir Edwin Lutyens, to lobby for artists to be added to the 'category 8' professions (scientists, researchers, academics) that qualified for release under the 1940 legislation, subject to Committee approval. The ARC also highlighted the injustice of arbitrary and summary internment and deportation to Australia and Canada 'without even an overcoat', separation from families, illness and death in camps due to lack of medical supplies, crowded housing, and poor conditions.[13] Internment, they said, was not worthy of the democratic and humane spirit that the nation championed. There were cases where tents on open moors lacked ground sheets, increasing illness, indicating the 'injustice and muddle' which many thought was a mark of an uncivilised nation.[14]

Two women, artist Helen Roeder (ARC Secretary) and AIA administrator Diana Uhlman (whose husband Fred was interned on the Isle of Man a week before the birth of their first child), were pivotal actors in the campaign.[15] The women undertook administration, correspondence, and daily management of rescuing and supporting refugee and interned artists, including Fred and his network.[16] Uhlman's father was Lord Henry Croft, Under-Secretary-of-State for War in Winston Churchill's cabinet. However, her political views and her marriage to a German Jew, who did not speak English, strained her relationship with her parents. On the other hand, Roeder was able to draw on her friendship with Sir Kenneth Clark, director of both the National Gallery in London and the War Artists Advisory Committee, two influential positions. Roeder provided him with a list of deported artists and information about them, singling out those who were in their network but also European artists whom they knew nothing about. Again, major artists were not ranked above lesser-known ones.

This advocacy work arose from political and social convictions, and shared belief in the importance of artistic freedom, activated through personal relationships and compassion. Offering to drop by for a chat, Roeder's handwritten note gently reminded Clark that some artists in English internment camps 'are very distinguished and most of them tragic'.[17] The brief biography in the inventory emphasised the artists' skills, successful exhibitions and prizes, and the all-important capacity to speak English, arming Clark with information he could use in making deputations to the Home Office. The testimony also described artists' experiences of Nazi imprisonment, cruelties and injuries sustained, as well as the brutal pace of arrests and deportation. Clearly, this testimony was gathered to emphasise credibility.

Contact with the National Gallery was vital. In 1938 Kenneth Clark acted as a patron of the mammoth exhibition *Twentieth Century German Art* (1938), at the New Burlington Galleries. It amassed over 270 works of European modernism, largely on loan from British and European collectors. This was London's speedy retort to the Nazis' 1937 Degenerate Art Exhibition in Munich, which infuriated Hitler. It was organised by a group of women artists, art historians, and dealers, gathering patronage from London art elites.[18] As director of the War Artists Advisory Committee, the scheme that turned the state into a patron, commissioning British (not refugee) artists to cover the war effort at home and abroad by recording what they witnessed, Clark personally kept many in employment at a perilous time.[19] He also held a role with the film unit of the powerful Ministry of Information (the War Office propaganda unit) and was well-acquainted with senior journalists. Helen Roeder thanked him: 'You have no idea what a relief it is to meet somebody who can pick up the telephones and suggest leaders to people like *The Times*. Please go on making them sit up and take notice'.[20]

The grassroots also relied on Clark's connections with major government figures. In chummy correspondence with Osbert Peake (1st Viscount Ingleby; Conservative MP), Undersecretary-of-State for Home Affairs, Clark divulged that he felt a 'personal responsibility' for the many refugee cases.[21] Significantly, the nation's preeminent art gallery director could communicate directly with the Home Office. He vouched for the professional standing and non-security risk of displaced artists, art dealers, art historians, archivists, book binders, picture restorers, and even more lowly roles in the art industry. The Warburg Library had been transferred to London from Hamburg in 1933, but its German staff, including archivist Otto Fein, were soon interned. The authorities possessed little information about these new arrivals, but Clark spoke to local police officers involved in arrests.[22] In 1940, Clark supported the naturalisation application of the Warburg Library's director Fritz Saxl, and reached out to Samuel Courtauld, the textile industrialist, art collector, and founder of the Courtauld Institute (1932). As Germany lay siege to Malta and occupied Greece, art historians Saxl and Rudolf Wittkower staged the successful exhibition *English Art and the Mediterranean* (1941), which Clark launched. Such exhibitions connected German and British interest in classicism and humanism, while indirectly proclaiming allegiance to British values.[23]

Soft power exercises could be more effective than direct lobbying. Boldly writing to Justice Asquith's Committee to personally vouch for the interned artists he had never met, Clark stated that 'art depends on freedom of expression and this was denied them in Germany'.[24] His attempt to appear before the Committee, however, was rebuked, indicating that the director's sway was limited.[25] The figure of greatest parliamentary influence in altering internment policy was the MP Eleanor Rathbone, who visited camps, questioned officials, and made tireless speeches on behalf of the interned, though not singling out artists.[26] Thus, the role of influential artist champions who could represent their specific interests was invaluable. Attestations of the good character of anti-Nazi 'cultured men' had to be credible. In July 1940, Muirhead Bone and his son Stephen Bone, as well as Vanessa Bell, Duncan Grant, Ian Gordon, James Bateman, Augustus John, Henry Moore, and John Piper all signed an ARC support letter.[27] Bone also lobbied Lord Cecil and the Foreign Office for fifteen artists to receive visas.[28]

An unlikely activist, Clark described this work as 'my advocacy', including writing personal letters to internees and their wives.[29] Its efficacy can be understood in the light of his class connections and the conventions of gentlemanly privilege and cultural patronage. Also crucial is that advocacy occurred at a time when the arbitrary character of refugee bureaucracy allowed a space for ad hoc benefaction. Thus, the protections that the art industry realised for its newest émigré and refugee members resulted from collaboration between the grassroots and the Establishment, united in the shared belief that art was the cornerstone of humanity, and that Nazism was its gravest threat. This broad 'generation' of creative agents – from elite, enlightened, liberals (of all classes) to Left-wing activists, pacifists and modernists – connected across the art industry to advance their compassion for the suffering of interned artists.[30]

The advocates also understood, however, that the cultural significance of modern art was heavily disputed. Roeder did not want the Royal Academy to be the body that would decide which internees met the criteria of 'distinction in the arts'. Encouraging Clark to appeal to Undersecretary-of-State Osbert Peake, she wrote: 'I can't tell you how glad we are that the artists have you to champion them'.[31] But Clark's suggestion of a modern art alternative, the Central Institute of Art and Design, curried no favour with Peake. He insisted that the respected Royal Academy would 'give an unprejudiced opinion' as to whether an 'alien artist is a "person of eminent distinction who has made outstanding contributions to Art" whatever the private opinion … of the merits of his particular School!', a jibe at the modernists.[32] Peake assumed that all the interned German and Austrian artists were modernists, which was not necessarily the case. Ultimately, we can see that different corners of the art world could collaborate effectively, and that institutional power played a role in negotiating with the government on behalf of displaced artists.

But what of the newcomer artists' careers? Sue Malvern argues that Clark promoted a 'middle brow', conservative aesthetic far from the avant-garde.[33] There is no evidence that he assisted the artists with exhibitions or other work after their release from internment. Displaced and interned artists struggled to earn a living. Those not yet naturalised might feel affinity with their new homeland but could not be included in British public collections. In wartime, the institutional vision was preserved for the native born. This also meant that the British artists sent overseas, such as Mary Kessell, could depict postwar refugees and displaced persons from the perspective of the outsider looking in – fleetingly and temporarily – at the catastrophe.

Where 'non-native' artists could participate was in anti-Nazi propaganda, such as in Ministry of Information commissioned posters. This was seen as a pragmatic use of the refugees' linguistic skills and graphic design expertise.[34] The limits of compassion and insight can also be seen in an anecdote of 1943, in which Clark suggested to Josef Herman, following his successful exhibition at Lefevre gallery, that the 'talented painter' might one day return to Europe. Stressing the 'humanity' of 'we English' (including himself) reflected the kind of antisemitism that was normalised among the upper classes.[35] These comments suggest Clark's profound failure to comprehend the nature of Nazi genocidal policies.[36]

The continuing hardship of displaced artists was reflected in museum collections. With a few exceptions, such as Josef Herman (a work purchased in 1946), Oscar Kokoschka (a work donated in 1943), and a Georg Ehrlich sculpture (donated in 1942), the Tate only began to acquire works of displaced artists in the 1990s. The Whitworth purchased work by Oskar Kokoschka in 1961. Support mostly came from private galleries, such as Ben Uri and ex-internee Jack Bilbo's Modern Art Gallery (1941), and the ARC activist and patron Margaret Gardiner.[37]

A consideration of both the efforts and limits of compassion and advocacy in Britain's wartime art industry leads to sobering reflections on the artists who were unable to escape Europe or lacked the networks in Britain to make a life in exile. The harrowing story of the brilliant, young Bauhaus fabric designer Otti Berger is a brutal reminder of what is at stake in the ongoing need for asylum and rights to work. In 1932, she opened her own atelier in Berlin, but was forced to close in 1936 due to the Third Reich's working bans on Jews. In 1937 she moved to Bolton near Manchester, working for the textile manufacturer Helios. Her unique style emphasised the tactility and optical illusions of textured fabrics for interior spaces (Figure 5.1).[38] In 1938, she was invited to the New Bauhaus in Chicago, where she hoped to join other Bauhaus refugees, but despite letters of recommendation from its (non-Jewish) leader Walter Gropius, who chose to leave Nazi Germany, she was unable to secure a visa.

Significantly, Berger's plight speaks to contemporary issues discussed in Chapter 2 concerning the intersectional barriers displaced artists encounter in their new country. Disconnected from British professional and social networks, and hampered by lack of English-language proficiency, as well as having a hearing impairment and being an avant-garde woman, Berger was unable to secure more work. She returned to Croatia in 1938 to care for her mother. Eventually she was deported to Auschwitz and killed in 1944. A small collection of her fabric samples and swatch books have survived at the Whitworth Art Gallery, precious remnants of her undervalued talent. The consequence of not speaking English or having a local education, patronage in the arts industry, or an advocate of Kenneth Clark's stature, had dire consequences. It is heart-breaking to consider that had she been able to live and work in Britain, she may have become a star of British design, along the line of Tibor Reich. In 1936, Reich fled to Leeds to study and establish his firm. Eventually, his interior textiles were showcased in the 1951 Festival of Britain, along with many other former refugee creatives.[39] This was the same year that the internationally recognised definition of a refugee came into force, with the 1951 Convention Relating to the Status of Refugees. As Linda Nochlin reminds, the fate of those exiled women artists was precarious and marginal

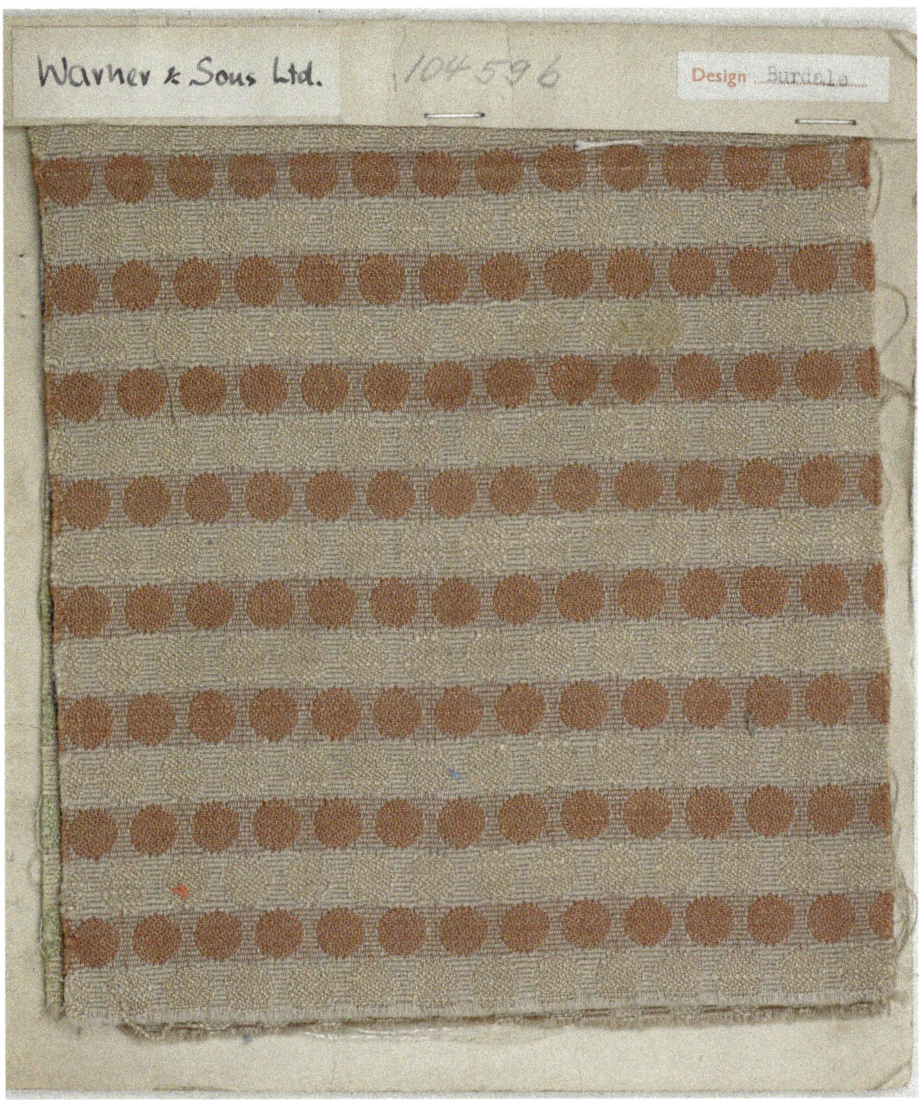

5.1 Otti Berger (1898–1944, Croatia), Helios Ltd (manufacturer), *Swatch for Burdale*, 1938. Image courtesy of the Whitworth, University of Manchester. Photo: Michael Pollard.

to the masculinist narrative of modernism. The now famous 1942 *Artists in Exile* exhibition (Pierre Matisse Gallery, New York) was, after all, an all-male exhibition.[40]

Compared with current hostilities towards refugees, as states are emboldened to refute the rights of asylum despite being signatories of the 1951 Convention Relating to the Status of Refugees, the 1940s was a time open to ad hoc possibilities for advocacy, lobbying, and behind-the-scenes initiatives on behalf of artists. Still, the fact cannot be ignored that the British government was especially hostile to non-European refugees and colonial exiles. For instance, Britain feared that some of the 45 million Chinese refugees might flee to its Hong Kong colony. Systematic exclusion was intrinsic to colonial power.[41] Humanitarian advocacy was possible due to collaborative efforts within the art industry itself, and institutional influence with the British state, but also because these displaced artists were White Europeans.

Stories of European humanitarian rescue during the Second World War are foundational to the narratives of art history, such as the recentring and movement of the art market from Paris to New York.[42] In Britain, the story should be understood in terms of class and status, which underpinned the institutional workings of displacement aesthetics. Nevertheless, while some artists and museum directors were more progressive in response to the refugee crisis and could exercise soft power that influenced the public and officials, there were limits. Institutional advocacy could change things for some exiled and refugee artists, but we have also seen the fatal instead of dire consequences of a lack of advocacy. The legacy of this is also profound. It is more than a tragic irony that the work of displaced artists, undervalued at the time, is now celebrated as part of Britain's national story. The history of institutional advocacy and collaboration remains under-recognised and only partially available in museum collections, aided by the fact that much clandestine activity went undocumented.

Reflecting on the current context of unprecedented global displacement, it is questionable how much influence museums and arts administrators can exert with governments. Instead, exhibitions and biennales appear today as primary sites for political advocacy. Despite this, the issue of displacement frequently remains dormant in art gallery collections, raising the question of how they might be awakened. Issues of institutional advocacy, collections and the connection to British art history were taken up directly in practice-led research at the University of Manchester. The result of this research was *Traces of Displacement*, a collaborative co-researched, co-produced temporary exhibition held at the Whitworth Art Gallery (2023–24).

Tracing displacement in a university art collection

Traces of Displacement addressed forced displacement as one of the major humanitarian concerns of the twentieth and twenty-first centuries, as conflict, persecution, and environmental devastation have led people to flee their homes and seek safety elsewhere. It engaged with global perspectives and stories, and many of the artists reflected on their family heritage or personal experience of displacement by making works and providing interventions that complicated the conventional narratives of refugees and experiences of displacement as they are told in art and in museum collections.

Two curators and three academic researchers at the Whitworth Art Gallery conducted the initial research and identification of potential works for conservation and display. The research faced the challenge of searching for traces of displacement in a database of 60,000 works. This also uncovered the collection's backstory and biases, as well as its missing and hidden stories. The fragmented and unacknowledged narratives of displacement proved challenging. Unearthing relevant stories and rendering them pertinent to histories, geographies, and experiences of displacement required collaboration with a group of creative practitioners with lived experience or a heritage of displacement, to act as advisors and co-curators.[43] A set of workshops responded to initial artworks and identified alternative works found to be personally meaningful. By mining the collection and discussing works together, key themes emerged to shape the exhibition spaces. To read and understand the traces of displacement in the collection, creative artists and communities have the skills, heritage, and cultural knowledge to activate this history. The exhibition was made up of collection works, some loans from other museums and contemporary artist galleries, as well as the co-curators' artworks.[44] As themes such as the forced displacement and trafficking of Africans emerged, expertise was sought from Laura Sandy (International Centre for Study of Slavery, Liverpool University) to better understand this brutal history and its legacy in collections.

The strongest themes became sections of the exhibition with wall texts, such as 'Detention and Detainment'. This was a burning issue at the time in UK immigration policy (indefinite detention and clandestine deportation). Yet this is rarely discussed in art. This section formed the first point of encounter in the space in the form of Cornelia Parker's large, bronze, floor-sculpture, *Jerusalem (Occupied Territory)* (2015), based on casts of pavements in East Jerusalem, the cracks and voids symbolic of displaced people. It was, however, especially important to have a work by the Palestinian conceptual artist Bashir Makhoul. His wallpaper piece entitled *Points of View* (1998) developed the theme of detainment in both public and private spaces (Figure 5.2). The work is based on his grandmother's flight to Lebanon following the Nakba in 1948. The wallpaper pattern derives from photos of bullet holes in walls. The scarred surface elicits an uncomfortable sensation from the juxtaposition of the supposed safety of home and the violence of pitted, textural, domestic wallpaper.

During the period of the exhibition, the Gaza War erupted, and public feedback suggested there was a desire for Palestinian art to fill a void in understanding the conflict. Although Makhoul's work is from 1998, it demonstrated the ongoing issue of protracted displacement.

Nana Varveropoulou's photos from the Colnbrook Immigration Removal Centre (*No Man's Land*, 2012–14) faced visitors as they entered the gallery and set the tone

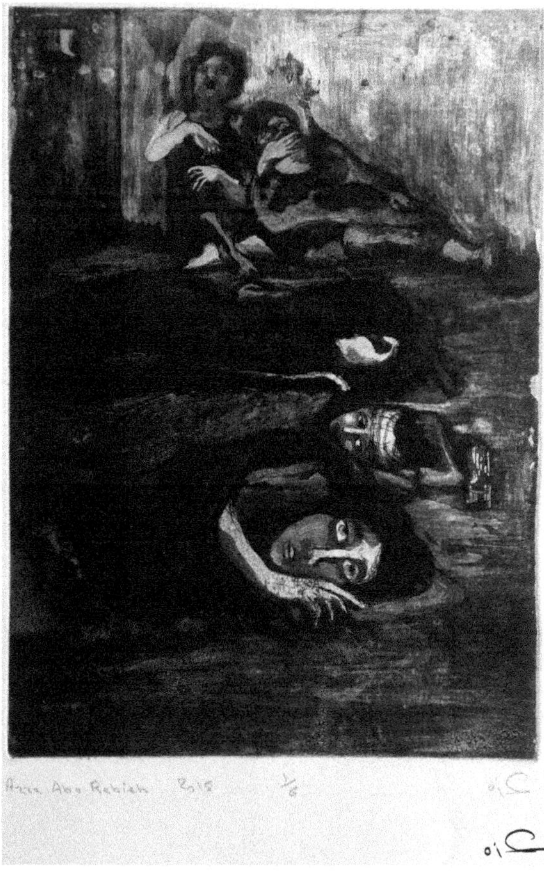

5.2 Azza Abo Rebieh, *Traces* (2018). Lithographic print. Image courtesy of the artist.

of critique of the dehumanising politics of current immigration removal in Britain. The work, on loan from the artist, is derived from a collaborative photography project with detainees. Pseudonyms protected their identities. Rare visual documents of the interior of the removal centre invisible to present-day photojournalists use first-person angles. The UK's policy of what amounts to indefinite detention (ie no maximum time limit) corresponds with Australia's notorious policy of onshore and offshore detention. Australia has pursued colonial-style agreements with poor Pacific-island nations to incarcerate asylum seekers (and their children) as though they have committed a crime. The UN and humanitarian agencies extensively criticised this policy. Including Australian artistic activism in the exhibition was crucial, therefore, to provide visitors with information. At the time of preparing the exhibition, Britain was contemplating a similar policy of deporting refugees indefinitely to Rwanda, which was a constant topic of public and political debate.

Australian artist Safdar Ahmed has worked extensively with survivors of extended offshore and onshore detention (at Villawood Immigration Detention Centre, Sydney), leading art classes with detainees. The exhibition installed one of his graphic comics entitled *Alien Citizen* (2022) featuring 'Manus Metal Man', made with the grassroots refugee-led arts organisation Refugee Art Project. An adjacent wall displayed the two-screen video work, *Border Farce* (2022), in which Ahmed collaborated with Kurdish Iranian heavy metal musician Kazem Kazemi, who had been detained for six years on Manus Island near Papua New Guinea, and cinematographer Alia Ardon. Kazemi talks about the trauma of detention and the relief that playing music brings.[45] The works threw into high relief the country's harsh detention policies, using humour and bitter irony as strategies of resistance to immigration politics and demonstrating resilience through creativity. As co-curator Chrisoula Lionis has argued, humour is a subtle weapon in mediating and transforming collective trauma in sites of protracted crisis such as Palestine, Greece, and Australia.[46] The use of humour in talking about this devastating policy was a critical addition to the exhibition.

Other artists work from the personal experience of incarceration. Azza Abo Rebeih's *Traces* (2018) is a harrowing set of etchings based on her time as an activist against and prisoner of Bashar al-Assad's brutal regime in Syria, before seeking asylum in Lebanon. For the exhibition, the Whitworth transformed the series into a digital book-display through which visitors could scroll. Abo Rebeieh depicts the harsh reality of state violence wrought upon protestors against the regime: beaten bodies, the abuse of pregnant women, the humiliation of strip-searching, and the ominous shadow of bats, echoing Goya's timeless themes. This is a deeply personal work that brings the viewer into the world of the female activist and prisoner who has suffered the trauma of incarceration and displacement. The plates have accompanying text. A bright green bus rushes through a ruined city: 'Millions of my countrymen have been displaced. The door of our homeland is open for departure, but closed for entry, even if this meant just another displacement to a huge prison'. *Traces* depicts extreme brutality and despair: 'in a one metre square room, we are fifteen women' (Figure 5.3). But it also shows the tenderness and care between female detainees crammed into confined spaces, who 'humour each other' before an interrogation.[47] Ultimately, the voice of female survivors of the regime emerges, transforming displacement into a story of resilience and resistance, which has since become even more resonant in the wake of Assad's fall in December 2024 , and world awakening to the horror of his torture prisons.

A significant outcome of this project resulted in the Whitworth adding to its displacement collections, purchasing a set of drawings by leading international artist Mounira al Solh, *I Strongly Believe in Our Right to be Frivolous* (2012–ongoing). Al Solh is a Lebanese-Dutch artist with a background of displacement that began when her parents fled to Syria in 1989 during the Lebanese Civil War. She documents in Arabic

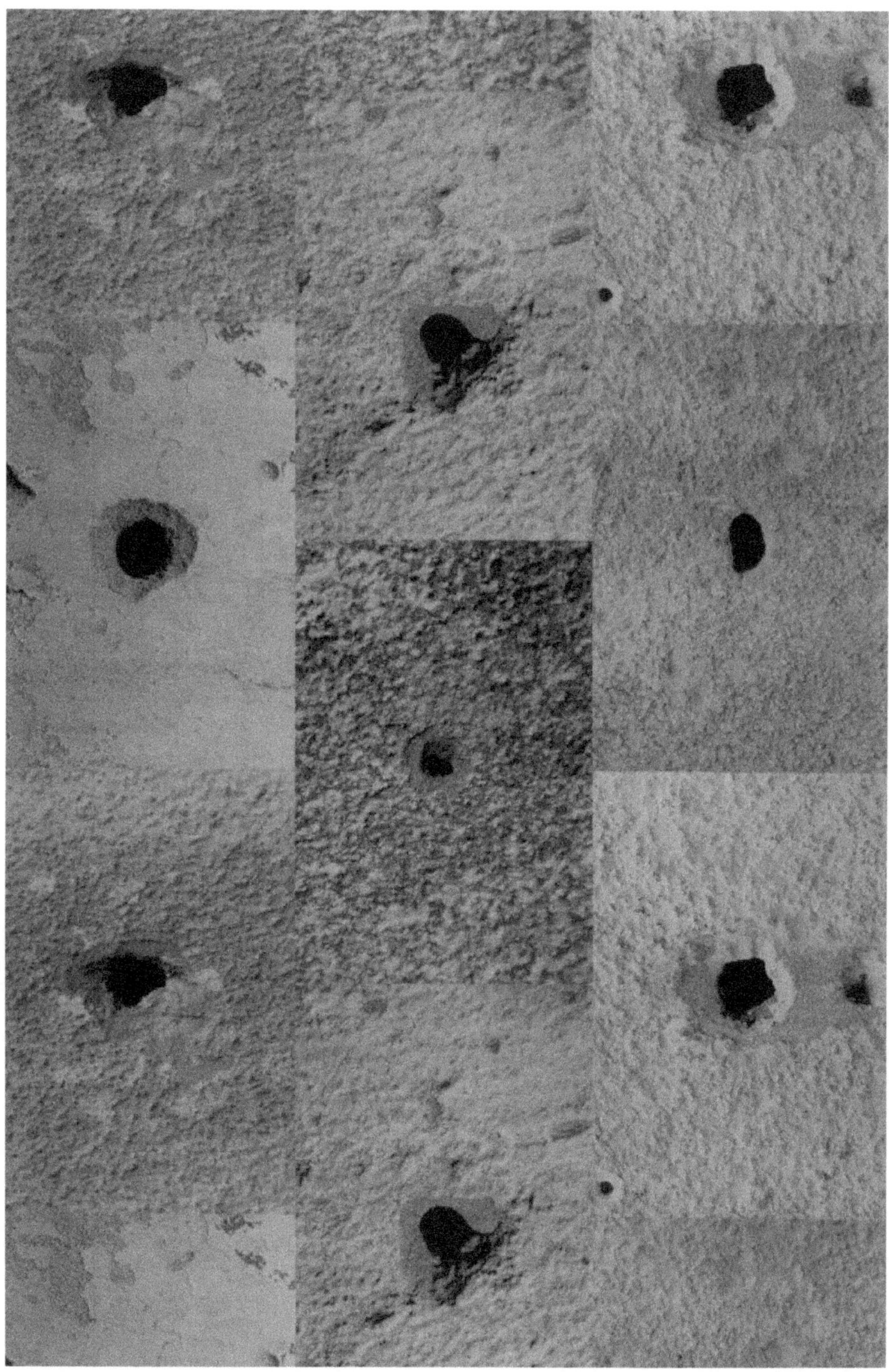

5.3 Bashir Makhoul, *Points of View* (1998). Wallpaper print. Image courtesy of the Whitworth, University of Manchester. Photo: Michael Pollard. Courtesy of the artist.

the stories of displaced people, while rendering quick portraits on yellow, lined, legal paper. This material refers to the bureaucracy, narrativisation, and 'burden of proof' involved when seeking asylum (as discussed in Chapter 2). The artist plays with the testimonies in legal practice but uses story fragments and portraiture to underscore experiences of displacement and resettlement. Some are portraits of children, suggesting the generational impact of displacement and referencing the compelling emotions that images of lone children arouse, as discussed in Chapter 1 (Figure 5.4). Another portrait tells the traumatic story of the imprisonment of one woman's husband in Syria (Figure 5.5). The title derives from Palestinian Poet Mahmoud Darwish and his writing on exile. This acquisition enabled a temporary exhibition to have a major legacy for the gallery's capacity to address displacement.[48]

As we have seen throughout this book, the foundations of displacement aesthetics were consolidated during the Second World War. Thus, the inclusion of a private archive relating to Jewish displaced artists interned on the Isle of Man was an important addition. It included drawings and prints by Paul Humpoletz, Ernst Eisenmeyer, and Hugo Dachinger, a camp gazette, and the poster for their camp exhibition, with

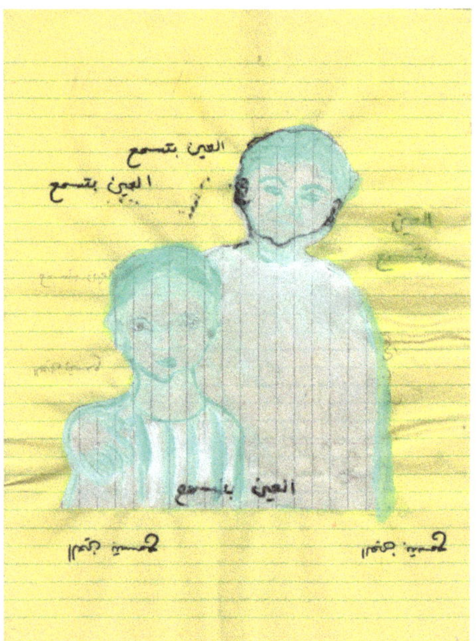 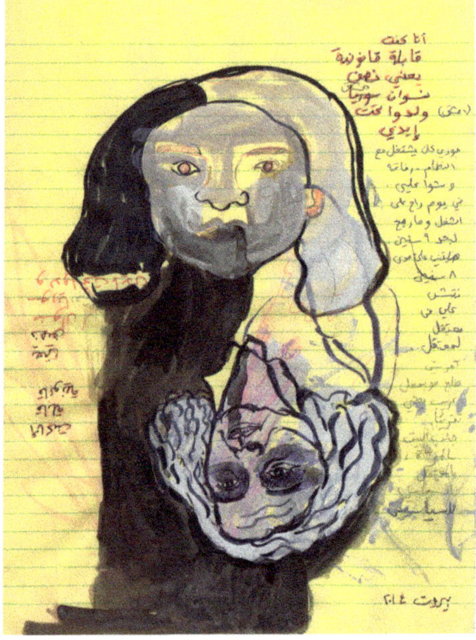

5.4 Mounira Al Solh, *I Strongly Believe in Our Right to Be Frivolous #99*, 2015, Mixed media drawing on legal paper, 28.6 × 21 cm. Courtesy of the artist and Sfeir-Semler Gallery Beirut/ Hamburg.

5.5 Mounira Al Solh, *I Strongly Believe in Our Right to Be Frivolous #155*, 2016, Mixed media drawing on legal paper, 28.6 × 21 cm. Courtesy of the artist and Sfeir-Semler Gallery Beirut/ Hamburg.

the redolent title of *Art Behind the Wire* (1941–42).[49] As discussed at the outset, the internment of artists, intellectuals, and professionals in Britain was of profound concern to the art world. The historical artworks in the show centred on the story of exiled and refugee artists from Nazi Europe during this critical period of seeking sanctuary. Collection works displayed included pieces by Oscar Kokoschka (*Head of Paul Westheim*, 1923), Frank Auerbach (*Head of E.O.W*, 1960), and Lucian Freud (*Man's Head, Self Portrait I*, 1963), all artists who came later in their lives to be celebrated as the most important British artists of their generation and beyond. However, also in the Whitworth's collection was a little-seen Max Ernst, *Danseuses* (1950). This artist was included in the infamous Nazi propaganda event, the 1937 Degenerate Art Show. Though a Catholic, the Nazi party had designated Ernst an enemy-alien due to his modernism and his affiliations. He was imprisoned in Camp des Milles, a French internment camp for 'undesirables' in 1939, where he, among other artists such as Hans Bellmer, made art as a form of resistance to their dehumanisation.

A further section in the exhibition, entitled 'The Politics of Rescue', was dedicated to the lesser-known story of European artists who escaped to the US and Mexico on the *SS Sinaia*. This was under the auspices of the Emergency Rescue Committee and the journalist Varian Fry, the American heiress Mary Jayne Gold, the artist Miriam Davenport, and the art historian Margaret Scolari, who was also the wife of Alfred Barr, director of the Museum of Modern Art in New York. During the research period, we discovered a stunning and rarely seen Marc Chagall pastel-on-paperwork in Manchester Art Gallery's collection, *Le Cirque au Cheval Blanc* (1967). This work is now listed in the public catalogue as a result. Complicating British and American narratives around rescuing Jewish artists and intellectuals was a way of talking about the contemporary criminalising of maritime rescue missions and the UK 'stop the boats' policy of the government at the time. 'The Politics of Rescue' also featured a set of Instagram photos from the Mediterranean refugee rescue vessel *MV Louise Michel*, which the street artist Banksy funded, and which has endured numerous legal challenges from European states.

By comparing historic and contemporary humanitarian rescues, and by focusing on different experiences of displacement, detention, and internment, the exhibition broadened the focus to allow a greater range of stories. Moreover, displacement aesthetics and the trauma of exile from war zones is sometimes opaque to the canon and its prioritisation of 'movements', such as Dada, Surrealism, and Abstract Expressionism. There is much more to understanding the traces of displacement in our public galleries than the story of modern art.

As we saw in Chapter 1, the foundation of the international refugee regime in the first half of the twentieth century underpinned displacement aesthetics. In this exhibition, it formed the grounding for the Anglo-European tilt of the show. Significantly, it also reveals how art was part of the cultural constitution of refugeedom in this era, even before the Convention Relating to the Status of Refugees (1951) and the 1967 Protocol. The latter ostensibly expanded from its Eurocentric, colonial origins to include refugees from across the world. However, by maintaining its persecution focus, it excluded Africans displaced in decolonising conflicts.[50] As we saw in Chapter One, the First World War had been a critical point in the legal categorisation of refugees, with around 9.5 million recorded in 1926. Racial hierarchies were abiding principles of empire that refused extending the rights of asylum to colonial subjects.[51] Representations of displaced Europeans, as well as Turks, Armenians, and Assyrians (from League of Nations mandated territories) generated common motifs of fleeing refugee crowds. The exhibition represented the theme of flight with the Belgian born Welsh 'official war artist' Frank Brangwyn's *The Leaving of Antwerp* (1914–16), depicted Belgian families traipsing along a road, also a trope of refugee movement that was reproduced in fund-raising posters for the Belgian and Allies Aid League.

Alongside the emotions linked to mobility, beauty was not just an aesthetic convention in portraiture, but was also a humanitarian aesthetic that feminised displacement. William Strang's *Belgian Peasant* (1915) is a portrait of a beautiful young woman, who we now know was one of the many refugees in Britain who earned money as a model for portrait painters. Her downcast eyes suggest modesty and the feminised state of refugee worthiness. This section, entitled 'Gendered Humanitarianism', problematised the tropes of refugees such as mobility, beauty, and 'womanandchild', as discussed in Chapter 1, and their use in artist-produced aid posters, which universalised women and children as refugee victims. Instead, the curation could juxtapose those images with works that reveal a counter narrative to tropes of passive, voiceless refugees. The display featured Armenian women's textiles made in the early twentieth century, including a baby's cap and embroidered fabric. The narrative focused on women's resilience as breadwinners and in continuing their cultural skills, in defiance of ethnic cleansing. However, to truly make sense of these stories, community voices were vital. In response, co-curator Ani Despanyan's *Poem for Armenian Fragments* (2022) speaks of 'the colours, the ornaments, the shapes of life that deprived us of the details of defining our home', but also of the courage of retaining 'the heritage I owe you'. Her poem was placed next to the textiles to enrich the interpretation and speak back to the long history of displaced women's silencing.

Holding the space and commanding new interpretations of the collection, the co-curators responded with their own works of poetry, painting, and audiovisual media, a critical shift in approach that occurred organically during the workshops. For the institution, their object labels and narratives were entered into the gallery's database, providing new information and a long-term legacy of a temporary exhibition. Scholars argue that such approaches emphasise the active role of creative practitioners in research, enhancing the activation of the meaning in the public domain and shifting the power from curators to community experts.[52] The cultural producer guiding the co-curation project noted that exhibitions do not often prioritise the voices of people with lived experience in curation, instead often relegating displaced artists to the limited role of Refugee Week.[53] Space was made for critical dialogue, personal testimony, resilience, and humour to enrich the conversations. Another co-curator reflected on the stimulating thoughts and interpretations that emerged and the way they revealed the value of unique, personal perspectives on how displacement can be understood through art.[54] Another co-curator noted that collaboration conveyed viewpoints and feelings through direct contact, observation and reflection, but also learning by listening to experiences of displacement other than one's own.[55]

To be sure, the pressured timescale of producing a temporary exhibition that was experimenting with co-curation, and resourced through a finite research project, had constraints. One of the co-curators also observed that their selections took the exhibition in a different direction to the early research because lived experience was at the forefront. The challenge in 'developing ideas with communities is to ensure that both the process and the final display are brought centre stage'.[56] Further, a gallery curator reflected that the challenge of collaboration is managing institutional procedures to consider whose 'authority and framework' remains core to co-production. Collaboration is about being 'caring, thoughtful and open', and questioning 'what it means to truly centre lived experience'. This might also include working with trauma-informed facilitators to 'mediate the encounter' between curators, academics, and focus groups, to 'hold the space' and 'advocate for constituents'.[57] An example of holding the space can be seen in a co-curator from Afghanistan, who selected an embroidered silk and cotton 'marriage kurta' (1950–99), displayed together with a film narrated in Dari about its 'historical and spiritual value'. Conducting his own tour for a delegation of Afghan dignitaries, including a minister in the former government, he reported that displaying the kurta was a proud moment of recognition.

Indeed, one significant outcome of this collaboration was understanding that expertise is multi-layered, and that it requires the mutual recognition of artists, communities, conservators, researchers, and curators. This follows on from the critical learning that the database is partial in its capture of knowledge. Most search results connected to displacement were returned through keywords related to borders and border-crossing, or geographies of conflict. The co-curators' valuable insights revealed the impact of reductive or marginalising discourse on their lived experience and informed curatorial decision-making. Thus, the database can be transformed with new data inputs from the different experts, especially those with lived experience, so that curators and conservators can better understand the significance of collection items for artists, communities, and future users. But valuing experiential expertise also requires resources to pay for time and contribution. This can be part of a wider decolonial strategy, although it is not always so simple. Academic collaborations are short-lived, and while resource priorities are built into a museum's business plans, it is widely known that the funding environment is dwindling.

A further challenge to bringing out these hidden stories is the contemporary moment. Extreme volatility and divisiveness around migration and refugee policy mean there is an even greater duty of care towards co-curators and artists with lived experience. Consideration is required of how to recognise and ameliorate the process of exhibition-making that involves a colossal and yet invisible burden of emotional labour. A senior gallery curator reflected on the 'emotional challenge of bringing people with lived experience of forced displacement into an institution', noting their 'brilliant specialist knowledge' existing alongside traumatic experiences. Because such 'embodied and raw' experiences go beyond any 'curatorial mission', 'listening and learning from them … was both a challenge and an opportunity'.[58] Recognition of these complexities can emerge to provide a 'transformative sphere' that is 'outside of established polarised discourses', as scholars suggest.[59] A diverse group of collaborators and a producer with lived experience allowed for mutual support among the group. An artist with a family heritage of displacement initially felt her views were not as valid as those among the group with direct experience, however, she said her fellow artists 'encouraged me to see that this was not so and from this experience my own art practice has developed'.[60] The impact of collaboration on the artists' own practices was a common point of reflection.

Another section, entitled 'After Images', problematised visual tropes of displacement. As discussed in detail in Chapter 2, these responses became a recorded conversation in the space, enabling the co-curators' voices to be even more present. An example of this artistic strategy was Lyndell Brown and Charles Green's *Sinjar 2* (2016–22), their response to a 2014 news story about a helicopter crash while rescuing Yazidi families from the advancing Daesh (ISIS) forces. The artists rendered photographs of the mediatised scene in watercolour before producing them in digital print. The faded quality of the image allegorises the impossibility of seeing and understanding through the media and of adequately empathising with the Yazidi's lived experience through the spectacle of rescue.

Deeply personal encounters with collection works became part of the shared experience of the workshops. Artist Vian K. Hussein was immediately taken with Edward Bawden's *Penjwin, Iraq, from the Hills* (1943). It 'created a sense of belonging for me', like a 'flashback to my childhood … the mountains in his painting took me straight away to the mountains of Kurdistan'.[61] Penjwin is in the Kurdistan region of Iraq where Bawden travelled as an official war artist. Contemporary conflicts in the area, including the Syrian Civil War (2011–ongoing) and the Islamic State's attempt to eradicate Kurdish cultural life in Iraq and Syria, resulted in Kurdistan taking in 2 million refugees and internally displaced people. The artist produced her own painting, *Women and Mountain* (2023), installed alongside the Bawden (Figure 5.6).

For Hussein, Bawden's landscape conjured up images of women fighters, including her own family members, who defended Kurdish identity and culture against annihilation. A line of women march toward a mountain, a site of refuge for Kurds fleeing persecution. Their garb refers to the 'woman, life, freedom' movement in support of Iranian women, and the olive branch in the foreground is a Kurdish symbol of peace. The artist recalls how 'creative conversations brought new facets to the stereotypes'.[62] Thus, through dialogue with historic art, making new art and redisplaying new and old works together, displacement aesthetics can be reimagined.

Diverging from the tropes of displacement and refugeedom, the section called 'The Body is the Record' referred to intricate ways in which the lived experience of displacement can be inscribed onto the human body as traumatic memories long after the event. The Whitworth has a special collection of so-called 'outsider art' (the Musgrave-Kinley Art Collection, named after Monica Kinley who was from a

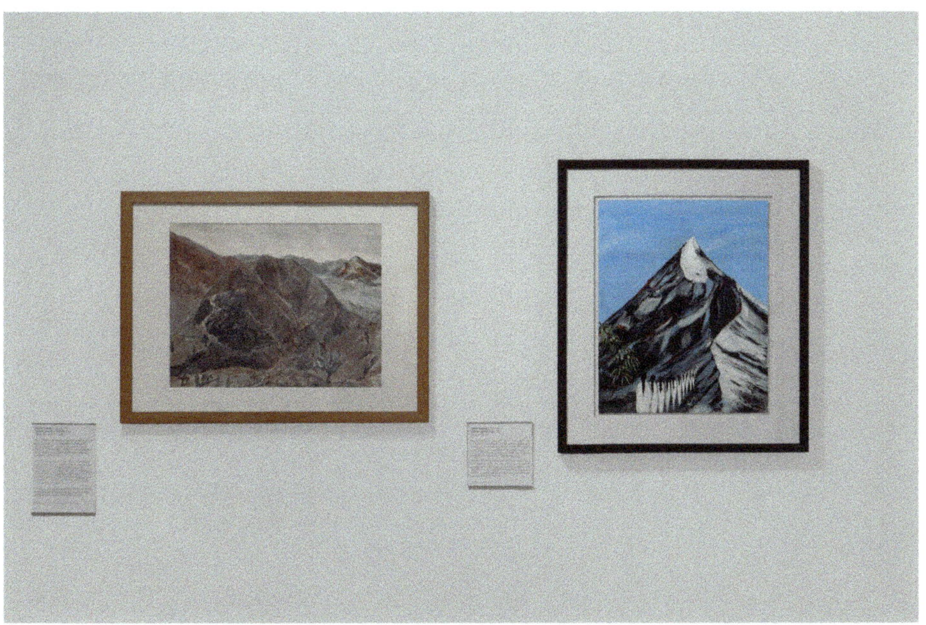

5.6 *Traces of Displacement* exhibition installation view. Edward Bawden (1903–89, UK), *Penjwin, Iraq, from the Hills*, 1943, watercolour and ink on paper [left] and Vian K. Hussein, *Women and Mountain*, 2023, acrylic on canvas [right]. Image courtesy of the Whitworth, University of Manchester. Photo: Michael Pollard. Copyright *Penjwin, Iraq, from the Hills*, 1943, Estate of Edward Bawden.

Jewish survivor family). She collected the work of Dusan Kusmic, a Croatian Italian who, during the Second World War, ended up in a prisoner-of-war camp in Sicily. Traumatised by the suicide of a friend and fellow prisoner, and unable to eat his bread ration, he moulded sculptures out of the materials (just as Kurt Schwitters did with porridge while interned on the Isle of Man). Work such as *Untitled (bread shoes on base)* (1948–50) channels a surrealistic materiality that transforms bread into symbols of life and luxury at the same time as helping the artist heal his trauma.

Collaboration brought new ways of thinking about lesser-known textiles. Helena Tomlin selected an embroidered, block-printed 'Russian table-top Mat' (1900–20), which was displayed inside a perspex box at coffee-table height (Figure 5.7). Around the mat her own works of watercolour and ink-coated paper, canvas, and thread were displayed. Although preceding the Holocaust, the nineteenth-century mat triggered a powerful 'post-memory' (how subsequent generations mediate memory through imaginative investment rather than personal recollection).[63] Tomlin's words in the object label declared: 'the mat marks a gathering space to reflect upon the generations weaving through the world, on paths newly connected'. This was not just about the trauma of lost ancestors but the threads of resilience and cultural continuity. The collection did possess many works made by refugees from Nazism, such as Josef

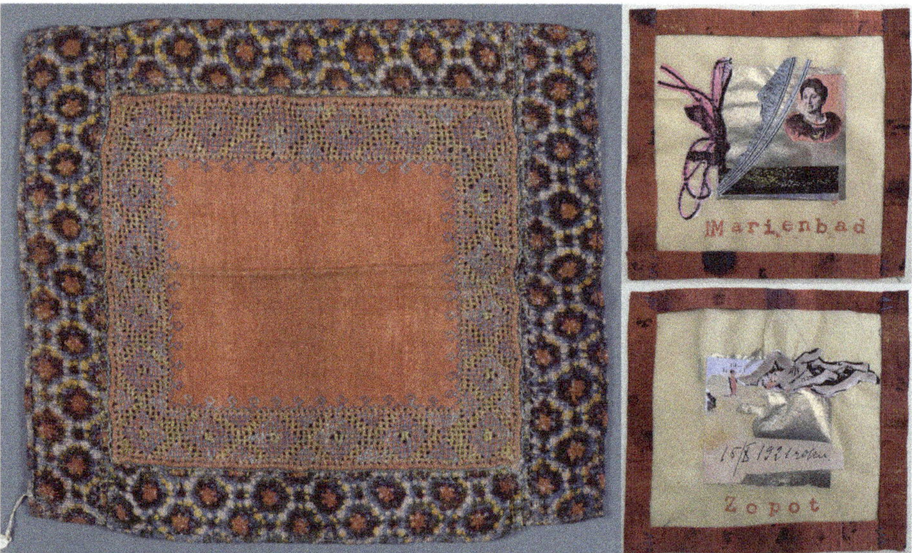

5.7 *Russian Table-Top Mat*, 1900–20, hand embroidered and hand block printed cotton or linen [left] and Helena Tomlin, *Russian Mat* (2023). [Top and bottom right; watercolour and stamped ink, coated paper, photocopy, canvas and thread]. Photo: Michael Pollard. *Russian Table-Top Mat*, Whitworth Art Gallery collection. *Russian Mat* image courtesy of the artist. Image files prepared by Daniel Wand, with permission.

Herman's Scottish miners series, but Tomlin was drawn to a narration of history and memory not overshadowed by the darkness of genocide. Thus, collaboration with these artists enabled a different perspective on stories of Jewish refugeedom, also highly pertinent to the city of Manchester, with its Jewish communities stretching back to the early 18th century.

Contemporary art in response to collections offers key insights into memory and forgetting of places, peoples, and emotions that displacement entangles. Raisa Kabir's textile work *It Must be Nice to Fall in Love* (2017) employs an 'unweaving' technique, to re-create a distorted pre-Partition map of India. This was an earlier commission in response to South Asian textiles in the Whitworth collection in Manchester (Figure 5.8). The 1947 Indian Partition generated new borders and new national identities, but the British policy also displaced 15 million people. In Tomlin and Kabir's work we are reminded of how tactile objects can trigger post-memories, which, as we will see, is a vital component emerging in decolonising museum collections.

Decolonising efforts seek to investigate the traces and legacies of colonialism and slavery in collections, responding to increasing public demand for truth-telling and reckoning with an imperial past in which collecting art and artefacts is entangled.[64] Art museums increasingly seek to understand how collections can be better interpreted and displayed in ways that are relevant to local communities. Nina Möntmann argues that 'de-centring' the dominant perspective of White, western, and male hegemonies implicates how themes are addressed in exhibitions, while also impacting community engagement.[65] Through this period of research came the slow recognition of the ongoing connections between colonial histories and displacement.

During the workshop discussions, it emerged that the collaborating artists felt it imperative that links between colonial history, enslavement, and mass displacement were highlighted in the exhibition. The curatorial scope of *Traces of Displacement* was therefore expanded to include a section simply titled 'The Trans-Atlantic Slave Trade'. It highlighted the 12.5 million Africans trafficked to the Americas between the fifteenth and nineteenth centuries. Drawing attention to the brutal trade and forced labour of enslaved people that underpins the wealth of modern industrial cities, including Manchester, was also a way of talking about dark histories of collecting. At the time of staging the exhibition, key institutions such as the *Manchester Guardian* and the University of Manchester were researching, publishing, and exhibiting their findings on their own historic links to slavery.[66] Responding to this research, the Whitworth (part of the University) publicly committed to investigating the link between slavery and its collections. In *Traces* this was explicitly acknowledged in exhibition wall text, a statement that has remained in the database system for future users. John Edward Taylor, the local cotton manufacturer and one of the *Guardian* founders, donated 266 drawings to the collection, including J.M.W. Turner's *Study of Boats* (1828–30).

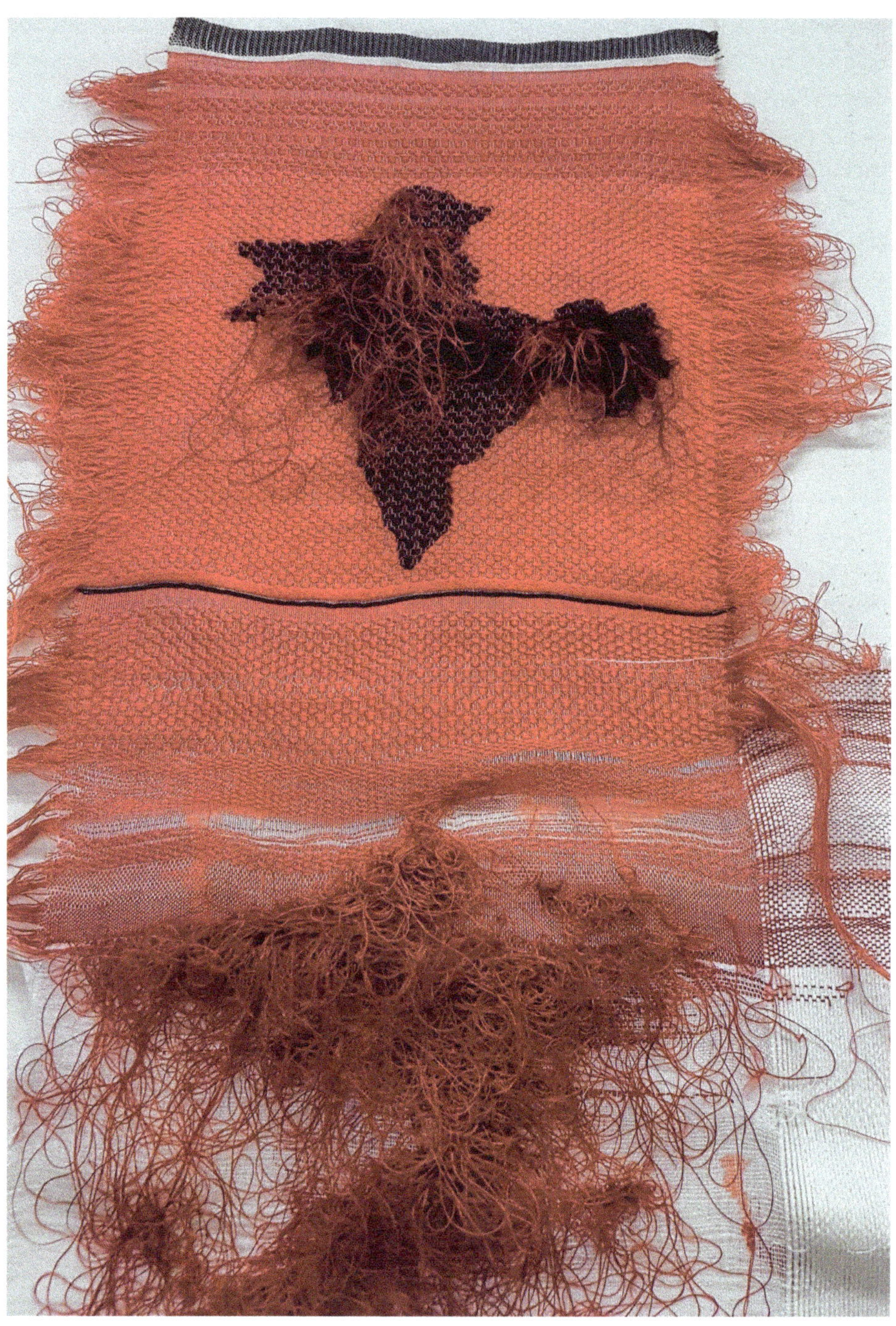

5.8 Raisa Kabir, *It Must Be Nice to Fall in Love...* (2017). Hand-dyed and hand-woven silk and cotton. Whitworth Art Gallery collection. Courtesy of the artist.

It was through the process of collaborative co-curation that slavery and colonialism were prioritised as crucial nodes in the longer trajectory of displacement aesthetics. This is significant because prior to collaboration with the artists, the research
concentrated on modern war and displacement over the last century. Historians have
challenged the view that international law was only the result of agreements between
nations. Rather, its colonial origins normalised the capacity for sovereign states (and
their settler colonies) to determine their exclusionary powers based on supremacist
markers of civilisation and racial difference.[67] Today, as Bosco Opi argues, 'refugee
coloniality' is still 'an ever-existing condition within the present globalised political system'.[68] For instance, Europeans institutionalised transit camps to detain and
forcibly displace enslaved Africans, which became a standard colonial and refugee
containment practice. The entanglement of displacement, colonialism, and slavery are
also ever-present in cultural objects, which demands investigation. In Manchester an
appetite was growing to understand this past and present, as the *Guardian's* research
revealed.

To address the intersections between the slave trade, Manchester, and forced
displacement, the exhibition included several key collection objects. These included
Theodor de Bry's 1590 engravings of the Algonquians (Roanoke Island, North
Carolina), and Frederic Etienne Joseph Feldtrappe's *Traite des Nègres* (*The Slave
Trade*), a French domestic textile with abolitionist images of African families being
separated, brutalised, and forced onto enslavers' boats (1815–20). After the launch,
one of the project's co-curators felt that the collection works emphasised White abolitionist narratives rather than enslaved people's resistance. For the co-curator, this
represented a wider problem of White privilege, marginalisation, and silencing, which
cultural spaces should seek to repair.[69] Returning to the collection with this critique
in mind, one of the gallery curators identified two new works that could highlight
activist stories. The Whitworth took a flexible approach to this turn of events after
the exhibition opening, investing resources into rehanging the section. The display
could now include Richard Cosway's etching of Ottobah Cugoano (with Mr and Mrs
Cosway, 1784), a trafficked activist and author of the first published work against
slavery, which inspired Abolitionists and transformed some enslavers in the art world.
Also included was William Ward's mezzotint portrait of Le Chevalier de St Georges
(1788), the influential composer and French Caribbean Abolitionist in the Society of
the Friends of Black People (Société des Amis des Noirs).

Thus, a longer history than planned in the original research was made possible
through collaboration with artists and additional advice from a slavery specialist.
The institution's genuine engagement with co-curation, and its rapid response to
critical input made the redisplay possible. Temporary exhibitions may seem more
agile in taking risks and adapting to changing circumstances, but they are often time

and resource constrained. When undertaking longer-term institutional change, the complexities widen, impacting multiple stakeholders, staff, and visitors, as well as involving invisible processes and added layers of consultation. Changing the way both galleries and researchers work means grappling with the subtleties of ongoing coloniality, of 'learning from being uncomfortable', possibilities that ideally emerge from the collaborative circle where trust is earned.[70]

Co-curating displacement in the redisplay of a public collection

Across the world, art museums are re-evaluating how they understand and display their collections, taking into account audiences' changing expectations. This work may redress missing stories, update with socially relevant narratives, highlight women and artists of colour (Reina Sofia; Metropolitan Museum of New York; Tate Britain), or decolonise conventional narratives with Indigenous artists, narrative voices, and audio-guides (Art Gallery of NSW; Baltimore Museum of Art). These approaches extend from African American artist Fred Wilson's groundbreaking project, *Mining the Museum* (1992). Although three decades ago, it is nevertheless true that for some audiences such experiments go too far, while for others they do not go far enough. Although museums are keen to welcome all visitors, this is no simple matter, especially when the reconsideration of empire, slavery, and colonialism has become a matter of public debate and culture wars. Academics and curators might be keen to revise the canon of western art, with all its perceived wisdom but some visitors navigate this uncertain terrain with trepidation, lack of historical knowledge, or resistance to previously unchallenged ideas. Unpicking the role of empire and the subtle constancy of imperialist thinking that underpins Eurocentrism has nevertheless generated new momentum to tackle difficult conversations.[71] Moreover, it is recognised that action is needed not just in reckoning with colonial heritage in the present-day, but to genuinely demonstrate that museums are safe and inclusive spaces for marginalised communities.

Certainly, it has become commonplace to talk about decolonisation within art museums where collections derive directly from imperial conquest. Yet art galleries (and White academics such as our research team) have more opaque relationships to privilege and, as discussed in Chapter 2, need to be continually reflective on the power and status they hold in the creation of knowledge. We know we have to try harder to ensure that collaboration does not feel extractive or burdensome in its hidden emotional labours. Moreover, genuine decolonisation, as Nina Möntmann and many others argue, demands greater liberation from western-centric forms of knowledge, such as universality, modernity, and the progressiveness of the avant-garde. Art museums, however, rest on the pillars that Walter D. Mignolo identified as a 'colonial matrix of power' of racism, sexism, and the exploitation of the natural world. Decolonising collections seeks to supplant these pillars, usually through telling multiple narratives from marginalised voices and decentring the European canon.[72]

This brings us to *The Grand Tour and Grand Style: The Influence of Travel* at Manchester Art Gallery. This was a decades-old installation of the collection, scheduled for an overhaul as part of a wider programme of redevelopment. The collaborative project – or 'rethink' – chimed with other initiatives undertaken, including Sonia Boyce's wildly misunderstood feminist intervention (*Six Acts* 2018), Jade Montserrat's investigation of race *Constellations: Care & Resistance* (2020–23), and American social practice artist Suzanne Lacy's *Uncertain Futures + 100 Women* (2023–24), a project with diverse women in Manchester, including migrant women workers.

Following on from this, we embarked on a collaboration between the authors, gallery curators, an external cultural producer, and four artists with backgrounds of migration and displacement. Together, we set out to locate alternative collection object and artworks, rallying around the themes of migration and displacement to see anew the history and art of *The Grand Tour*. The project took over a year to bring together and resulted in a redisplay entitled *Rethinking the Grand Tour*.

Centring displacement and migration within a revised history of art acknowledged the legacy of colonialism, trade, and the mobility of heritage through collecting, including the creation of transnational markets for art and artefacts. Reconsidering celebrated European art of the eighteenth and nineteenth century showed its role, as Katrin Sieg and others have observed, 'in supporting Eurocentric and imperialist understandings of the world', which served the power relations underpinning the supremacy of western aesthetic values.[73] Travellers to Europe often adopted an 'ethnographic posture' when encountering its local peasantry, and saw in classical art and antiquities the cultural superiority that valued Europe as the seat of civilisation. Such ideas would later shape the interests of nineteenth-century imperial power. Grand tourism produced ideas of the 'other' as 'exotic, inferior, quaint, and picturesque'.[74] However, the cultural education of aristocratic youth was not its only form. Middle-class gentlemen and merchants became avid travellers, keen to exploit new commercial opportunities.[75] Alongside imperial expansion, grand tourism and the passion for travel extended to India and to the Ottoman lands, where coveted classical antiquities were bought, stolen, and vandalised by a wide range of travellers. Vast quantities of objects entered Britain.[76] As tourism became less 'grand', it was implanted in colonised lands and in imperial armed service: 'tourism was inseparable from the west's conquest of the Middle East'.[77] Today, scholars note how the colonial origins of globalisation and the world-wide tourist industries reflect how its 'colonial overtone never fades'.[78]

Economic factors, such as extractive forms of colonial capitalism, have come under increasing scrutiny. Decolonial strategies in museums seek to challenge where the money comes from, which can be a fraught and complex endeavour when collection provenances are hard to locate. This relates to the history of the Grand Tour. Conventionally, it seems an innocuous form of aristocratic education that revered classical antiquity and produced an appetite for adventure and collecting. Not as well known is that some British grand tourists paid for this luxury from wealth derived from enslavement plantations, such as William Thomas Beckford, whose family owned thirteen sugar plantations with 3,000 enslaved Africans in Jamaica.[79] In the nineteenth century, American planters also undertook such tours, imitating the English genteel classes while seeking to affirm their racial and cultural superiority.[80] To embark on rethinking the Grand Tour through the lens of migration and displacement, then, was to make both explicit and implicit connections to the colonial past that were slowly revealed over time through research and collaboration with artists with lived experience.

Multivocality is a key approach to decentring dominant discourses and Eurocentric art collections that valorise 'the western canon and the associated (re)production of knowledge'.[81] Challenging the Grand Tour and the imperial language that underpins the canon chimed with Manchester Art Gallery's wider mission of exploring complicated histories through recognition and dialogue. *Rethinking the Grand Tour* thus shone a light on the privilege of European tourism (the Grand Tour) and its fervour for collecting that saw swathes of art and antiquities enter many countries, including Great Britain. To engage in this conversation, artists with backgrounds of migration and displacement helped to inform institutional knowledge by making art and installing a different set of collections that would replace an older arrangement the gallery was eager to update.

This collaboration with artists emanated from earlier projects and relationship building. One of the key learnings from In Place of War, a Creative and Social Entrepreneur Programme hosted at the Whitworth and Manchester Art Gallery, was to invest in long-term connections with minority artists. This can advance the careers of artists who, for instance, may have experienced interruptions from forced migration. Four artists from that programme came together for the rethink project: Kani Kamil, Mahboobeh Rajabi, Kofo Kego Oyeleye, and Khalda Alkhmri. Over many months, the artists worked with an external cultural producer Jason Cyrus, the authors of this book, and Manchester Art Gallery curators to investigate a vast collection across three large sites of stored and displayed items.

Co-curation entails institutional collaboration with people skilled in brokering relationships and logistics to do participatory and mediational work informed by co-curators' insight. This is far from a simple task as artworks can trigger unanticipated emotional responses that then inform curation and interpretation, but also build new ways of understanding the past and present. As one curator later reflected when listening to an artist speak about being forced to leave their country and feeling brutalised by the UK asylum system:

> I can remember … having a dawn of understanding about how complicated feelings must be about home for someone who has been forced out of it … It just came upon me, all at once, the enormity of having your whole life sliced from you and yet carrying on with the everyday holding down a life here and now.[82]

To be sure, art is about people, and the affective emotions that it generates impact collaborators in unique and bonding ways, which curators and institutions can only understand with time and trust-building with marginalised artists and communities.

Across a diverse team, the role of the cultural producer, drawing on expertise in decolonial methods and textile histories, was important in furthering understanding. Professional guidance and emotional support were provided for the artists through the decision-making process of the redisplay and when encounters with objects were challenging. For gallery curators, the producer acted as 'a buffer between the gallery's assumptions and the artists' individual wants and needs'.[83] Power-sharing in curating collections requires shifts in long-established curatorial strategies or organisational cultures, so that a broker and advocate provides an empathetic bridge. Rachel Minott has advised that the voices of community co-curators should not be filtered, neutralised, or silenced.[84] The Museums Association also declares, 'collaboration is critical to decolonising museums'.[85] In *Rethinking the Grand Tour*, the gallery was keen to prioritise lived experience, appreciated as curatorial knowledge and expertise. This was an ambitious step for a collection redisplay. The co-curators selected collection items, including painting, photography, posters, textiles, and objects they found especially meaningful, which triggered memories or brought compelling stories to the fore. But since they were artists, they also responded to them creatively, drawing their own personal interpretations. Certainly, artists acting as co-curators is one key strategy in institutional efforts to share power, diversify community access, and reinterpret collections.

One challenge in undertaking collection-based collective research and co-curation is to anticipate differing expectations, institutional practices, and modes of communication that are a normal part of day-to-day business, though often invisible to external collaborators. In addition, priorities and resources can shift, which impacts how discrete projects are understood across an institution. Artists with lived experience also draw on their (sometimes unexpressed) emotional labour, alongside the energy that the opportunity of collaboration and access brings. The process of 're-thinking' was also about 're-doing' the space.

One of the crimson walls (a Victorian heritage colour) was now repainted with sombre yellow, indicating the new display. This colour was arrived at collectively: the aim was to shine a bright light onto the past with the artists' new narratives. Signage, didactic wall panels, object labels, and artist statements were also yellow. The labels of the original *Grand Tour* artworks, which remained on the red walls, were rewritten to draw out stories of migration from those artist histories as well as linking to contemporary displacement. For instance, the label for James Barry's enormous painting *The Birth of Pandora* (1741–1706) describes how international organisations today use the myth of Pandora's box to discuss the 'unforeseen consequences' of conflicts such as population displacement, but also suggests that hope remains to finding solutions. The label for William Hodges' *View of Calcutta (Kolkata)* (c.1790) describes his commissions on Captain Cook's second voyage to the Pacific (1771–76) and for the Governor General of India, and the East India Company. The painting is described as a 'quiet celebration' of colonial migration that 'dispossessed local people of their land, resources and culture'. The label for William Blake's drawing of *Homer* (1757–1827) notes the themes of war, displacement, and hospitality in the epic poems *The Iliad* and *The Odyssey*, often used today as 'cultural reference points to understand contemporary refugee crises'. Other classical and Grand Tour works highlight the privilege of free movement, in dialogue with the contemporary works on the yellow wall that refer to contemporary restrictions on mobility and how art collecting implicates colonialism. The online museum catalogue was updated to reflect the shifts and new understandings about names and descriptions of collection items, all based on research by the co-curators. This would embed power-sharing and new knowledge, leaving a long-term legacy. But, as we learned, embedding also takes time.

Indeed, the cultural producer reflected that this co-curatorial work may be enriched by 'the breadth of experiences and perspectives', however the challenge remains in 'collating and aligning' this within a relatively short time-frame.[86] Echoing this, a gallery curator noted, 'Co-curating? Triple the amount of time you think you need'.[87] Collaboration with universities and marginalised artists brings resources and wide expertise, but there were other pressures placed upon this important art museum, as we shall see.

Affective encounters with collections

In 2022, the co-curators visited Manchester Art Gallery's collections at Queen's Park, an offsite building with many hidden treasures that the gallery is bringing to the public through its intensive capital redevelopment programme. The co-curators also visited Platt Hall (an eighteenth-century home that had once been a costume gallery and had even housed Belgian refugees in 1915), which contained 24,000 objects. The works discovered here were captivating.

At Queen's Park, the artists' attention was drawn to a set of Empire Marketing Board posters depicting the River Niger with a British colonial lens focused on its riches, an orientalist tile panel made by the Pilkington factory, a contemporary photowork, and two paintings – an Argentinian port and a Manchester streetscape. Encounters with the ghosts of art past, and with collections unseen by the public but holding curious tales, hinged around the British Empire and its collecting passions, defy description. An artistic explosion soon followed. This was the joy of collaboration and making something new out of the timeworn and mysterious. What emerged were personal stories of the migration of objects and art, like people, across the world. Stories told by artists who have experienced restrictions on their capacity to travel contrasted with the privileged artists of the Grand Tour. Other emotions soon followed.

The idea of home, and its material link with belonging resonated particularly with Khalda Alkhmri. She was surprised to find a small painting of a house and shop in Manchester (by the soldier-artist Harry Kingsley, *New Street*, 1956), surrounded by slum-cleared land. The red bricks, square design, and bright colour reminded the artist of Syrian villages. Alkhmri's artist label states: 'the painting speaks to me of isolation and distance, a haven for families and friends … and looking to the future outside'. The painting she made in response was placed in a perspex box alongside archival documents about Kingsley. *The Damascene House* (2022), with its windows covered in roses and jasmine, 'depicts my identity and tradition', and the archway connects families and houses (Figure 5.9).

Alkhmri also selected a large painting from Queen's Park that had not been displayed in a long time. Benito Quinquela Martin's *Morning Sun, Buenes Aires* (1930) depicts a bustling harbour with boats and workers, expressing the joy of everyday life in bright colours. Boats, here, are seen in a positive light, as signs of free trade and travel, unlike the boats associated with displacement and migration. Subsequently, this work has resonated with gallery visitors.

For Mahboobeh Rajabi, a photowork by the collective Artists Anonymous captured her imagination. It was only later, when its title *Swan Lake* (2007) was retrieved from the catalogue, that its uncanny significance emerged. As a child, she had yearned to be a dancer, but this was forbidden in her home country. The artwork seemed to liberate her from the traumatic origins of her own displacement. This is the unintended consequences of art and collaboration, but it is also the nub of creativity. She returned to Platt Hall to make a video piece about her encounter with the Persian textiles, dancing on its grand staircase, which was installed in the rethink space (*Untitled*, 2022) (Figure 5.10), where she draws on poetic discourse to explore her encounters with

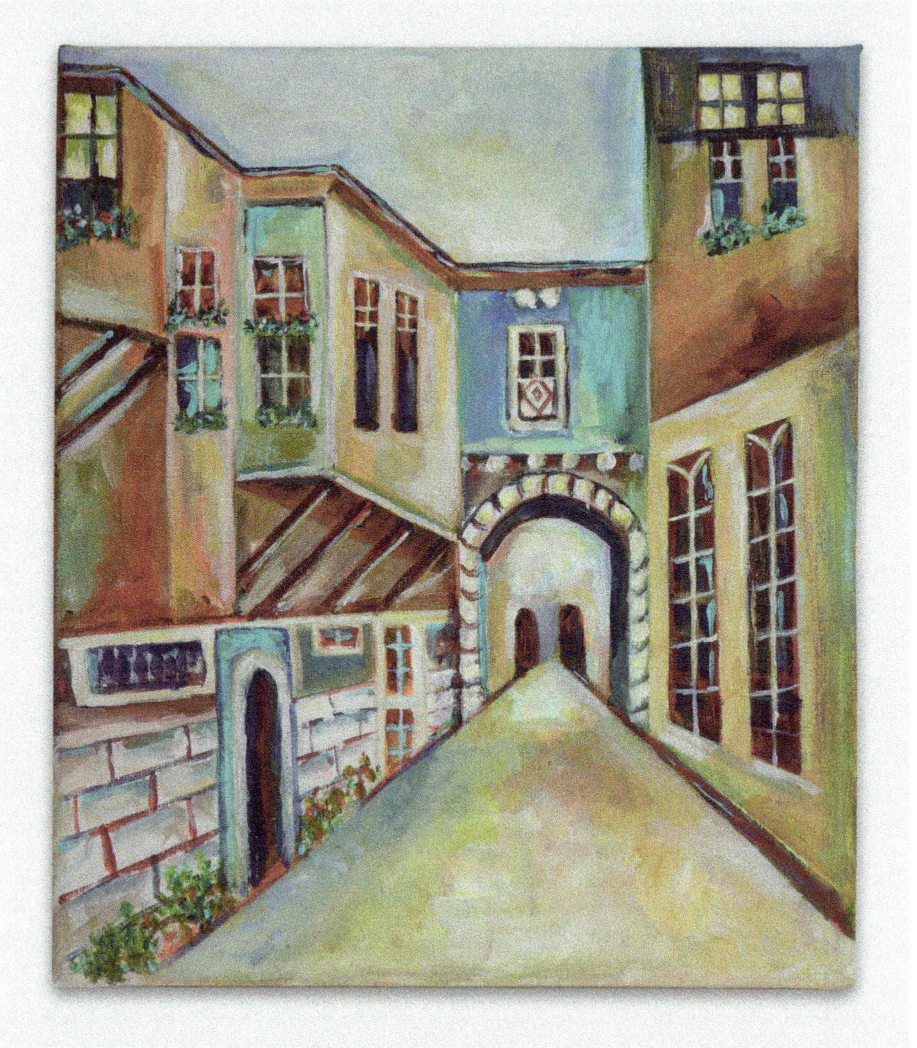

5.9 Khalda Alkhmri, *The Damascene House* (2022). Acrylic on canvas. Photo: Michael Pollard. Courtesy of the artist.

this past heritage in the museum. Over at Platt Hall, a wooden Victorian doll's house and a leather suitcase turned Rajabi's mind to incongruous sensations of leaving and belonging. Her curatorial intervention involved placing one object inside the other, with both displayed inside a perspex box (Figure 5.11).

On the label, the artist writes how objects remind 'of how my Iranian heritage is with me, even though I am far away … My heritage is my home. It's as if I packed it in my suitcase at the age of 21'. This reaction was akin to Helena Tomlin's mat in *Traces*.

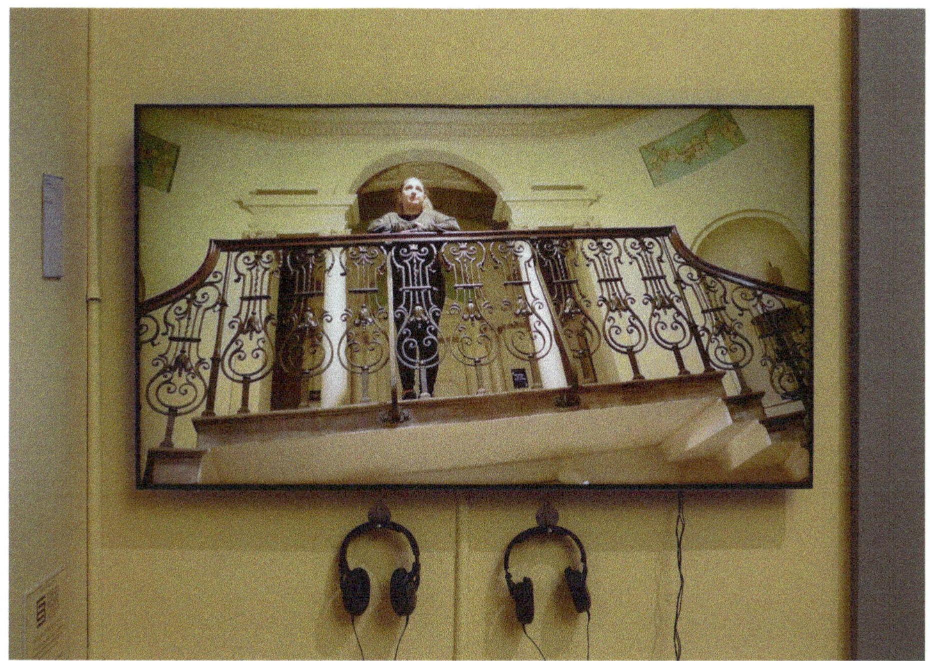

5.10 Mahboobeh Rajabi, *Untitled* (2022). Video still. *Rethinking the Grand Tour* redisplay (installation view). Photo: Michael Pollard. Courtesy of the artist.

Despite no direct link, objects can be invested with meaning, eliciting personal and post-memories, and intangible resonances. We might recall the suitcases mentioned in Chapter 1 and their role as relics of displacement with longstanding significance for artists.

In the attic of this grand building, the textile curator showed us an array of boxes of textiles. Artistic minds were set awhirl. As each box was carefully opened, the precious samples of textiles from pre-twentieth-century Nigeria, Syria, and Iran, were touched through the protective barrier of blue gloves (Figure 5.12).

Something magical happened in this haptic encounter. Is this why textiles are sensory touchstones to the past, with the sustained power to resonate with our ancestors? Belying their quietude, the textiles, woken from their slumber, spoke to the artists in ways that could not have been anticipated. Such 'affective artefacts' – with their material capacity to engage senses and memories, reaching into past lives and cultures – draw time together, as Stefan Hanss argues.[88] However, one of the textile boxes was labelled 'Moorish embroideries'. It was a stark reminder of the inaccuracies and ignorance of colonialism and the racialised capitalism that also buoyed Manchester's industrial wealth. It is recognised that colonial trade

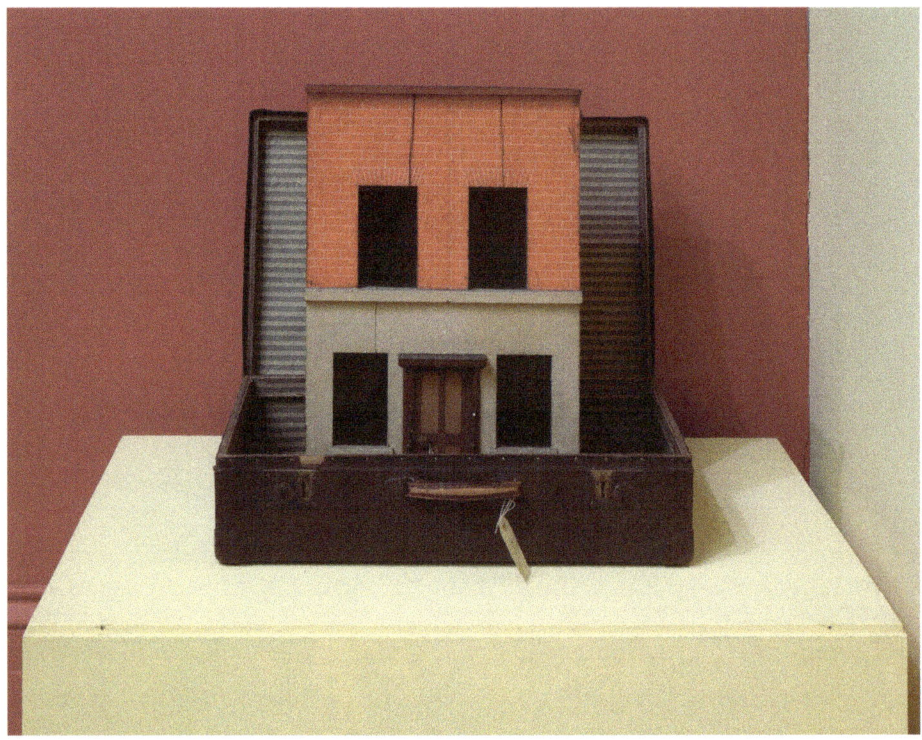

5.11 Doll's house, date and maker unknown, painted wood and glass; suitcase, vulcanised fibre with leather and paper (1920–30). Selected by Mahboobeh Rajabi for *Rethinking the Grand Tour* redisplay (installation view). Manchester Art Gallery collection. Photo: Michael Pollard.

produced asymmetrical relations that harmed local craft industries and decimated cultural knowledge.[89] But from this encounter, the emotions aroused in the process of discovering these rare textiles also generated momentum for the redisplay.

This became the subject matter of Kani Kamil's artistic response. In *A Whisper Behind the Grand Tour* (2022), she reprised the encounter at Platt Hall with a traditional costume from Iraq, a Hashmi dress contained in the 'Moorish' box, which incorrectly identified the item as a 'waistcoat' (Figure 5.13). However, the dress could not be displayed due to its fragility and conservation requirements. Inscribed in Kurdish on the gallery walls, positioned above the empty box contained in perspex on a plinth, Kamil's storytelling ponders the complexity of cultural heritage. Addressing the audience directly:

I've been meaning to ask you … Do you know how many people's stories, cultures, and histories are hidden … closed in dark and invisible places for a century? How long will these objects remain there?

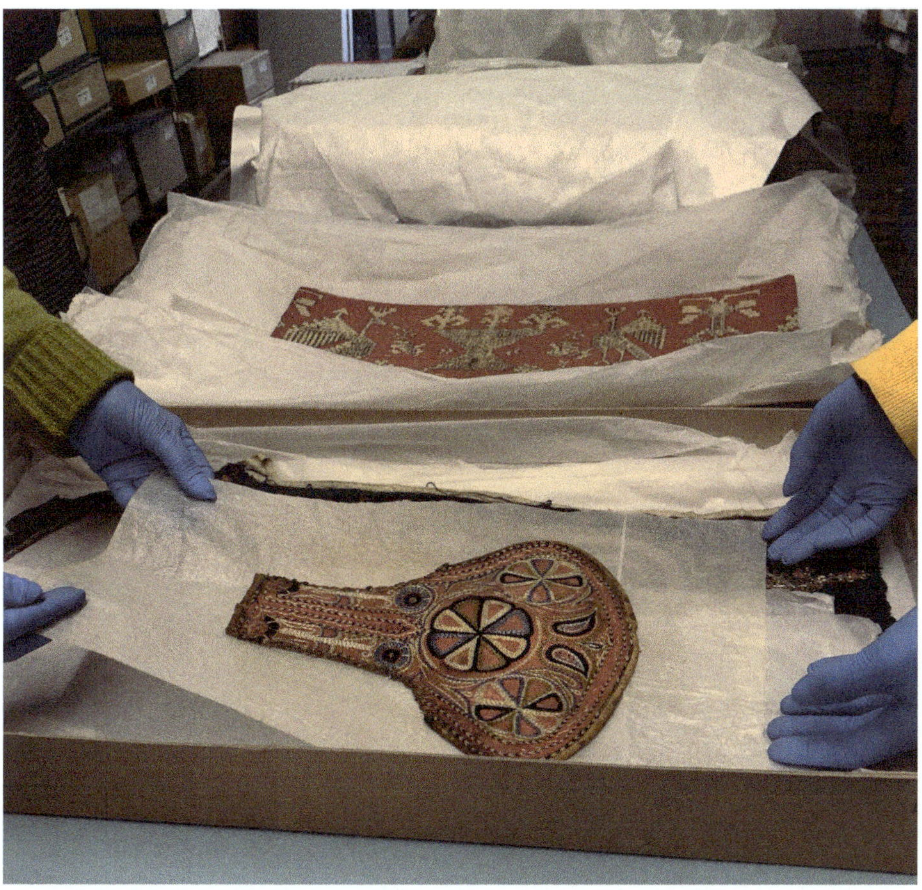

5.12 *Rethinking the Grand Tour* collections research at Platt Hall, Manchester Art Gallery, 2022. Image: Ana Carden-Coyne.

The object triggered a memory of her mother's 'beautiful and precious' Hashmi dress at a time when the Iraqi people were impoverished by economic sanctions and food scarcity. The dress was sold for the family to survive. The label was powerfully felt as 'an act of barbarism that further marginalises and silences cultures, histories, people. To me, the word 'Moorish' might as well read "Others"'. She laments that the dress 'stays in this box, in company with the "Others", each waiting for you to hear, see, and feel their stories'. A unique engagement with grand tourism and its legacies disclosed the emotions aroused when decolonising displacement. As Kamil's object label states, the work is 'about all the voiceless and unseen pieces that have been brought to this country by grand tourists'. Thus, deeply, personal art emerges from the trauma of colonial collecting, which lingers in the present day.

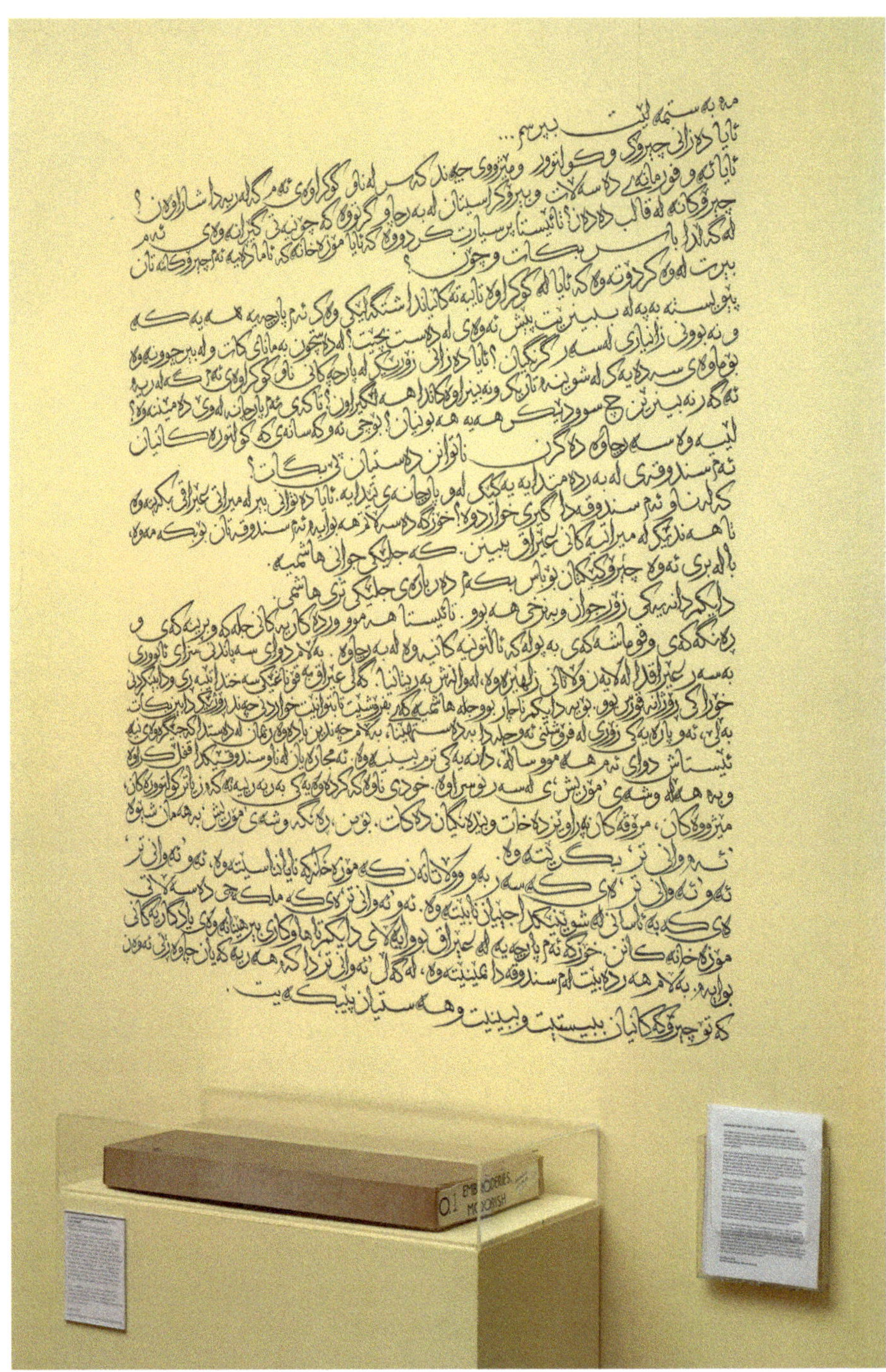

5.13 Kani Kamil, *A Whisper Behind the Grand Tour* (2022). Kurdish calligraphy and 'Moorish' box from Platt Hall, Manchester Art Gallery collection. Photo: Michael Pollard. Courtesy of the artist.

Certainly, it also intimates the complexities of collaboration, and the reality of risking and caring for precious objects. The gallery acknowledged that the artist's work 'identifies core questions around the identity, value, and use of historic objects', and that it 'powerfully expresses the wider impact of such decisions, and highlights the complex questions we need to consider in deciding how to prioritise limited resources'.[90] As one curator later reflected, it was the first time the gallery had worked with contemporary artists with lived experience of migration and displacement in order to explore the collection, but it was necessary and much needed. Significantly, examining these barely documented textiles also revealed their fragility and 'increased the urgency' to develop this decolonial work further, such as in reviewing collections, documentation, and 'addressing historical languages and classification systems that reinforce legacies of inequality'.[91] For an institution keen to explore new horizons and make changes, it had, as another gallery curator noted, 'influenced our approach to permanency … this experience has shown us that the star works are not always the one you think they are. Sometimes they are Pre-Raphaelite paintings. Sometimes they are Kurdish calligraphy on a yellow wall'.[92] This is the promising ambition of lasting change, and it points to the pertinence of contemporary artists being able to hold a light up to the world. Indeed, for the public the work had an ongoing impact, as the artist noted: 'Many visitors to the gallery have been inspired and touched by my piece, and some have even recreated the Hashmi dress that remains mysterious'.[93]

Although the aspirations of decolonial strategies in projects around displacement have their strengths and their limitations, it is the striving to learn that is encouraging. Artists and galleries will continue to pursue their desire to bring lost heritage to light with diverse community users. As Fred Wilson observed, there are 'multiple meanings' in objects present at the same time, and objects can be understood 'from many different vantage points'. Museums do not just collect objects, 'they collect memories, meanings, emotions and experiences'.[94] Thus, objects and memories are interdependent, and intrinsic to the process of rethinking and renegotiating the past.

Artist Kofo Kego Oyeleye found a way around a similar display issue. He had identified an evocative Nigerian textile at Platt Hall, one of 200 cloths that the family of Charles A. Beving gifted to the British Museum and then Manchester Art Gallery. A Manchester cotton merchant and manufacturer, Beving acquired the fabrics during his tour of West Africa in the nineteenth century. The hand-woven samples were collected 'to provide samples for imitation by the Manchester export trade'.[95] Bentinck Mill remade and sold the textiles back to places such as Nigeria, impacting the local economy and continuity of cultural skills. The artist was acutely aware of this loss, as his own family had been in the textile trade. The *Aso Oke* ('top cloth' woven in Iseyin, Oyo state, with cotton and metallic thread) is indigenous to the Yoruba people of Nigeria. It represented 'the spirit of royalty, community and stability', he remarked.

The cloth was an emblem of pride, which, the artist wrote, reminded him of 'a time when people were safe in their homeland. There was no need to escape to the west'. However, this original nineteenth-century cloth was only able to be displayed for six months in a glass case due to conservation guidelines. Ingeniously, the artist had a replica made to replace the original, at the sixth-month mark. This act of replacement sparks questions of appropriation and imitation that are embedded in colonial encounters of the past and present day. Accompanying this piece, was a film entitled *Aso Oke* (2022), installed on the yellow walls about the cloth, including interviews with makers and traders in Nigeria (Figure 5.14).

For Kofo Kego Oyeleye the cloth symbolised his rich cultural heritage and 'that we can build a great nation, fit for the coming generation'. Indeed, he later hosted a public event about the history and contemporary use of *Aso Oke*, discussing the importance of culture and language. This event enthralled audiences, including many from the Nigerian community who had never been to the gallery before. The artist wanted to 'get people from under-represented communities into these spaces because they are

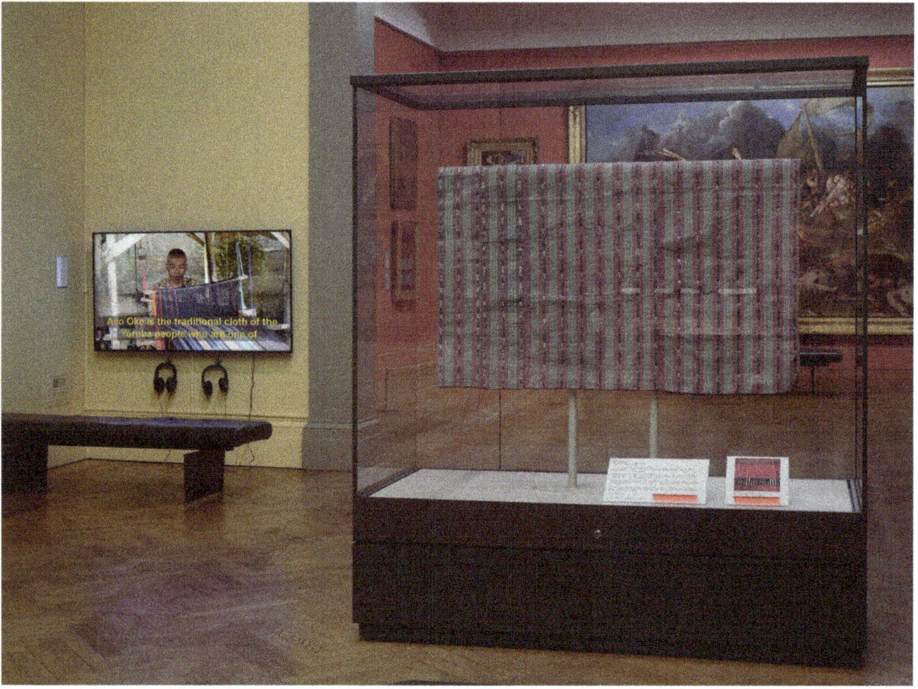

5.14 Kofo Kego Oyeleye, *Aso Oke* (2022) [left] and the original textile, Aso Oke (pre-1934, unknown designer, Yoruba people, Nigeria, Silk and cotton) [right, in display case]. Textile selected by Kofo Kego Oyeleye for *Rethinking the Grand Tour* redisplay (installation view). Photo: Michael Pollard.

in this business … [and] if we want to foster cohesion in our divided communities, people need to mix … to come together'.[96] An atmosphere of pride in Yoruba culture was shared with a range of visitors in the revitalised space, addressing European art history with empowered knowledge. As Manchester Art Gallery's Creative Lead, Inbal Livne, reflected, the gallery's collection is owned by the people of Manchester and seeks to reflect the city's diverse residents, so they can 'see the threads of their histories within our telling of global history and the history of art'.[97]

Another recent research project offers guidance for museums that is pertinent to this discussion of collaborating with artists from source communities and engaging with contested heritage. Investigating calls for the restitution of African colonial era collections in UK museums, it observes that: 'The weight of the colonial past is so embedded in many museums' entire structure that doing this meaningfully raises a host of fundamental issues about museums' existence and purpose', such as practical/institutional challenges and under-funding.[98] Further, it articulates the 'emotional charge' of contested collections, which can be 'demanding, for members of descendant communities and for museum staff'.[99] Some progressive practices in grappling with colonial history, conservation, and the diverse expectations of source communities have come from work with Indigenous heritage.[100] National museums in Africa, especially those founded in the colonial period, have been 'burdened with dealing with a violent past' of minority domination and dispossession, which affect people's 'everyday realities'. Scholars warn against 'using decoloniality to avoid critical introspection', 'cosmetic' approaches to participation, and ignoring the multilingualism of local visitors.[101] Curators argue that the 'tainted histories of cultural dislocation through its collecting practices can, in the postcolonial moment, be a platform for retrieving objects to offer spaces for the previously silenced voices', thus increasing inclusivity by reconnecting communities with their heritage.[102] This is highly pertinent to collaborating with displaced artists and co-curators, and centring communities in guiding change.

Overarchingly, the 'rethink' revealed that collaboration with displaced artists brings original, new perspectives, and new user communities to gallery spaces, while increasing the presence of marginalised artists. It also discovered the emotional labour of working with collections and cultural heritage, and that there is limited information and provenance of objects. Displacement aesthetics is tethered to concealed colonial histories that surface in the process of research, and which intensify the ambitions of long-term change. Such aspirations require considerable financial and emotional resources for all involved to reimagine and transform a future museum and what it can achieve for its collections and communities.

Displacement aesthetics and the crisis of collections

Since the turn of the twenty-first century, scholars have emphasised that different kinds of museums – archaeological, ethnological, and artistic – have faced a 'crisis of curation'.[103] Collections have increasingly come under scrutiny, as their historical origins and contemporary political and social relevance are contested. The crisis has been underpinned by funding cutbacks, shrinking museum storage, and the loss of specialised staff necessary for ensuring the coordination and resourcing vital to maintaining the safety of collections.[104] This was particularly pronounced in the wake of the recession that followed the global financial crisis, the COVID-19 pandemic, and the effects of the Rhodes Must Fall and Black Lives Matter movements.[105] As Michelle Moon points out, in the aftermath of COVID-19, two major changes have faced museums (particularly in the US and in the UK): the loss of staff of colour, and a distinct paradigm shift within museums; a change from being 'about somebody, to being *for* somebody'. Accordingly, this emerging paradigm is more acutely attuned to racial and cultural diversity, wage equity, better work practices, and community care.[106] This emerging paradigm looks to the 'use' value of collections for communities, while exploring the historical legacies embodied by collections.

It is striking that across many museums in the Global North, it was not until recently that the collection and display of non-western objects was viewed as problematic. Objects were often naturalised within a colonial paradigm, which regarded the acquisition and display of such objects as essential to European self-understanding. These objects were a logical and consistent material aspect or embodiment of a colonial outlook.[107] Reckoning with the legacies of colonialism in museums was seen in Manchester Museum's world-leading programme of repatriating First Nations' artefacts, ongoing since the 2000s. At the other end of the scale, as mentioned previously, in 2019, the Netherlands banned the term 'Golden Age' in museums, as it was thought to be an outmoded glorification of its enslaving empire during the seventeenth century. However, the issue of restitution and collections is, as Louise Tythacott and Kostas Arvanitis point out, moving far more quickly in museum practice than in museum history and theory.[108] Museums and their collections are thus at the forefront of negotiating nationalism, cultural diplomacy, and community discourse.[109]

Displacement aesthetics is closely bound to these museological challenges and debates surrounding the relevance and political charge of museum collections. The intersection between displacement aesthetics and the challenges currently facing museum collections come into sharper focus when considering both changes to the approach to collection objects in recent curatorial practices, and the increasing use of collections by artists with backgrounds of forced displacement. However, it is useful to begin by considering the most internationally recognised example of contestation over objects and their repatriation, that of the Parthenon Marbles. After Lord Elgin forcibly removed them from the Acropolis in the early nineteenth century, the British Museum continue to hold onto these famous sculptures despite decades-long international repatriation campaigns. As the most well-known case of refused restitution of cultural heritage, the Parthenon Marbles continue to cause heated debate focused on cultural heritage and colonial acquisition within museums, governments, universities, and the public at large.[110]

The ownership and display of the Parthenon Marbles in the British Museum is significant because, as Nicholas Mirzoeff argues, classical art holds pride of place across major institutions in the Global North (such as the British Museum, the Metropolitan Museum, or the Altes Museum in Berlin, and as mentioned earlier, Manchester Art Gallery). The common style of imperial, classical architecture parallels the power and inequality of collecting cultures. As Mirzoeff argues, these classical objects, as well as others acquired through colonial expansion, are part of a 'colonial aesthetic'.[111] Whereas museums such as the British Museum centre their colonial aesthetic (and architectural design) around these objects, a consciously dissimilar aesthetic is employed at the Acropolis Museum in Athens. Opened in 2009, the Acropolis Museum stands as a bold reminder of the *absence* of the Parthenon Marbles, not only on the Acropolis Hill, but within a Greek national collection. The curatorial approach continually reinforces a sense of absence within the Museum's collection. For instance, labels identify where the statues' missing body parts are located in other museums in the Global North, alluding to the destructiveness of colonial collecting.

Architecturally and symbolically orbiting around the concept of absence (rather than presence) the museological approach of the Acropolis Museum is one that can be traced across several large-scale and important museums that deal with the issue of displacement. The two most notable in this regard are the Jewish Museum in Berlin, and the Palestinian Museum in Ramallah. Designed by Daniel Libeskind, the Jewish Museum opened in 2009 without objects in order to highlight the deliberately claustrophobic and menacing architecture of the zinc-clad building. While the building was designed to commemorate and celebrate Jewish contributions to Berlin, the lasting feelings the museum evoke are fear and disorientation. An architecture centred around what Libeskind describes as 'voids', the museum purposefully reminds us of the limitations of collections in representing the trauma of ethnic cleansing, genocide, and displacement.

While the focus on emptiness and 'voids' has been well received in the decades since the opening of Libeskind's museum, the same cannot be said of the focus on absence which characterises the Palestinian Museum. Opening in 2016, the Palestinian Museum was launched without a collection on display. This was intended to demonstrate the Palestinian experience of having material culture destroyed, confiscated, disappeared, or sublimated within the archive. Yet, as Hanan Toukan notes, while the tradition of an empty museum might have been an apt framework for highlighting the Palestinian condition, this was not how the museum was received locally at its opening. The emptiness of the museum at that time reinforced a distinct trauma that Palestinians face, namely a sense of perpetually having to convince the world of their existence, history, and collective identity.[112] The museological debate around emptiness has particular valence in the context of Palestine, where the museum in effect performs the role of national institution in the absence of a sovereign Palestinian state.

The debate around the Palestinian Museum thus focused on emptiness and invisibility, highlighting recognition of the potential and limits of collections to represent stories of displacement. In this specific context, the displaced object is a reminder of historical loss, and yet also the privilege of a museum aimed at preserving and displaying its endangered cultural heritage. Given the role of collections in negotiating representations of history, forging collective identity, and facilitating cultural debate, it is little wonder that contemporary artists have worked with museum collections as part of their practice.

This turn toward artistic projects focusing on interventions in collections has meant that museums are increasingly 'awash with artists' invited to reassess, activate, and trouble collections.[113] Building on strategies of institutional critique, such interventions question the significance of the archive, institutional framings of art, and systems of governance within museums. Since the 1980s, so-called 'institutional critique' became a response to museum collections and spaces, with artists such as Hans Haacke, Andrea Fraser, Mierle Laderman Ukeles, and Marcel Broodthaers.[114] Today, museums take for granted such strategies when they commission artists, including when they want to focus on the legacies of colonial histories in exhibition programming.

As already mentioned, the pivotal moment of what we would now understand as a decolonising strategy came in the 1990s. Fred Wilson's *Mining the Museum* intervention at the Maryland Historical Society (1992) provided a landmark rupture to the museological conventions of the Global North.[115] *Mining the Museum* displayed collection objects (most memorably ornate silverware cups alongside a pair of metal shackles used on enslaved peoples), to confront and challenge perceptions of race and legacies of slavery. Opening within a week of the acquittal of four White officers accused of beating Rodney King, Wilson's intervention shed light on the links between museum collections and systems of oppression, violence, and inequality in the present. Thus, while Wilson's intervention marks a watershed moment in the use of museum collections to reflect on brutal colonial histories, it also emphasises the importance of linking these histories to their ongoing consequences in the present. This curatorial and artistic practice continues to proliferate internationally, as we saw with the decolonial efforts of Manchester Art Gallery and the Whitworth Art Gallery. These interventions are poignant for displaced communities whose histories and experiences are often sublimated within the archive. Such practices are also important for creative practitioners with backgrounds of forced displacement.

One recent example is the Vietnamese American artist Tuan Andrew Nguyen. Born in Ho Chi Minh City (formerly Saigon), Nguyen's family migrated to the US as refugees in 1979 when the artist was aged three. Stories of displacement, colonisation, and the fault lines of collective memory proliferate across Nguyen's sculpture, film, and video works, which frequently blur the line between 'real' places and objects, and those of distant and speculative futures. In films such as *The Island* (2017), Nguyen returned to the island of Pulau Bidong (off the coast of Malaysia), which was the oldest refugee camp of the Vietnam War, and the place where he and his family lived before securing asylum in the US. *The Boat People* (2020) is set in an unspecified future at the edge of humanity's extinction and is shot in multiple areas of the Philippines, including the Philippine Refugee Processing Centre. Nguyen presents a group of children who travel the seas by wooden boat in order to collect stories and objects that have survived the ruins of human civilisation, such as a head of Buddha (Figure 5.15). *The Boat People* engages with 'real' heritage objects to explore experiences of displacement, interconnected histories of colonialism and displacement, as well as speculative futures in the wake of accelerated crises.

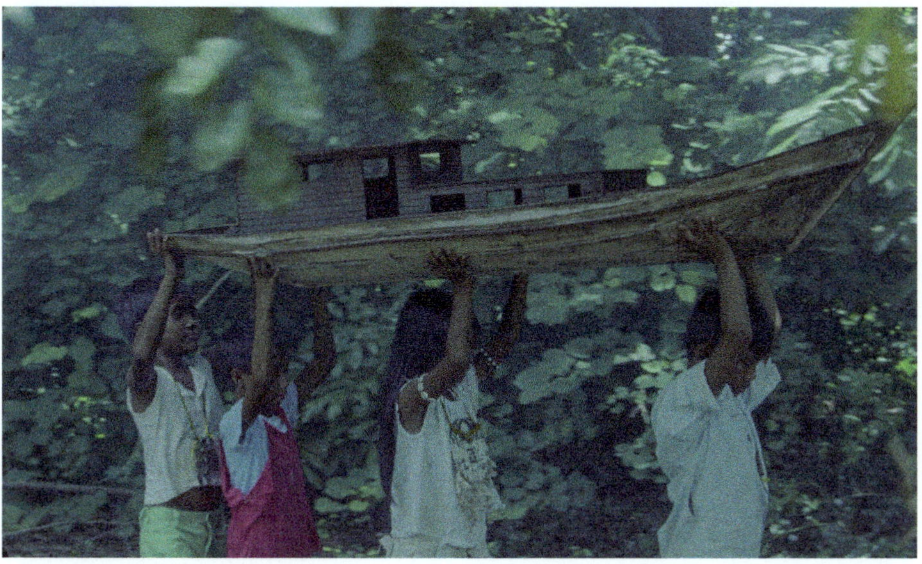

5.15 Tuan Andrew Nguyen, *Boat People* (2020). Single-channel video, 20 min. Courtesy of the artist and Cohen gallery.

Nguyen's work engages with objects as a means of reflecting on processes of memorialisation, and histories of displaced communities which have not yet achieved substantial archival presence. It is useful here to turn our attention to artists who engage with collections as a means of performing 'institutional critique' regarding unequal forms of institutional exchange. Several of the interventions discussed in this chapter could be said to utilise strategies of institutional critique (whether by individual artists, or by curators and administrators working within museums and galleries). However, contemporary artists also engage with collections to directly address, and indeed mediate, the *conditions* of displacement. In other words, their art practice instigates the 'operational' mode of displacement aesthetics.

Two significant examples in this regard come from the work of Palestinian artist Khaled Hourani and Iraqi-American artist Michael Rakowitz. Both artists instrumentalise their positionalities as internationally renowned artists to highlight, mediate, and alter museological infrastructure, which reflects and perpetuates a central condition of forced displacement – that of mobility – both for people and for objects.

Identified as one of the most significant Palestinian works of the decade, Khaled Hourani's *Picasso in Palestine* (2011) is often cited for laying bare the systems of unequal exchange within art markets and culture industries when they deal with conflict, forced displacement, and foreign occupation.[116] Over two years in development, *Picasso in Palestine* involved collaboration between the International Academy of Art Palestine in Ramallah (IAAP) and the Van Abbemuseum in Eindhoven. The premise of the work was simple. Hourani, who was also Director of the IAAP, asked the Van Abbemuseum's director, Charles Esche, for a loan from the collection. This was his response to Esche's own invitation during a Van Abbemuseum workshop, when Esche asked a group of international artists, curators, and museum directors to choose one work from the museum's collection and to propose an artistic or curatorial activity connected with that object. When Hourani presented his idea – the loan of Pablo Picasso's *Buste de Femme* (1943) to the IAAP in the West Bank – the workshop participants at the Van Abbemuseum responded with amusement and disbelief.

While Hourani's suggestion was initially received as though it were a joke, the artist was completely serious.[117] The reaction was a measure of the fact that, while Palestinian art's visibility had mushroomed across international art circuits in the first decade of the twenty-first century, this had too often been a one-way exchange. In other words, while Palestinian art toured major art centres in the Global North, art from great collections did not travel to Palestine. Indeed, the loan of *Buste de Femme* would be the first time a masterpiece was poised to make such a journey. Valued at \$7.1 million in 2011, arranging the loan was incredibly complex. Museum protocols had to be radically adjusted, and legal frameworks pertaining to transportation and insurance had to be revised to fit West Bank realities. The complex obstacles encountered by the IAAP and Van Abbemuseum underscore the reality of life under Israeli occupation and the constraints under which museums of the Global North engaged with such a politically and physically volatile space.

The choice of *Buste de Femme* also highlighted the restrictions on Palestinians' mobility: several Picasso paintings were coincidentally on view at the Israel Museum, a mere 15 kilometres away in Jerusalem, yet Palestinians holding West Bank IDs could not visit.[118] Mentioned in *Frieze* (2011), and documented in Michael Baers' artwork *An Oral History of Picasso in Palestine* (2014), Hourani's project drew major arts figures to the West Bank for the first time (including philosopher Slavoj Žižek).[119] This amplified the profound concern that Picasso's work would never make it through the multitude of legal and military hoops necessary to arrive in Ramallah. Indeed, right up until the final days before the exhibition's opening in 2011, there was a very real fear the exhibition would open with an empty gallery space. To this end, Hourani invited filmmaker Rashid Masharawi to document the project, resulting in a film (also titled *Picasso in Palestine*) that would eventually tour to major international art spaces and events, including *documenta13* (2012).

The eventual success of the project meant that audiences in the West Bank queued during a hot summer to see Picasso's painting, which was guarded around the clock by two armed Palestinian officers.[120] This image was replicated by Hourani in numerous works (photographic, painting, and installation) in the decade after the project opened in Ramallah. Significantly, it was not just Hourani's work that built the aura of the project long after Picasso's painting was returned to the Netherlands. Many visitors to the IAAP would later come merely to see the empty space in which a Picasso was once hung.

Picasso in Palestine had at least three afterlives: ongoing artistic networks between the IAAP and the flurry of international visitors; international collections exchanges; and import and insurance protocols ahead of the opening of the Palestinian Museum (2016). From his positionality as an artist and a senior cultural figure in Palestine, Hourani was able to broker a collaboration which marked a watershed moment between art spaces of the Global North and Palestinian institutions. An artist's positionality is thus vital to projects which mitigate the operational conditions of displacement aesthetics in museum collections.

This was also evident in the art of Michael Rakowitz, which was a reminder not only of the forced migration of people through conflict, but also of the displacement of cultural objects, as seen in his celebrated work, *The Invisible Enemy Should Not Exist* (Figure 5.16). Begun in 2006, three years after the US-led invasion of Iraq began, it recreated 7,000 collection objects destroyed or looted from the Iraqi Museum and from archaeological sites in Iraq. In 2018, Rakowitz was commissioned to install part of the work for the Fourth Plinth in London's Trafalgar Square. Now the most

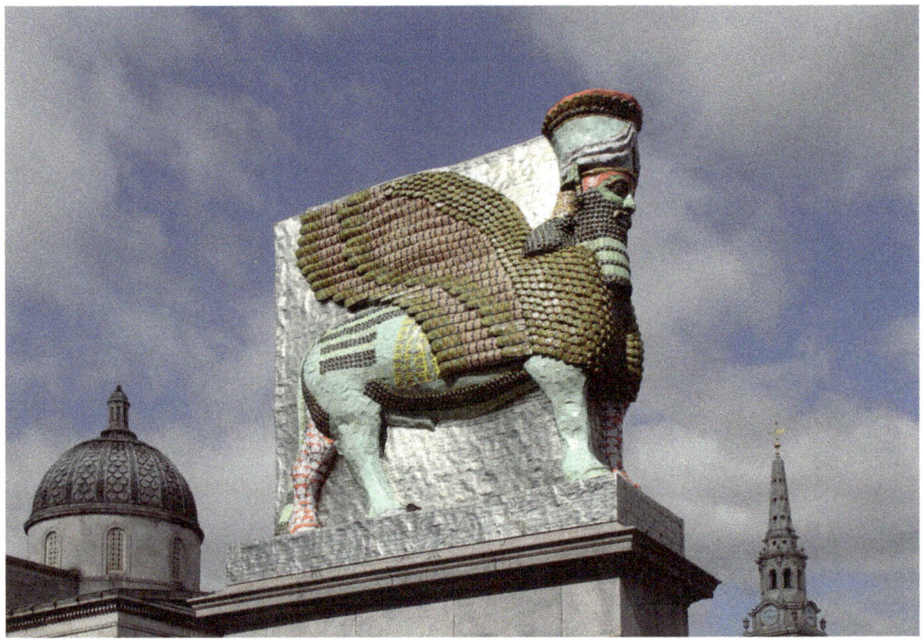

5.16 Michael Rakowitz, *The Invisible Enemy Should Not Exist (Lamassu of Nineveh)* (2018). 10,500 Iraqi date syrup cans, metal frame. Commissioned for Trafalgar Square's Fourth Plinth, London UK (installation view). (https://www.flickr.com/photos/hisgett/41530407000/in/photostream/). Photograph by Tony Hisgett (CC by 2.0).

celebrated work of the artist's oeuvre, Rakowitz's striking sculpture is a true-to-scale replica of the winged bull, *Lamassu*, a protective deity which once stood at the entrance to Nineveh, near contemporary Mosul, from 700 BCE until it was destroyed by Daesh (ISIS) in 2015. Installed facing away from the National Gallery and gazing toward the Foreign Office and the Houses of Parliament, *Lamassu* was made of 10,500 empty Iraqi date syrup cans, a material used often by the artist as a reflection on the once-renowned date palm industry of Iraq, which was devastated by the second Gulf War (also known as the Iraq War, 2003–11).

For art historian Anthony Downey, Rakowitz's *Lamassu* reflects a multitude of historical displacements. As Downey argues, 'through the commerce of dates and the symbolism associated with their packaging, [the Lamassu] bears plaintive testimony to a contentious history of forced migration, topographical dislocation, precarious resettlement, and the usurpation of cultural and natural diversity'.[121] Forced displacement and exchange of cultural objects is a reoccurring theme in the artist's work, not least because of his own biography. Identifying as Iraqi-American, Rakowitz has never been to Iraq. His grandfather, an Iraqi Jew, made the decision to leave Iraq in 1946, fearing for the safety of his family and resettling in the US, where he developed an import-export business.

While Rakowitz's art is concerned with the reconstruction of cultural objects as a means to, in Downey's words, 'understand global politics of cultural destruction and reconstruction', the artist also explores the possibilities of repatriation.[122] In early 2023, Rakowitz made public his efforts to repatriate an Assyrian Lamassu sculpture from the British Museum. Rakowitz's public letter proposed that the museum should return one of the two Lamassu sculptures in their collection, which had been excavated by English archaeologist, art historian, and diplomat Sir Austen Henry Layard (1817–94). In return, the repatriation would replace the 700 BCE Lamassu that Daesh (ISIS) had destroyed in their raid on the Mosul Museum in 2015. Rakowitz's Fourth Plinth commission (one of the most prestigious in the UK) was leverage in his proposition to the British Museum.

Rakowitz's Fourth Plinth sculpture was acclaimed, and Tate Modern expressed an interest in acquiring the work for its permanent collection. Rakowitz offered to gift his artwork to the Tate on the condition that the gallery would share ownership with the state of Iraq. He also stipulated that, as part of the acquisition, the British Museum would repatriate one of the two Lamassu sculptures in its collection back to Mosul. In the spirit of the pioneering anthropologist Marcel Mauss, Rakowitz offered a reminder that gifts are never truly free. Instead, they are a social contract to encourage reciprocal exchange.[123]

Blurring the line between commission, decommission, and cultural gift, Rakowitz enacted a very particular type of institutional critique. Like *Picasso in Palestine* (2011) before, this centred on museological exchange. It also speaks to the way that the mass displacement of people and objects results from colonialism, neocolonialism, and conflict. Further, Rakowitz's art troubles the institutional critique that is instrumentalised in some galleries to an extent that it has perhaps lost its bite.

The acute awareness of their positionality as internationally recognised artists informed the institutional critique of both Hourani and Rakowitz. Their projects call for a conscious, long-term restructure and revaluation of the often invisible and unequal mechanisms of museum exchange and collaboration across the Global North. Within their short-term commissions, both artists focused on legacy and impact. Both Hourani and Rakowitz used their positionalities to create projects geared towards lasting change, a form of institutional critique characterised by what Janet Marstine described as 'critical practice'. It is an institutional critique centred on the reconciliation between museums and publics. Such reconciliation would embody museum ethics to be geared toward redress, pluralism, and shared authority.[124]

Temporary exhibitions might represent displacement, but they only occasionally allow displaced artists to have their own platforms. The legacy of understanding displacement aesthetics lies in recognising this. Realising change across every art museum department, however, requires contending with years of austerity impacting collections and acquisitions. Even as contemporary artists and activists attempt to intervene, to encourage institutional change and restitution, it is vital that museums themselves acknowledge the invisible aspects of displacement aesthetics as a criterion for change.

Conclusion

This chapter discussed the advocacy of art institutions and grassroots arts collectives in Britain during the foundational period of displacement aesthetics, when the legal refugee regime was coming into being. This history reveals that art museums leveraged their power in the service of European artists whose lives were at risk. This demonstrated the shift from representation to the active and *operational*, key modes identified in displacement aesthetics. Several decades later, the interventions of Manchester Art Gallery and the Whitworth Art Gallery reveal just how important collaborations had become with artists who have backgrounds of migration and displacement. Artist collaborations and co-curation can 'open up new modes of social connection', disrupting 'top-down models of colonial authority', as Nikos Papastergiadis argues.[125] These galleries recognise displaced people and refugees as agents who can shape the future of the art institution. This was officially recognised when British charity City of Sanctuary awarded both galleries the status of Gallery of Sanctuary, which is dedicated to building a welcoming movement for refugees and asylum seekers.

We argued that engaging with displacement is a necessary part of decolonisation and is a crucial step forward for museums. Significantly, the relationship between forced displacement and histories of colonialism are often treated as discrete. The result of this is that populations forced to flee in periods prior to the Second World War (and the 1951 Refugee Convention) are often not understood as forcibly displaced. As exhibitions are spaces in which the intersections between complex histories can be brought to the surface, museums can highlight the relationship between histories of colonialism and displacement. This was evident in the exhibition *Traces of Displacement*, which drew lines of connection between experiences of asylum seekers in the present and those in the past who suffered mass displacement arising from the Trans-Atlantic slave trade and the Partition of India. While this chapter's focus is on the nexus between displacement and museum collections and collaborations, the issues explored are equally relevant to decolonial scholarship in museum studies concerned with co-curation, funding, language and terminology, the creation of spaces of care, and cultural mediation. Understanding displacement as part-and-parcel of decolonial work will be fundamental for the future of the art museum.

Through advocacy and collaboration between galleries, universities, and artists, displacement aesthetics can be transformative for how stories are shared with and by diverse communities. In addressing the modes of displacement aesthetics, we found that the past can be made visible in the present. Collaboration enables art museums to be sites of multivocality, and to be both humble and hopeful spaces working towards a connective and equitable future.

Notes

1 Stuart Hall, *Representation: Cultural Representations and Signifying Practices* (London: Sage, 1997).

2 Anna Müller-Härlin, 'It All Happened in This Street, Downshire Hill': Fred Uhlman and the Free German League of Culture', in Shulamith Behr and Marian Malet (eds), *Arts in Exile in Britain, 1933–1945: Politics and Cultural Identity* (Leiden: Brill, 2005), p. 244.

3 Mary Adshead, widow of Stephen Bone, cited in Lynda Morris and Robert Radford, *AIA: Artists International Association 1933–1953* (Oxford: Museum of Modern Art, 1983), p. 52

4 Morris and Radford, *AIA*, p. 52

5 Vinzent Jutta, *Identity and Image: Refugee Artists from Nazi Germany in Britain (1933–1945)* (Weimar: Verlag, 2006), p. 31.

6 Francis Klingender, cited in Morris and Radford, *AIA*, p. 59.

7 Morris and Radford, *AIA*, pp. 59, 78.

8 Monica Bohm-Duchen (ed.), *Insiders/Outsiders: Refugees from Nazi Europe and the Contribution to British Visual Culture* (London: Lund Humphries, 2019); Vinzent Jutta, 'The Making of Modern Art through Commercial Galleries in 1930s London', *Visual Culture in Britain*, 21:2 (2020): 145–176; Philip McEvansoneya, 'Estella Solomons (1882–1968) and the Irish Contribution to the Artists' Refugee Committee', *British Art Journal*, 24 (2023): 27–32; Lucy Wasensteiner, *The Twentieth Century German Art Exhibition: Answering Degenerate Art in 1930s London* (New York: Routledge, 2018).

9 Aaron Goldman, 'Defence Regulation 18B: Emergency Internment of Aliens and Political Dissenters in Great Britain in World War II', *Journal of British Studies*, 12:2 (May 1973): 122–123.

10 Charmian Brinson and Richard Dove, *A Matter of Intelligence: Political Refugees from Germany and Austria after January 1933* (Manchester: Manchester University Press, 2014), p. 25

11 Artist's Refugee Committee, 21 August 1940, Tate Archives, 8812/1/4/182/4.

12 Artist's Refugee Committee, 21 August 1940, Tate Archives, 8812/1/4/182/4.

13 Artist's Refugee Committee, 21 August 1940, Tate Archives, 8812/1/4/182/4.

14 Artist's Refugee Committee, 21 August 1940, Tate Archives, 8812/1/4/182/4.

15 Fred Uhlman describes internment coming 'out of the blue' and its injustice suggests it left a deep mark on his memory. IWM Sound archive 4441 (1979). www.iwm.org.uk/collections/item/object/8000440

16 Muller-Harlin, 'It All Happened in This Street', p. 248.

17 Letter from Helen Roeder, AIA, to Sir Kenneth Clark, Tate Archives, 8812/1/4/182/5.

18 Wasensteiner, *The Twentieth Century German Art Exhibition*.

19 Brian Foss, *War Paint: Art, War, State and Identity in Britain 1939–1945* (New Haven, CT: Yale University Press, 2008).

20 Letter from Helen Roeder to Sir Kenneth Clark, 3 September 1940, Tate Archives, 8812/1/4/182/17.

21 Letter from Osbert Peake, Home Office, to Sir Kenneth Clark, 28 August 1940, Tate Archives, 8812/1/4/182/19.

22 Such as of Dr Meier of the Warburg Library. Letter from Sit Kenneth Clark to Fritz Saxl, 28 June 1940. Tate Archives.

23 Christy Anderson, 'War Work: English Art and the Warburg Institute', *Common Knowledge*, 18:1 (Winter 2012): 149–159.

24 Letter from Sir Kenneth Clark to Hon. Mr Justice Asquith, 29 August 1940, Tate Archives, 8812/1/4/182/11.

25 Letter from Edmund Matthews, Secretary, Advisory Committee on the Internment of Aliens, 2 September 1940, Tate Archives, 8812/1/4/182/16.

26 Susan Cohen, 'Eleanor Rathbone: MP for Refugees', in Anthony Grenville and Andrea Reiter (eds), *Political Exile and Exile Politics in Britain after 1933* (Amsterdam: Rodopi, 2011), pp. 6–7.

27 ARC letter, July 1940. Tate Archives.

28 Cordula Frowein, 'German Artists in Wartime Britain', *Third Text*, 5:15 (1991): 52.

29 Sir Kenneth Clark to Count Antoine Seilern (art collector and historian), 8 November 1940. Tate Archives; Letter from Diana Uhlman to Sir Kenneth Clark, 22 September 1940. Tate Archives, 8812/1/4/182/14.

30 As described by Lord Noel Annan *Our Age: British Intellectuals between the Wars: A Group Portrait* (New York: Random House, 1990).

31 Letter from Helen Roeder to Sir Kenneth Clark, 6 September 1940, Tate Archives, 8812/1/4/182/19.

32 Letter Osbert Peake, Home Office, to Sir Kenneth Clark, 13 November 1940, Tate Archives 8812/4/182/21.

33 Sue Malvern, review of Brian Foss, *War Paint*, *Journal of British Studies*, 49 (2010): 217.

34 Charmian Brinson, 'The Contribution of German-Speaking Refugee Artists to British Wartime Propaganda' in Bohm-Duchen (ed.), *Insiders/Outsiders*, pp. 203–209.

35 Cited in Bohm-Duchen, 'Accents in Art: Émigré Painters and Sculptors in Britain after 1933', in Bohm-Duchen (ed.), *Insiders/Outsiders*, p. 27.

36 We are indebted to Monica Bohm-Duchen for this point and other advice in this chapter.

37 Joanna Gardner-Huggett, 'Margaret Gardiner: Collecting as Activism', *British Art Journal*, 6:2 (2005): 76–82.

38 Otti Berger, sample fabric swatch card, courtesy of he Whitworth Art Gallery.

39 Harriet Aktinson, in Bohm-Duchen (ed.), *Insiders/Outsiders*.

40 Linda Nochlin, 'Art and the Conditions of Exile: Men/Women, Emigration/Expatriation', *Poetics Today*, 17:3 (1996): 317–337.

41 Lucy Mayblin, 'Colonialism, Decolonisation, and the Right to Be Human: Britain and the 1951 Geneva Convention on the Status of Refugees', *Journal of Historical Sociology*, 27:3 (2014): 429.

42 Anthony Heilibut, *Exiled in Paradise: German Refugee Artists in American from the 1930s to the Present* (New York: Viking, 1983).

43 The collaborative team included the authors of this book and curators Dr Leanne Green and Hannah Vollam, with advice from the textile curators Ann French and Amy George. Co-curators included heritage professional Yuiwai Chung, poet Ani Daspanyan, artist Vian K. Hussein, poet and journalist Ambrose Musiyiwa, artist and producer Mahboobeh Rajabi, actor Noor Seddiqi, and artist Helena Tomlin.

44 Link to the fully illustrated catalogue: www.whitworth.manchester.ac.uk/whats-on/exhibitions/upcomingexhibitions/tracesofdisplacement/

45 Ahmed's multi award-winning graphic novel *Still Alive: Notes from Australia's Immigration Detention System* (2021). Border *Farce* was also shown at *documenta15*. https://safdarahmed.com/documenta-fifteen/; https://documenta-fifteen.de/en/mediathek/trailer-for-border-farce-a-video-artwork-by-lumbung-artist-safdar-ahmed/

46 Chrisoula Lionis, *Laughing in an Emergency: Weaponising Humour in Contemporary Art* (Cham: Springer, 2023), p. 2.

47 https://www.azzaaborebieh.com/traces

48 Funded with the support of the Friends of the Whitworth.

49 Private collection of Professor Janet Wolff, Emeritus Professor, University of Manchester.

50 Bosco Opi, *Refugee Coloniality: An Afrocentric analysis of prolonged encampment in Kenya* (Cham: Palgrave Macmillan, 2024), p. 59ff.

51 Mayblin, 'Colonialism, Decolonisation, and the Right to Be Human', pp. 426–428.

52 Umut Erel, 'Collaborations between Academics, Artists, and Activists: Transforming Public Understandings and Representations of Migration Issues', in W. Sievers (ed.), *Cultural Change in Post-Migrant Societies: Re-imagining Communities through Arts and Cultural Activities* (Imiscoe: Springer, 2024), p. 183.

53 Feedback from cultural producer and artist Maboobeh Rajabi, 2024.

54 Feedback from poet Ani Despanyan, 2024.

55 Feedback from museum and heritage professional, Yuiwai Chung, 2024.

56 Feedback from artist Helena Tomlin, 2024.

57 Feedback from Whitworth assistant curator Hannah Vollam, 2024.

58 Curator Dr Leanne Green, cited in www.thefourdrinier.com/interview-may-2024-the-whitworth-traces-of-displacement

59 Erel, 'Collaborations between Academics, Artists, and Activists', p. 182.

60 Feedback from artist Helena Tomlin, 2024.

61 Correspondence with the artist, 2024.

62 Correspondence with the artist, 2024.

63 Marianne Hirsch, *The Generation of Postmemory: Writing and Visual Culture After the Holocaust* (New York: Columbia University Press, 2012).

64 Dan Hicks, *The Brutish Museum: The Benin Bronzes, Colonial Violence and Cultural Restitution* (London: Pluto, 2020).

65 Nina Möntmann, 'Small-Scale Art Organisations as Participatory Platforms for Decolonising Practices and Sensibilities', *Journal of Aesthetics and Culture*, 13:1 (2021): 2.

66 www.theguardian.com/news/ng-interactive/2023/mar/28/slavery-and-the-guardian-the-ties-that-bind-us; www.manchester.ac.uk/about/news/founders-and-funders/#:~:text=O pening%20at%20the%20John%20Rylands,funded%20the%20cultural%20and%20educ ational

67 Glen Peterson, 'Colonialism, Sovereignty and the History of the International Refugee Regime', in M. Frank and J. Reinisch (eds), *Refugees in Europe, 1919–1959: A Forty Year Crisis?* (London: Bloomsbury, 2017), pp. 213–228.

68 Opi, *Refugee Coloniality*, p. 13.

69 Feedback from poet and journalist Ambrose Musiyiwa, 2024.

70 Wayne Modest and Robin Lelijveld (eds), *Words Matter: An Unfinished Guide to Word Choices in the Cultural Sector* (Leiden: Research Center for Material Culture, 2018).

71 Alice Proctor, *The Whole Picture: The Colonial Story of the Art in our Museums and Why we Need to Talk About It* (London: Cassell, 2021).

72 Nina Möntmann, *Decentring the Museum: Contemporary Art Institutions and Colonial Legacies*. Translated by Gerrit Jackson, (London: Lund Humphries, 2023) p. 32.

73 Katrin Sieg, *Decolonizing German and European History at the Museum* (Ann Arbor: Michigan University Press, 2021), p. 204.

74 Julie Codell, 'Reversing the Grant Tour: Guest Discourse in Indian Travel Narratives', *The Huntington Library Quarterly*, 70:1 (2007): 173.

75 Margaret Hunt, 'Racism, Imperialism and the Traveler's Gaze in Eighteenth-Century England', *Journal of British Studies*, 32:4 (1993): 348.

76 Michael Greenhalgh, *Plundered Empire* (Leiden: Brill, 2019).

77 F. Robert Hunter, 'Tourism and Empire: The Thomas Cook and Son Enterprise on the Nile, 1868–1914', *Middle Eastern Studies*, 40:5 (2004): 28.

78 Denis Linehan, Philip Xe, and Ian Clark, *Colonialism, Tourism and Place* (London: Edward Elgar, 2020), p. 2.

79 See UCL's Legacies of British Slavery. www.ucl.ac.uk/lbs/person/view/22232

80 Daniel Kilbride, 'Travel, Ritual and National Identity: Planters on the European Tour, 1820–1860', *Journal of Southern History*, 69:3 (2003): 549–584.

81 Möntmann, *Decentring the Museum*, p. 12

82 Feedback from curator Hannah Williamson, 2024.

83 Feedback from curator Hannah Williamson, 2024.

84 Rachael Minott, 'The Past is Now: Confronting Museums' Complicity in Imperial Celebration', *Third Text*, 33:4–5 (2019): 569–570.

85 www.museumsassociation.org/campaigns/decolonising-museums/supporting-decolon isation-in-museums/collaboration/

86 Feedback from cultural producer Jason Cyrus, 2024.

87 Feedback from curator Hannah Williamson, 2024.

88 Stefan Hanss, 'The Material Creativity of Affective Artifacts in the Dutch Colonial World: Imaging and Imagining Early Modern Feather Fans', *Current Anthropology*, 65:2 (April 2024): 196–199.

89 Lucio Menezes Ferreira, 'Who's Affected by Colonialism? The Asymmetric World of Symmetric Approaches', *Cultural Anthropology*, 65:2 (2024): 224–226.

90 Published on the Gallery website: https://manchesterartgallery.org/event/rethinking-th e-grand-tour/

91 Feedback from curator and communities learning manager Ruth Edson, 2024.

92 Feedback from curator Hannah Williamson, 2024.

93 Feedback from artist Kani Kamil, 2024.

94 Mark A. Graham, 'Interview with Artist Fred Wilson', *Journal of Museum Education*, 32:3 (Fall 2007): 215.

95 The Charles Beving Collection of Textiles, *The British Museum Quarterly*, 8:4 (May 1934): 151.

96 Interview with Kofo Kego Oyeleye, 2023.

97 Senior Creative Lead, Inbal Livne, Manchester Art Gallery, 2024.

98 *Making African Connections: Decolonial Futures for Colonial Collections*, Executive Summary, Point 9, p. 10.

99 *Making African Connections*, Point 11, p. 11.

100 Renata Peters et al., *Heritage Conservation and Social Engagement* (London: UCL press, 2020).

101 Farai Mudododzi Chabata and Jesmael Mataga, 'Beyond the De-Colonial: Rethinking the Future of Museums in Africa', in Kerstin Barndt and Stephan Jaeger (eds), *Museums, Narrative and Critical Histories* (Berlin: De Gruyter, 2024), pp. 151, 155.

102 Jesmael Mataga and Farai Mudododzi Chabata, 'The Power of Objects: Colonial Museums Collections and Changing Contexts', *International Journal of the Inclusive Museum*, 4:1 (2012): 92.

103 Zanna Friberg and Huvila Isto, 'Using Object Biographies to Understand the Curation Crisis: Lessons Learned from the Museum Life of an Archaeological Collection', *Museum Management and Curatorship*, 34:4 (2019): 362–382.

104 Kate Arnold-Foster, 'A Developing Sense of Crisis': A New Look at University Collections in the United Kingdom', *Museum International*, 52:3 (2000): 10, 11.

105 Katja Lindqvist, 'Museum Finances: Challenges beyond Economic Crises', *Museum Management and Curatorship*, 27:1 (1990): 1–15.

106 Michelle Moon, 'Retooling for the Revolution: Framing the Future of Museum Management After COVID-19', *Journal of Cultural Management and Cultural Policy/ Zeitschrift für Kulturmanagement und Kulturpolitik*, 6:2 (2020): 193.

107 Moon, 'Retooling for the Revolution', p. 210.

108 Kostas Arvanitis and Louise Thyacott (eds), *Museums and Restitution: New Practices, New Approaches* (London: Routledge, 2014).

109 Jack Green, 'Museums as Intermediaries in Repatriation', *Journal of Eastern Mediterranean Archaeology & Heritage Studies*, 5:1 (2017): 6.

110 Herman Alexander, *The Parthenon Marbles Dispute: Heritage, Law, Politics* (London: Bloomsbury, 2023).

111 Nicholas Mirzoeff, 'Empty the Museum, Decolonize the Curriculum, Open Theory', *The Nordic Journal of Aesthetics*, 53 (2017): 15

112 Hanan Toukan, 'The Palestinian Museum', *Radical Philosophy*, 2 (2018): 13.

113 Simon Stephens, 'Artistic Merits', *Museums Journal*, 112 (2012): 22.

114 Anne Ring Petersen, *Migration into Art: Transcultural Identities and Art-Making in a Globalised World* (Manchester: Manchester University Press, 2017), pp. 113–114.

115 Fred Wilson, et al., 'Objects and Identities: An Interview with Fred Wilson', *ASAP/Journal*, 2:1 (2017): 3–28.

116 'The Best Art Shows of the Decade', *Hyperallergic*, 23 December 2019, accessed 29 May 2024. https://hyperallergic.com/533861/the-best-art-shows-of-the-2010s/

117 Chrisoula Lionis, *Laughter in Occupied Palestine: Comedy and Identity in Art and Film* (London: I.B Tauris, 2016), p. 183.

118 Johanna Lamoureux, Melanie Boucher, and Marie Fraser, 'Looking at the One and Only: The Return of the Single-Work Show', *Stedelijk Studies*, 20:5 (2017): 12

119 Nick Aitkins, 'Picasso in Palestine: Taking a Modern Masterpiece to Ramallah', *Frieze* (6 July 2011), accessed 13 September2024. www.frieze.com/article/picasso-palestine; Michael Baers, *An Oral History of Picasso in Palestine* (Berlin: Haus der Kulteren der Welt, 2014). https://archiv.hkw.de/en/media/publikationen/2014_publikationen/michael_ba ers_an_oral_history_of_picasso_in_palestine.php

120 https://www.frieze.com/article/picasso-palestine

121 Anthony Downey, 'After Mosul: The Cultural and Political Economy of Destruction and Reconstruction, in Jonathan Harris (ed.), *Terrorism and the Arts: Practices and Critiques in Contemporary Cultural Production* (London: Routledge, 2021), p. 82.

122 Downey, 'After Mosul', p. 82.

123 Marcel Mauss, *The Gift: The Form and Reason for Exchange in Archaic Societies* (London: Taylor & Francis, 2001).

124 Janet Marstine, *Critical Practice as Reconciliation: Artists, Museums, Ethics* (London: Routledge, 2017).

125 Nikos Papastergiadis, *Museums of the Commons: L'internationale and the Crisis of Europe* (London: Routledge, 2020), pp. 86, 88.

Conclusion

Displacement aesthetics is not new. It is an historical long durée phenomenon that came into force in the first half of the twentieth century in tandem with the emergence of the international refugee regime, and the rising influence of humanitarian and UN agencies. This, we argued, continues to shape representations of displacement and refugees, and how humanitarian emotions impact visual culture and art-making in the present day. Artists, scholars, and curators have also been shown to play an important role in crafting and mediating displacement aesthetics in artworks and exhibitions. Vitally, these different agents have shaped the cultural figure of the refugee and how the conditions of refugeedom were visualised in the past and now in the present. The historicising of contemporary representations of displacement has offered a significant contribution to interdisciplinary research.

The inspiration for this book began as an insight that histories and experiences of displacement are sublimated in art institutions – in museum practices and vast collections of art textiles and objects. This includes famous artworks and textiles, and those with little-known origins, information and provenance. During four years of interdisciplinary academic research, it was only through collaborative research and exhibition projects, with both galleries and, crucially, artists from backgrounds of forced migration and displacement, that the meaning and consequences of displacement aesthetics could be understood, as the title of this book indicates.

Displacement aesthetics is the result of a long history of visual representations of refugees and cultural conditions of refugeedom. These histories are born in relation to other key factors, such as language and identities, institutions, labour conditions, and art-making. Significantly, we found that in grounding displacement aesthetics in its history, what emerges in its ongoing afterlife is a fuller recognition of both its visible and invisible forces, particularly as they operate in the creative industries. This also means that the legal, social, and economic barriers impacting displaced people's everyday lives produce aesthetic outcomes. Displacement aesthetics, therefore, entangles the past and the present in *representational, lived, and operational* dynamics.

We have argued that displacement aesthetics offers a way of understanding what is seen, felt, and activated when refugees and displaced people are visualised or undertake artistic practice. Central to this argument is the identification of its four main modes. One mode is the visual themes, motifs, and tropes that persisted across visual forms, time, and geographies. This fundamentally recognises that the aesthetics of displacement are deeply embedded in human emotions and sensory responses, and that artists make use of motifs such as mobility, stasis, beauty, and alone children, for diverse purposes. The second mode is in the language of refugeedom, such as terminologies, identities, and typologies of artists. The third mode focused on art institutions and how they inform displacement aesthetics, with both visible and invisible factors shaping how collections are hidden and used, and how exhibitions are curated. Fully understanding the impact of displaced artists' lived experiences was key to understanding how this mode works in practice. Mode four highlighted the role of labour in its operational impact. This includes the emotional labour of making exhibitions and collaborating with institutions, as well as the actual labour of making art and undertaking commissioned projects.

Understanding displacement aesthetics also means acknowledging that there are significant legal, social, and economic barriers that impact displaced people's everyday lives – and that they also *produce aesthetic outcomes*. We have argued that representation is not separate from the lives of forcibly displaced people; it both impacts on them and is engineered by them, as we saw with many different types of artists across the century. Following this, and drawing upon close examples from Britain and elsewhere, we identified a set of challenges unique to displaced artists, including temporal injustice, visa, work and travel restrictions, with consequent social and economic precarity, as well as labour and gender-based inequalities. Nevertheless, recognising artists' agency is also key in shaping aesthetics. Artists, as we have seen, undertake creative work, and public museum interventions, that holds a light up to the aesthetics of displacement. Crucially, we insist that displacement aesthetics should not be seen as a cultural pathology but, rather, a hitherto misrecognised cultural phenomenon.

Ultimately, in drawing out the nuances of displacement aesthetics, we have emphasised a more holistic approach to aesthetics that centres lived experiences. This approach suggests that the cultural figuring of refugees and refugeedom cannot be reduced only to the sensory and affective, or even to politics. Nor should it be separated from people's lives and from institutional practices. As a team of interdisciplinary researchers, we found that this way of framing aesthetics will be particularly productive in the wide fields of cultural history, art history and theory, and museum/curatorial studies.

Since the turn of the twenty-first century, the field of aesthetics has been steadily broadened to both challenge conventional and historical associations of the term and to formulate alternative ways of thinking about art history and visual culture. Although these developments have not yet impacted disciplines such as cultural history, this book has made inroads into sharing these ideas and approaches.

The interdisciplinary approach to aesthetics, thus, challenged how representation is conceptualised in social and cultural history. Historians ground visual representations in historical contexts, but investigating the aesthetics of displacement has provided a new way of understanding this complex human experience. For, aesthetics captures the mixture of affective emotions, lived experiences, artistic practices, as well as the social and cultural contexts that have been key to the analysis.

This book has made apparent the ways in which aesthetics can be a useful framework for understanding how refugees and displacement are visually imagined, culturally perceived, and are generative beyond the production and dissemination of the image. Moreover, it has demonstrated how the art industry, experiences of migration, and displacement have been folded together as the conditions of twentieth-century modernity and, more recently, of twenty-first-century contemporaneity.

Another key finding is that by focusing on displacement and not collapsing migration, voluntary movement, statelessness, and people forced to flee into one overarching category, we have been able to disentangle the assumption of equality between these forms of mobility and immobility. Migrant images and migrant aesthetics tend to do this, whereas displacement aesthetics is based on the recognition of unequal rights to mobility and its consequences in people's lives.

Lived experience (often considered distinct from aesthetics) directly influences art practice, curatorial practice, and results in aesthetic outcomes, some of which are visible. Chapter 2, for example, demonstrated this by making clear the intersectional challenges which serve to both differentiate displaced artists from other migrants and to directly shape the education, career opportunities, and artistic practices of artists with backgrounds of displacement. Chapters 3 and 4, which focused on the issues of language and labour respectively, highlighted how artists with backgrounds of displacement are often 'spoken for', and how employment regulations, legal barriers, and work conditions shape the artistic labour of displaced artists. Chapter 5 argued that displacement is an important but under-acknowledged factor in artistic collaboration, co-curation, and collections-based exhibitions. Through advocacy and collaboration between galleries, universities, and artists, we found that displacement aesthetics can be transformative for museums, artists, and communities.

The key arguments of this book are the result of interdisciplinary methods, discussions, analysis, and reading across these fields together as co-authors and as practice-based researchers. Many of the findings on displacement aesthetics would not have been possible without this interdisciplinary approach. One key example was how visual culture and art revises or, alternately, replicates the repeated motifs, metaphors, and tropes that constitute the figure of the refugee. None of this would be fully comprehensible if we just focused on the present or indeed only on the past, as disciplines tend to do within their silos. The danger in this is that modern and contemporary art's assumptions sometimes go unchallenged. Another important factor is that the impact of art (including of socially engaged art projects) remains negligible on the lived experiences and professional development of artists with backgrounds of forced displacement.

We argue that displacement aesthetics provides museum and curatorial studies with a new way of considering decolonial efforts in art institutions, and of understanding the gaps in collections and approaches to collaboration with artists. This book explored five key issues which underscore displacement aesthetics: visual tropes, intersectional barriers, language and identity, labour, and institutional practices. While these key issues are directly relevant to analysis of the relationship between art and displacement, they are equally relevant to decolonial scholarship. Indeed, as we have demonstrated, without the understanding of displacement as an integral part of decolonial work, admirable efforts in museum studies, curatorial practice, and art history can only ever be partial. In cultural history, decolonising archives and images is part-and-parcel of analysing power differentials, prejudice, social and cultural inequalities, and the way that the historical record replicates colonial thinking based on racial hierarchies. Institutions and archives shape the way historians understand people on the move. Colonial history is far too often isolated from refugee history, however. To put displacement into the heart of this matrix is to draw out the connections between colonised *and* displaced populations, to understand the ongoing coloniality of refugee policy and its cultural resonances, which, as we argued, are deeply rooted in visual histories and repeated in current forms of refugee visuality and displacement aesthetics.

Displacement aesthetics is underpinned and formulated through interdisciplinarity. It brings cultural history together with art history – working with primary sources, artworks, artist testimonies, and co-curation – and on local art histories that underpin art. In doing so, this book sought a shift beyond the well-meaning but inconsistent performance of human rights that cultural institutions and artists enact, even in gestures of solidarity. For, as demonstrated, this does not alter the 'operational' aspect of displacement aesthetics, such as the legal, social, and economic barriers impacting displaced people's everyday lives.

Interdisciplinarity, we have found, is especially pertinent when researchers are 'learning as doing'. Our practice-led curatorial research was symbiotic: artistic projects were informed by cultural history, art history, and museum/curatorship studies, and our research was directly informed by the outcomes and processes of artistic projects. We assisted galleries in making curatorial and infrastructural changes, addressing gaps in resourcing and research, and developing new knowledge. We discovered the role and value of working closely, over several projects and with a degree of continuity and longevity, with a group of creative practitioners from a heritage of displacement.

Together with the partner artists and galleries, we learned that collaboration needs time and sincere, long-term relationship building. True collaboration requires trust and that requires real resources to implement long-term change in the culture industry. Small often temporary projects can be too piecemeal and do not allow for learning and people to evolve together. The significance of community expertise is crucial to re-interpreting collections, both in terms of accessing and using collections in innovative ways. The significance of community expertise was crucial to re-interpreting collections, both in terms of accessing and using collections in innovative ways. There is an immense but untapped potential for communities to hold spaces of cultural authority and reimagine the heritage often hidden away in storage.

Understanding displacement aesthetics now, and in the future, will require many more in-depth studies into the colonial origins of collections, their evolving stories, and the longer history of forced displacement with the trafficking of enslaved peoples. For a project ostensibly focused on the twentieth and twenty-first centuries, this discovery was quite unexpected and came about as a result of the collaborative process, with artists and curators, of investigating the permanent collections. It also meant that something as celebrated and as seemingly innocuous as the Grand Tour could be understood through a different set of questions and artistic interpretations. Thus, fully embracing the degree to which lived experiences of displacement constitute in-depth knowledge and expertise, deployed, for instance, in interpreting collections and rewriting object labels and providing new information for databases, is of crucial importance to the culture sector. Moreover, this method produced clear insights into our concept of displacement aesthetics as emanating from the interconnected phenomena of representation, lived experience, and institutions.

Finally, we reflect on how displacement aesthetics can be useful for future researchers, who we hope will identify further modes. Further research is needed into the history of images and the humanitarian context in which images are circulated, analysing their cultural impact across diverse geographical contexts. In addition, the relationship between displacement and colonialism, which has been overlooked across many disciplines, demands much more intense investigation than was possible here. Nuances to our arguments may also be uncovered by future research on established artists who became displaced, and how they managed their transformations, networks, linguistic challenges, and breaking back into the art industry in a new home.

This book has drawn some key arguments from the context in the UK, a post-migrant society grappling with the history and contemporary legacy of empire and colonialism that is often hidden in collections. We saw that British institutions are increasingly engaged with co-curation and community consultation, and open to shared decision-making on what should be displayed and how stories can be narrated. It is our hope that future researchers will examine alternative geographies and those that are not post-migrant nations, such as in Southeast Asia, or non-signatories to the international refugee laws, such as Jordan, Thailand, Uganda, or Iran, but which nevertheless host large refugee populations. As well, research into the role of private galleries in sustained support of displaced artists' careers, and the context of the art market and private collectors, as opposed to the short-lived role of discrete art projects in public galleries and museums, will strengthen understanding of how displacement aesthetics are constituted historically and in the present day.

Select bibliography

Books

Adey, Peter, Janet C. Bowstead, Katherine Brickell, Vandana Desai, Mike Dolton, Alasdair Pinkerton, and Ayesha Siddiqi (eds), *The Handbook of Displacement* (London: Palgrave Macmillan, 2020)

Ariese, Csilla E., and Magdalena Wroblewska (eds), *Practicing Decoloniality in Museums: A Guide with Global Examples* (Amsterdam: Amsterdam University Press, 2021)

Bishop, Claire, *Artificial Hells: Participatory Art and the Politics of Spectatorship* (London: Verso, 2012)

Boreus, Kristina, *Migrants and Natives – 'Them' and 'Us': Mainstream and Radical Right Political Rhetoric in Europe* (London: Sage, 2020)

Bourke-White, Margaret, *Halfway to Freedom* (Bombay: Asia Publishing, 1950)

Burgess, Greg, *The League of Nations and the Refugees from Nazi Germany* (London: Bloomsbury, 2016)

Chatta, Ilyas, *Partition and Locality: Violence, Migration and Development in Gujranwala and Sialkot, 1947–1961* (Oxford: Oxford University Press, 2011)

Clayton, Gina, and Georgina Firth, *Immigration and Asylum Law (9th edition)* (Oxford: Oxford University Press, 2021)

Clifford, Rebecca, *Survivors: Children's Lives After the Holocaust* (New Haven: Yale University Press, 2020)

Demos, T.J., *The Migrant Image: The Art and Politics of Documentary During Global Crisis* (Durham, NC: Duke University Press, 2013)

Derrida, Jacques, and Anne Dufourmantelle, *Of Hospitality*, trans. Rachel Bowlby (Stanford, CA: Stanford University Press, 2000)

Dimitrakaki, Angela, *Gender, artWork, and the Global Imperative: A Materialist Feminist Critique* (Manchester: Manchester University Press, 2013)

Downey, Anthony, *Dissonant Archives: Contemporary Visual Culture and Contested Narratives in the Middle East* (London: Bloomsbury, 2015)

Elkins, James, *The End of Diversity in Art Historical Writing: North Atlantic Art History and Its Alternatives* (Berlin: De Gruyter, 2021)

Enloe, Cynthia, *Bananas, Beaches and Bases: Making Feminist Sense of International Politics* (Oakland, CA: University of California Press, 2014)

Fiddian-Qasmiyeh, Elena (ed.), *Refuge in a Moving World: Tracing Refugee and Migrant Journeys Across Disciplines* (London: UCL Press, 2020)

Gatrell, Peter, *Free World? The Campaign to Save the World's Refugees, 1956–1963* (Cambridge: Cambridge University Press, 2011)

Gatrell, Peter, *The Making of the Modern Refugee* (Oxford: Oxford University Press, 2013)

Gatrell, Peter, *The Unsettling of Europe: The Great Migration, 1945 to the Present* (London: Allen Lane/Penguin Books, 2020)

Gigliotti, Simone, *Restless Archive: The Holocaust and the Cinema of the Displaced* (Bloomington, IN: Indiana University Press: 2024). https://doi.org/10.2979/RestlessArchive.0.0.02

Green, Charles, and Anthony Gardner, *Biennials, Triennials and Documenta: The Exhibitions That Created Contemporary Art* (Boston: Wiley-Blackwell, 2016)

Hariman, R., and J.L. Luciates, *No Caption Needed: Iconic Photographs, Public Culture and Liberal Democracy* (Chicago, IL: Chicago University Press, 2007)

Kershen, Anne J. (ed.), *Language, Labour and Migration* (New York: Taylor and Francis, 2017)

Krasny, Elke, and Lara Perry (eds), *Curating with Care* (London: Routledge, 2023)

Lionis, Chrisoula, *Laughter in Occupied Palestine: Comedy and Identity in Art and Film* (London: I.B. Tauris, 2016)

Malkki, Liisa, *Purity and Exile: Violence, Memory, and National Cosmology among Hutu Refugees in Tanzania* (Chicago, IL: University of Chicago Press, 1995)

Malkki, Liisa, *The Need to Help: The Domestic Arts of International Humanitarianism* (Durham, NC: Duke University Press, 2015)

Mannik, Lynda, *Photography, Memory and Refugee Identity: The Voyage of the SS Walnut, 1948* (Vancouver: UBC Press)

Meskimmon, Marsha, *Transnational Feminisms, Transversal Politics and Art: Entanglements and Intersections* (London: Routledge, Taylor and Francis Group, 2020)

Möntmann, Nina, *Decentering the Museum: Contemporary Art Institutions and Colonial Legacies* (London: Lund Humphries, 2023)

Papastergiadis, Nikos, *Cosmopolitanism and Culture* (Boston: Wiley, 2012)

Papastergiadis, Nikos, *Museums of the Commons: L'internationale and the Crisis of Europe* (London: Routledge, 2020)

Petersen, Anne Ring, *Migration into Art: Transcultural Identities and Art-Making in a Globalised World* (Manchester: Manchester University Press, 2017)

Rahman, M.D. Mahbubar, and Willem Van Schendel, '"I am Not a Refugee": Rethinking Partition Migration', *Modern Asian Studies*, 37:3 (2003): 551–584

Ramírez, Catherine Sue, Sylvanna M. Falcón, Juan Poblete, Steven C. McKay, and Felicity Amaya Schaeffer (eds), *Precarity and Belonging: Labor, Migration, and Noncitizenship* (New Brunswick, New Jersey: Rutgers University Press, 2021)

Ross, Christine, *Art for Coexistence: Unlearning the Way We See Migration* (Cambridge, MA: MIT Press, 2022)

Said, Edward, *Reflections on Exile and Other Essays* (Cambridge, MA: Harvard University Press, 2000)

Salvatici, Silvia, 'Sights of Benevolence: UNRRA's Recipients Portrayed', in H. Fehrenbach and D. Rodogno (eds), *Humanitarian Photography: A History* (New York: Cambridge University Press, 2015): 200–222

Schnapp, Jeffrey T., and Matthew Tiews, eds, *Crowds* (Stanford, CA: Stanford University Press, 2006)

Schramm, Moritz (ed.), *Reframing Migration, Diversity and the Arts: The Postmigrant Condition* (New York: Routledge, 2019)

Sergi, Domenico, *Museums, Refugees and Communities: Communities, Collections and Representations* (London: Routledge, 2021)

Shabout, Nada, 'Framing the Discipline of Contemporary Art of the Arab World through the Press', in Hamid Keshmirshekan (ed.), *Contemporary Art from the Middle East: Regional Interactions with Global Art* (London: IB Tauris, 2015): 51–68

Singh, Julietta, *Unthinking Mastery: Dehumanism and Decolonial Entanglements* (Durham, NC: Duke University Press, 2018)

Thompson, James, *Care Aesthetics: for Artful Care and Careful Art* (London: Routledge, 2022)

Yildiz, Yasemin, *Beyond the Mother Tongue: The Postmonolingual Condition* (New York: Fordham University Press, 2012)

Zahra, Tara, *The Lost Children: Reconstructing Europe's Families after World War II* (London: Harvard University Press)

Zarzycka, Marta, *Gendered Tropes in War Photography: Mothers, Mourners, Soldiers* (New York: Routledge, 2016)

Articles and chapters

Alcoff, Linda, 'The Problem of Speaking for Others', *Cultural Critique*, 20 (1991): 5–32

Banko, Lauren, Katarzyna Nowak, and Peter Gatrell, 'What is Refugee History, Now?', *Journal of Global History*, 17:1 (2022): 1–19

Banks, Mark, and Kate Oakley, 'The Dance Goes on Forever? Art Schools, Class, and Higher Education', *International Journal of Cultural Policy*, 22:1 (2015): 41–57

Burman, Erica, 'Beyond "Women vs Children" or "WomenandChildren": Engendering Childhood and Reformulating Motherhood', *International Journal of Children's Rights*, 16:2 (2008): 177–194

CAMP and Nora El Qadim, 'On CAMP, Copenhagen: The Politics of Curating Art on Migration. A Conversation between Frederikke Hansen, Tone Olaf Nielsen and Nora El

Qadim', *Parse*, 10 (Spring 2020): 1–8. https://parsejournal.com/article/on-camp-copenha gen-the-politics-of-curating-art-on-migration/

Campanioni, Chris, 'The Right to a Dignified Image: The Fashioning and Effacement of the Refugee within the Celebrity System', *Journal of Cinema and Media Studies*, 61:1 (2021): 27–50

Derrida, Jacques, 'The Principle of Hospitality', *Parallax*, 11:1 (2005): 6–9

Diamond, Hanna, 'Representing Defeat: Photographic Images of the French Exodus of 1940', *Journal of War and Culture Studies*, 1:3 (2008): 275–292

Fehrenbach, Heidi, 'Children and Other Civilians: Photography and the Politics of Humanitarian Image-Making', in H. Fehrenbach and D. Rodogno (eds), *Humanitarian Photography: A History* (New York: Cambridge University Press, 2015): 165–199

Freilich, Toby Perl, 'Blazing Epiphany: Maintenance Art Manifesto 1969! An Interview with Mierle Laderman Ukeles', *Cultural Politics*, 16:1 (2020): 14–23

Gatrell, Peter, 'Refugees: What's Wrong with History?', *Journal of Refugee Studies*, 30:2 (June 2017): 170–189

Gatrell, Peter, Anindita Ghoshal, Katarzyna Nowak, and Alex Dowdall, 'Reckoning with Refugeedom: Refugee Voices in Modern History', *Social History*, 46:1 (2021): 70–95

Goodman, Simon, Ala Sirriyeh, and Simon McMahon, 'The Evolving (Re)categorisations of Refugees Throughout the "Refugee/Migrant Crisis"', *Journal of Community and Applied Social Psychology*, 27:2 (2017): 105–114

Hesler, Eva, 'Mounira Al Solh, *Mother Tongues*', *Asymptote*, accessed 20 June 2023. https:// www.asymptotejournal.com/visual/eva-heisler-mounira-al-solh-mother-tongues/

Holman, Valerie, 'Representing refugees: migration in France 1940–44', *Journal of Romance Studies*, 2:2 (2002): 53–69

Huhn, Sebastian, '"Plausible Enough": The IRO and the Negotiation of Refugee Status After the Second World War', *Journal of Contemporary History*, 58:3 (2023): 398–423

Jiang, Zhe, and Marek Korczynski, 'The Art of Labour Organizing: Participatory Art and Migrant Domestic Workers' Self-Organizing in London', *Human Relations*, 74:6 (2021): 842–868

Johnson, Heather L., 'Click to Donate: Visual Images, Constructing Victims, and Imagining the Female Refugee', *Third World Quarterly*, 32 (2011): 1015–1037

Khan, Mehre Y, '"Shaking Up" Vision: The Video Diary as Personal and Pedagogical Intervention in Mona Hatoum's Measures of Distance', *Intercultural Education*, 18:4 (2007): 317–334

Kim, Nora Hui-Jung, 'Cold War Refugees: South Korea's Entry into the International Refugee Regime, 1950–1992', *Journal of Refugee Studies*, 35:1 (March 2022): 435–453

Kirkegaard, Ane Marie Ørbø, and Sisse Mari-Louise Wulff Nat-George, 'Fleeing Through the Globalised Education System: The Role of Violence and Conflict in International Student Migration', *Globalisation, Societies and Education*, 14:3 (2016): 390–402

Kushner, Tony, 'Truly, Madly, Deeply … Nostalgically? Britain's On-Off Love Affair with Refugees Past and Present', *Patterns of Prejudice*, 52:2–3 (2018): 172–194

Lionis, Chrisoula, 'A Past Not Yet Passed: Postmemory in the work of Mona Hatoum', *Social Text*, 32:2 (2014): 77–93

Malkki, Liisa, 'National Geographic: The Rooting of Peoples and the Territorialization of National Identity among Scholars and Refugees', *Cultural Anthropology*, 7:1 (1992): 24–44

Malkki, Liisa, 'Speechless Emissaries: Refugees, Humanitarianism, and Dehistoricization', *Cultural Anthropology*, 11:3 (1996): 377–404

Michaelsen, Anja Sunhyun, '"Locked Out in Nature": Films on the European Asylum System, Latent Violence, and Ghosts', in *Weathering: Ecologies of Exposure*, ed. by Christoph F.E. Holzhey and Arnd Wedemeyer, *Cultural Inquiry*, 17 (Berlin: ICI Berlin Press, 2020): 207–225

Milevska, Suzana, 'Solidarity and the Aporia of "We": Representation and Participation of Refugees in Contemporary Art', in K. Lynes, T. Morgenstern, and I. Paul (eds), *Moving Images: Mediating Migration as Crisis* (Bielefeld: Verlag, 2020): 245–262

Minh-ha, Trinh T., 'The Image and the Void', *Journal of Visual Culture*, 15:1 (2016): 131–140

Minott, Rachael, 'The Past is Now: Confronting Museums' Complicity in Imperial Celebration', *Third Text*, 33:4–5 (September 2019), 559–574

Morrice, Linda, 'The Promise of Refugee Lifelong Education: A Critical Review in the Field', *International Review of Education*, 67 (2021): 851–869

Morrice, Linda, Linda K. Tip, Michael Collyer, and Rupert Brown, '"You Can't Have a Good Integration When You Don't Have a Good Communication": English-Language Learning Among Resettled Refugees in England', *Journal of Refugee Studies*, 34:1 (2021): 681–699

Ndikung, Bonaventure Soh Bejeng, 'The Curious Case of Olu Oguibe's Monument for Strangers and Refugees', *Frieze*, 22 March 2021, accessed 6 September 2023. https://www.frieze.com/article/olu-oguibe-monument-strangers-refugees-controversy

Ng, Wendy, Syrus Marcs Ware, and Alyssa Greenberg, 'Activating Diversity and Inclusion: A Blueprint for Museum Educators as Allies and Change Makers', *Journal of Museum Education*, 42:2 (2017): 142–154

Paynter, Eleanor, 'Border Crises and Migrant Deservingness: How the Refugee/Economic Migrant Binary Racializes Asylum and Affects Migrants' Navigation of Reception', *Journal of Immigrant and Refugee Studies*, 20:2 (2022): 293–306

Petersen, Anne Ring, 'The Square, the Monument and The Re-Configurative Power of Art' in Anna Meera Gaonkar, Astrid Sophie Ost Hansen, Hans Christian Post, and Moritz Schramm (eds), *Postmigration: Art, Culture, and Politics in Contemporary Europe* (Bielefeld: Transcript Verlag, 2021): 235–264

Phu, Thy, 'Refugee Photography and the Subject of Human Interest', in Tanya Sheehan (ed.), *Photography and Migration* (London: Routledge, 2018): 135–149

Pinnock, Andrew, 'The Menace of Meritocracy: Unmasking Inequality in the Creative and Cultural Industries', *Cultural Trends*, 28:2–3 (2019): 249–260

Rajaram, Prem Kumar, 'Humanitarianism and Representations', *Journal of Refugee Studies*, 15:3 (2002): 247–264

Rodrigo, Javier, and David Alegre Lorenz, 'Before the Convention: The Spanish Civil War and Challenges for Research on Refugee History', *Refugee Survey Quarterly*, 41:2 (2022): 196–217

Rotas, Alex, 'Is 'Refugee Art' Possible?', *Third Text*, 18:1 (2004): 51–60

Sigler, Friederike, 'Santiago Sierra's *Workers Who Cannot Be Paid*: Precarious Labour in Contemporary Art', in A. Halsema, K. Kwastek, and R van den Oever (eds), *Bodies That Still Matter: Resonances of the Work of Judith Butler* (Amsterdam: Amsterdam University Press, 2021): 127–138

Stevenson, Jacqueline, and John Willott, 'The Aspiration and Access to Higher Education of Teenage Refugees in the UK', *Compare*, 37:5 (2007): 671–687

Targarona Rifa, Nuria, and Giorgia Donà, 'Forced Unemployment or Undocumented Work: The Burden of the Prohibition to Work for Asylum Seekers in the UK', *Journal of Refugee Studies*, 34:2 (2021): 2052–2073

Tello, Verónica, 'What is Contemporary About Institutional Critique?', *Third Text*, 34:6 (2020): 635–649

Tip, Linda K., Rupert Brown, Linda Morrice, Michael Collyer, and Matthew J. Easterbrook, 'Improving Refugee Well-Being With Better Language Skills and More Intergroup Contact', *Social Psychological and Personality Science*, 10:2 (2019): 144–151

Wright, Terence, 'Moving Images: The Media Representation of Refugees', *Visual Studies*, 17:2 (2002): 53–66

Zarzycka, Marta, and Martijn Kleppe, 'Awards, Archives and Affects: Tropes in the World Press Photo Contest, 2009–11', *Media, Culture and Society*, 35:8 (2013): 977–995

Exhibition catalogues

Barron, Stephanie, Sabine Eckmann, and Matthew Affron (curators and eds), *Exiles + Emigrés: The Flight of European Artists from Hitler*, exhibition catalogue (Los Angeles: LA County Museum of Art, 1997)

Biesenbach, Klaus, Anna-Catharina Gebbers, and Susanne Pfeffer (curators and eds), *Christoph Schlingensief* (New York and Berlin: MoMA PS1 and KW Institute for Contemporary Art, 2013)

Bonyhady, Tim and Nigel Lendon, *I Weave What I Have Seen: The War Rugs of Afghanistan*, exhibition catalogue (Canberra: Australian National University School of Art Gallery, 2003)

Cooke, Lynne, Mark Godfrey, and Christian Rattemeyer (curators and eds), *Alighiero Boetti: Game Plan*, exh. cat. (New York: Museum of Modern Art, 2012)

Enwezor, Okwui, Katy Siegel, and Ulrich Wilmes (curators and eds), *Postwar: Art between the Pacific and the Atlantic, 1945–1965*, exhibition catalogue (Munich: Haus der Kunst, 2016)

Gioni, Massimiliano (curator and ed.), *The Restless Earth* (La Terra Inquieta; Milan: Trussardi Foundation and Triennale de Milan, 2017)

Pollock, Griselda, 'Glimpsing the Work of the World or What Painting Invites Us to Notice', *Caroline Walker: Women's Work*, Midlands Art Centre catalogue (2021)

Sussman, Elisabeth (curator and ed.), *1993 Whitney Biennial*, exhibition catalogue (New York: Whitney Museum of American Art & Harry Abrams, 1993)

Traces of Displacement, exhibition catalogue, www.whitworth.manchester.ac.uk/whats-on/ exhibitions/upcomingexhibitions/tracesofdisplacement/

Reports

Patel, Bharti, and Nancy Kelley, *The Social Care Needs of Refugees and Asylum Seekers* (Bristol: Social Care Institute for Excellence, 2006)

Index

Page numbers in **bold** refer to figures.

EU authorised representative for GPSR:
Easy Access System Europe, Mustamäe tee 50,
10621 Tallinn, Estonia
gpsr.requests@easproject.com

www.ingramcontent.com/pod-product-compliance
Ingram Content Group UK Ltd.
Pitfield, Milton Keynes, MK11 3LW, UK
UKHW062120150726
7214IPUK00009B/68